DISCARD

RACE ON
THE BRAIN

———

JONATHAN KAHN

RACE ON
THE BRAIN

What Implicit Bias Gets Wrong

About the Struggle for Racial Justice

COLUMBIA UNIVERSITY PRESS
NEW YORK

Columbia University Press
Publishers Since 1893
New York   Chichester, West Sussex
cup.columbia.edu
Copyright © 2018 Columbia University Press
All rights reserved

Library of Congress Cataloging-in-Publication Data

Names: Kahn, Jonathan, 1958– author.
Title: Race on the brain : what implicit bias gets wrong about the struggle
for racial justice / Jonathan Kahn.
Description: New York : Columbia University Press, [2017] | Includes
bibliographical references and index.
Identifiers: LCCN 2017010254 | ISBN 9780231184243 (cloth : alk. paper) | ISBN
9780231545389 (e-book)
Subjects: LCSH: Discrimination in criminal justice administration—United
States. | Discrimination in justice administration—United States. |
Racism—Psychological aspects. | Racism—United States. |
Discrimination—Law and legislation—United States.
Classification: LCC HV9950 .K34 2017 | DDC 364.3/400973—dc23
LC record available at https://lccn.loc.gov/2017010254

∞

Columbia University Press books are printed on permanent
and durable acid-free paper.
Printed in the United States of America

Cover design: Noah Arlow

CONTENTS

PREFACE

I n 2012, I came across a study out of Oxford University purporting to show that taking a particular drug (the beta blocker propranolol) could eliminate implicit bias.[1] I had just completed a book on BiDil, the first drug ever approved by the U.S. Food and Drug Administration with a race-specific indication—to treat heart failure in a "black" patient.[2] Where BiDil involved the problematic implications of developing a drug to treat a "race," the Oxford study raised the no less troubling issue of developing a drug to treat "racism." Where the former raised the specter of biologizing race, the latter biologized racism. As I began to explore the background to the Oxford study, I found it grounded in two decades of psychological and neuroscientific research on the cognitive basis of implicit bias—a field of science known as implicit social cognition. This research, in turn, led me to the field of behavioral realism, where a distinct set of legal scholars and policy makers had taken up the findings of implicit social cognition to make arguments about the nature of racial bias in contemporary American society and the best ways to address it. While I was tracing the path back from pills for racism to the beginnings of behavioral realism and then forward again to the present, Ferguson erupted, the Black Lives Matter movement emerged, and the language of implicit bias suffused media discussions of policing practices in America. But the more I learned about the foundations of implicit bias and the ways it was being deployed in legal and policy contexts, the more concerned I became about how it was being used as a primary lens through which to view issues of racial justice. The idea of a pill for racism, it turned out, was merely an extreme form of what was already logically present in the racial frame created by behavioral realism—the ideal of a neat, technical fix for racism. And so what began as an article on pills for racism grew into a much larger project on constructing and contesting the common sense of racism in law, science, and society.

In order to identify and address persistent racial inequality and injustice, we must first consider how we understand the basic nature of the problem. In their pathbreaking book *Racial Formation in the United States*, Michael Omi and Howard Winant examine how "race becomes 'common sense'—a way of comprehending, explaining or acting in the world."[3] My book instead examines how a distinctive conception of *racism* has become common sense in contemporary American society. It focuses in particular on how law and science can come together to shape and inform this common sense of racism and provides an extended critique of how the idea of implicit bias is being used to understand and address issues of racial justice in contemporary American law and society. At the outset, I want to be clear that I do not deny the significance of implicit bias or the potential utility of bringing it to light. I consider many of the people engaged in exploring and promoting implicit bias research and interventions to be allies in the fight for racial justice. Nonetheless, I am deeply concerned that in many quarters implicit bias has morphed from a useful psychological theory of cognitive function into a master narrative framing legal and policy responses to race and racism in America today. As this one particular tool for understanding certain aspects of racial dynamics has grown into a dominant story of contemporary race relations, I believe it is having certain profound and problematic unintended impacts on the underlying assumptions that shape the law and policy of racial justice in America.

Foremost among these impacts are (1) the reinforcement of the logic of conservative equal-protection jurisprudence that embraces a color-blind ideal, denies the importance of history, and holds up "diversity" as the sole rationale for affirmative action; (2) the reduction of racism to merely another form of "bias" in a manner that erases the distinctive legacy and meaning of racism in the United States; (3) the obscuring of the relations of power that undergird contemporary race relations; (4) the promotion of a mirage of easy, pain-free ways to fight racism; (5) an overenthusiastic and uncritical embrace of the idea of a technological fix for what is fundamentally a complex social, political, and historical problem; and (6) an open door to the biologization of racism, which casts it as a neurological or biochemical phenomenon susceptible to biochemical interventions—the ultimate technical fix.

My aims here, therefore, are to uncover how the discourses and technologies (both legal and scientific) of implicit bias are being deployed in ways that threaten to undermine broader progress on racial justice and to propose alternative approaches that bring implicit bias back into balance with other understandings of and approaches to racial justice.

■ ■ ■

Early on in my work on this book, I had occasion to discuss it over lunch with Troy Duster. I expressed some concern that it might seriously ruffle some feathers among my colleagues who worked on implicit bias and asked Troy if he had any advice. He simply said, "That's right. There are likely going to be some people who are unhappy with this book." At first, I thought (uncharitably) something to the effect of "Thanks—that and a buck will get me a cup of coffee." Of course, as I progressed with the project, I came to realize that Troy's statement, although simple, was acutely apt. As I developed my analysis of the making and unmaking of the common sense of racism in American society, I realized that one of my greatest concerns with work on implicit bias is its insistence on *not ruffling feathers*—not making people uncomfortable with the persistence of racial injustice and racism in this country. If I *do not* ruffle any feathers with this book, then perhaps it is not the book it should be. Thus, Troy's generous spirit and intellectual acuity have continued to inform my work throughout this project.

Along the way, many other scholars have offered critical insight and support. Foremost among them have been Osagie Obasogie and Lundy Braun, who have enthusiastically urged me to "get the book out" and generously offered thoughtful comments and close readings along the way. I was privileged to present an early version of the first two chapters at the workshop "Race and Empirical Legal Studies" at the University of Wisconsin School of Law, where I was fortunate to have Joan Fujimura offer extensive and helpful comments as a primary reader of the paper. I also presented aspects of the project at the annual meeting of the Science and Democracy Network and Duke University's Conference on the Present and Future of Civil Rights Movements: Race and Reform in 21st Century America; the annual meetings of the Association of Law, Medicine, and Ethics and the American Anthropological Association; and the University of California at Irvine conference "Race, Biological Causation, and Science Communication." I am also grateful to Dayna Matthew for our spirited and enlightening conversations during several shared conference panels over the past few years. As in all my work on race and science over the past decade, the RaceGen listserve has provided me with a vital and supportive virtual intellectual community. As ever, Jay Kaufman and Jon Marks have been especially helpful (and diverting) colleagues within this online village. Among the many others to whom I am indebted for continuing conversation and support are Ruha Benjamin, Rina Bliss, Deborah Bolnick, Simon Cole, Martha Crossley, Duana Fullwiley, Evelynn Hammonds, Terrence Keel, Alondra Nelson, Aaron Panofsky, Kimani Paul-Emile, Dorothy Roberts, Carolyn Rouse, and Patricia Williams. As with my previous book, Patrick Fitzgerald and the staff at Columbia University Press have been wonderful to work with. Supportive and responsive, they have been exemplary partners in these endeavors. This book is for Emma, who has grown into a remarkable young woman, and for Karen-Sue, who with loving grace and equanimity shares our newly empty nest with me.

RACE ON
THE BRAIN

———

INTRODUCTION

Rethinking Implicit Bias—the Limits to Science as a
Tool of Racial Justice

The election of Donald Trump in 2016 has surely and finally disabused
Americans of the illusion that the election of Barack Obama in 2008
somehow ushered in a postracial era. As incidents of hate speech proliferate in the aftermath of Trump's election, it is time to rethink the nature
of implicit bias and racism in America today. I would like here to put the
phenomenon of Trump's rise in a broader perspective and begin by looking
at legal authorities and their construction of appropriate uses of race in law
and public policy over the past several decades. To put it starkly, when it
comes to racial justice in this country, things seem to be getting worse. What
do you do when an area of the law you care about seems to have reached a
dead end? Or, rather, what do you do when your preferred reading of the
purpose and value of an area of the law appears to have been superseded or
simply cast aside by a dominant reading that threatens to consign it to the
dustbin of history? This question has been facing scholars of the left with
increasing urgency ever since the Burger Court began curbing and rolling
back the advances in progressive jurisprudence of racial justice attained
under the Warren Court. Perhaps beginning with *Milliken v. Bradley* in 1974
or maybe with *Washington v. Davis* in 1976, but in any event most certainly
by 1978 with *Regents of the University of California v. Bakke*,[1] scholars (and
jurists) of the left seem to have been fighting a rear-guard action to protect
the civil rights advances of the Second Reconstruction of the 1950s and
1960s.[2] As Berkeley law professor Ian Haney-López notes, "Since the end of
the civil rights era in the early 1970s, the emancipatory potential of the Fourteenth Amendment has been thoroughly undone. Today, its guarantee of
'equal protection' no longer promotes reform but rather protects the racial

status quo. This undoing has spanned four decades, with sharp plunges followed by ever-lower plateaus."[3]

Owen Fiss issued the clarion call in 1976 with his foundational article "Groups and the Equal Protection Clause,"[4] which inaugurated what has come to be known as the antisubordination school of equal-protection jurisprudence.[5] Fiss wrote of a "group disadvantaging principle" embedded in the history of the Reconstruction amendments under which laws may not "aggravate" or "perpetuate . . . the subordinate status of a specially disadvantaged group."[6] Under this approach, state laws and policies that classify by race are suspect primarily to the extent that they stigmatize or otherwise subordinate the specified group. It therefore allows for remedial uses of racial classifications, as in affirmative action. Under this principle, the Warren Court's focus on stigma in *Brown v. Board of Education* looms large.[7] Fiss invoked an anticaste interpretive tradition that goes back to Justice John Marshall Harlan's famous dissent in *Plessy v. Ferguson* (1896), where he stated that "in view of the constitution [*sic*], in the eye of the law, there is in this country no superior, dominant, ruling class of citizens. There is no caste here. Our constitution is color-blind, and neither knows nor tolerates classes among citizens. In respect of civil rights, all citizens are equal before the law."[8] The tricky thing about Harlan's statement, however, is that it also contains the reference to a "color-blind" Constitution, and therein lies the rub. For whereas contemporary scholars in the antisubordination tradition focus on Harlan's invocation of caste as central to understanding the meaning of the Equal Protection Clause, those in the distinct but related anticlassification tradition focus on the concept of "color blindness" to argue that *all* racial classifications should be suspect and subjected to strict scrutiny, which requires that any use of a racial classification be narrowly tailored to serve a compelling state interest, even where such classifications are intended to benefit rather than burden a historically subordinated group.

The anticlassification color-blind approach has come to dominate the modern Supreme Court's jurisprudence at least since *City of Richmond v. J. A. Croson Co.* in 1989, where a majority of the Court held for the first time that all race-conscious programs would be judged by strict scrutiny.[9] This decision provided a conservative bookend to the rollback of progressive approaches to racial justice concerning direct discrimination inaugurated in *Washington v. Davis* (1976) and *Personnel Administrator of Massachusetts v. Feeney* (1979).[10] The latter two cases undermined disparate-impact theories of liability, which had allowed plaintiffs claiming discrimination to make their case by showing how the challenged law or policy *affected* racial minorities. The Court instead moved toward a theory of disparate treatment under which plaintiffs have to make the nearly impossible showing of the defendant's subjective intent to discriminate.[11] Some see recent decisions under the Roberts Court (particularly in *Shelby County v. Holder* [2013][12]) as marking the effective end of judicial solicitude for civil rights in America.[13]

Focusing on issues of legal doctrine arising around the concept of discriminatory intent and its relation to the Court's development of a jurisprudence of color blindness, Haney-López notes,

> Colorblindness today applies when a government actor explicitly employs a racial classification. In practice, this covers affirmative action policies and little else. Under colorblindness, the remedial motives behind affirmative action are irrelevant. Indeed, frequently the Court asserts that whether the government's motives are benign or invidious is inherently unknowable. Distrusting its ability to parse the state's intentions, the Court under colorblindness subjects all affirmative action policies to the most stringent level of "scrutiny," which is to say, it requires the highest level of governmental necessity before such programs will be allowed. This scrutiny is so onerous that, since colorblindness gained five adherents on the Court in 1989, only one affirmative action case has been held to meet that standard.[14]

Haney-López contrasts color blindness with intent doctrine, which "applies to allegations of discriminatory treatment where a racial classification is *not* explicitly used. In effect, this covers all contemporary cases of discrimination against non-Whites, since instances of frank and open mistreatment are now virtually nonexistent." He notes that current intent doctrine in effect demands that plaintiffs prove a state of mind akin to an explicit malicious intent to discriminate. This standard is so exacting that "since this test was announced in 1979, it has never been met—not even once." Haney-López refers to this sorry state of affairs as one of "intentional blindness" by the Court to the persistence of racial discrimination against nonwhites.[15] Reva Siegel echoes this concern in discussing how the conservative majority's lack

4   **INTRODUCTION**

of empathy for nonwhites' experience of the law has informed the Court's recent decisions on race.[16]

So here we are. The prospect is not very encouraging, but it is important to note that the line of cases rolling back more expansive, antisubordination-informed readings of equal protection have been closely divided. Going back to *Bakke*, one can note that William J. Brennan and Thurgood Marshall's stirring opinions failed to garner majority status by only one vote, and *Shelby* similarly succeeded in striking down section 5 of the Voting Rights Act with a bare five-vote majority. On this reading, but for one judicial appointment, things might be very different.[17] But, of course, they are not different, so we must consider how to proceed if one is committed, as I am, to antisubordination principles and a more robust approach to identifying and redressing racial injustice.

One approach is to try to revivify surviving strands of antisubordination principles in existing precedent. Scholars such as Jack Balkin and Reva Siegel argue that the distinction between anticlassification and antisubordination has been overdrawn, that the two have always been intertwined, and that it is therefore possible to find within existing precedent the basis for bringing antisubordination principles more clearly to the fore.[18] In a recent article considering the possibilities raised for racial justice by the Court's more progressive holdings recently on gay rights and same-sex marriage (where Justice Anthony Kennedy's concerns for individual dignity figure prominently), Siegel asks the reader to

> imagine a Court enforcing equal protection by asking whether a law's enforcement "tells" minorities they are "unworthy," or by asking whether a law's enforcement "demeans" and "humiliates" them. Imagine a case on suspect apprehension that explained that when government classifies by race, even for benign purposes, judicial oversight is required to ensure that government employs means that respect people's dignity and treat them fairly, as individuals, in order to avoid racially divisive messages. Imagine a Court even suggesting that the constitutionality of a law might require attention to these matters. Imagine a Court at least prepared to get out of the way when minorities secure protection through the political processes. Or, imagine a Court prepared to intervene in politics to guard against laws that violate expectations of fair dealing and engender social division, for

minority as well as majority groups. The resources are in our equal protection tradition. Imagine.[19]

The key point here is that Siegel is not asking us to imagine some remote alternative universe of legal doctrine; rather, she argues, "the resources are in our equal protection tradition." Perhaps this statement expresses a hope that Justice Kennedy will draw upon this tradition to expand his concerns regarding human dignity more fully into the realm of racial justice. Indeed, one gets an inkling of this expansion in his recent opinion in *Fisher v. University of Texas* (2013), where he provided a crucial vote for upholding the university's affirmative action admissions program.[20] Yet the great caveat here is that Siegel begins the passage by asking the reader to "imagine if an appointment to the Supreme Court" reasoned this way.[21] So there is still a great deal of political contingency embedded in this hope—contingency highlighted by the recent presidential election. Moreover, even if we were to get such an appointment, the potential for advancing racial justice might be severely constrained if certain underlying assumptions about the nature of racism in contemporary American society go uninterrogated.

IMPLICIT BIAS AND THE LAW

Writing squarely within the antisubordination tradition, Haney-López, Balkin, and Siegel are challenging the basic tenets of the conservative approach to race and equal protection. Over the past twenty years, however, another approach has emerged from within this tradition on the left that works to challenge the Court's "intentional blindness" largely on its own terms.[22] This approach takes on the very concept of intent that Haney-López identifies as setting an impossibly high hurdle to equal-protection claims and tries to reconfigure it in a manner more conducive to serving the interests of racial justice. Specifically, it invokes recent findings in the psychology and neuroscience of implicit social cognition (ISC) to argue that whereas *explicit* intent or bias may be vanishingly difficult to identify, *implicit* intent or bias remains pervasive and deeply salient in society to an extent that both supports the findings of discrimination and justifies the taking of affirmative action to redress resulting racial inequities.[23] Many of the researchers

adopting this approach refer to themselves as "behavioral realists"[24]—
"behavioral" because they are looking primarily at the cognitive foundations of individual attitudes and "realists" because they are grounding their
work in rigorous empirical methods and quantitative measurement. This
book is concerned mainly with this new, hybrid interdisciplinary approach
to law and racial justice.

In 2005, Jerry Kang, a leading scholar working to integrate the findings
of ISC into the law, declared that "race talk in legal literature feels like it is at
a dead end."[25] Most scholars in the antisubordination tradition probably
have shared this feeling at one time or another. These scholars' critical work,
I would argue, has turned primarily to a deeper analysis of existing legal
doctrine embedded in past cases as a means to circumvent this dead end. In
contrast, Kang suggested that "no new philosophical argument or constitutional theory seems to persuade those sitting on one side of the fence to jump
to the other. One way to break current deadlocks is to turn to new bodies of
knowledge uncovered by social science, specifically the remarkable findings
of social cognition. Not only do they provide a more precise, particularized,
and empirically grounded picture of how race functions in our minds, and
thus in our societies, they also rattle us out of a complacency enjoyed after
the demise of de jure discrimination."[26] Kang and other behavioral realists
look *outside* the law to the science of ISC to help break the deadlock by
using its empirical findings to jump-start a new approach to racial justice in
the law.

As the term *implicit* indicates, the science of ISC purports to examine
mental processes that function without the subject's "conscious awareness
or conscious control but [that] nevertheless influence [his or her] fundamental evaluations."[27] More specifically, with respect to intergroup bias, ISC
theory argues that "cognitive structures and processes involved in categorization and information processing can in and of themselves result in stereotyping."[28] Stereotyping is nothing special. Categorizing observed phenomena
is part of how we make sense of the world. Nonetheless, such stereotypes
fundamentally affect judgments and decision making about different groups.
A key point here for behavioral realists is that such biases are cognitive
rather than motivational. That is, they occur "beyond the reach of decisionmaker self-awareness."[29] Thus, in contrast to explicit attitudes or
biases, implicit biases are "introspectively unidentified [and] . . . triggered

automatically, often without awareness."[30] For those concerned with racial justice, problems arise not from the stereotypes themselves but from the ways in which they become layered with positive or negative valences.[31]

Scholarship exploring ISC and its implications for policy and law tends to be highly interdisciplinary.[32] Although ISC is grounded primarily in psychology, researchers in the field of cognitive neuroscience have increasingly been employing new brain-scanning technologies, such as functional magnetic resonance imaging (fMRI), to explore how subjects' brains respond to performing implicit bias–related tasks.[33] In addition, behavioral economists have also shown considerable interest in this work, using it to provide a new angle on traditional law and economics approaches to understanding human behavior.[34]

As Kang summarized in 2005, research from the field of ISC "demonstrates that most of us have implicit biases in the form of negative beliefs (stereotypes) and attitudes (prejudice) against racial minorities. These implicit biases, however, are not well reflected in explicit self-reported measures. This dissociation arises not solely because we try to sound more politically correct. Even when we are honest, we simply lack introspective insight. Finally, and most importantly, these implicit biases have real-world consequences."[35]

These attitudes form the basis of the type of cognitive biases with which the law should be concerned.[36] Given the pervasiveness of such attitudes, scholars who employ ISC findings argue that legal understandings of the intent standard need to be reconfigured away from an exclusive focus on explicit bias to take into account the presence, here and now, of extensive *implicit* biases that shape existing decisions, practices, and policies.[37]

One of the foundational advances in applying ISC theories to specific social problems was the development of the Implicit Association Test (IAT) by psychologists Anthony Greenwald, Mahzarin Banaji, and Brian Nosek in the mid-1990s.[38] One can use the IAT to measure implicit attitudes toward any number of paired categories—for example, young versus old, gay versus straight, male versus female. The test basically evaluates how closely any two concepts, such as "old" and "bad," are associated by measuring how quickly a subject is able to match them. To measure implicit attitudes toward the racial categories "black" and "white," a subject sits at a computer and responds to racially coded stimuli, such as a picture of a person's face, and is then shown words coded with positive or negative valences, such as *smart* and *kind* or *violent* and *lazy*. The subject is first asked for one response (say, pressing the *e* on the keyboard) when she sees either black faces or positive words and for a different response (pressing the *i* key) when she sees white faces or negative words. The test is then flipped, so black faces are matched with negative words and white faces with positive. The test measures how quickly the subject can make these associations, down to the millisecond. The basic idea is that a subject will respond more quickly to associations that she or he has already cognitively made. Thus, if a subject consistently associates positive words more quickly with white faces and negative words more quickly with black, the researcher can infer an already-existing implicit bias in favor of whites.[39]

Among the first legal scholars to use ISC theory was Linda Krieger, who in her foundational article "The Content of Our Categories: A Cognitive Bias Approach to Discrimination and Equal Employment Opportunity" in 1995 applied ISC theory to the context of Title VII (Civil Rights Act of 1964) employment-discrimination law in an attempt to address the sort of deadlock Kang later identified. Krieger used ISC theory to challenge the "entire normative structure of anti-discrimination law," which is "based on an assumption that decision makers possess 'transparency of mind,' that they can accurately identify why they are about to make, or have already made, a particular decision."[40] Where previous critics of *Washington v. Davis* argued for revivifying disparate-impact theory, Krieger, in effect, embraced the dominant disparate-treatment theory but proposed to use ISC to turn that theory on its head so as to support broad claims of systemic discrimination in employment contexts. Instead of focusing on an actor's conscious motivation to discriminate, Krieger argued that underlying implicit "stereotypes cause discrimination by biasing how we process information about other people"; that is, "we judge other people by the content of our categories."[41] This move allows plaintiffs to satisfy the requirement of showing "intent" to discriminate by shifting the focus from conscious to unconscious motivation.

A decade later Jerry Kang described such categorization in terms of "racial schemas" or cognitive structures developed in social contexts that provide individuals with "implicit and explicit racial meanings associated with that category, [which] . . . then influence our interpersonal interaction." The point for Kang is "not merely that certain mental processes will execute automatically; rather, it is that those implicit mental processes may draw on racial meanings that, upon conscious consideration, we would expressly disavow. It is as if some 'Trojan Horse' virus had hijacked a portion of our brain."[42] Critically, for scholars of ISC the influence of implicit biases on our "interpersonal interactions" can be empirically, quantitatively measured. This ability to measure such influence distinguishes ISC fundamentally from the approach taken by antisubordination theorists such as Charles Lawrence III, who, although concerned with the individual psychology of racism, examine "cultural meaning" more broadly as a means to establish pervasive prejudice in society that needs legal redress.[43] Kang recently asserted that "in the past decade, the branch of science that has arguably most destabilized antidiscrimination law is implicit social cognition," in large part because of its empirical rigor.[44]

Kang and Mahzarin Banaji have asserted that findings from ISC are particularly destabilizing in the field of affirmative action law, where critics have long argued that such preferential treatment circumvents an accurate consideration of true merit. They argue that findings from ISC research make a firm "scientific case" that implicit bias can lead to the "mismeasurement of merit." This insight, they suggest, "reframes certain affirmative action programs not as 'preferential treatment' but as an opportunity for more accurate measures."[45] They characterize more accurate measures as more "fair" and hence as providing a new way to conceptualize social interventions to favor equality.

This approach also provides a new temporal frame, focusing not on past injustices but on present, ongoing manifestations of implicit bias that cause unfair discrimination in everyday practices.[46] This "presentist framing," Kang and Banaji argue,

> also avoids problems with forward-looking "diversity" justifications of affirmative action. These justifications were politically attractive—arguably necessary—because we, as a society, lost political consensus on the magnitude of bias and discrimination that persisted. With evidence from ISC, the forward-looking frame becomes optional. We do not need to argue about the empirical benefits of diversity— although we can. We do not need to explain why such real-world benefits trump the supposed moral or constitutional imperative of colorblindness— although we can. Instead, by

demonstrating discrimination *now*, this fire can be fought with narrowly
tailored fire. Put another way, color consciousness in the form of pervasive
implicit bias is what requires color consciousness in the form of prevention
and remedies.[47]

The implications of this reframing are both political, speaking "to the many
Americans who are willing to adopt fair measures that take race and gender
into account only to stop and prevent unwarranted discrimination on the
basis of those very attributes," and doctrinal, articulating how responding
to the discrimination found by ISC is a compelling interest sufficient to satisfy the strict standards of review set forth in cases such as *Grutter v. Bollinger* (2003).[48]

Scholars such as Kang, Fiske, and Banaji contrast "behavioral realism" to
what they see as relatively uninformed folk or commonsense understandings of how human beings make judgments.[49] Behavioral realists argue that
such unarticulated lay understandings of psychology often diverge from the
best empirical evidence provided by cognitive science.[50] They work to
"identif[y] naïve theories of human behavior latent in the law and legal
institutions" and then "juxtapose these theories against the best scientific
knowledge available to expose gaps between assumptions [e.g., about the
existence of bias] embedded in the law and reality described by science."
Finally, behavioral realists argue that when those gaps become substantial,
"the law should be changed to comport with science."[51]

SOME CONCERNS

Behavioral realism is very appealing in many respects. Leveraging the
authority of science to break through the deadlock of conservative racial
backlash seems tactically astute and clearly holds some promise. Moreover,
we may use it to supplement rather than supplant the sorts of arguments
being made by antisubordination theorists working primarily within a doctrinal legal frame. Kang, for example, makes clear that he embraces the pursuit of "multiple methodologies" and does not believe that "hard science" is
the only way to engage in critical thinking about the relationship between
law and race.[52] Nonetheless, the authority of science in contemporary

American culture is very powerful, especially among elites. Nor does the application of science to legal questions happen in a vacuum. The "hard science" itself is being developed, applied, and interpreted in a social context that frames the frames, as it were, that ISC theorists and their legal counterparts are employing. Despite Kang's well-considered caveats, when he and others apply ideas from ISC theory to legal and policies issues, the authority of science tends to predominate. Thus, for example, when Kang and Banaji assert that "the law should be changed to comport with science," they are clearly placing the authority of science *above* that of the law and implicitly making totalizing claims for the ISC framework they are proposing. My primary concern, therefore, is that in the hands of its most ardent practitioners, ISC theory or its application in law as "behavioral realism," rather than complementing existing analyses of the relations between race and law, is becoming a master narrative and primary frame for understanding and addressing all contemporary approaches to racial justice.

And it is a master narrative with a great deal of traction. Talk of "implicit bias" pervades contemporary discussions of race relations in America. In the first presidential debate in 2016 between Democratic candidate Hillary Clinton and Republican candidate Donald Trump, moderator Lester Holt asked Secretary Clinton if she "believed that police are implicitly biased against black people." She responded, "Implicit bias is a problem for everyone, not just police," and emphasized that as president she would devote considerable resources to training police to help address the problem.[53] Protests and analyses of the numerous policing incidents that gave rise to the Black Lives Matter movement are replete with references to implicit bias as they call for reforms in police training and practice. Major American legal institutions, including the National Center for State Courts,[54] the American Bar Association,[55] and the U.S. Department of Justice,[56] have implemented significant initiatives to study and address implicit bias in the law. In October 2016, President Barack Obama issued the "Presidential Memorandum—Promoting Diversity and Inclusion in the National Security Workforce," which called on executive agencies to "expand training on unconscious bias, inclusion, and flexible work policies" as well as to "expand their provision of training on implicit or unconscious bias."[57] To meet such demands, a multi-billion-dollar diversity-training industry has emerged that is premised largely on applying ISC theories to address issues of implicit bias in the workplace.[58]

In the second edition of their pathbreaking book *Racial Formation in the United States*, published in 1994, Michael Omi and Howard Winant observe that "the distinct, and contested, meanings of racism which have been advanced over the past three decades have contributed to an overall crisis of meaning for the concept today. Today, the absence of a clear 'common sense' understanding of what racism means has become a significant obstacle to efforts aimed at challenging it."[59]

Omi and Winant's theory of "racial formation" recognizes that racism is not a static thing but, like race itself, changes over time and space. They define racial formation "as the sociohistorical process by which racial categories are created, inhabited, transformed, and destroyed." This process, in turn, involves historically situated *racial projects* that "connect what race *means* in a particular discursive practice and the ways in which both social structures and everyday experiences are racially *organized*, based upon that meaning." They go on to note that "a racial project can be defined as *racist* if and only if it *creates or reproduces structures of domination based on essentialist categories of race*."[60] Behavioral realism generally *does not* employ essentialist categories of *race*, but it *does* tend to create or reproduce essentialist understandings of *racism*—that is, it constructs racism as a natural, biological process. Behavioral realism, therefore, can be understood as a sort of racial project insofar as it creates a master narrative that connects what *racism* means to ways in which legal and policy interventions are organized based on that meaning.

In itself, this connection might not be a big issue, but I believe that within such a master narrative there are some highly problematic and underappreciated implications of creating a regime that is so focused on individual psychology and that asks us simply to "follow the science" in identifying, interpreting, and responding to racial injustice in law and society. In this book, I intend to explore some of these implicit problems with the use of the notion of implicit bias. Perhaps foremost among these problems is the concern that much scholarship on implicit bias fundamentally accepts the conservative frame elaborated in cases from *Bakke* and *Washington v. Davis* to *Grutter v. Bollinger* and *Shelby County v. Holder*. Central to this frame are a commitment to the ideal of color blindness, a belief that "diversity" is the only compelling interest sufficient to justify affirmative action in education, and an understanding that *explicit* racism is largely a thing of the past.

I see additional problems with how behavioral realism valorizes the scientific method as an autonomous means to resolve complex social, historical, and political issues. The first problem involves what I call the "deracination of the legal subject." It builds on my concerns that the implicit bias approaches, in particular those emphasizing the IAT, employ a color-blind ideal insofar as they imply that subjects should have *identical* responses to black and white (or other paired) categories. Although reasonable in many respects, this approach effectively asks us to stop "seeing" race—to erase race, its history and meaning, from our perceptions.

Second, the implicit bias approach tends to obscure significant relations of power. It casts bias as pervasive but also as invisible, submerged below our conscious awareness. Moreover, many proposed responses operate in similarly obscure ways, often trying to shape or manipulate unconscious attitudes without the subject's full awareness.

Third, this approach also evidences a basic distrust of the citizenry by placing in expert hands the paramount authority to identify, measure, evaluate, interpret, and administer remedies to address persistent racial injustice in society. These remedies not only obscure power relations but also tend to manipulate rather than engage citizens directly in the hard work of achieving racial justice. The implicit bias approach is perhaps most evident in Richard Thaler and Cass Sunstein's behavioral economic concept of "paternalistic libertarianism," elaborated in their best-selling book *Nudge*,[61] but it also suffuses many other proposed remedies grounded more directly in ISC theory.

Fourth, when ISC legal scholars suggest that the law should be changed to comport with science," they are constructing a highly problematic relation between the authority of law and science that is grounded in seeking a clean technical fix for highly complex and messy political and social problems. Just as some of the proposed remedies to implicit bias evince a distrust in the citizenry, seeking a technical fix reveals a similar distrust in the democratic legal institutions of judge and jury, elevating technologies of measurement and quantification over interpretive legal traditions grounded in more humanistic approaches to law and justice.

Finally, as psychological research involving implicit bias has increasingly been integrated with neuroscience and attempts to locate racially coded responses in distinct brain regions through imaging technologies such as fMRI, the combination has opened the door to an ultimate technical fix that effectively renders racism primarily a function of biological activity in the brain. Specifically, these technologies have been used to measure how exposure to chemical compounds such as the hormone oxytocin or the beta blocker propranolol affect brain activity and IAT responses to racially coded stimuli—exploring the possible ways in which pharmaceuticals might be used in the future to combat racism.[62] This "pills for racism" approach threatens to use science to supersede law altogether, privatizing the fight against racism to the commercial world of pharmaceutical marketing.

Despite these concerns, I believe there are many positive and productive avenues to be pursued by means of ISC theory and its relation to law. The critical thing, however, is to fully explore and appreciate the implications and limitations of the science and to place it in a true *dialogue* with law and policy, a dialogue in which neither is made to "comport" with the other but rather they all are used mutually to inform, construct, and deepen our understanding and engagement with both past and ongoing realities of racial injustice in American life.

This book deals in turn with each of the issues raised here and outlined in the preface.

Chapter 1 explores in greater depth the science of implicit social cognition. It examines the basic concepts of implicit and explicit bias and the models of cognitive functioning that underlie them. It considers the rising connection between cognitive psychology and developments in neuroscience, with particular focus on new brain-imaging technologies and the study of what has come to be known as the "neural correlates of race."[63] It then moves on to examine the IAT in depth, its connections to neuroscience, and ongoing work being done to establish its validity as a predictor of behaviors ranging from everyday social encounters to conduct in healthcare settings, employment, law enforcement, and criminal justice. The IAT is particularly significant because of its widespread influence and strong uptake among certain sectors of the legal academy. Chapter 1 concludes by discussing some of the interventions proposed to address pervasive implicit bias.

Chapter 2 discusses in greater detail the uptake of ISC theory in general and of the IAT in particular in the legal academy. It contrasts early iterations of behavioral realism with alternative interpretive frameworks for understanding pervasive bias and considers the appeal of ISC's apparent empirical rigor to legal scholars. It also examines specific sites across the law where ISC insights into implicit bias have been brought to bear in considering specific proposed remedies. The chapter then moves on to review some existing critiques of both the science and legal application of ISC in general and of the IAT in particular. First, critics who are often though not universally from the right contest the basic interpretation of the meaning and significance of results from tests such as the IAT; some of these critics also raise less-political technical issues, particularly with the application of neuroscience in the complex fields of behavioral and cognitive psychology. Second, critics generally from the left are particularly concerned with behavioral realism's tendency to reduce discrimination primarily to a function of individual attitudes at the potential expense of appreciating the significance of larger historical and structural forces that shape such attitudes.

Chapter 3 addresses the first of my own concerns with behavioral realism in the law: its tendency to accept the conservative frame for modern civil rights jurisprudence. This chapter deals the most extensively among all the chapters with the specific holdings of the Supreme Court and related legal doctrine. It considers the relationship of behavioral realism to four key aspects of the conservative frame: time, color blindness, diversity, and intent.

Time involves the implications of casting explicit racism as largely a thing of the past. Behavioral realism's focus on the "here and nowness" of implicit bias in contrast to the "pastness" of explicit racism tacitly reinforces conservative arguments that racism is largely a thing of the past and hence not a concern sufficient to justify policies such as affirmative action. The conservative embrace of a *color-blind* ideal as a rationale for striking down affirmative action similarly resonates with the IAT's implicit norm that subjects should respond the same to both black and white faces—that is, that they should be "blind" to the color of the target stimulus. Also embedded in this implicit norm is the idea that racial categories should not carry distinctive positive or negative valences so that subjects respond to them neutrally as just another attribute among many. Although laudable in the abstract, this approach treats race in a manner similar to the conservative holdings in *Bakke* and *Grutter* that drain racial identity of its distinctive character and history by treating it as merely yet another "factor" among many to be considered in serving to promote "diversity"—the only interest recognized as sufficiently compelling to justify the use of racial categories in affirmative action. Finally, the focus on subjective "intent" so central to the behavioral realist approach to racial discrimination basically embraces the conservative disparate-treatment framework of cases such as *Washington v. Davis* and *Personnel Administrator v. Feeney*. I argue that this approach places an inordinate faith in the power of empirical data and quantitative measurement to do the heavy ideological lifting of making arguments for addressing structural discrimination, particularly in employment settings.

Chapter 4 examines some of the more direct implications of adopting the behavioral realism frame as the primary explanatory frame for racial injustice in law and policy. It argues that behavioral realism ultimately allows conservative justices to pick and choose among the numbers and empirical methodologies that suit their purposes without challenging any of these methodologies' underlying assumptions. It further considers how concepts central to behavioral realism have come to dominate areas of policy, in particular the diversity-management and training business, in ways that serve to legitimate existing structures of inequality and insulate them from legal challenge.

Chapter 5 explores behavioral realism's broader tendency to deracinate the subject. Drawing on political philosopher Michael Sandel's influential article "The Procedural Republic and the Unencumbered Self,"[64] it argues that identity matters. The norm of color blindness embedded in the IAT not only accepts a conservative legal framework but also fails to consider that perhaps there are times when one *should* respond differently to racially coded information. To have the same response time to both black faces and white faces on an IAT *may* in some contexts be a good thing, but in others perhaps it is not. As an uninterrogated norm, it implicates what Martha Minow has characterized as the "dilemma of difference"—namely, "When does treating people differently emphasize their differences and stigmatize or hinder them on that basis? And when does treating people the same become insensitive to their differences and likely to stigmatize or hinder them on *that* basis?"[65] In addition, the typically binary structure of tests such as the IAT (e.g., testing black versus white for positive versus negative associations) also constructs a thin representation of race and subordinated categories in society that elides other coexisting categories (such as gender, sexuality, and class), whose significance the extensive scholarship on law and intersectionality has been fruitfully exploring for more than two decades.[66]

Chapter 6 considers how the logic and application of behavioral realism tends to obscure significant power relations in ways that may undermine long-term efforts to engage and transform racial relations and status in our country. It makes use of the work of political scientist Suzanne Mettler on what she has characterized as the "submerged state" to argue that in characterizing racism primarily in terms of unconscious, implicit attitudes, behavioral realism effectively renders it invisible to the common person.[67] In the behavioral realist approach, racism is brought to light only through expert intervention, tests, measurement, and interpretation. The chapter moves on to explore how particular interventions proposed by behavioral realists involve similarly invisible or subliminal manipulations of the environment or individuals that are meant to work beyond conscious apprehension. These interventions, in turn, feed into a phenomenon I characterize as "privatizing antiracism," wherein behavioral realism's focus on individual cognition locates responsibility for identifying and addressing racism primarily in the private sphere, as exemplified by the multi-billion-dollar diversity-management industry.

Chapter 7 examines how behavioral realist interventions and indeed the IAT itself feed into a related phenomenon I call "recreational antiracism." Here, I argue that the IAT and related interventions constitute technologically mediated routes to self-knowledge that can become almost a form of entertainment or a low-cost route to self-improvement—a sort of antiracism analogue to the type of phenomena Barbara Ehrenreich describes in her book *Bright-Sided: How Positive Thinking Is Undermining America*[68]— which, instead of promoting the "power of positive thinking," promotes the power of positive subliminal nudging. As a heuristic to draw out the implications of this approach, chapter 7 compares the paternalistic ISC models of "nudging" and "unconsciousness raising" to the "consciousness-raising" mobilizations of the 1960s and 1970s that grew out of second-wave feminism.[69] In contrast to challenging and engaging citizens in a common civic enterprise, as the civil rights movement of the 1950s and 1960s did, these ISC-informed interventions manipulate and mollify citizens in an attempt to provide a painless path to racial justice.

Chapter 8 follows up in depth on the behavioral realist idea that the law should be made to "comport with the science" to consider the broader implications of seeking what is essentially a technical fix to a complex historical, social, and political set of problems. Drawing on the work of science and technology studies scholars, such as Sheila Jasanoff and Bryan Wynne, it extends the critique of behavioral realism's construction of citizenship to explore how its foregrounding of empirical science necessarily privileges the status of experts over judges and juries.[70] Behavioral realism additionally privileges the authority of empirically based quantitative-measurement-related expertise over that of other interpretive models of legal judgment and meaning making. In this, it evinces a profound discomfort with uncertainty and interpretive judgment, which I argue are integral to democratic governance. It further is grounded in highly problematic technocratic assumptions regarding the objectivity of such measurement and the related clear separation of facts from norms in evaluating racial discrimination.

Chapter 9 examines the ultimate technical fix to racism: pharmaceutical interventions. This chapter begins by reviewing a strand of the psychological analysis of racism that casts it as a disease that demands diverse forms of medical intervention. It then considers how the increasing use of tests such as the IAT in tandem with advanced brain-imaging technologies, such as fMRI, is "biologizing" racism—that is, locating it in specific organic regions of the brain as a physiological phenomenon. As this new, powerful technological frame purports to render racism a function of direct biological measurement, it renders racism susceptible to similar biological interventions—that is, pharmaceuticals. In particular, studies have been conducted on the effects of the beta blocker propranolol on racial attitudes and intergroup dynamics, often as measured by both the IAT and fMRI scans of test subjects. This chapter explores the implications of these cases and considers how drawing upon pharmaceuticals to fight bias has an unsettling tendency to further privatize the fight for racial justice as a function of market-based sales and consumption of self-improvement remedies.

The conclusion presents an alternative model for using the IAT and behavioral realists' findings to *inform* rather than to *guide* law and policy. It proposes that what is really going on in contests between progressive and conservative approaches to racial justice, between antidiscrimination and antisubordination approaches to equal protection, between behavioral realists and their critics are arguments about constructing and interpreting the common sense of race and racism in American society. The conclusion builds on earlier critiques of behavioral realism to explore how its findings might nonetheless play an important role in shaping these arguments, while emphasizing that it is important to keep such findings in perspective lest the unintended consequences of behavioral realism's implicit technological triumphalism overwhelm the underlying democratic commitments of the fight for racial justice. Finally, it circles back to Reva Siegel's call for us to "imagine a Court enforcing equal protection by asking whether a law's enforcement 'tells' minorities they are 'unworthy,' or by asking whether a law's enforcement 'demeans" and 'humiliates' them." But where Siegel looks exclusively to the "resources . . . in our equal protection tradition," I argue that setting her antisubordination concerns into *dialogue* with the findings of behavioral realism may instead allow us to build explicitly upon the substantive due process dignitary strains of Justice Kennedy's jurisprudence in a manner that revivifies and gives legal force to the foundational concerns for stigma so forcefully articulated in *Brown*. I hope with this analysis to engage, anchor, and extend the implications raised by Justice Sonia Sotomayor in her forceful dissent in *Schuette v. BAMN* (2014), where she declared that "the way to stop discrimination on the basis of race is to speak openly and candidly on the subject of race, and to apply the Constitution with eyes open to the unfortunate effects of centuries of racial discrimination."[71]

1

DEFINING AND MEASURING IMPLICIT BIAS

The study of implicit social cognition "examines those mental processes that operate without conscious awareness or conscious control but nevertheless influence fundamental evaluations of individuals and groups."[1] It is grounded primarily in the field of psychology but has been taken up by many other fields, including neuroscience.[2] Ralph Adolphs, professor of psychology and neuroscience at the California Institute of Technology, has complained that "social cognition is a domain with fuzzy boundaries and vaguely specified components." Nonetheless, he recognizes that it can be understood as guiding "both automatic and volitional behavior by participating in a variety of processes that modulate behavioral response: memory, decision-making, attention, motivation and emotion are all prominently recruited when socially relevant stimuli elicit behavior."[3]

ISC's potential for political applications is made abundantly clear in an article titled "Political Neuroscience: The Beginning of a Beautiful Friendship," in which an interdisciplinary group of coauthors assert that "the application of neuroscience to political topics offers a powerful set of research methods that promises to integrate multiple levels of analysis. As E. O. Wilson (1998) wrote in *Consilience: The Unity of Knowledge*: 'the social sciences are intrinsically compatible with the natural sciences. The two great branches of learning will benefit to the extent that their modes of causal explanation are made consistent.'"[4]

Psychologists Curtis Hardin and Mahzarin Banaji assert that "implicit prejudice" itself "(a) operates unintentionally and outside awareness, (b) is empirically distinct from explicit prejudice, and (c) uniquely predicts consequential social judgment and behavior."[5] Thus, as other authors assert, "people can have implicit prejudices—feelings, favorable or unfavorable, toward persons or groups that they did not endorse or even realize that they possessed."[6]

ISC emerged from a history of psychological studies of prejudice that John Dovidio has broadly characterized as happening in three waves. The first wave, from the 1920s through the 1950s, cast prejudice as form of psychopathology involving "not simply a disruption in rational processes, but as a dangerous aberration from normal thinking." The second wave, lasting until the early 1990s, "began with an opposite assumption: Prejudice is rooted in normal rather than abnormal processes." This approach conceived of prejudice, stereotyping, and bias as "outcomes of normal cognitive processes associated with simplifying and storing information of overwhelming quantity and complexity that people encounter in daily life." Beginning in the mid-1990s, a third wave—the current wave—emerged that "emphasizes the multidimensional aspect of prejudice and takes advantage of new technologies to study processes that were earlier hypothesized but not directly measurable." During this wave, psychologists developed the IAT and more recently fMRI studies of neuropsychological processes to produce "a more comprehensive, interdisciplinary, and multidimensional understanding of prejudice."[7] This current interdisciplinary approach is notable for its focus on quantifiable, measurable, and (in the case of fMRI) visualizable metrics of prejudice.

Despite this rather sequential characterization, it bears noting that each "wave" did not simply supersede and render prior research irrelevant. Rather, these waves are best understood as building upon, interweaving with, and influencing one another—more like marbled layers of research than distinct historical strata. Thus, for example, many scholars remain deeply concerned with what they see to be the pathologies of racism—particularly in its most extreme forms—though they may also embrace current work on ISC.

HEURISITICS AND BIASES

Amos Tversky and Daniel Kahneman's profoundly influential article "Judgment Under Uncertainty: Heuristics and Biases" was published in 1974, during the "second wave," but it remains of fundamental significance to the work of ISC theorists in general and of behavioral realists in the law in particular.[8] Among scholars during the "third wave," Mahzarin Banaji and Anthony Greenwald, writing from within the discipline of psychology, as well as Richard Thaler and Cass Sunstein, writing from within economics and law, draw directly and heavily on this work. Banaji and Greenwald refer to the "heuristics and biases" identified by Tversky and Kahneman as "mind bugs," which are "ingrained habits of thought that lead to errors in how we perceive, remember, reason, and make decisions."[9] Thaler and Sunstein simply call them "rules of thumb."[10] They identify these mind bugs or rules of thumb with three key heuristics analyzed by Tversky and Kahneman as centrally shaping the way people use shortcuts to make sense of the complicated array of information that we encounter in everyday life: anchoring, availability, and representativeness.

Banaji and Greenwald observe that "the mind does not search for information in a vacuum. Rather, it starts by using whatever information is immediately available as a reference point or 'anchor' and then adjusting."[11] Thaler and Sunstein illustrate the concept of anchoring by considering how they, living in Chicago, might respond to a request to guess the population of Milwaukee, about two hours away. They know little about Milwaukee other than that it is the largest city in Wisconsin. So they start with something they *do* know, the population of Chicago, which is roughly three million. This is their *anchor*. Working from this number, they consider that Milwaukee is a major city but clearly isn't as big as Chicago, perhaps one-third its size, so they estimate its population at one million. Then, they compare this process to that of a hypothetical resident of Green Bay, Wisconsin, who uses Green Bay's population of one hundred thousand as his anchor and guesses that Milwaukee is three times as big—three hundred thousand. Like Banaji and Greenwald, Thaler and Sunstein refer to this process as "anchoring and adjustment"—in conditions of uncertainty, you start with the anchor you know and adjust from there. The problem is that the adjustment is often insufficient, creating a bias toward the anchor. In their example, they note that the population of Milwaukee is actually about 580,000 people.[12]

Banaji and Greenwald illustrate the availability heuristic by asking the reader, "Pick the correct answer in each of the following three pairs: Each year, do more people in the United States die from cause (a) or cause (b)?"

1. (a) murder (b) diabetes
2. (a) murder (b) suicide
3. (a) car accidents (b) abdominal cancer[13]

They note that most people chose (b) for question 1 and (a) for questions 2 and 3. In fact, the correct answer to each question is (b). The availability heuristic means that "when instances of one type of event (such as murder rather than suicide) come more easily to mind than those of another type, we tend to assume that the first event also must occur more frequently in the world."[14]

Thaler and Sunstein characterize "representiveness" simply as the idea "that when asked to judge how likely it is that A belongs to category B, people . . . answer by asking themselves how similar A is to their image or stereotype of B (that is, how 'representative' A is of B)."[15] Given representativeness's direct connection to stereotyping, one can readily appreciate its implications for understanding implicit prejudice.

EXPLICIT AND IMPLICIT BIAS

Such cognitive heuristics are understood as operating largely at an unconscious or implicit level in contrast to realms of more conscious, explicit deliberation and awareness. Daniel Kahneman popularized this "dual-system" model in his best-selling book *Thinking, Fast and Slow*, where he describes it as follows:

- System 1 operates automatically and quickly, with little or no effort and no sense of voluntary control.
- System 2 allocates attention to the effortful mental activities that demand it, including complex computations. The operations of System 2 are often associated with the subjective experience of agency, choice, and concentration.[16]

This dual-system model applies across a wide range of cognitive tasks but has been particularly significant in framing discussions of ISC and drawing distinctions between implicit and explicit bias. It suffuses Thaler and

Sunstein's work, who state baldly that it is "how we think." They describe the dual-system model as involving "a distinction between two types of thinking, one that is intuitive and automatic and another that is reflective and rational."[17]

Among psychologists, David Amodio and Saaid Mendoza use the terms *implicit* and *explicit* to refer to a subject's own awareness of a particular psychological process, such as bias: "an *explicit* process can be consciously detected and reported (regardless of whether it was triggered spontaneously). Any process that is not explicit is referred to as *implicit*. Hence, 'implicit' describes a process that cannot be directly inferred through introspective awareness."[18]

Psychologists Brian Nosek and Rachel Siskind offer a slightly different definition, asserting that "implicit social cognition" is *not* a specific psychological process but rather "is a descriptive term encompassing thoughts and feelings that occur independently of conscious intention, awareness, or control."[19] Anthony Greenwald and Linda Hamilton Krieger also emphasize awareness and control, noting that "a belief is *explicit* if it is consciously endorsed," whereas *implicit* cognition involves "processes of social perception, impression formation, and judgment" over which a person "may not always have conscious, intentional control."[20]

Implicit bias involves three basic steps: the mental recognition or construction of a social group; the association of a stereotype with that group; and the layering of a positive or negative association or attitude on top of the stereotype. Social psychologists define a social stereotype as "a mental association between a social group and a category or trait."[21] Stereotypes in themselves are not necessarily normative. In contrast, an attitude is "an evaluative disposition, that is, the tendency to like or dislike, or to act favorably or unfavorably toward someone or something."[22] Implicit biases, therefore, "are discriminatory biases based on implicit attitudes or implicit stereotypes."[23] Implicit attitudes may be related to explicit attitudes, "but [the two] are distinct in that neither is robustly predictive of the other."[24] Of particular interest are situations in which explicit and implicit attitudes toward the same object differ. These dissociations are most commonly observed with respect to stigmatized groups, such as racial minorities.[25]

MEASURING IMPLICIT BIAS

As Amodio notes, "Many of the central components of intergroup bias (e.g., the construct of implicit bias) are exceedingly difficult to study using the traditional methods of social psychology, as they appear to be impervious to introspection, and thus to self-report."[26] The science of ISC began to gain traction in the 1990s as psychologists developed new techniques for measuring and quantifying it. At a larger social level, bias (both implicit and explicit) may often be inferred from significant statistical disparities in the treatment of racial groups with respect to a particular practice. Thus, for example, the phenomenon of differential traffic stops by police that has come to be known as "driving while black" became the basis for a number of successful lawsuits challenging racial profiling.[27] One early study done in 1993 found that in a particular place where more than 98 percent of the cars on the New Jersey Turnpike were speeding, the police essentially had discretion to pull over anyone they chose. Although African Americans made up only 15 percent of the speeders, not statistically different from their proportion of the driving population, 35 percent of the drivers pulled over were black. The average black driver was almost four times more likely to be pulled over than a nonblack driver.[28] Such statistics provided strong evidence of the impermissible use of race in police practices. This statistical approach has given significant ammunition not only to those bringing racial-profiling cases to court but also to those seeking to establish claims of systemic employment discrimination.[29] Such statistics in themselves, however, do not reveal anything about whether the officers' intent involved explicit or implicit bias. Nor do they say anything about particular officers' individual motivations.

Controlled audit studies also rely on statistical information but are more tightly framed as controlled experiments rather than as observational studies. A typical example of an audit study of hiring practices might involve matched pairs of white and minority job applicants with similar qualifications and credentials. Any resulting significant net difference between groups in hiring could therefore be logically attributed to racial or ethnic discrimination. In one study, researchers mailed out more than two thousand pairs of matched résumés in response to a large number of help-wanted advertisements in Boston and Chicago. The only thing they systemically varied was the first name of each applicant, for which they alternated between names suggestive of a black American (e.g., Aisha, Ebony, Darnell, Hakim) and names suggestive of a white American (e.g., Kristen, Meredith, Neil, Todd). The callback rate for white-named applicants was about 50 percent higher than for black-named applicants (9.7 percent versus 6.5 percent).[30] Even more striking is an audit study led by Princeton sociologist Devah Pager that found not only that black applicants were half as likely as equally qualified whites to receive a callback or job offer but also that white applicants identified as just having been released from prison actually received more callbacks (17 percent) than comparable black applicants with no criminal record (14 percent).[31] Audit studies have produced similar findings in settings ranging from health care to housing to car purchasing.[32]

Priming studies also involve controlled experiments to assess the workings of System 1 automatic cognitive functions. They cover a wide range of subjects, including racial attitudes. Priming studies "show how causing someone to think about a particular domain can trigger associative networks related to that domain. Activating these associative networks, which can include stereotypes, can affect people's decision-making and behavior, often without their conscious awareness."[33] The basic idea is that providing people with certain cues can unconsciously affect their cognitive processes and behavior. A classic example of the effects of priming comes from a famous study done in 1996 in which participants unwittingly exposed to the stereotype of old age walked slower when exiting the laboratory.[34] In a typical example of the effects of racial priming, a study in 2001 found that participants identified objects as guns more quickly when primed with black faces than when primed with white faces. In a second experiment, participants misidentified pictures of tools as guns more often when primed with a black face than with a white face.[35] In these studies, relative speed and accuracy became quantifiable measures of racial effects implying possible bias.

A great breakthrough in the systematic measurement of implicit attitudes at the individual level came in the 1990s with the development of the Implicit Association Test. Greenwald developed the first iteration of the IAT in 1994,[36] and he coauthored the first article about the use of the IAT in 1998.[37] That same year Greenwald and Banaji, together with their graduate student Brian Nosek, launched an Internet demonstration site for the IAT, which later developed into the website for Project Implicit, a nonprofit corporation created "to foster dissemination and application of implicit social cogni-tion."[38] Project Implicit describes the process of taking an IAT as follows:

> When doing an IAT you are asked to quickly sort words into categories that are on the left and right hand side of the computer screen by pressing the "e" key if the word belongs to the category on the left and the "i" key if the word belongs to the category on the right. The IAT has five main parts.
>
> In the first part of the IAT you sort words relating to the concepts (e.g., fat people, thin people) into categories. So if the category "Fat People" was on the left, and a picture of a heavy person appeared on the screen, you would press the "e" key.
>
> In the second part of the IAT you sort words relating to the evaluation (e.g., good, bad). So if the category "good" was on the left, and a pleasant word appeared on the screen, you would press the "e" key.
>
> In the third part of the IAT the categories are combined and you are asked to sort both concept and evaluation words. So the categories on the left hand side would be Fat People/Good and the categories on the right hand side would be Thin People/Bad. It is important to note that the order in which the blocks are presented varies across participants, so some people will do the Fat People/Good, Thin People/Bad part first and other people will do the Fat People/Bad, Thin People/Good part first.
>
> In the fourth part of the IAT the placement of the concepts switches. If the category "Fat People" was previously on the left, now it would be on the right. Importantly, the number of trials in this part of the IAT is increased in order to minimize the effects of practice.
>
> In the final part of the IAT the categories are combined in a way that is opposite what they were before. If the category on the left was previously Fat People/Good, it would now be Fat People/Bad.
>
> The IAT score is based on how long it takes a person, on average, to sort the words in the third part of the IAT versus the fifth part of the IAT. We would say that one has an implicit preference for thin people relative to fat people if they are faster to categorize words when Thin People and Good share a response key and Fat People and Bad share a response key, relative to the reverse.[39]

In 2001, Nosek and Banaji introduced a variant on the IAT: the Go/No-Go Association Test (GNAT) which could be used to examine automatic social cognition of a single target category. A GNAT measures implicit attitudes by having participants simply respond to stimuli that represent the target category (e.g., "black" or "white") and the attribute category (e.g., "good") but do nothing in response to other stimuli.[40]

The key thing about the IAT is that researchers believe it captures attitudes that the test taker is not necessarily consciously aware of. Thus, for example, a person may consciously be very explicitly committed to the tenet of racial equality and yet have an IAT score that indicates an implicit preference for whites over blacks as measured by the speed and accuracy of his or her association of the category "white" with positive words or of the category "black" with negative words or both. Indeed, Banaji and Greenwald have noted that the IATs they took indicate that they themselves harbor such implicit prejudices.[41]

The latter admission indicates the social situatedness of the IAT. Researchers working with the IAT readily acknowledge the significance of structural social and cultural influences in shaping implicit attitudes,[42] clearly understanding that "awareness of shared cultural stereotypes . . . [is] indeed a major source of implicit bias."[43] Or as Banaji put it in one interview, "The Implicit Association Test measures the thumbprint of the culture on our minds."[44] Psychologist John Dovidio elaborated on this idea: "The way to think about this is that particularly these implicit biases are habits of mind. They are things that have been associated with race all your life. And in our society, which historically has had racist traditions and is characterized by racial disparities, we develop these automatic associations with people of color that are more negative than the associations with whites so that they become habitual ways of thinking, and they're like habits."[45]

Thus, for example, differential levels of implicit pro-white bias among test takers of different races are thought "to reflect cultural and social learning of race attitudes and stereotypes."[46] Though some ISC researchers look closely at the role of society in structuring implicit associations, Greenwald and Banaji tend to focus primarily on how these attitudes manifest in individuals' distinct psychological attitudes.[47] Thus, for example, when declaring in their book *Blind Spot* that "institutional discrimination as a cause of Black disadvantage is an undeniable historical fact," they provide as examples of contemporary institutional discrimination reports of "discriminatory acts" at polling places in the 2000 and 2004 presidential elections, where precinct workers rigorously applied voter-qualification laws to black voters but not to white voters.[48] Although structural in the sense of involving the applications of laws, this example is telling in that it circles back away from structure to a focus on individuals' particular attitudes and behaviors.

What, therefore, does the IAT find regarding race? Basically, it finds implicit bias against blacks—lots of it. In 2006, summarizing nearly a decade of IAT research, Greenwald and Krieger found the evidence showed that the magnitude of implicit bias is large, that it often conflicts with explicit attitudes, that it affects behavior, and that it is malleable and therefore amenable to corrective interventions.[49] Assessing the state of the field in 2013, Greenwald and Banaji found subsequent data confirming these findings and concluded that data from the IAT have clearly established (1) "that automatic White preference is pervasive in American society," and (2) that "the automatic White preference expressed on the Race IAT is now established as signaling discriminatory behavior. It predicts discriminatory behavior even among research participants who earnestly (and, we believe, honestly) espouse egalitarian beliefs."[50] Most significant, perhaps, as Jennifer Kubota, Mahzarin Banaji, and Elizabeth Phelps report, is the finding for white Americans that "even when weak or no race preference is apparent on explicit, self-report measures, substantial levels of preference for positive stereotypes of white rather than black are observed on the IAT." The pattern is more complex in the results for black Americans, with 40 percent showing pro-white attitudes, 40 percent showing pro-black attitudes, and 20 showing neutral attitudes.[51]

The issue of predicting behavior is of central concern to IAT researchers. This centrality raises critical concerns regarding the significance of IAT test results beyond the controlled setting of a computer-based test. As Elizabeth Phelps and Laura Thomas noted as early as 2003 in a review of studies connecting IAT measures to fMRI studies of brain function, "Showing a behavior 'in the brain' does not say something more important or fundamental about who we are than our behavior. Functional neuroimaging techniques pick up on signals indicating brain activity. These signals, by themselves, do not specify a behavior. Only by linking these brain signals with behavior do they have psychological meaning."[52]

In 2006, Greenwald and Krieger argued that early evidence of predictive validity established that racial differences on IAT measures reflected actual implicit biases, not merely awareness of broader cultural attitudes or stereotypes.[53] In 2009, Banaji and Greenwald, together with Andrew Poehlman and Eric Uhlmann, published a meta-analysis of 122 research reports on the relation between IAT measures and predictions of "behavioral, judgment, and physiological measures." They concluded that their review justified "a recommendation to use IAT and self-report measures jointly as predictors of behavior." They interpreted the findings as being particularly strong concerning prediction of racially discriminatory behavior.[54] Commenting on this meta-analysis, Brian Nosek and Rachel Riskind concluded in 2012 that "accumulated evidence leaves no doubt that the implicit measures predict behavior."[55] Nonetheless, critics of the IAT vigorously dispute such claims,[56] and the controversy is unlikely to be resolved definitively anytime soon.

One of the first experiments to test for a relation between scores on a Race IAT and discriminatory behavior was conducted in 2001. In it, researchers covertly videotaped forty-two white college undergraduates during two brief interviews, one conducted by a white woman, one by a black woman. The students also took a Race IAT. Those whose scores indicated strong implicit preference for white relative to black displayed an array of behaviors that indicated greater comfort with the white interviewer than with the black interviewer. Researchers assessed such subtle behaviors as eye contact and leaning toward or away from the interviewer. They found that the students hesitated less and made fewer speech errors when speaking to the white interviewer than to the black interviewer; the students also spoke more to and smiled more at the white interviewer than the black interviewer. Drawing on past psychological studies of such behaviors, the researchers concluded that these results indicated a higher level of comfort and friendliness toward the white interviewer or greater discomfort or coolness toward the black interviewer or both.[57] Subsequent studies found similar results correlating IAT scores to behavior in hiring situations, doctor–patient encounters, and perceptions of anger.[58] One study even found that implicit racial preferences predicted the reported vote in the presidential election of 2008 between Barack Obama and John McCain.[59]

Such behavior is sometimes characterized as "racial microaggression."[60] Psychologists John Dovidio and Samuel Gaertner prefer to call it "aversive racism." They contrast aversive racism with "dominative racism," which they characterize as the "'old-fashioned,' blatant form." Aversive racism typically manifests in the behaviors of white people who are consciously committed to contemporary egalitarian ideals and do not overtly express any racist attitudes but who, according to Dovidio and Gaertner, "also develop some negative feelings toward or beliefs about blacks, of which they are unaware or which they try to dissociate from their nonprejudiced self-images. These negative feelings that aversive racists have toward blacks do not reflect open hostility or hatred. Instead, aversive racists' reactions may involve discomfort, uneasiness, disgust, and sometimes fear."[61]

This basic duality of attitudes and beliefs can produce a "racial ambivalence" that can lead to apparent contradictions between these white people's avowed beliefs and their sometimes "unintentionally" biased actions against blacks.[62]

Significantly, some prominent researchers are reluctant to call either the attitudes adduced from the IAT or the connected behavior as "prejudiced," let alone "racist." Thus, for example, in their book *Blind Spot*, Banaji and Greenwald note that ISC research grounded in the IAT does not find "*overtly* racially hostile acts." Because the sort of subtle social behaviors they observe in interracial interviews in hiring contexts "are not the types of negativity or hostility that are generally taken to be characteristics of 'prejudice,'" they answer "no" to the question "Does automatic White preference mean 'prejudice'?" Indeed, although embracing Dovidio and Gaertner's basic findings, Banaji and Greenwald explicitly "choose a different label" than *aversive racism*, concluding that "it is unwarranted to attach a 'racist' label to the many people who show an automatic White preference on the IAT." They suggest the term *uncomfortable egalitarians* as a possible alternative. Thus, they conclude, "it is a mistake to characterize modern America as racist."[63]

IAT MEETS FMRI

Researchers have also long engaged in trying to measure physiological responses to racially coded stimuli. Early efforts included measuring how skin sweats and how facial muscles twitch.[64] More recent studies have focused on assessing eyeblink startle responses to black versus white faces, cardiovascular reactivity, and event-related potential measures of the brain's electrophysiological response to racially coded stimuli.[65] Summarizing these studies, Jennifer Eberhardt concludes that they "consistently reveal significant response differences as a function of race even when traditional, more direct, measures of racial attitudes do not."[66] Perhaps the most sophisticated technology currently being used to measure physiological responses to race is functional magnetic resonance imaging.

A standard MRI uses a pulse of radio waves to temporarily knock protons out of alignment and then a giant magnet to measure the radio waves the protons emit as they relax back into alignment. Computers then take these data and process them to create an image of the subject's brain. An fMRI is "functional" in the sense that it is able to measure the flow of blood to particular parts of the brain during specified tasks undertaken while the subject is in the MRI machine. It is able to do this because measureable levels of iron in the blood vary depending on the blood's degree of oxygenation. Because blood oxygenation varies according to the levels of neural activity, these differences can be used to detect brain activity.[67] The device gathers information about the subject's Blood Oxygen Level Dependent (BOLD) response. In a comparison of the subject's BOLD response signals and a control state, small changes in signal intensity are detectable and can provide information about brain activity.[68]

The use of the IAT to measure implicit bias thus reached an entirely new level of technological complexity when researchers began combining it with fMRI to produce images of how people's scores on an IAT correlated with how their brain responded to racially coded stimuli. In 2000, Banaji along with Elizabeth Phelps, professor of neuroscience and psychology at New York University, and others in her lab coauthored the first study using fMRI in conjunction with the IAT "to explore the neural substrates involved in the unconscious evaluation of Black and White social groups." This study used fMRI to focus on a portion of the brain known as the amygdala, then understood to play a role in "emotional learning and evaluation," to assess the strength of its activation when white subjects viewed unfamiliar black and white faces. The fMRI results were then correlated with IAT results (and an additional unconscious measure of "potentiated startle") for the same test subjects. The study found greater amygdala activation, as measured by fMRI detection of BOLD patterns, in response to black faces, leading the authors to conclude that "these results suggest that amygdala and behavioral responses to Black-versus-White faces in White subjects reflect cultural evaluations of social groups modified by individual experience."[69]

Since 2000, a growing number of studies have explored correlations between racial perception, activation of particular brain regions, and Race IAT measures.[70] The amygdala has been a primary though not the sole focus of this work. It is a small, almond-size part of the brain (its name derives from the Greek word for "almond") that has been studied extensively with respect to implicit emotional learning and memory.[71] Early studies connected the amygdala strongly with classical fear conditioning, but more recent work has suggested that it might simply be more generally connected with the recognition of cognitively salient stimuli, which might also be positive.[72] Other studies suggest that familiarity and norm violation might also play a significant role in race-related amygdala activation.[73] The range of study findings suggests the "flexibility of [the] amygdala," showing that its activation may be broadly "sensitive to representations of any valence when they are motivationally relevant."[74] Thus, one recent review of numerous findings of greater amygdala BOLD activity in response to out-group race faces versus in-group race faces took this greater activity to indicate not fear but rather the "emotional salience of race in American culture."[75]

One recent review by Kubota, Banaji, and Phelps identifies, in addition to the amygdala, several other areas of particular interest to those studying what they call the "neural systems of race." Prominent among these areas are the anterior cingulate cortex (ACC), the dorsolateral prefrontal cortex (DLPFC), and the fusiform face area (FFA). Neuroscientists have observed ACC activation when individuals experience conflict between automatic and intentional responses to stimuli.[76] One might see such observations as the physiological indicia of conflicts between Kahneman's System 1 and System 2 modes of cognition.[77] In the context of racially coded stimuli, the ACC may be activated through detecting a conflict between automatic, implicit biases and conscious egalitarian intentions.[78] The DLFPC is thought to be implicated in top-down, conscious, executive-control function. Many studies report that the DLPFC is also activated when the ACC is activated, which suggests that once the ACC detects a conflict, the DLPFC may be activated to inhibit implicit racial biases.[79] The FFA, as its name suggests, is an area of the brain involved in processing visual perceptions of faces. Studies show that the ability to distinguish among faces is influenced by race, indicating a likely role for the FFA in facilitating the recognition of in-group versus out-group faces.[80] In one particularly provocative recent study, researchers successfully predicted the race of faces shown to subjects based on interpretations of the BOLD activation patterns in the FFA detected by fMRI. Moreover, the researchers also found a correlation with IAT measures indicating that a stronger pro-white bias "decreases the similarity of neural representations of Black and White faces."[81]

In 2008, David Amodio cautioned that "one cannot assume a one-to-one mapping of a psychological process onto a particular neural structure, nor can one assume that a particular experimental task elicits a process-pure instantiation of the phenomenon of interest."[82] More recently, a review of literature in political neuroscience put forth the following useful caveat in considering how to read data from fMRI in relation to complex social behaviors, which should be kept in mind in reviewing work on neuroscience and race:

> Our review of the literature reveals that most studies thus far have concentrated simply on "brain mapping," that is, seeking to identify correlations between neural functions (or region-specific activation) and political attitudes and behaviors. This is a necessary step in the research process, but it is also important to bear in mind problems associated with the drawing of "reverse inferences," that is, concluding that because a given brain region (e.g., the amygdala) is generally involved in a certain type of task or function (e.g., the processing of emotionally salient information) that its activation in a given instance must indicate the presence of a specific mental process (e.g., the experience of emotion). As Poldrack has pointed out, the method of reverse inference provides only weak evidence concerning the operation of specific mental processes "because of the fact that activation is rarely selective," insofar as "regions are often activated by a wide range of mental tasks."[83]

This well-stated caution to avoid overclaiming for basic observed correlations between brain-region activation and a particular stimulus leads the authors of this review of the literature to posit a more dynamic and interactive model of brain functioning and to hypothesize that "differences in neurocognitive structure and functioning are linked to a constellation of social and psychological processes that unfold over time and *both reflect and give rise to the expression of political behavior.* In other words, we favor a dynamic, recursive theoretical framework in which the connection between physiological (and psychological) functioning and political outcomes is conceived of as bidirectional rather than unidirectional."[84]

This dynamic, recursive model of brain functioning stands in stark contrast to Tversky and Kahneman's dual-system model and to related ISC scholarship that is premised on a clear distinction between automatic and deliberate or controlled brain functions.[85] As one recent paper by Jay Van Bavel, Jenny Xiao, and Leor Hackel remarks, "Although dual process models serve as a useful heuristic for the human mind and have sparked numerous studies, advances in social and cognitive neuroscience suggest that the human evaluative system is more widely distributed and dynamic than that proposed by traditional dual process models."[86]

Similarly, in a paper published in 2012, William Cunningham and his coauthors argue that "recent developments in the cognitive and neural sciences suggest that human information processing is better characterized in terms of dynamical system models, rather than dual-process models."[87]

Along these lines, a recent study by Christian Kaul, Kyle Ratner, and Jay Van Bavel investigated the influence of processing goals on how the fusiform gyrus (FG, where the FFA is located) processes representations of race. Investigators assigned subjects to one of two teams, the Leopards and the Tigers. Each team had six black and six white members, represented by matched faces presented to the subjects. Subjects were given three minutes to memorize the faces belonging to each team. In a series of fMRI trials, participants were then asked to categorize each face either by *skin color* or by *group membership*. The study found that "race decoding was higher in the FG during the group vs skin color categorization task. The results suggest that, ironically, explicit racial categorization can diminish the representation of race in the FG." The authors conclude that these results suggest that "the representation of race is dynamic, reflecting current processing goals that arise from the social environment."[88] A more dynamic-systems model of brain functioning challenges (but does not necessarily undermine) the idea of automaticity so central to much of the IAT research. It does, however, lend perhaps even greater support to a central concern noted by those employing a dual-system model: the basic malleability of automatic implicit evaluations.[89] Studies suggest that the sort of rapid social perception underlying implicit bias may be flexible and hence susceptible to modification through manipulation of the context that influences different individual motivational states.[90]

Malleability is central because the goal of much of this research is not simply to understand how the brain responds to perceiving race but to provide a scientifically grounded basis for developing specific interventions to help reduce, contain, or manage racial bias—that is, the project of implicit social cognition is also largely a project concerned with racial equity. As Amodio puts it,

> A major goal of research on intergroup bias is to find ways to reduce prejudice in society. Most contemporary approaches to prejudice reduction in the field of social psychology have focused on changing prejudiced attitudes and reducing the strength of race-biased associations in implicit memory. Indeed, the ultimate goal of a prejudice reduction intervention is to rid a person of all implicit and explicit racial biases. But prejudice may be reduced in others ways as well, such as through the enhancement of self-regulation and through the modulation of situational factors. In the end, the goal of prejudice reduction efforts is to eliminate the expression of discriminatory behaviour, and thus any strategies that accomplish this goal are worth considering.[91]

It is important to note here Amodio's direct emphasis on individuals' particular attitudes. Even while acknowledging the relevance of "situational factors," his primary focus is interventions that engage the individual qua individual, ridding him or her of bias on a case-by-case basis, whether through particular external interventions or through enhancing "self-regulation."

Central to ISC scholars' hopes and programs, therefore, is an understanding of human cognitive perception and bias as malleable. As Mary Wheeler and Susan Fiske put it in 2005, "The malleability of stereotyping matters in social psychology and in society."[92] Malleability means that implicit bias is not intractable. If it is not intractable, then there is space for social psychologists and neuroscientists to craft interventions to help lessen such bias or even to eliminate it altogether. The key for these researchers, then, is to understand how manipulating particular contexts may affect implicit bias. Hence, "the Holy grail of implicit race bias research is to change the underlying associations that form the basis of implicit bias."[93]

Specifically with regard to implicit bias, ISC researchers emphasize that racial attitudes are not hard-wired. The human brain may have evolved to create categories for sensory stimuli, but it seems unlikely that phenotypic racial categories (e.g., skin pigmentation) are primary among them, for the simple reason that when the human brain was evolving, our ancestors were not highly mobile. Their neighbors were likely to look very much like them; therefore, as psychologist Robert Kurzban has noted, "there would be no adaptive advantage to a mental module that automatically took note of someone's race."[94] Moreover, the results of one recent study suggest that "differential amygdala response to African American faces does not emerge until adolescence, reflecting the increasing salience of race across development."[95] Thus, as psychologists Nosek and Riskind note, "the key implication for policy considerations is that implicit social cognition is not a fixed entity; it is dynamically interrelated with the social situation."[96] Another key implication is that the perception of racial difference is not "natural" in the sense of being evolutionarily programmed into us. We all perceive difference, yes, but the meaning and salience of those differences are mediated primarily through social not physiological forces.

The question then becomes how to mitigate implicit bias. The Leopard/Tiger study, for example, indicates that it is possible to alter the salience of racial categorization. As William Cunningham, a coauthor of the study, noted, "You can build a larger 'we' . . . [and] mitigate or even override the original prejudice. That means that racism is neither intractable nor inevitable."[97] Similarly, a study of children found that "greater peer diversity was associated with attenuated amygdala response to African American faces,"[98] suggesting that interventions promoting intergroup racial contact may reduce the salience of race.

All of this comes under the general heading "debiasing," which ISC scholars see as the critical type of intervention to develop from their work. In a discussion of the policy implications of ISC, Nosek and Riskind argue that ISC research can influence social policy in at least two ways: first, by simply applying insights from ISC to design and evaluate policies and, second, by using instruments such as the IAT to further particular policy goals. For them, the key is to develop interventions that effectively derail the translation of implicit biases into particular behaviors. The critical point is that "having thoughts is not the same as acting on those thoughts." They discuss a four-step model of debiasing in which people must "(1) detect their unwanted thoughts, (2) be motivated to remove the biasing influence, (3) detect the size and direction of the biasing thoughts, and (4) redirect their own judgments or behaviors so that they are not contaminated by the biasing thoughts." To achieve these steps, Nosek and Riskind suggest three possible interventions, each largely educational: first, working to reduce the existence of bias itself; second, teaching key decision makers (such as judges or juries) to prevent unwanted biases from being activated or influencing judgment; and third, manipulating the context in which decisions are made so as to lessen the influence of unwanted biases. Nosek and Riskind see the IAT as an important tool here to be used in training key decision makers to see and understand their own personal implicit biases. Other specific strategies such as developing identity-blind evaluations in employment settings involve manipulating the context to lessen the influence of implicit biases.[99]

Along the lines of the Leopard/Tiger study, researchers have argued that promoting intergroup contact may be a constructive intervention to lessen implicit bias. Adam Pearson, John Dovidio, and Samuel Gaertner also speak more generally of creating a larger "we" by inducing members of different racial groups to think of themselves as a "single superordinate in-group rather than as two separate groups."[100] In addition, populating particular social situations with high-status, well-liked people who are known to hold egalitarian values appears to call out like minds in those around them.[101] Amodio and Mendoza note three particular basic areas of intervention to moderate the effects of implicit bias: first, "changes in representation," which, for example, might involve examining the effect on IAT performance among subjects who are first primed by viewing pairings of black faces with positive images and white faces with negative images; second, "goal effects," which can be as simple as exposing subjects to positive exemplars of a stigmatized groups (e.g., pictures of Martin Luther King Jr.) or to egalitarian messages; and third, "situational effects," wherein context can affect implicit attitudes, as in how viewing a picture of a black man in the context of a dark alley elicits more biased responses than viewing him in a church context.[102]

One basic idea here is to "decoupl[e] more gut-level affective responses from images of stigmatised group members."[103] ISC scholars argue that the malleability of implicit bias opens the door to well-crafted expert interventions through training, education, and context manipulation that hold out the hope of mitigating or even eradicating implicit bias.

2

THE UPTAKE OF IMPLICIT SOCIAL COGNITION BY THE LEGAL ACADEMY

Given ISC's focus on the nature and dynamics of bias, it should come as no surprise that certain segments of the legal academy concerned with persistent social inequality have turned to it for insights, support, and programmatic remedies. Since the 1990s, legal scholars have been drawing upon the science of ISC to make new arguments concerning the legal recognition of subtle yet pervasive forms of discrimination, in particular claims for employment discrimination under Title VII of the Civil Rights Act of 1964, and the assertion of the constitutional legitimacy of affirmative action remedies to redress such inequity.

In 1995, Linda Krieger's influential article "The Content of Our Categories: A Cognitive Bias Approach to Discrimination and Equal Employment Opportunity" sounded a clarion call to shift the frame of disparate-treatment analysis from a motivational focus to a cognitive focus. Krieger argued that the latter was the best way for the law to address subtle and unconscious forms of bias as they manifest in concrete decisions and actions in employment settings.[1] She built much of her argument around exploring the limitations of the then recent Supreme Court decision in *Price Waterhouse v. Hopkins* (1989).[2] At the trial, Krieger's later coauthor, psychologist Susan Fiske, testified as an expert witness that the plaintiff, Ann Hopkins, likely was the victim of sex stereotyping in adverse employment decisions by her employer, Price Waterhouse.[3] Justice William J. Brennan's plurality opinion in *Price Waterhouse* was notable for articulating a "mixed-motive" theory of Title VII discrimination, under which a defendant might be held liable even if some legitimate reasons underlay its employment decisions. Brennan asserted that "so long as the plaintiff . . . shows that an impermissible motive played a motivating part in an adverse employment decision . . .[she] has thereby placed upon the defendant the burden to show that it would have made the same decision in the absence of the unlawful motive."[4]

Though Hopkins won the case, Krieger was concerned that Brennan's analysis confounded "concepts of motive, intent and causation," premised liability wholly on "the presence of conscious discriminatory animus," and "in essence direct[ed] the trier to fact to take a snapshot of the decisionmaker's mental state at the moment the allegedly discriminatory decision was made." She drew on social cognition theory to argue that much discrimination, particularly when based on stereotypes, operates at a cognitive level below that of conscious intent and must be understood in a broader temporal context. She asserted that such stereotypes can cause discrimination by biasing how we process information about other people; in short, "we judge other people by the content of our categories." Such discrimination is automatic and operates independently of motive or intent. Nonetheless, according to Krieger, "it can be controlled, sometimes even eliminated, through careful process re-engineering. Cognitive biases in intergroup perception and judgment, though unintentional and largely unconscious, can be recognized and prevented by a decision maker who is motivated not to discriminate and who is provided with the tools required to translate that motivation into action."[5] Here we see early on how the idea of cognitive malleability creates space for imbuing psychologically based interventions with legal salience.

Early in her article, Krieger carefully distinguished her social cognition perspective on disparate-treatment law from the perspective that legal scholar Charles Lawrence III offered in his article "The Id, the Ego, and Equal Protection: Reckoning with Unconscious Racism" (1987).[6] Krieger noted that Lawrence drew on psychoanalytic theory to assert "that much of what is classified as disparate treatment discrimination results from subconscious instincts and motivations," but she argued that although "Professor Lawrence does mention cognitive bias as a potential source of discriminatory decisionmaking, he focuses primarily on discussing motivational rather than cognitive antecedents."[7]

At this point, it is useful to review briefly some key aspects of Lawrence's earlier work to more fully appreciate the distinctions between his more psychoanalytic approach to prejudice and Krieger's ISC-grounded approach. In his article, Lawrence explicitly pathologized racism as a "disease" and focused on how "a common historical and cultural heritage" that attaches negative feelings and opinions to nonwhites has infected us all and, in effect, "turned us all into racists." Yet, he noted, "most of us are unaware of our racism. We do not recognize the ways in which our cultural experience has influenced our beliefs about race or the occasions on which those beliefs affect our actions. In other words, a large part of the behavior that produces racial discrimination is influenced by unconscious racial motivation."[8]

At first blush, Lawrence's foregrounding of unconscious racism would seem to comport well with notions of implicit bias employed by Krieger and ISC theorists. Lawrence, however, was much more broadly focused on the dynamics in the production and circulation of cultural meaning as a basis for the legal assessment of discriminatory acts. For Lawrence, "racism in America is much more complex than either the conscious conspiracy of a power elite or the simple delusion of a few ignorant bigots. It is a part of our common historical experience and, therefore, a part of our culture. It arises from the assumptions we have learned to make about the world, ourselves, and others as well as from the patterns of our fundamental social activities."[9] Where ISC tends to focus on the psychological state of particular biased individuals, Lawrence concentrated on cultural context and stigma—that is, on the harm suffered by those who experience racist acts rather than on the state of mind of those committing such acts.

ISC is grounded in tests such as the IAT that employ expert technical measurements of individual responses to particular stimuli. In contrast, Lawrence proposed a "cultural meaning" test to trigger judicial recognition of race-based behavior, a test that was primarily interpretive in nature and looked to broad cultural and historical phenomena to evaluate whether a particular act conveys a shameful or stigmatizing message. Lawrence suggested that the cultural meaning of an act was "the best available analogue for, and evidence of, a collective unconscious that we cannot observe directly." He argued that such cultural meaning was a sort of social text or "text-analogue" that courts were well suited to interpret, just as they had long engaged in interpreting a wide array of social phenomena.[10] The reference to "collective unconscious" contrasts strikingly with ISC's focus on specific individual cognition. Twenty years later, reflecting back on his original article, Lawrence explained, "My reference to the 'collective unconscious' rather than [to] the individual actor's unconscious was meant to convey my belief that the harm resided in the continued existence of a widely shared belief in white supremacy and not in the motivation of the individual actor or actors charged with discrimination."[11]

Krieger's characterization of Lawrence's work as focusing on motivational states is thus curious insofar as it seems to overlook Lawrence's primarily cultural or social focus. The cultural meaning test does not depend on evaluating the motivational state of the individual or entity that commits a particular act; rather, the test interprets the functioning of that act as it plays out in a social and historical context. Krieger's obscuring of Lawrence's focus on the significance of cultural meaning is both striking and significant. It laid the foundations for a decisive move by legal scholars applying ISC theory away from Lawrence's broad interpretive approach in evaluating societal racism toward a more narrow and technical focus on causation and evaluating individual attitudes and biases through quantitative, controlled, expertly constructed and mediated interventions, such as the IAT.

Christine Jolls, another early and influential advocate of integrating ISC into a behavioral realist approach to the law, similarly distinguished Lawrence's work, noting that his cultural meaning test simply had not caught on and that "prominent antidiscrimination law scholars who strongly support the focus on implicitly biased behavior have argued that the cultural meaning test is difficult if not impossible to apply or is flawed on other grounds." Nonetheless, she cast Lawrence's work as part of an emerging "consensus" around the idea that "the problem of bias on the basis of race and other traits in American society today is primarily a problem of *implicit* rather than conscious bias."[12]

The contrast between the ISC approach and Lawrence's cultural approach perhaps becomes clearer in an article Krieger coauthored with Susan Fiske in 2006, in which they refer to judge and jury as "intuitive psychologists" who act on "implicitly held theories of human behavior" in reaching their decisions.[13] Although there is certainly much to recommend this reference as a commonsense characterization of what happens in the judicial system, Lawrence's focus on the judge's role as an interpreter of cultural texts located authority and expertise firmly within an existing tradition of jurisprudential practice, whereas Krieger and Fiske introduce the discipline of psychology as a new source of authority to guide and instruct the courts. As Jerry

Kang succinctly states the contrast, "Lawrence's methodology divines cultural meaning, whereas the 'implicit bias' research measures bias through individuals' reaction-time differentials."[14] Kang's distinction between the two basic stances toward understanding racism could not be clearer: the cultural "meaning" of acts and expressions that come to be understood as racist through an interpretive enterprise versus empirical measures of the "fact" of racism. Similarly clear is Kang's privileging of precise empirical measurement over interpretation, which merely "divines cultural meaning," much as an augur might consult bird entrails for portents of the future.

This, then, is the space within which the legal school of behavioral realism has come to engage issues of implicit bias. Krieger and Fiske posit that

> behavioral realism in law stands for the proposition that legal theories, no less than their epistemological counterparts, both can and should be naturalizing. Behavioral realism, like naturalism, stands for the proposition that judges should not generate the behavioral theories sometimes used in the construction or justification of legal doctrine through a solely conceptual, *a priori* process. To the extent that legal doctrines rely on stated or unstated theories about the nature of real world phenomena, behavioral realism argues, those theories should remain consistent with advances in relevant fields of empirical inquiry. And where the real world phenomena relevant to a particular area of law concern human social perception, motivation, and judgment, the relevant domains of empirical inquiry with which legal theories should remain consistent include cognitive social psychology and the related social sciences.[15]

By "naturalizing," they mean that law, in particular antidiscrimination law, should be "behaviorally realistic," such that it "remain[s] continuous with progress in psychological science." This in turn means that when drawing on models of real-world phenomena (such as the psychology of ISC), "judges should take reasonable steps . . . to make sure they have the science right."[16]

For Jerry Kang and Mahzarin Banaji, behavioral realism "takes ISC seriously" and "identifies naïve theories of human behavior latent in the law and legal institutions. It then juxtaposes these theories against the best scientific knowledge available to expose gaps between assumptions embedded in law and reality described by science."[17] Kang notes elsewhere that behavioral realism asks lawmakers and legal institutions to account for any discrepancies between naive, commonsense theories of human behavior and the findings of ISC. Such an accounting "requires either altering the law to comport with more accurate models of thinking and behavior, or providing a transparent explanation" of reasons for retaining the less-accurate view.[18]

Behavioral realists see the science of ISC as transforming the law. Kang and Banaji straightforwardly assert that "new facts recently discovered in the mind and behavioral sciences can potentially transform both lay and expert conceptions of affirmative action. Specifically, the science of implicit social cognition (ISC) can help us revise the very meaning of certain affirmative action prescriptions by updating our understanding of human nature and its social development." They identify four key areas where, they argue, a behavioral realist application of ISC theory can transform the law of affirmative action, effectively revitalizing what has become a relatively moribund area of law. First, behavioral realists can change the temporal frame of affirmative action by casting it as a response to ongoing discrimination "in the here and now." Second, they can "update the scientific case for the mismeasurement of merit" by showing how implicit bias skews the evaluation of merit. In this context, affirmative action is cast not as preferential treatment but as "an opportunity for more accurate measures."[19] Third, they suggest that ISC findings can be used to craft affirmative action programs more effectively to serve as debiasing agents. Effective debiasing is a particularly important part of the legal scaffolding because, as Kang later states in a separate article, "the point of debiasing is to directly counter (implicit) racial bias that has been found to predict discrimination. And preventing race from influencing behavior—has always been recognized as a compelling interest."[20] Finally, ISC theory addresses an additional temporal component of affirmative action—namely, When will it end? Kang and Banaji propose that

> the lifespan for certain affirmative action programs should be guided by evidence of bias rather than [by] any arbitrary or hopeful deadline. Now that we can measure threats to fair treatment—threats that lie in every mind—such data should be a crucial guide to ending affirmative action. We suggest a terminus when measures of implicit bias for a region or nation are at zero or some rough behavioral equivalent. At this point, implicit bias

would align with an explicit creed of equal treatment. It would fulfill collective aspirations to behave in accordance with explicitly held values.[21]

This data-driven approach to measuring bias clearly falls in the behavioral realist tradition enunciated by Krieger in 1996, in contrast to Lawrence's more humanistic interpretive approach.

It is perhaps precisely the empirically based scientific framing of the behavioral realist approach that has given it such powerful traction in certain segments of the legal academy over the past decade. As Kang and psychologist Kristin Lane put it in 2010, "Once upon a time, the central civil rights questions were indisputably normative. . . . Today, the central civil rights questions of our time turn also on the underlying empirics."[22] The focus on empirics marks behavioral realism as a sort of answer from the left to the more conservative law and economics movement. We see this when Krieger and Fiske concede with grudging respect, "Two of the core insights of the law and economics movement are that people respond to incentives and that law can serve as a powerful tool for structuring those incentives in socially beneficial ways. It is testimony to the enormous success of this movement that legal rules are increasingly crafted with an eye toward structuring incentives so as to encourage people and organizations to act in particular ways and forbear from acting in others."[23]

Krieger and Fiske hold out the hope that a new awareness of implicit bias will provide a basis for crafting legal interventions that might "profoundly alter [a] decision maker's judgment and behavior" so as to reduce discrimination.[24]

Legal scholars have identified a wide array of contexts where ISC findings can be relevant to identifying relevant implicit bias and to crafting remedial or preventative interventions. Kang and Banaji's idea that debiasing might form a constitutionally compelling interest sufficient to justify state intervention has broad implications for both educational and employment programs seeking to implement affirmative action policies. For example, the amicus brief submitted by the American Psychological Association in support of the respondents in *Grutter v. Bollinger* (2003) referenced psychological studies to argue for the ameliorating effects that a diverse student body would have upon implicit bias.[25] And the association's amicus brief in the more recent case *Fisher v. University of Texas* (2013) explicitly drew on findings from IAT studies to develop arguments on the positive debiasing effects of affirmative action.[26]

Christine Jolls and Cass Sunstein provide the following two hypothetical situations to illustrate the possible working of implicit bias in an employment context:

> [1.] An employer is deciding whether to promote Jones or Smith to a supervisory position at its firm. Jones is white; Smith is African-American. The employer thinks that both employees are excellent, but it chooses Jones on the ground that employees and customers will be "more comfortable" with a white employee in the supervisory position. [2.] An employer is deciding whether to promote Jones or Smith to a supervisory position at its firm. Jones is white; Smith is African-American. The employer thinks that both employees are excellent, but it chooses Jones on the basis of a "gut feeling" that Jones would be better for the job. The employer is not able to explain the basis for this gut feeling; it simply thinks that "Jones is a better fit." The employer did not consciously think about racial issues in making this decision; but, in fact, Smith would have been chosen if both candidates had been white.[27]

Jolls and Sunstein note that the first example clearly runs afoul of antidiscrimination law, but the second case, although perhaps equally troublesome, is far more problematic.[28] There is no clear prohibited act or rationale in the second case, and yet the sort of "gut feeling" underlying the idea of a "better fit" is precisely the sort of situation where implicit bias can come into play. Such gut feelings may play a role not only in promotion but in initial hiring and a host of other employment-related decisions, including performance evaluation and compensation.[29] Thus, Jolls and Sunstein suggest, "It should not be controversial to suggest that in formulating and interpreting legal rules, legislatures and courts should pay close attention to the best available evidence about people's actual behavior," evidence supplied by behavioral realists employing ISC theory and methods such as the IAT.[30]

Similar dynamics may come into play wherever individual judgment and discretion are at issue. A collection of essays on "implicit bias across the law" contains chapters covering property law, criminal justice, torts, employment, health care, education, communications, corporate law, intellectual property, tax law, environmental law, and federal Indian law.[31] In noting the persistence of broad-based racial disparities in the United States, the volume editors argue that the effects of implicit bias are so "powerful and pervasive that they help explain not only the continued subordination of historically subordinated groups but also the legal system's complicity in the subordination."[32]

One chapter on property law recounts a study where participants evaluated particular houses according to specified buyer needs. The study found that participants who evaluated a house for sale by a black family viewed it more negatively than participants who evaluated the exact same house when told it was for sale by a white family.[33] The chapter on criminal justice references studies showing implicit bias against blacks in a range of law enforcement contexts. So-called Shooter Bias studies figure prominently, where in a typical scenario subjects play a video game that instructs them to shoot at perpetrators holding a weapon but to refrain from shooting bystanders holding a nonthreatening object, such as a book or cell phone. Results consistently show subjects shooting at black figures more frequently and more quickly than at white figures and conversely refraining from shooting at white bystanders more frequently and more quickly than refraining from shooting black bystanders. Thus, the authors conclude, "literally, the 'face' of crime in America is black, and, more, . . . being white is actively disassociated with (at least street) crime."[34] The chapter on health care builds on extensive work in the field of health disparities, finding broad, persistent, and significant implicit bias in the health-care system.[35] This chapter draws on a report by the Institute of Medicine issued in 2003 that cited ISC studies in finding, inter alia, that "bias, stereotyping, prejudice, and clinical uncertainty on the part of healthcare providers may contribute to racial and ethnic disparities in healthcare."[36] Yet the authors of the chapter note that "because the behaviors operate at the subconscious level, meeting the proof requirement (intentionality) and litigating such cases will be difficult under current civil rights law."[37] And so each chapter of this volume on "implicit racial bias across the law" goes, documenting it at work and assessing its legal implications.

Of particular note is the chapter on communications law,[38] where Jerry Kang builds on his earlier extensive treatment of the subject in his influential article "Trojan Horses of Race." In both chapter and article, Kang explores the power of the electronic media in perpetuating and fostering pernicious racial stereotypes that feed broader implicit biases throughout society. Kang argues that as we consume local media images "replete with violent crime stories prominently featuring racial minorities," we "download a sort of Trojan Horse virus that increases our implicit bias." These images both construct and exacerbate racial schemas—cognitive structures that "automatically, efficiently, and adaptively parse the raw data pushed into our senses."[39] The law is implicated because the Federal Communications Commission regulates these entities and might both monitor content more effectively and propose rules that might counter the effects of such images, such as "debiasing public service announcements."[40]

We come now to the issue of remedy or interventions to address such pervasive implicit bias across the law. Most suggested interventions involve education or training or the manipulation of context to achieve debiasing effects. In considering possible interventions, Kang and Banaji "proffer no silver bullets, for the science provides none." They instead "provide a few modest interventions that address both perceiver and target effects." These suggestions provide a good basic framework for assessing the range of possible interventions and tend generally to reflect the types of interventions suggested by many behavioral realists and ISC scholars. Kang and Banaji begin by suggesting action to "motivate decision makers to correct bias by increasing self-awareness." This action basically takes the form of promoting broad self-diagnosis of implicit basis by encouraging "those who admit, hire, select, and evaluate" others to "experience their bias directly" through such interventions as taking the IAT online, free of charge. Next, they speak generally of the need to "prevent the influence of implicit bias." More specifically, where feasible, they recommend "cloaking social category in order to prevent biased perceptions."[41]

A classic of example of such "cloaking" is taken from a policy implemented by the American Symphony Orchestra in the 1970s to use blind auditions to address gender bias in hiring. Here, a candidate for a position with the orchestra would audition from behind a curtain so that those in a position to evaluate the performance and make hiring decisions would do so solely on the basis of the performance, having no indication of the candidate's gender to implicitly bias their decisions. As a result, the number of female musicians hired rose significantly.[42] In the educational context, Kang and Banaji suggest blind grading of a student's work, and they note that cyberspace offers many opportunities for cloaking a subject's identity so as to mitigate possible implicit bias.[43] Under this heading, they also suggest decreasing "subjective discretion in the merit measurement" by discounting "the emphasis on traditional interviews" in hiring or other evaluative settings.[44]

Kang and Banaji also urge measures to address "stereotype threat," which affects the targets of implicit bias. Stereotype threat, generally speaking, involves the danger that certain circumstances will promote the likelihood that those subject to negative stereotypes will perform in ways that conform to the stereotype—an example might be a situation where girls taking a math test are primed to think of their gender and as a result perform worse on the test than when primed with non-gender-specific references. The idea here would generally be to educate people to avoid using triggers that might produce stereotype-threat responses.[45] Finally, Kang and Banaji propose "breaking ties in favor of bias targets" on the theory "that any candidate who registers a tie on an instrument that is biased against her is likely to be the stronger candidate."[46]

Beyond these rather specific employment-based interventions, Kang and Banaji also discuss more general debiasing strategies with potentially broader societal application. They cite numerous studies for the proposition that increasing intergroup contact can ameliorate bias. They go on to note that ISC research suggests that exposing people to "countertypical exemplars" may also reduce implicit bias.[47] For example, they discuss one study by Nilanjana Dasgupta and Anthony Greenwald that found that exposing subjects to the names and images of positive black exemplars, such as Martin Luther King Jr., and of negative white exemplars, such as serial killer Jeffrey Dahmer, could significantly affect scores on subsequent IATs.[48] Similarly, they note studies showing how "countertypical visualizations"—merely imagining positive exemplars—and having "countertypical teachers" in an educational setting might also mitigate implicit bias. Considering the power of images to shape bias, they explore a range of possible microinterventions that might be available "for private, individual, voluntary, 'do it yourself' attitude makeovers. How do you decorate your room? What is on your screensaver?"[49] (Indeed, Kang suggests elsewhere that debiasing screensavers might be ordered as part of the settlement of a discrimination lawsuit.[50]) A recent study even argues that putting oneself in the place of a black avatar in a video game can reduce implicit bias.[51]

Perhaps most provocatively, Kang and Banaji go on to consider the possible implications of hiring what they call "debiasing agents" for affirmative action policies. They describe a debiasing agent as "an individual with characteristics that run counter to the attitudes and/or the stereotypes associated with the category to which the agent belongs. Examples include women construction workers, male nurses, Black intellectuals, White janitors, Asian CEOs, gay boxers, and elderly marathon runners."[52]

Kang and Banaji note that in contrast to the "role model" rationale of much diversity rhetoric, the purpose of debiasing is actually to reduce discrimination. This reduction, they argue, would constitute a compelling interest sufficient to legally justify the use of such measures. As they conclude, the ultimate rationale for using debiasing agents "is not self-esteem; it is disinfection"—that is, the removal of the "virus" of implicit bias.[53]

Most of these interventions ultimately involve some form of education or training or manipulation of context, all crafted and administered by experts in ISC. Targets of education might include everyone from police officers to judicial officers and juries, employers, real estate agents, and media executives.[54] In the realm of legal practice, it is particularly noteworthy that the American Bar Association has created a task force on implicit bias that "support[s] the presentation of programming on the topic by judges, bar leaders, and others across the country."[55] A centerpiece of this project is a series of three videos developed by the Judicial Council of California to educate officers of the court about implicit bias. Produced by the Center for Judiciary Education and Research, the videos come under the heading "The Neuroscience and Psychology of Decisionmaking." The hosting website also contains links to Project Implicit at Harvard University, where subjects can take an online IAT free of charge as well as download a counterstereotype screensaver.[56] Many of the experts discussed earlier, including Kang and Banaji, appear in the videos. In the first sixty-minute video, titled *A New Way of Learning*, experts discuss research in neuroscience and social psychology, describing how unconscious processes may affect our decisions. It specifically considers research using fMRI to show how the brain reacts when different images, voices, or written work are presented.[57] The second video, *The Media, the Brain, and the Courtroom*, also combines recent fMRI research with an analysis of the media images that may affect our view of women and numerous other groups. Early in this video, Jerry Kang discusses the power of media imagery to shape our perceptions; the video then turns to Anthony Greenwald for a discussion of the IAT.[58] The final video, *Dismantling and Overriding Bias*, highlights neuroscientific and psychological evidence that we can indeed dismantle and override bias using specific techniques—for example, computer screensavers that present counterstereotypical exemplars.[59]

Beyond California, the National Center for State Courts (NCSC) maintains a website that offers educational resources to help courts learn about and address implicit bias, noting that California, Minnesota, and North Dakota have been serving as pilot test states for extensive engagement in judicial education programs in implicit bias.[60] In 2012, the NCSC issued the report *Helping Courts Address Implicit Bias: Resources for Education*, which elaborated more fully on the sorts of strategies described in the *Dismantling and Overriding Bias* video.[61] The report describes the need for extensive training sessions and methodologies for mitigating the effects of implicit bias, many along the lines proposed by Kang and Banaji, such as presenting counterstereotypical exemplars in a systematic manner grounded in consistency and reinforcement.

A recent article authored by Kang and others describes the NCSC initiative and nicely reviews some key suggested interventions. The authors present the program as a way for judges to "to gain actual scientific knowledge about implicit social cognitions," with the goal "to persuade judges, on the merits, to recognize implicit bias as a potential problem, which in turn should increase motivation to adopt sensible countermeasures."[62] They also recommend the following tactics to address implicit bias:

First, training should commence early, starting with new-judge orientation when individuals are likely to be most receptive. Second, training should not immediately put judges on the defensive, for instance, by accusing them of concealing explicit bias. Instead, trainers can start the conversation with other types of decisionmaking errors and cognitive biases, such as anchoring, or less-threatening biases, such as the widespread preference for the youth over the elderly that IATs reveal. Third, judges should be encouraged to take the IAT or other measures of implicit bias.[63]

Concerns to address implicit bias, then, have gained significant traction both within the legal academy and more broadly in the bar and in the courts. Building on the research in ISC, legal scholars in conjunction with practitioners and psychologists have also developed educational and training materials that are being actively disseminated to address implicit bias.

SOME EXISTING CRITIQUES

Given the policy implications of the rise of ISC studies in general and in the use of the IAT in particular, it is not surprising that a range of critiques have emerged over the past decade or so. The critiques fit into two general categories: those coming from within the disciplines of psychology and neuroscience that challenge some of the technical aspects of the testing, data, and interpretation; and those coming from other disciplines such as sociology and law that question more generally the focus and framing of these studies. In the brief review of existing critiques given here, the point is not to resolve the disputes but to integrate them into our understanding of the terrain in which ISC theory and behavioral realism are playing out in broader discussions of the nature of bias in contemporary American society.

As Justine Tinkler notes, "There is little scholarly disagreement that results from the IAT reveal that most Americans . . . have an easier time associating positive words with White people and negative words with Black people than the other way around. Where researchers disagree is on whether the results from an IAT reflect personally held attitudes towards groups or something else."[64] Perhaps foremost among the technical critics are psychologists Gregory Mitchell and Philip Tetlock. In a series of articles, they have argued, first, that results from the IAT, far from revealing "bias" per se, might be explained by other factors, such as familiarity with the stimuli, anxiety over the test, sympathy for disadvantaged groups, and cognitive dexterity. Quite simply, they contend that it is impossible to know whether the individual IAT test taker's response times are a function of personal implicit bias or merely an awareness of larger societal attitudes toward the disfavored group.[65] They also raise some technical concerns regarding the IAT's reliability, asserting that its varying correlations with explicit measures of attitudes indicate a high possibility of error and may be improperly calibrated to show more bias than actually exists.[66] In addition, they challenge the basic foundational assertion that IAT scores translate into biased behavior. Finally, they raise an issue that is common to much experimentally based social psychology: the results derived in the context of controlled laboratory settings will not translate well into the world of everyday lived experience.[67]

Of particular concern to IAT researchers has been Tetlock and Mitchell's contention, raised in 2009, that "there is no evidence that the IAT reliably predicts class-wide discrimination on tangible outcomes in any setting."[68] This argument directly takes issues with findings of Greenwald and his colleagues' meta-analysis published that same year, purporting to show just such a connection.[69] In a forceful response, John Jost and his colleagues take on Tetlock and Mitchell's charges and argue that evidence from existing studies clearly establishes that IAT measures do in fact "predict socially and organizationally significant behaviors, including employment, medical, and voting decisions made by working adults." They also take on the criticism that IAT results may reflect shared cultural stereotypes rather than personal animus by noting that "most implicit bias researchers have been arguing (for nearly 30 years) that (a) it is possible for people to be biased without feeling personal animus (or wanting to be biased in any way), and (b) awareness of shared cultural stereotypes (and objective inequalities among groups in the social system) are indeed major sources of implicit bias"—that is, it is possible for an individual's attitudes to reflect both cultural stereotypes and personal biases.[70] Kang and Lane argue that Tetlock and Mitchell make unrealistic and unfair claims for a level of scientific rigor and certainty regarding ISC that Tetlock and Mitchell themselves do not meet in their own work.[71]

In 2012, the patron saint of behavioral realists, Daniel Kahneman, wrote an open email to psychologists working in the field of social priming to address a "storm of controversy" over the "robustness of priming results." He noted numerous sources of concern, including "the recent exposure of fraudulent researchers, general concerns with replicability that affect many disciplines, multiple reported failures to replicate salient results in the priming literature, and the growing belief in the existence of a pervasive file drawer problem that undermines two methodological pillars of your field: the preference for conceptual over literal replication and the use of meta-analysis." For all these reasons, he concluded, "your field is now the poster child for doubts about the integrity of psychological research."[72] Priming studies are just one component of a broad array of the work being done on implicit bias, but they are a significant component.

Other technical critiques engage more broadly with issues common to social psychology and neuroscience, particularly with studies using fMRI. Perhaps foremost among these issues is the "WEIRD problem" in psychology and neuroscience research. The acronym WEIRD stands for "Western, Educated, Industrialized, Rich, and Democratic," which aptly characterizes the demographic characteristics of most subjects studied in neuroscience research. One review of a comparative database across the behavioral sciences suggests "both that there is substantial variability in experimental results across populations and that WEIRD subjects are particularly unusual compared with the rest of the species—frequent outliers."[73] The basic concern is that studies done using WEIRD subjects—in particular university undergraduates, who often provide a readily accessible pool of research subjects for psychology professors—form the empirical foundation for claims being made more broadly about the basic characteristics of human nature and the functioning of the brain.[74] Other concerns with fMRI studies include a recent analysis showing that "the average statistical power of studies in the neurosciences is very low," leading to "overestimates of effect size and low reproducibility of results."[75]

Perhaps most infamous is a controversy that recently arose around what one scholar terms "the salmon of doubt."[76] The salmon at issue was a dead one, purchased at a fish market by neuroscientist Craig Bennett, who then took it to his lab at Dartmouth, placed it in an fMRI, and showed it "a series of photographs depicting human individuals in social situations with a specified emotional valence,"[77] as is done with human subjects in many of the race and brain-activation studies. In the fMRI scan, it looked as if the dead salmon were *actually thinking* about the pictures it had been shown. "By complete, random chance, we found some voxels that were significant that just happened to be in the fish's brain," Bennett told *Wired* magazine.

"And if I were a ridiculous researcher, I'd say, 'A dead salmon perceiving humans can tell their emotional state.'"[78]

The point is not that fMRI is illegitimate or produces ridiculous results. Rather, the salmon experiment highlights the fact that fMRI results are not direct and transparent representations of brain functioning but rather are highly complex, technologically mediated statistical constructions of results that have many steps involving human interventions to set parameters and construct results in a manner that can actually be highly subjective.[79] As science studies scholar Joseph Dumit argues in his study of positron emission tomography (PET) scans, these images are not simply captured but rather critically *produced* in four stages: first, designing the experiment, which "involves choosing participants for the study and designing their state and behavior in the scanner"; second, "measuring brain activity," where "a scanner must properly collect the data, and then a computer must algorithmically reconstruct the data into a three dimensional map of activity, based on assumptions about the scanner and brain activity"; third, "making data comparable," which entails transforming and normalizing scans so that an individual's "brain locations can be correlated with those of others;" and, fourth, "making comparable data presentable." The fourth stage typically involves two steps: "first, colors are used to substitute for the numbers in the dataset, and second, specific colored brainsets are selected, to be produced and published. Coloring involves transforming numeric variation into a contour map, highlighting some differences at the expense of others."[80]

One particularly controversial paper exploring some of these implications for fMRI studies of such subjective choices was initially titled "Voodoo Correlations" and later renamed "Puzzlingly High Correlations in fMRI Studies of Emotion, Personality, and Social Cognition." The paper examines the widespread finding of "nonindependence error" in many social neuroscience papers that attempt to correlate activity in certain parts of the brain (measured using fMRI) with behavioral or self-report measures of "social" traits—essentially personality. Nonindependence error involves not the measurement of data per se but the subjective selection of data within larger sets, wherein researchers tend to pick out results with higher values. The overall average of such chosen numbers will tend to show significant results where such results might not really exist.[81] It deserves note, however, that among the many studies the authors of this paper reviewed, they found examples of research by Mahzarin Banaji and Elizabeth Phelps that did meet high standards of methodological rigor.[82]

Of those critiques expressing concern over larger framing and interpretive issues, it is perhaps best to start with Charles Lawrence III, whose own work provides such an important background and point of contrast for later behavioral realists. In 2008, reflecting back on developments in ISC and behavioral realism since his foundational article "The ID, the Ego, and Equal Protection" was published in 1987, Lawrence argued that "while this scholarship's focus on the mechanisms of cognitive categorization has taught us much about how implicit bias works, it may have also undermined my project by turning our attention away from the unique place that the ideology of white supremacy holds in our conscious and unconscious beliefs." Of particular concern for Lawrence was that "cognitive psychology's focus on the workings of the individual mind may cause us to think of racism as a private concern, as if our private implicit biases do not implicate collective responsibility for racial subordination and the continued vitality of the ideology and material structures of white supremacy." Moreover, the focus on how the mind or, more particularly, the brain categorizes information tends to cast racism as "biological, normal, automatic, an inevitable product of the workings of the brain" and obscures "the question of our responsibility for what our history has wrought."[83]

Lawrence argued that, in contrast to this casting of racism, "racism's harm [is] greater than the biased actions of individuals." His "cultural meaning test" did not ask "whether bias infects the decisions of the individual actors. Rather, it demonstrates the continuing presence of racist belief in the larger society by discerning the racial (or racist) meaning or interpretation that the relevant community would give an act or decision that is not articulated or justified in explicitly racial terms." His project, therefore, was very different from that of the behavioral realists. He saw the latter as accepting "the central premise of the *Davis* intent requirement—that the harm of race discrimination lies in individual acts infected by bias," whereas his cultural meaning approach "rejects that premise and finds the harm of racism in the pervasive effects of shared racist ideology."[84]

Sociologist David Wellman shares many of Lawrence's concerns but focuses more explicitly on issues of structure and substance. Wellman argues, along with sociologists such as Eduardo Bonilla-Silva,[85] that historical accumulations of institutional practices embedding racism deep in the structures of American society mean that "bias need not be critical to the formation of racial inequality." Therefore, asserts Wellman, behavioral realists' focus on individual prejudice may play into existing neoconservative approaches to racism that emphasize individual attitudes rather than structure and power. Wellman is also deeply troubled by what he sees as ISC researchers' tendency to "naturalize racism"—that is, to reduce race to a function of "raw data processed in the brain[,] not a relationship between groups," thereby diminishing "persistent, durable racial inequality" into simply "a part of the natural order of things." In short, "it takes political issues associated with structure, domination and advantage off the legal agenda and replaces them with a theory based on neurons."[86]

Wellman further argues that by focusing on the intent or attitudes of individuals harboring racial biases, ISC theory tends to adopt or reproduce a white perspective on racism, whereas for black people "the fact of racial oppression exists largely independent of the motives or intentions of its perpetrators." Moreover, by rendering racist actions as primarily a function of biological processes, "the explanations for them are lifted to scientific status, and they are transformed from social into individual troubles, rendering solutions private not public."[87] This focus on individual bias fits into the model of what sociologists Laurence Bobo and Ryan Smith characterize as "free market racism," where, as Wellman explains, "instead of looking for the causes of racial inequality in a historical-structural, state-based account, this discourse looks for them in the actions of self-interested and self-motivated individuals on either side of the color line. In this frame, race in the post–civil rights era is a problem of individual (mis)behavior."[88]

From within the legal academy, Ralph Richard Banks and Richard Thompson Ford have written one of the most trenchant critiques of the application of ISC theory to the world of law and policy. While echoing some of Tetlock and Mitchell's concerns regarding the ambiguity of IAT findings, their deeper concern, like Wellman's, is with the danger that the discourse of implicit bias may actually subvert the goals of achieving racial justice more broadly in society.[89]

Banks and Ford begin by noting that the idea of unconscious bias is politically palatable because it does not level accusations of blame "so much as it identifies a quasi-medical problem buried deep within us all." This focus, they argue, promotes a superficial consensus by eliding more contentious issues, in particular the historical accretion of substantive inequalities in areas ranging from education and employment to incarceration and housing that have fueled conscious and unconscious bias alike. The goal of racial justice efforts, they contend, "should be the alleviation of substantive inequalities, not the eradication of unconscious bias." In the field of antidiscrimination law, they argue that the discourse of implicit bias is not even necessary, for the simple reason that "neither statutory nor constitutional antidiscrimination law requires a distinction" between unconscious bias and simple hidden or covert conscious bias. They assert that the concept of unconscious bias is largely irrelevant to claims of discrimination under Title VII of the Civil Rights Act of 1964 because courts "have developed a doctrinal framework that does not require the fact finder to make any determinations as to the state of mind of the defendant." They observe that a "prima facie case of intentional discrimination does not require the plaintiff to prove intentional discrimination." Rather, the focus is on "whether the [defendant's] proffered legitimate, nondiscriminatory reason is credible." They assert that neither Justice Brennan's mixed-motive analysis in *Price Waterhouse* nor the amendments to Title VII made in 1991 "turn on the existence, or absence, of conscious bias."[90] Similarly, the Supreme Court's constitutional race discrimination jurisprudence going back to *Washington v. Davis*, which admittedly was very directly focused on questions of intent and purpose, simply does not turn on making distinctions between conscious and unconscious bias.[91]

Banks and Ford conclude their critique by noting several specific risks attendant upon an overzealous embrace of implicit bias discourse. The first they characterize as "Goal Distortion," by which they mean a confusion of means and ends such that the strategy of lessening implicit bias becomes mistaken for the larger goal for achieving racial justice. Second, they caution against a creeping "technocratic authoritarianism" embedded in the logic of implicit bias discourse that seeks generally to attack all "bias" in decision making. This technocratic focus might lead to efforts "to eradicate any decision-making process that is not rational in a narrow instrumental sense," with the results that "the goal of eliminating bias then becomes an effort to enforce a principle of strict rationality, the sort of instrumental logic associated with computers and technology" that can promote the profound "alienation and disenchantment that follows from the technical bureaucratization of social life." Finally, they come back to their original concern that the focus on implicit bias discourse, with its predominant concentration on individual acts of discrimination, inadequately explains persistent racial disparities, "siphons energy away from substantive reform projects," and may further legitimize a color-blind conservative antidiscrimination framework that casts all efforts to consider race as suspect.[92]

Stephen Rich is similarly concerned by the potential of the cognitive account of discrimination to crowd out alternative, more-expansive conceptions of discrimination, noting, for example, that Title VII disparate-treatment doctrine does not require proof of prejudice—explicit or implicit—to succeed. The critical focus of disparate-treatment doctrine is not on the presence of prejudice but on whether a "plaintiff has been treated differently from other similarly situated persons because of his or her status." Where the cognitive account of discrimination focuses on individual states of mind, Rich argues, "disparate treatment's commitments lie with enforcing equal treatment in the service of the statute's overarching vision of equal employment opportunity rather than [with] purging employment decisions of invidious mental states."[93]

Among behavioral realists, Jerry Kang in particular has responded directly to some of these criticisms. He is sensitive to critiques "from the left" (as he terms them) that suggest that behavioral realism's reliance on science might be "naïve or unsophisticated," not to mention "reductionist, because it fails to capture the bigger picture, in the forms of 'institutional,' structural,' or 'societal' racism." He recognizes such criticisms as "sincere and important" but argues that they "mostly miss the mark." He presents the science of ISC as a useful tool that should not be lightly cast aside:

> Again, I am merely describing the brute fact that scientific evidence culled through standard hypothesis-testing procedures deploying modern statistics and published in peer-reviewed journals is considered to be the "gold" standard for policymaking, including legal reform. Accordingly, if the Left wants to be pragmatic about its agenda, it seems sensible to pay attention to what science says. This is not to recommend putting all eggs in the scientific basket, but it is an argument not to abandon it altogether.

Kang clearly appreciates the significance of structural issues but argues "there is no reason why they cannot be integrated with Implicit Social Cognition." He believes that the only way to see whether the focus on ISC is presenting untenable opportunity costs, draining resources and attention away from other approaches, is to assess net benefits after the fact—though he does suggest that one surrogate measure might simply be "to see how much the science (as compared to other forms of progressive discourse) upsets the right."[94]

In the following chapters, I move on to develop my own critiques of behavioral realism. Much of my approach builds on and extends the critiques of those who, like Wellman, Banks and Ford, and Rich, share the behavioral realists' antidiscrimination goals but believe that the behavioral realists' work contains many problematic aspects and troubling implications for the fight for racial justice. In developing and extending these critiques, I take the ISC theorists' findings largely on their own terms, choosing to engage issues raised by the interpretation and deployment of their findings rather than to contest the underlying scientific validity of those findings. In doing so, I am sympathetic to Kang's call to avoid abandoning ISC research altogether. There is much in the ISC theorists and behavioral realists' work that I think is of great value and significance. My concerns arise primarily from the framing and presentation of many of these findings in what has tended to approach a grand-master narrative for addressing contemporary racial injustice—despite many often thoughtful and well-intentioned caveats from behavioral realists that nonetheless tend to be rather abstract and overwhelmed in practice by suggested interventions that focus almost exclusively on the individual, psychologically based dynamics of bias assessment and intervention.

3

ACCEPTING CONSERVATIVE FRAMES

Time, Color Blindness, Diversity, and Intent

Much of the behavioral realist approach to racial justice strikes me as an attempt at a sort of legal jujitsu that uses the weight of conservative doctrine concentrating on the defendant's mental state against itself. It embraces the conservative focus on intent and then applies ISC theory to show how shifting from conscious to unconscious mental states allows behavioral realists to make clear and strong cases for redressing racial bias in ways that pass muster under existing conservative legal doctrine. In building on the critiques of behavioral realism discussed in the previous chapter, I want to examine more fully the implications not simply of what behavioral realism elides or ignores with respect to structural racism but also of what it affirmatively creates, even if one accepts its arguments on their own terms.

This approach examines critiques of behavioral realism and ISC theory as part of a broader debate over the costs and benefits of accepting the ascendant conservative frame for understanding racial inequality in American society. It is very much in line with the concern Charles Lawrence III expressed in 2012 regarding racial disparities in education: "When we make the pragmatic argument that we must accept piecemeal and inadequate reforms because there is no political will to make structural change, I fear that we have accepted the status quo so easily because we have lived with inequality for so long that it seems natural—that we have lost our sense of outrage because we believe some part of the nature story that says this is where poor black children are supposed to be."[1]

Political scientist Suzanne Mettler expresses similar concerns in her analysis of the influence of behavioral economics on contemporary liberal approaches to governance more broadly: "For too long, progressives have accepted the conservative playbook, creating and expanding tax expenditures on the assumption that they can tilt some of their benefits to low- and middle-income Americans. As long as this cornerstone of the submerged state is left intact, it fosters the delusion that governance is generally ineffective and unhelpful to most Americans, and it prompts people to attribute to markets more credit than they are due."[2]

I will have much more to say about Mettler's metaphor of the "submerged state" in chapter 6, but for now suffice it to say that she defines this state as "a conglomeration of federal social policies that incentivize and subsidize activities engaged in by private actors and individuals . . . [in ways that] have shrouded the state's role, making it largely invisible to most ordinary citizens, even beneficiaries of existing policies."[3] Behavioral economists share much of the same theoretical orientation as behavioral realists in that both apply cognitive theories to address pressing legal and policy issues. There are overlaps among proponents of these approaches, perhaps most prominently in the person of Cass Sunstein, professor of law at Harvard University and formerly administrator of the White House Office of Information and Regulatory Affairs in the Obama administration.[4] Lawrence and Mettler clearly are concerned that the costs of adopting a tactical embrace of behavioralist theories may outweigh the benefits.

In this chapter, I examine in greater depth four particular aspects of the conservative frame: time, color blindness, diversity, and intent. By "time," I mean the tendency to frame racial discrimination as largely a phenomenon of the past or soon to be past that has been transcended by historical progress. "Color blindness" is fairly self-explanatory and refers to the ideal of transcending not the past perception but the present perception of racial difference. My critique of "diversity" examines the problematic implications of embracing Justice Lewis Powell's finding in *Regents of University of California v. Bakke* (1978) that diversity constitutes the only state interest sufficiently compelling to justify race-conscious, affirmative action remedies. "Intent" addresses some distinctive ways the behavioral realist narrative frames the concepts of intent required under cases such as *Washington v. Davis* (1976) and *Personnel Administrator of Massachusetts v. Feeney* (1979) to establish a claim for discrimination. Finally, I explore some of the practical implications of adopting this frame by examining how select key Supreme Court opinions have engaged the sort of social scientific evidence of bias that behavioral realists champion as the game changer to break through the deadlock of racial jurisprudence. I analyze some of the strengths and weaknesses of the behavioral realist approach and argue that, in fact, far from changing the game, it may be inadvertently reinforcing some of the game's more pernicious rules.

TIME

Jerry Kang and Mahzarin Banaji speak of "using behavioral realism as our legal approach and ISC as the science . . . to revise the affirmative action conversation" by providing "a new temporal framing for much affirmative action discourse." They argue that findings of existing implicit bias enable us to view affirmative action programs "as responses to discrimination in the here and now" instead of as the "backward-looking frame of corrective justice (e.g., compensation for slavery) and a forward-looking frame of utilitarian engineering (e.g., potential pedagogical benefit)." They elaborate on their critique of the "backward-looking frame," noting that it does not fit traditional tort models of compensation because the perpetrators, "slave owners[,] are long dead" and the beneficiaries "are not regarded as the specific victims of prior discrimination." Under this dominant model, the resulting benefits of affirmative action are therefore regarded as "unjust enrichment."[5] Rather than challenge head on this characterization of the significance of the past or its enduring legacies and effects on the present, Kang and Banaji implicitly accept its frame, dismissing the past to focus on implicit bias in the present. As Kang puts it elsewhere, the findings from ISC can be used to argue that "the disparate results long evinced by summary statistics across racial and gender groups could not be entirely attributed to merit differences or historical maldistributions of resources. Instead, we would now have reason to believe that these disparate results are also caused—at least in part—by implicit social cognitions operating right now."[6]

Kang clearly cares about these historical injustices, yet, apparently for tactical reasons concerned with addressing the current dominant conservative understandings of tort law, he utterly dismisses the need for historical understanding to address racial injustice. For Kang, ISC operates "right now,"

but history does not. This is a curious understanding of history, yet it resonates with Justice Powell's profoundly influential opinion in *Bakke*, where he
asserted that the goal of "remedying past societal discrimination" was
insufficient to justify affirmative action because it promoted "an amorphous
concept of injury that may be ageless in its reach into the past."[7]

As Jack Balkin and Reva Siegel have observed, the debates around affirmative action in the 1970s were not just about law or politics but also "over
cultural memory." By turning toward a strict color-blind anticlassification
frame, "white America could more easily believe that racial inequality was
a thing of the past."[8] ISC thus feeds the trope "the past is the past," which
Eduardo Bonilla-Silva identifies as central to constructing what he characterizes as "color-blind racism." He notes that this sentiment typically manifests itself in attitudes such as "I didn't own slaves" or "if Jews, Italians and
Irish have made it, how come Blacks have not?"[9]

One corollary of the assertion that implicit bias is distinctively *present* is
the assumption that explicit racism, at least explicit racism that matters, is
largely a thing of the *past*—an historical artifact—and hence not of central
concern to contemporary struggles for racial justice. We see this assumption in widespread discussions of how American has now entered a "postracial" era, particularly in light of the election of Barak Obama as president in
2008.[10] Thus, we have Mahzarin Banaji and Anthony Greenwald in their
book *Blind Spot* (2013) citing recent surveys that make the case "that America is no longer racist" and noting that Americans' broad adoption of egalitarian principles further "support[s] the conclusion that American society
is not presently racist."[11] The modifier *presently* is particularly notable here,
again emphasizing the new temporal frame that distinguishes implicit from
explicit bias. This distinction is underlined by Banaji and Greenwald's assertion that "explicit bias is infrequent; implicit bias is pervasive."[12] Similarly,
as behavioral realist Christine Jolls puts it, "Not so long ago in American
society, conscious discrimination was a frequent occurrence."[13] She acknowledges its reality but consigns it to the dustbin of history. Psychologist John
Dovidio contrasts explicit racism with the existence of "subtle contemporary
biases, such as 'aversive racism'" to demonstrate that "discrimination is not
a 'thing of the past.'"[14] Or as Sophie Trawalter and Jenessa Shapiro put it,
"Despite improving explicit racial attitudes, many white individuals continue

to have negative implicit racial biases."[15] In this frame, bias still matters in the present, but only in its implicit form.

Neuroscience studies of implicit bias also marginalize the ongoing significance of explicit racism. We see a clear example of this marginalization in some statements made by psychologist and neuroscientist Elizabeth Phelps in regard to an article she wrote with Banaji and Jennifer Kubota reviewing the neuroscience of racial perception. In an interview with the journal *Nature* following the publication of the article, Phelps was asked about conducting fMRI scans on people who are "overtly prejudiced." "Finding differences in people with extreme views wouldn't be too surprising," she responded, "but I'm not sure we'd see anything more than an exaggerated [emotional] response. We're more interested in 'normal' people."[16] There is a great deal to unpack in these two brief sentences. First, there is the idea that "overt prejudice" is an "extreme view." Certainly, as Banaji and Greenwald note, egalitarian principles have been widely adopted in U.S. laws and institutions and "now appear routinely in informal public discourse,"[17] or as Phelps and her coauthors put it in their article, "equality norms in American society dictate that behaving in a racially biased manner is unacceptable and many individual Americans share that aspiration."[18] In this sense, one might argue that overt expressions of prejudice are "extreme" insofar as they deviate from this public standard, but Phelps seems to be implying that such views are also rare and marginal. Second, her lack of interest in finding what she assumes would merely be an "exaggerated [emotional] response" indicates she considers such data to be relatively uninteresting and insignificant. Third, it is "normal" people who interest her; that is, she casts overt prejudice as abnormal or atypical or implicitly largely a thing of the past. This view hearkens oddly back to the first wave of psychological research on prejudice from the 1920s to the 1950s, which presented explicit prejudice as a pathological aberration from normal thinking.[19] Thus, the normalizing of implicit bias as common and pervasive here carries with it the implication that explicit bias is abnormal, uncommon, and even scientifically uninteresting.

Cliven Bundy would likely qualify as one of those overtly prejudiced people whose extreme views render his brain of relatively little interest to ISC researchers. Bundy is a rancher in Nevada. He is in his late sixties, white, and male, and he hates the federal government—on whose public land he has been illegally grazing his herd since 1993. In April 2014, Bundy became a darling of the conservative media after he and some fifty or so armed supporters drove away a number of Bureau of Land Management rangers who, acting on a court order, had tried to confiscate five hundred of his cattle. Soon after the initial confrontation with the bureau rangers, however, Bundy's media star began to fade as he was caught on video saying things about black people receiving government support, such as "They abort their young children, they put their young men in jail, because they never learned how to pick cotton. And I've often wondered, are they better off as slaves, picking cotton and having a family life and doing things, or are they better off under government subsidy? They didn't get no more freedom. They got less freedom."[20]

Not surprisingly, these remarks were widely condemned as racist. Yet, as Megan Carpentier noted in a column for the *Guardian*, "despite the outcry that followed . . . some of Bundy's supporters still seem unwilling to call the man himself a racist." Sure, they called his remarks "repugnant" and "ignorant" and "racist," but they would not call Bundy himself a racist, and Bundy, of course, denied that he was racist or that his remarks were racist. All of this denial led Carpentier to wonder, "What the hell do you have to say, believe or do in America these days to actually, personally, be considered a racist? George Zimmerman, who shot the teenager Trayvon Martin for walking in a hoodie while black, was declared 'not a racist.' The GOP official who passed around pictures portraying President Obama as a monkey was 'not racist.' People who use the n-word if black people use it are 'not racist.' Even the Ku Klux Klan declared 'We are not racists.'"[21]

This example demonstrates that nobody, not even Cliven Bundy or the Klu Klux Klan, thinks of himself, herself, or themselves as "racist."[22] As Carpentier indicates, we have set the bar for actually calling someone a racist so impossibly high that it naturally seems that explicit racism is largely a thing of the past.[23] I call this trend the "dumbing down" of racism, meaning the condition where cognizable racism has been reduced to its most explicit and virulent forms—forms stripped of all subtlety and nuance, so obvious that even the most obtuse, benighted idiot would recognize them as racist. Pernicious in its own right, such dumbing down also allows us to ignore subtler or more nuanced forms of racism—or frankly any form of racist practice that does not look the same as what came before.

This is not new. Generally speaking, racist people do not think of them-selves as racist. Cliven Bundy was merely echoing a theme that goes back at least to John C. Calhoun's speech to the U.S. Senate in 1837, when he spoke of slavery as a "positive good," in part because "never before has the black race of Central Africa, from the dawn of history to the present day, attained a condition so civilized and so improved, not only physically, but morally and intellectually."[24] This theme winds up in the majority opinion in *Plessy v. Ferguson* in 1896, which declared that if "the enforced separation of the two races stamps the colored race with a badge of inferiority . . . it is not by reason of anything found in the act, but solely because the colored race chooses to put that construction upon it."[25] In the immediate post-*Brown* era, we have the following statement from the white citizens of Levittown, Pennsylvania, when confronted in 1957 with the prospect of residential integration: "We, the citizens and homeowners of Levittown, Pennsylvania, protest the mixing of Negroes in our previously all-White community. As moral, religious and law-abiding citizens, we feel that we are unprejudiced and undiscriminating in our wish to keep our community a closed commu-nity. In as much as having equal rights, the Negroes have an equal opportu-nity to build their own community of equal value and beauty without intermingling with our community."[26]

In this statement, the white citizens of Levittown formally acknowledged the equal rights of African Americans, believing that this acknowledgment absolved their sentiments of any taint of racism. They embraced ideologies of equal opportunity and "separate but equal" in the same breath. Always there is the explicit disavowal of racism, but an explicit disavowal does not mean that explicit racism is not present—that is, unless, perhaps, you are a behav-ioral realist.

The reluctance of conservatives (and many liberals) to call Bundy a racist must be understood in relation to ISC researchers' tendency to character-ize people like Bundy as outside the American mainstream. Recall that John Dovidio and Samuel Gaertner contrast their conception of aversive racism with the dominative form, which they characterize as " 'old-fashioned,' [and] blatant"—that is, belonging to a past era.[27] Similarly, Banaji and Gre-enwald assert in good faith that "although racially discriminatory attitudes persist in American society, it is a mistake to characterize modern Amer-ica as racist—at least not in the way that the label of 'racism' has long been understood. Most Americans—a large majority—advocate racial equality."[28]

Where racism has been dumbed down and marginalized as a phenomenon of the past or of extreme elements of society, it is not difficult to conclude that modern America is not racist.

Contrast this view with Ta-Nehisi Coates's observations, also made in the aftermath of the Bundy controversy, regarding entrenched white supremacy among American conservatives: "Whether it's the Senate minority leader [Trent Lott] claiming that America should have remained legally segregated, a beloved cultural figure [*Duck Dynasty* star Phil Robertson] fondly recalling how happy black people were living under lynch law, a presidential candidate [Newt Gingrich] calling Barack Obama a 'food-stamp president,' or a campaign surrogate [Ted Nugent] calling Barack Obama 'a subhuman mongrel,' the preponderance of evidence shows that modern conservatism just can't quit white supremacy."[29] All of these examples reflect a point Coates makes in another article: that even bigots can be conflicted about their racist attitudes. Writing about Senator Strom Thurmond, he notes that, on the one hand, Thurmond "tried to raise an entire political party on the basis of segregation," yet, on the other hand, "he had a black daughter to whom he gave financial support, sired the career of black conservative Armstrong Williams, supported Historically Black Colleges and Universities." These things do not mean Thurmond was not a racist, but, Coates emphasizes, they do indicate he and other racists, going back to the era of slavery, "were conflicted, complicated, and bigoted."[30]

As sociologists Lawrence Bobo and Camille Charles put it in reflecting on the state of race in America in their article "Race in the American Mind," "First and most centrally, we offer a story of complexity. Despite the tendency in lay discourse and much social science work to rely on simple phrases or sweeping characterizations, 'racist America' versus 'the end of racism,' we believe attitudes and beliefs about race have long been internally complex and have only become more so since the time of the Moynihan Report."[31]

For Bobo and Charles, real racial progress has indeed been made, yet that progress must be "juxtaposed with clear and convincing evidence of persisting racial tensions," not least of which is the fact that "negative racial stereotypes remain the norm in white America."[32] An Associated Press poll in 2012 found that 51 percent of Americans "express explicit anti-black attitudes."[33] These analyses offer a far more complex and contested portrait of the nature and meaning of contemporary racism than the basic explicit/implicit binary portrayed by behavioral realism.

Republican presidential candidate Donald Trump drew enthusiastic crowds of thousands to rallies, where they avidly embraced thinly veiled, dog-whistle racist references to Latinos, blacks, Muslims, Asians, and Jews.[34] Yet even as commentators and politicians were willing to characterize certain of Trump's individual statements as racist, they continually referred more generally to issues of racism in the campaign in terms of implicit bias.[35] Thus, we had the striking spectacle of Republican Speaker of the House Paul Ryan denouncing Trump's remarks concerning the integrity of a Latino judge as "the textbook definition of a racist comment," even as Ryan continued to maintain his support for Mr. Trump's candidacy.[36] This stance echoes those made by conservatives about Cliven Bundy, trying to distinguish particular remarks from the person who made them—and erasing racism in the process. And so in this through-the-looking-glass world of contemporary racial politics, conservatives present us with a curious perversion of Bonilla-Silva's idea of "racism without racists"—we have racist statements without racists.

Perhaps even more troubling, a more recent analysis of trends in racial attitudes hypothesizes that there may be a growing sense of "racial apathy" among whites, characterized as a sense of emotional distance from blacks and "a growing indifference to talk of race and racial distinctions altogether."[37] In a similar vein, Michelle Alexander identifies "racial indifference" as central to maintaining racial caste systems throughout U.S. history, perhaps never more so than now in an era of mass incarceration of black men, which she characterizes as "the new Jim Crow."[38]

Racism, in short, is not some static "thing" that exists only in one particular form under all circumstances. To the contrary, as Alexander notes, "any candid observer of American racial history must acknowledge that racism is highly adaptable. The rules and reasons the political system employs to enforce status relations of any kind, including racial hierarchy, evolve and change as they are challenged."[39] Similarly, as historian George Fredrickson has observed, "a culture of racism, once established, can be adapted to more than one agenda and it is difficult to eradicate."[40] This culture endures and adapts, as Reva Siegel has noted, through a process of "persistence and transformation."[41] Or as Coates tersely puts it, "Racism is never simple."[42] The trick is to identify it in real time. It seems we are ready and able either to marginalize contemporary instances of racism as aberrant or to consign racism itself to the past. Yet, as Siegel also notes, "that which we retrospectively judge evil was once justified as reasonable."[43] *Plessy*, for example, was a very popular opinion when first decided; that is, *at the time* most (white) people did not see it as racist. Similarly, it is important to recognize that current Supreme Court decisions "may be rationalizing practices that perpetuate historic forms of stratification, much as *Plessy v. Ferguson* once did."[44] That some do not perceive such recent decisions as racist does not mean that the country has transcended racism—anymore than it had in 1896.

We see a particularly telling analysis (one might even say celebration) of the adaptability of racism in a statement from Republican political operative Lee Atwater, who was responsible for the infamous "Willie Horton" ad during the presidential contest between George H. W. Bush and Michael Dukakis in 1988. In an interview on the Republicans' "Southern Strategy" of using race to court white voters in the South, Atwater observed, "You start out in 1954 by saying, 'Nigger, nigger, nigger.' By 1968 you can't say 'nigger'— that hurts you, backfires. So you say stuff like, uh, forced busing, states' rights, and all that stuff, and you're getting so abstract. Now, you're talking about cutting taxes, and all these things you're talking about are totally economic things and a byproduct of them is, blacks get hurt worse than whites. . . . 'We want to cut this,' is much more abstract than even the busing thing, uh, and a hell of a lot more abstract than 'Nigger, nigger.'"[45] And so today a white person might answer a survey about racial attitudes by stating that he believes in formal equality but is against busing or raising taxes. Behavioral realists would not see the connection to racism in what this person says, only the potential implicit bias in how this person might not make eye contact with or smile less at a person of color.

Ironically, ISC researchers who have devoted so much attention to exploring the malleability of racist attitudes at a cognitive level in individual subjects, have devoted remarkably little thought to the malleability of the manifestations of racism itself. So malleable are these manifestations that anthropologist Leith Mullings has observed how scholars, "struggling to interpret these complex new forms of racism, . . . have bestowed [on racism] such appellations as 'laissez-faire racism'; postracism; racism in consequence rather than by formal institution; 'unmarked racisms'; neoracism or cultural racism; and cultural fundamentalism."[46]

Add Bonilla-Silva's "color-blind racism" and Alexander's "racial indifference" to the diverse definitions Mullings has identified, and you see that these multifarious, ongoing attempts to pin down contemporary forms of racism go far beyond the traditional "individual versus structural" and "intent versus impact" binaries of much legal discourse. They attempt to name and understand the complex, shifting, and sometimes elusive manifestations and meanings of racism in contemporary society.

At the very least, then, we should acknowledge that it is quite possible to be racist and still espouse formally egalitarian principles or, rather, to harbor at one and the same time both a racist attitude and an antiracist attitude. Who among us is not even a little bit at war with ourselves? And might not the same be said of American society as a whole?

This argument is more than just about whether or to what extent American society is racist or whether some conservatives are white supremacists. When brought into conversation with the orientations of ISC theory and behavioral realists, the argument is also about the temporal location of racism, which has serious implications for current law and policy. Even while acknowledging the continued salience of race for understanding pervasive implicit bias, behavioral realism's consignment of explicit racism to the past or to the margins of contemporary society approaches the sort of "postracialism" decried by Ian Haney-López as helping us to "diffuse our moral responsibility to directly challenge these dimensions of race as well as the persistent inequality they protect and produce."[47] In a conceptual frame where only implicit bias matters, how can one be held responsible for attitudes that by definition are beyond one's conscious control? Moreover, if explicit racism is pervasively understood as a thing of the past, then it is no wonder that white Americans are expressing the sort of racial apathy Bobo and his colleagues identify.

Perhaps the most dramatic recent exposition of the conservative relegation of racism to the past comes not in an equal-protection or Title VII case but in the Supreme Court's Voting Rights Act decision in *Shelby County v. Holder* in 2013. In a five-to-four decision, the *Shelby* Court held section 5 of the Voting Rights Act of 1965 to be unconstitutional, with the result that the section's formula for evaluating proposed changes to voting laws can no longer be used as a basis for subjecting specified jurisdictions with a history of discrimination to preclearance. Central to the logic in Justice John Roberts's opinion for the Court was how he temporally grounded the sorts of racially discriminatory practices that gave rise to the Voting Rights Act in 1965 firmly in the past. "Nearly 50 years later," Roberts declared emphatically, "things have changed dramatically." Roberts then went on to recite a long list of achievements since 1965, particularly in voter registration and the election of African Americans to public office, achievements that he readily acknowledged were brought about "in large part *because of* the Voting Rights Act." Nonetheless, because in his view things *had* changed—that is, because the explicitly racist practices of the past have been transcended—there is no further need to continue to single out specific jurisdictions for preclearance based on a formula that looks to a historical past that is no longer legally relevant.[48]

Roberts's conclusion is particularly striking not simply for the way it dismisses the ongoing significance of the historical legacy of the fifty-year struggle for voting rights but also, as Reva Siegel notes, for the way his elevation of concerns for individual states' equal sovereignty over citizens' equality and dignity "effaces the history of the Civil War and the Second Reconstruction."[49] I would perhaps modify that assessment to characterize Justice Roberts's treatment of history not as "effacement" but as "dismissal." He simply did not deem history relevant to current practices. As Patricia Williams notes, "The Roberts majority is prone to an extreme ahistoricism. In *Shelby County v. Holder*, Roberts threw out the oversight provisions of the Voting Rights Act based on an apparent commitment to live entirely in the 'present'—a present entirely disconnected from reality."[50] Perhaps the greatest irony of Roberts's ahistoricism is the way it echoes similarly retrograde Supreme Court opinions from the past. Thus, for example, we have in 1883 the Supreme Court striking down the Civil Rights Act of 1875 and declaring that "when a man has emerged from slavery, and, by the aid of beneficent legislation, has shaken off the inseparable concomitants of that state, there must be some stage in the progress of his elevation when he takes the rank of a mere citizen and ceases to be the special favorite of the laws."[51] Thus, just a few years after emancipation, the Court was already determining that sufficient *time* had passed to deny legal solicitude to claims of racial discrimination. The Court in 1883 might as well have said, "Nearly eight years later, things have changed." From this very early case to *Bakke* to *Shelby*, this sentiment, so blind to social and historical reality, can easily be taken as the guiding principle of racial justice backlash.

We have here a jurisprudential instantiation of what Ta-Nehisi Coates contends that white America does best when it comes to racism—forget. "The forgetting is habit," observes Coates, "yet another component of the Dream. They [white Americans] have forgotten the scale of the theft that enriched them in slavery; the terror that allowed them, for a century, to pilfer the vote; the segregationist policy that gave them their suburbs. They have forgotten because to remember would tumble them out of the beautiful Dream and force them to live down here with us, down in the world."[52]

This myopic focus on the present resonates all too easily with behavioral realism's emphasis on addressing discrimination in the "here and now."[53] The issue is not that Kang or Banaji would endorse Roberts's view of history— far from it. But they and other behavioral realists grant Roberts's approach a huge concession in agreeing to focus primarily on the present as a distinct time frame, separate from and more important than the past. This critique of behavioral realism does not deny the fact that times have indeed changed—slavery and formal Jim Crow are gone, and a black man, Barak Obama, was elected president—but it does contest the *meaning* of that change. It acknowledges Bobo and Charles's recognition of persisting racial tensions in American society and challenges the Whiggish characterization of racial progress implicit in Roberts's opinion as ever forward, with no potential for regression or backlash.[54] It adopts the skepticism of critical race scholars such as Jerome Culp, Angela Harris, and Francisco Valdes, who urge us to assume that "unless the system proves it is not subject to or complicit in entrenched structures of subordination, trust no one and question everything."[55] It would ask judges to pose commonsense questions that rely on interpretive judgment rather than on expert quantitative measurement— questions such as "Why did Shelby County adopt its voting changes if not to limit the voice of black people?" or, more generally, "Why are Republican-led state governments everywhere trying to restrict access to the ballot box through voter ID laws when there is no evidence whatsoever of systemic or widespread voter fraud?" Many people are asking these obvious questions, but such questions are not relevant to behavioral realists because to ask them is to imply that such laws are *explicitly* racist yet at the same time *mainstream.* ISC theorists, along with Justice Roberts, have told us that "things have changed"—explicit racism is marginal or a thing of the past.

In the conservative frame, not only is the past the only place where explicit racism lives, but it is also the place where all race consciousness should dwell. Thus, in his opinion for the Court in *Schuette v. BAMN* (2014)—holding that an amendment to Michigan's constitution prohibiting state universities from considering race as part of its admissions process does not violate the Constitution's Equal Protection Clause—Justice Anthony Kennedy asserted that "the electorate's instruction to governmental entities not to embark upon the course of race-defined and race-based preferences was adopted, we must assume, because the voters deemed a preference system to be unwise, on account of what voters may deem its latent potential to become itself a source of the very resentments and hostilities based on race that this Nation seeks to put behind it."[56]

For Kennedy, it is all about putting racial hostility behind us—about, as he put it in his opinion on *Schuette*, trying "to transcend the stigma of past racism."[57] Certainly, these goals are reasonable, even admirable. But the critical idea embedded in Kennedy's language here is not the all-too-easy reference to the idea that stigma is bad. No, it is his use of the ideas of "transcending" the stigma of "past" racism, of putting racial hostility "behind" us. He thus creates a temporal framework for "assuming" that the voters of Michigan had a benign reason for singling out affirmative action for state constitutional prohibition.

There is a difference, though, between "transcending" racial conflict and merely suppressing or repressing it. There is no working through race here, no engagement or discussion; there is instead a denial of racism by both Kennedy and the state constitutional amendment, yet Kennedy "assumes" that voters meant their prohibition to help heal racial wounds. Ultimately, the only evidence to support this assumption is his appeal to the temporal desire to move beyond race and leave it in our collective wake. This appeal reveals an understanding of race and racism that no amount of testing for implicit bias will ever be able to identify or redress. It constructs the framework for a commonsense understanding of the place of race in American society that cannot be undone by behavioral realist measurements but only by arguments over the interpretation and meaning of the actions at issue.

Kang and Banaji attribute the current impasse in affirmative action discourse in part to the fact that affirmative action, "as traditionally understood,"
does not fit the narrow model of tort-based compensation: "As for perpetrators, slave-owners are long dead, and those who have inherited advantages
are not held directly accountable for what their ancestors did decades or
centuries ago. Not surprisingly, Whiteness is not viewed as a corporation
that carries its specific debts forward. Further, the beneficiaries of affirmative action today (e.g., recent minority immigrants) are not regarded as the
specific victims of the prior discrimination, or even their heirs. Thus, any
benefit they receive is decried as 'unjust enrichment.'"[58]

Yet as Kang and Banaji describe "traditional understandings" of affirmative action in terms of corporate debt, nothing comes so readily to mind
as Justice Antonin Scalia's ringing declaration in his concurrence in *Adarand Constructors, Inc. v. Peña* (1995) that "under our Constitution there can
be no such thing as either a creditor or a debtor race."[59] Scalia's view may be
influential, but to characterize it as "traditional" seems a stretch, to say the
least.

Certainly, vigorous dissents—from Justice William Brennan's position in
Bakke to Justice Sonia Sotomayor's position in *Schuette*—would challenge
this view. Writing in *Bakke* in 1978, Justice Brennan observed that "a glance
at our docket and at dockets of lower courts will show that even today offi-
cially sanctioned discrimination is not a thing of the past."[60] Writing decades
later in *Schuette* in 2014, Justice Sotomayor declared, "Race matters. Race
matters in part because of the long history of racial minorities being denied
access to the political process. . . . Race also matters because of persistent
racial inequality in society—inequality that cannot be ignored and that has
produced stark socioeconomic disparities."[61] Sotomayor evoked history and
made it presently real. Scalia's view may be momentarily dominant, but the
difference between a frame of momentary dominance and "traditional
understanding" points up yet another powerful aspect of the temporal framings embedded in much behavioral realist discourse. Such easy-to-overlook
elisions may have the unintended consequence of legitimizing the very same
conservative racial discourse that the behavioral realists seek to challenge.

Kang and Banaji's acceptance of the conservative frame here constitutes
an odd sort of mirror image to Roberts's Whiggish view of racial progress

in which older, more progressive understandings of racial justice are consigned forever to literal and figurative "minority" status. Yet this acceptance overlooks the deep contingency of the current composition of the Court. David Cole suggests in a recent article on the Roberts Court that it was really born in the aftermath of the *Bush v. Gore* (2000) decision, which effectively awarded the presidency to George W. Bush. As Cole notes, "Had a Democratic president been able to replace Rehnquist and O'Connor, constitutional law today would be dramatically different. Affirmative action would be on firm constitutional ground. The Voting Rights Act would remain in place," and a host of other recent conservative decisions would likely have come out differently.[62]

Conceding that the current view of the conservative Court is grounded in a traditional understanding of affirmative action therefore concedes far too much. The trope "debtor and creditor races" and images of long-dead slave owners reinforce the idea that prior harms are cordoned off from the present—as if U.S. history were some sort of temporal Las Vegas where "what happens in the past stays in the past." Contrast this trope with the work done by political scientist and historian Ira Katznelson, who in his book *When Affirmative Action Was White* carefully traces the impact of an array of governmental laws and policies dating back to the New Deal that significantly disadvantaged African Americans in ways that they *directly* experience today. These laws and policies range from how the Social Security Act of 1935 excluded the disproportionately black job categories of domestic and agricultural workers to how the GI Bill of 1944 ensured discriminatory implementation by locating oversight and administration powers in local bodies controlled by the existing white power structure.[63] Melvin Oliver and Thomas Shapiro made similar points in their earlier book *Black Wealth/ White Wealth: A New Perspective on Racial Inequality*, pointing in particular to the ways in which federal housing law and policy directly inhibited the accumulation of intergenerational wealth by black families in ways that are still felt today.[64]

More recently, in his cover article for the *Atlantic*, "The Case for Reparations," Ta-Nehisi Coates compellingly chronicles the stories of African American individuals such as Clyde Ross to show how specific racist attitudes and practices of the past continue to affect people's lives today. Ross, a black man born in Mississippi in 1923 whose family's land was effectively stolen by local authorities in the 1920s, continued to suffer from systematic acts of discrimination up through the 1940s. After returning to the United States from fighting in World War II, he moved north to Chicago, only to find himself shut out of the legitimate market for home mortgage loans by precisely the sort of racially discriminatory programs examined by Oliver and Shapiro. His only recourse was a predatory mortgage lender, which in the 1970s in turn led to a situation in which he, like thousands of other African Americans, was effectively dispossessed of his home and the potential for accumulated wealth that it represented.[65]

Even more viscerally, recent work by public-health experts has shown how the vestiges of racism literally live on in the bodies of black people. In a review of scientific research on racism and health, sociologists David Williams and Selina Mohammed found in 2013 that in addition to institutional and cultural racism, "experiences of racial discrimination are an important type of psychosocial stressor that can lead to adverse changes in health status and altered behavioral patterns that increase health risks."[66] These health effects can accumulate cross generationally. Recent epigenetic studies exploring the impact of environmental stressors on individuals at the genetic level have found that the physiological effects of persistent experiences of racism over time can actually cause changes at the molecular level that can be passed on to later generations—racism of the past literally manifests itself in the bodies of the present.[67]

The point here is not that the people in Coates's article or those excluded under the Social Security Act or the GI Bill are experiencing specific discriminatory acts in the "here and now," as the behavioral realists would say, but that the accumulated weight of history continues to matter in the present in a manner that law and policy can and should recognize.

The other critical aspect of the behavioral realist temporal framing of racial discrimination involves remedies that specifically establish terminal points of affirmative action initiatives in the future. We see such framing most explicitly in Kang and Banaji's assertion that ISC theory can provide a "*new ending* for affirmative action" because "now that we can measure threats to fair treatment—threats that lie in every mind—such data should be a crucial guide to ending affirmative action. We suggest a terminus when measures of implicit bias for a region or nation are at zero or some rough behavioral equivalent. At this point, implicit bias would align with an explicit creed of equal treatment. It would fulfill collective aspirations to behave in accordance with explicitly held values."[68]

In this account, explicit bias is a thing of the past, but implicit bias exists in the present and must be dealt with through affirmative action. The same measure that establishes the current existence of implicit bias, the IAT, can be used as well to provide a clear ending point for the application of affirmative action remedies in the future.

Just as the relegation of explicit racism to the past resonates with Justice Roberts's notion that "things have changed," so too does the concern to provide a new, finite ending to remedies resonate with and indeed reinforce Justice Sandra Day O'Connor's statement in *Grutter v. Bollinger* (2003) that "race-conscious admissions policies must be limited in time." She suggests subsequently that "it has been 25 years since Justice Powell first approved the use of race to further an interest in student body diversity in the context of public higher education.... We expect that 25 years from now, the use of racial preferences will no longer be necessary to further the interest approved today."[69] Justice Roberts expressed a similar sentiment in *Parents Involved in Community Schools v. Seattle School District No. 1* (2007) when he noted that using racial balancing as a compelling interest in making pupil assignments has "no logical stopping point" and then went on to reference O'Connor's twenty-five-year time horizon.[70] The specification of twenty-five years is also implicitly Whiggish insofar as it presumes a steady march forward to racial justice. Yet the irony of this requirement of finitude is that if you cannot clearly project the end to a remedy, then you can never begin the process of remediation. Kang and Banaji do an effective job of presenting the IAT as a means to address this problem, but they do so at the cost of accepting the underlying premise of the necessity of specifying a clear temporal end point for a policy meant to address centuries of racial subordination.

Understanding the significance of temporal frames also illuminates a key aspect of Justice Roberts's much commented upon statement in *Parents Involved* that "the way to stop discrimination on the basis of race is to stop discriminating on the basis of race."[71] This opinion is not simply an exhortation toward color blindness (though it certainly is that) but also a statement about how we as a society and how the Supreme Court as an arbiter of constitutional values should act *now* in the present in a country where, as Roberts would proclaim six years later in *Shelby*, "things have changed."[72]

The relegation of explicit racism to the past, whether by Roberts or by behavioral realists, enables the dismissal of the need to address the enduring legacy of racism in the present and legitimizes the requirement of a "logical end point" to the few currently permissible uses of affirmative action in the future.

COLOR BLINDNESS

Embedded in Kang and Banaji's construction of the IAT as a means to provide a technologically mediated terminus for affirmative action is the implicit embrace of a second key aspect of the conservative frame: color blindness. The basis for finding bias through an IAT is premised on the idea that subjects *see* different races differently. An IAT result that shows no bias is one where race itself makes no difference—where the subjects are blind to race. This is perhaps ironic, given behavioral realists' avowed goal of dismantling current conservative color-blind jurisprudence—a goal evidenced, for example, by the title of Jerry Kang and Kristin Lane's article "Seeing Through Colorblindness: Implicit Bias and the Law."[73] Behavioral realism tends to foster an idea that the visual perception of racial difference is simply a natural phenomenon. But as Osagie Obasogie has argued in *Blinded by Sight*, his study of how blind people perceive race, the visibility of race should not be "conceptualized as existing anterior to any social process." Rather, he shows, "our eyes are trained to see race in particular ways—so much so that even blind people see race."[74]

Justice Powell's opinion in *Bakke* in 1978 marks the initial elaboration of contemporary color-blind jurisprudence by the Supreme Court. His analysis was adopted a decade later by a majority of the Court in *City of Richmond v. J. A. Croson Co.* (1989).[75] In his *Bakke* opinion, Powell rejected the idea that so-called benign uses of race, such as affirmative action, should be subject to lesser judicial scrutiny than invidious uses. "Racial and ethnic distinctions of any sort," he declared, "are inherently suspect and thus call for the most exacting judicial examination." In the context of higher education, Powell found the promotion of "diversity" to be a sufficiently compelling state interest to warrant consideration of race in admissions policies, but only under very proscribed conditions where race is considered as merely one factor among many and no specific quotas are used.[76] In *Croson*, Justice

O'Connor looked back to Powell's lone opinion in *Bakke* to articulate, now for a majority of the Court, a new standard that *all* state uses of racial categories must be subject to strict scrutiny, requiring that such uses be narrowly tailored to serve a compelling state interest.[77] Ian Haney-López has referred to O'Connor's analysis in *Croson* as "the cornerstone of today's colorblind constitutionalism." Haney-López argues that in a series of decisions following upon *Croson* "colorblindness took on a life of its own—not only justifying certain outcomes and doctrinal changes, but establishing a way of seeing race and equal protection that fueled hostility toward affirmative action as well as skepticism regarding claims of racial mistreatment."[78] This context effectively established color blindness as the new jurisprudential common sense of equal protection.

This new common sense, however, has not been uncontested; scholars writing in the antisubordination tradition have consistently attacked O'Connor's color-blind approach.[79] It has also been contested from the Supreme Court bench. Dissenting in *Croson*, Justice Marshall invoked temporal concerns, asserting that the majority opinion in effect cast "racial discrimination as largely a phenomenon of the past."[80] Angela Davis has marked the connection between temporal frames and color blindness in neoliberal approaches to racism in American society:

> Neoliberalism sees the market as the very paradigm of freedom[,] and democracy emerges as a synonym for capitalism, which has reemerged as the telos of history. In the official narratives of U.S. history, the historical victories of Civil Rights are dealt with as the final consolidation of democracy in the U.S., having relegating racism to the dustbin of history. The path toward the complete elimination of racism is represented in the neoliberalist discourse of colorblindness. Equality can only be achieved when the law, as well as individual subjects, become blind to race and fail to apprehend the material and ideological work that race continues to do.[81]

Time and color blindness are also linked in the discourses of behavioral realism and ISC theory. Just as ISC theory consigns explicit racism largely to the American past, it also embraces the ideal of color blindness for the American present and future. But it is color blindness with a twist: it can be identified, measured, and quantified through expert interventions and evaluations, most prominently in the form of the IAT and related uses of fMRI. Moreover, the IAT measures color blindness as a function of time, specifically the millisecond differentials between connecting black faces or white faces with good or bad associations.

The connections between the neoliberal embrace of markets as ordering mechanisms for society and ISC theory is also evident in the latter's emphasis on the notion that biases get in the way of perceiving an individual's "true" merit and hence ultimately undermine economy and efficiency. Not only does this notion presume an ideal, objectively verifiable conception of "merit," but it also implies that an underlying basis for nondiscrimination is to be found first and foremost in economic ideas of rational functionalism rather than in concerns for social justice.[82] Kang and Banaji, for example, accept the basic conservative frame of affirmative action as being about merit, noting that "critics of affirmative action argue that affirmative action circumvents merit." Rather than challenge the idea that employer-defined conceptions of merit should be the central legitimating concern of affirmative action, they posit that ISC theory can be used to "update the scientific case [that] the *mismeasurement of merit*" is caused by implicit bias. "This insight," they assert, "reframes certain affirmative action programs not as 'preferential treatment' but as an opportunity for more accurate measures."[83]

The very conception and structure of the IAT are premised on an ideal that subjects should be blind to race. Race is not supposed to make a difference. Subjects should respond in the *same* way to representations of white targets and black targets. It is precisely the difference in response that becomes the measure of implicit bias. Kang and Banaji's suggestion that IAT measurements of "zero" be taken as marking terminal points for affirmative action remedies indicates the power of the color-blind ideal embedded in behavioral realism.[84]

Behavioral realists also embrace the trope of color blindness quite literally in proposing possible remedies to implicit bias. One favorite example used by behavioral realists and ISC theorists involves the practice, implemented by several American symphony orchestras in the 1970s and noted in chapter 2, of using a screen to conduct "blind" auditions for aspiring instrumentalists. The lesson here is that the implicit biases of the judges, who hitherto had been improperly influenced by stereotypes associating musical virtuosity with men, could be corrected through blinding them, here primarily to gender (though, of course, they could not see color either).[85] Psychologists Brian Nosek and Rachel Riskind, exploring how blindness might be strategically employed to improve policy outcomes, suggest such possible interventions as having employment supervisors "review performance reports or other performance indicators with identifying information redacted." They suggest that "comparing identity-conscious and identity-blind evaluations can identify discrepancies and provide fodder for investigating whether social bias could be a contributing factor."[86] The issue here is not that these ideas are necessarily bad; to the contrary, they have much to commend them. It is rather that, presented as a primary way to understand and address bias, they endorse an ideal of identity blindness in such a broad and generally uncritical manner that they actually go to support the broader frame of color blindness put forth in cases such as *Croson* and *Parents Involved*.[87]

We see this support for color blindness in how, though somewhat tongue in cheek, Banaji and Greenwald invoke the Dr. Seuss story *The Sneetches* as an aspirational ideal. The story involves two groups of typically Seussian fantastical creatures called "Sneetches," one with stars on their bellies, one without. Sneetches with stars discriminate against those without. An entrepreneurial character shows up with a new machine that will for a fee put a star on the bellies of starless Sneetches. As plain-bellied Sneetches take advantage of this machine, the original Star-Bellies grow increasingly angry at losing their distinctive privilege. The entrepreneur takes advantage of this anger by presenting them with a new machine that will, again for a fee, *remove* stars, thus making them seem distinctive. In the ensuing free-for-all, confusion results:

> Until neither the Plain nor the Star-Bellies knew
> Whether this one was that one . . . or that one was this one
> Or which one was what one . . . or what one was who.[88]

By the end of the story, both groups of Sneetches come to understand that with or without stars "Sneetches are Sneetches." "Would that human society were as enlightened," remark Banaji and Greenwald after recounting the tale.[89] It is just such an enlightened society that behavioral realists seek, where racial distinctions become as inconsequential as the stars on

Sneetches' bellies, and they see ISC as a path toward achieving it. For behavioral realists, however, color blindness is not only an ideal to be strived for but also a means to achieve that enlightened society, as in the musician audition example, and a literal metric for assessing when affirmative action remedies are no longer needed, as discussed in the previous section on temporal framing. Behavioral realists may use ISC to show that individuals in contemporary American society are not color-blind, but they embrace the ideal of color blindness nonetheless.

fMRI scans add yet another, more complex layer of technological intermediation that renders the measurement of color blindness even more literal. In the pictures of subjects' brains generated by fMRI technicians during IATs and related tasks, blindness to race becomes visually represented in terms of similarity or difference in brain-activation patterns measured in response to racially coded target stimuli. The goal here is to have color-blind brains that respond the same to both black and white targets. In their review of the neuroscience of race, Kubota, Banaji, and Phelps suggest that fMRI data can be used the help "discover the means by which we can control or eliminate" the effects of implicit bias.[90]

"Neuroskeptic," a neuroscientist blogger for *Discover* magazine, pointed up one problem with this color-blind ideal, particularly as measured by IATs and fMRIs: "So there have been studies investigating which bits of Americans' brains activate in response to looking at photos of black people vs. white people. It emerges that 'a network of interacting brain regions' light up. But so what? Sure, the brain reacts differently to seeing people of different races. Of course it does—it reacts differently to everything, so long as we can perceive a difference; that's how we perceive a difference."[91]

The blogger here does not contest the validity of the scientific measurement, merely its *meaning*. Ralph Richard Banks, Jennifer Eberhardt, and Lee Ross elaborate on this contention when they observe that "the distinction between being racially biased and racially unbiased cannot be a distinction between race blindness and race consciousness, or between according race significance and not, for everyone is race conscious and vests race with more meaning than physical characteristics such as eye or hair color. On this view, if the findings of the Race IAT constitute evidence of racial bias it cannot be because they confirm that people deviate from some ideal of being (nearly) blind to race."[92]

The contingency of IAT and fMRI findings (understanding how context shapes not only outcomes but also the meaning of those outcomes or, alternatively, how such findings are not transparent unmediated representations of some objective fact of bias) is particularly significant in light of the changing interpretations of just what different BOLD patterns signify. For example, much research on the "neuroscience of race" has focused on the amygdala. Early articles asserted that different levels of brain activation (meaning different levels of oxygenation in blood flowing to the amygdala) indicated different levels of *fear* in response to black or white faces. Later studies reconsidered this interpretation, asserting that these different levels merely indicated differential response to *in groups or out groups* more generally. Still more recent studies posit that amygdala activation simply indicates general levels of a perceived object's *salience*—perhaps more specifically, its emotional salience.[93]

In this context, then, just what would fMRIs that do not show any different response to the perception of black versus white faces mean? And why should this lack of difference be something to aspire toward? As Neuroskeptic indicated, the brain simply responds differently to difference. In some respects, black faces are different from white faces. In other respects, any given white face is going to be different from another white face. The brain will likely register those differences as well. The issue is not difference per se; it is the *meaning* of difference, which is something that current levels of technology that simply measure levels of blood oxygenation in vessels going to specified parts of the brain cannot determine with any specificity.

As early as 2003, Elizabeth Phelps and Laura Thomas offered the following useful caveat: "Showing a behavior 'in the brain' does not say something more important or fundamental about who we are than our behavior. Functional neuroimaging techniques pick up on signals indicating brain activity. These signals, by themselves, do not specify a behavior. Only by linking these brain signals with behavior do they have psychological meaning."[94]

To this, I would add that the meaning of the term *behavior* is also not transparent. Anthropologist Clifford Geertz provides an example of this simple reality in his classic discussion of the meaning of the behavior we call a "wink." Discussing the work of Gilbert Ryles, Geertz asks us to consider "two boys, rapidly contracting the eyelids of their right eyes. In one, this is an involuntary twitch; in the other, a conspiratorial signal to a friend. The two movements are, as movements, identical from an I-am-a-camera, 'phenomenalistic' observation of them alone. . . . Yet the difference, however unphotographable, between a twitch and a wink is vast."[95]

Geertz goes on to discuss the gesture of a third boy, who parodies the first boy's "wink" to amuse his cronies. His gesture, again, is the same as that of the other two boys, but he is neither twitching nor winking; he is parodying. Another boy might be unsure of his winking ability and try rehearsing winks in the mirror. And so on. Geertz contrasts the "thin description" of the "I-am-a-camera" approach with the "thick description" needed to understand fully the behavior at issue, which requires engaging "a stratified hierarchy of meaningful structures in terms of which twitches, winks, fake-winks, parodies, rehearsals of parodies are produced, perceived, and interpreted and without which they would not . . . in fact exist, no matter what anyone did or didn't do with his eyelids."[96] Even a direct connection between certain brain-activation patterns and particular behaviors occurs in a cultural context and must still be interpreted. We can understand the differential response to black or white faces only by connecting the fMRI images to broader social and cultural understandings of the current meaning and significance of racial difference in contemporary America.

An overfascination with technologies of precise measurement can obscure the underlying normative choices that determine why, when, how, or, more generally, under what circumstances we are or should be "blind" to which particular differences. As Banks, Eberhardt, and Ross observe, it is imperative to recognize "the indeterminacy of our antidiscrimination and antibias ideals" because "identifying racial bias . . . must entail deciding that some forms of race consciousness are more, or less, morally objectionable than others, a determination with respect to which reasonable minds may differ."[97] Identifying and addressing racism cannot be reduced to a technical or purely empirical problem. Forms of "race consciousness" as made manifest through IATs or fMRIs are not transparent, unmediated representations of some underlying objective reality of racial perception. As Joseph Dumit's work makes clear, the process of producing an fMRI (no less than a PET scan) involves all sorts of very human subjective choices that will shape the outcome.[98] Researchers *choose* particular subjects to study (largely the WEIRD, who often are college students); they *choose* to focus on particular parts of the brain and to look at how they respond to particular types of stimuli; they *manipulate* the data to average them and present them graphically and then to *interpret* what those differences mean.

Part of this understanding that racism cannot be reduced to a norm-free technical problem comes back to critiques made by Philip Tetlock and Gregory Mitchell as well as by others who question whether the IAT measures actual bias or merely awareness of cultural stereotypes.[99] But it involves more. Many ISC researchers have taken to heart Phelps and Thomas's caveat about connecting brain function to behavior, and their work has gone far to demonstrate such connections.[100] Color blindness, understood as a sociolegal concept (as opposed to the physiological inability to distinguish between red and green) cannot be reduced to a purely empirical question of measurement—whether by fMRI or the IAT. Yet Kang and Lane imply otherwise when they make statements such as, "Even when we put aside difficult philosophical questions about equality, justice, and fairness, we still run into tough empirical questions of whether we are, in fact, 'colorblind.' Thankfully, there has been a recent explosion of scientific knowledge on this front. At the nexus of social psychology, cognitive psychology, and cognitive neuroscience has emerged a new body of science called 'implicit social cognition' (ISC)."[101]

According to Kang and Lane, ISC provides the tools for empirically verifying whether we are "in fact" color-blind. The potential power of this empirical approach is made evident in Kang and Banaji's proposals that such measurements provide the basis for a "specific and objectively measurable" terminus to affirmative action remedies.[102] This conclusion further implies that there is some objective and "true" way to respond to an IAT or fMRI that would definitively indicate a lack of bias. We have perhaps a new conceptualization of the postracial ideal as mediated through fMRI: the color-blind amygdala—a brain scan that reveals no difference in BOLD activation patterns when a subject is viewing a black face or a white face. One might well wonder what this lack of difference really would mean. Might it possibly indicate blindness not only to color but to history?

Behavioral realists may be understood as trying to use empirical data showing the continued presence of implicit bias as a means to dismantle narrow conservative constructions of color blindness that focus only on conscious attitudes. As Kang and Lane put it, "The data force us to see through the facile assumptions of colorblindness."[103] This statement assumes, however, that the conservative argument for color blindness is primarily an empirical claim rather than a normative (or straightforwardly ideological) claim. It reads the conservative reluctance to accept affirmative action remedies or to find acts of discrimination as grounded in the empirical problems of defining measurable outcomes or identifying subjective intent. The idea is to overwhelm the conservatives' objections with data. This approach has some merit and may gain some traction in particular cases. Certainly, it is gaining traction in the American Bar Association Task Force on Implicit Bias and in the related pilot programs to train members of the judiciary in California, Montana, and Minnesota.[104] Nonetheless, it is deeply constrained by its assumption that "scientific evidence" on its own, without norms, can answer questions about discrimination and racial bias definitively and uncontestably.[105] But data alone cannot undermine Justice Roberts's assertion that "the way to stop discrimination on the basis of race is to stop discriminating on the basis of race." This claim is not an empirical one. Data alone cannot undo an ideological tautology.

A further irony of behavioral realism's embrace of empirically verified individual color blindness is that one can readily imagine a future where racial differences are erased from individual IAT scores or fMRI BOLD patterns, and yet deeply embedded structural racial disparities in health, income, and other measures of well-being persist. Under such circumstances, however, the behavioral realists would have no basis for making any claims for redress because their "specific and objective measures" would indicate that society is now "truly" color-blind. Their terminus will have been reached, and they will be forced to exit the train.

These points raise an underlying issue with the color-blind frame established by behavioral realists: its reduction of racial justice to a function of empirically verifiable metrics, as if empirics obviate the need to engage in interpretation or to articulate normative commitments. In this regard, the frame mirrors Roberts's conservative approach to color blindness that embraces a rigid anticlassification principle on the misguided belief that it is somehow more objective than antisubordination analysis, which must look at particular actions, laws, or policies in context to make subjective judgments about whether they improperly stigmatize vulnerable groups.[106] As Balkin and Siegel argue, however, "the seeming objectivity of the anticlassification principle is illusory; a variety of social concerns shape its application, including but not limited to, interests in preserving, and in disestablishing, status relations."[107]

DIVERSITY

"Diversity" is the slender reed upon which contemporary affirmative action programs precariously balance. In *Bakke*, Justice Powell elevated diversity to the level of a state interest sufficiently compelling to justify the use of racial classifications in higher-education admissions processes. His conception of the relation between race and diversity was quite distinctive, however. "The diversity that furthers a compelling state interest," he asserted, "encompasses a far broader array of qualifications and characteristics of which racial or ethnic origin is but a single though important element. Petitioner's special admissions program, focused *solely* on ethnic diversity, would hinder rather than further attainment of genuine diversity."[108]

According to Justice Powell, an admissions process that reviews all aspects of an applicant *as an individual* may consider "race or ethnic background [to be] . . . a 'plus' in a particular applicant's file." Race, in short, "is only one element in a range of factors a university properly may consider in attaining the goal of a heterogeneous student body."[109] Given the Court's sharp divisions and multiple opinions in *Bakke*, the status of the diversity rationale was somewhat uncertain until *Grutter v. Bollinger* in 2003, where Justice O'Connor, writing for a majority, reaffirmed Powell's framing of diversity, proclaiming, "Today we endorse Justice Powell's view that student body diversity is a compelling state interest that can justify the use of race in university admissions."[110] Since the decision in *Bakke*, Powell's focus on diversity has been widely analyzed and critiqued, not least in the opinions written by other justices in the fractured *Bakke* Court.[111]

Treating race as just another "factor" in affirmative action programs in effect strips race of its distinctive history and meaning. In the context of higher-education admissions programs, this treatment places race on a par with individual's geographic origin, sports ability, or participation in extracurricular activities. Thus, in *Grutter* the Court approvingly noted that the admissions policy at issue made clear that "there are many possible bases for diversity admissions, and provides examples of admittees who have lived or traveled widely abroad, are fluent in several languages, have overcome personal adversity and family hardship, have exceptional records of extensive community service, and have had successful careers in other fields."[112]

Each attribute may be considered as a factor in admissions, and all factors are the same in this regard. Race may matter so long as it is not "RACE"—that is, the culturally specific and historically freighted legacy of subordination of a people in this country.

The diversity frame as invoked by behavioral realists accepts and reinforces the idea that racism is just like any other cognitive glitch or "mind bug" we might have. In this framing, as in *Bakke*'s just-a-"factor" language, race matters not as "RACE" but simply as a cognitively constructed category like any other. Hence, Banaji and Greenwald's reluctance to say the findings from the IAT indicate racism—they prefer the nonspecific term *bias*.[113] We have "race bias," just as we have biases regarding age or height or any other binary we might subject to an IAT.

In *Parents Involved*, Chief Justice Roberts, writing for the Court, struck down city student assignment plans that used racial classifications as a "tiebreaker" to allocate slots in particular high schools. In this clear formulation of a formalist anticlassification, color-blind approach, he declared that all uses of racial classifications must be subject to strict scrutiny no matter their purpose.[114] His opinion reveals the thinness of the diversity rationale as a basis for upholding affirmative action programs. He found in *Parents Involved* that the "diversity" interest in *Bakke* and *Grutter* was insufficient to justify such assignment schemes because "race is not considered as part of a broader effort to achieve 'exposure to widely diverse people, cultures, ideas, and viewpoints.'"[115] Charles Lawrence III argues in his critique of Roberts's opinion that "it achieves the pretense of reason only by taking the question of racial meaning off the table. Desegregation can only inflict the same injury as segregation if we ignore the question of what each signifies. Only in this *Alice in Wonderland* world, where racial classifications are devoid of meaning, can a remedy to the injury identified in *Brown v. Board of Education* become the injury itself."[116]

Parents Involved brings us back to Clifford Geertz's discussion of the "wink." For Roberts, a wink is always transparently a wink. For Lawrence, who focuses on the importance of cultural meaning, a wink—or a racial classification—can be understood only in context. It is not the contraction of the eyelid that matters; it is what the contraction signifies that counts. Lawrence asks us to engage in a thick-description understanding of racial classifications, in contrast to Roberts's formalistic thin-description understanding.

Behavioral realists, however, concede Roberts's point, abandon antisubordination arguments that go back to Owen Fiss's work in the 1970s and to Brennan's and Marshall's dissents in *Bakke*, and give full weight to the conservative Court's dominant decontextualized approach. In answer to opinions such as *Grutter* and *Parents Involved*, behavioral realists propose "debiasing" as an additional science-based compelling interest to justify affirmative action. Christine Jolls and Cass Sunstein characterize debiasing as a way to address the problem of people's "bounded rationality" in everyday affairs by using the law to "steer people in more rational directions."[117] Kang and Banaji directly connect the notion of debiasing to affirmative action by positing that taking the race of a person into account in making hiring or admissions decisions might serve the "compelling interest" of debiasing the workplace or school by providing counterstereotypical and counterattitudinal exemplars.[118]

Kang and Lane assert that "the end sought by this intervention is not to inflate minority student self-esteem via role modeling; to redistribute goodies between racial groups or genders; or to correct hard-to-measure general societal discrimination. The Supreme Court has rejected all three such goals as not quite compelling. Rather, the point of debiasing is to directly counter racial bias that has been found to predict discrimination. And fighting racial discrimination has always been recognized as a compelling interest."[119]

The first thing to note in Kang and Lane's assertion is the contempt they express for antisubordination approaches toward racial classification in general and toward affirmative action in particular. Although correct in recognizing the Supreme Court's cramped view of what constitute permissible rationales for affirmative action, Kang and Lane's dismissive characterization of role modeling, redistribution, and remediation not only accepts the conservative frame but also embraces and legitimizes it. They throw decades of antisubordination argumentation under the bus in order to redirect attention toward their shiny new object: science-driven debiasing remedies. These remedies are not actually oriented toward helping those who have historically experienced the degradations and deprivations of racial discrimination but rather, like diversity itself, toward benefiting those who hold biases (whether explicit or implicit) by trying to make them into better people who will not discriminate in the future. Kang and Lane's characterization casts such remedies as therapy for those whom psychiatrists might call the "worried well"—or, as Banaji and Greenwald like to call them, the "uncomfortable egalitarians."[120]

INTENT

Debiasing thus boils down to an adjunct to the diversity rationale, hopped up by references to cognitive psychology and neuroscience but ultimately reinforcing the conservative move away from examining the *harm* visited upon the subjects of discrimination toward the mindset or the *intent* of the perpetrators of such discrimination. This approach tries to outflank conservatives with "science," but the authority of science alone cannot resolve the fundamentally normative questions that underlie calls for racial justice, nor can it fully vitiate the effects of accepting the conservative frame.

As Ian Haney-López has observed, the conservative Court's intent doctrine "applies to allegations of discriminatory treatment where a racial classification is *not* explicitly used. In effect, this covers all contemporary cases of discrimination against non-Whites, since instances of frank and open mistreatment are now virtually nonexistent. In its modern incarnation, intent doctrine demands that plaintiffs prove a state of mind akin to malice on the part of an identified state actor."[121]

Whereas the doctrine of color blindness typically applies to affirmative action cases, the Court usually applies intent doctrine to claims of discriminatory treatment against nonwhites. Nonetheless, color blindness and intent doctrine are intertwined. Both ultimately turn on questions of discerning intent, but they do so asymmetrically or, one might simply say, in a manner rigged against redressing racial injustice. As Haney-López puts it, "Colorblindness denies that the state's purposes can be discerned; intent doctrine demands proof of malicious purpose. Colorblindness consistently imposes the most stringent form of scrutiny; intent cases always default to the most lenient form of constitutional review. Plaintiffs challenging affirmative action under colorblindness virtually always win; parties challenging discrimination under intent doctrine almost invariably lose."[122]

Behavioral realists' proposal that debiasing be elevated to a compelling state interest attempts to modify this dynamic, not by trying to discern the "state's purposes" but by claiming to be able to modify the *future* intents of actors who might otherwise discriminate.

In contrasting his "cultural meaning" approach to behavioral realism, Lawrence notes that

> the "cultural meaning" test does not ask whether bias infects the decisions of the individual actors. Rather, it demonstrates the continuing presence of racist belief in the larger society by discerning the racial (or racist) meaning or interpretation that the relevant community would give an act or decision that is not articulated or justified in explicitly racial terms. These are two very different projects. One accepts the central premise of the *Davis* intent requirement—that the harm of race discrimination lies in individual acts infected by bias. The other rejects that premise and finds the harm of racism in the pervasive effects of shared racist ideology.[123]

Behavioral realism accepts and reinforces the conservative premise of *Washington v. Davis* (1976) not only by focusing on the intent of individual actors in discrimination claims but also by elevating the intent of future individual actors to a matter of sufficiently compelling state interest to satisfy conservative color-blind doctrine.[124] In both cases, the focus is directed away from the harm done to minorities and instead toward the mindset of the (presumably white) perpetrators of discrimination.

Devon Carbado and Daria Roithmayr, although arguing for a closer collaboration between critical race theory and social science, nonetheless acknowledge (along with Charles Lawrence as well as Ralph Richard Banks and Richard Ford) that uncritically drawing on social psychology in particular "risks undermining [critical race theory] critiques of objectivity and neutrality and potentially limits the theory's ability to combat structural forms of racial inequality." Carbado and Roithmayr make some powerful points about how "proposed remedies for implicit bias target the individual" and that the effects of such limited approaches "can be quite pernicious." Yet as an example of connecting behavioral realism to "structural claims," they present an article by Kang and his colleagues (including Carbado as a coauthor), "Implicit Bias in the Courtroom," that explores "the cumulative effect of implicit biases at crucial decision-making points in the criminal justice system."[125] The latter study itself is interesting and revealing, yet as an example of structural critique it is extremely limited. Like many studies of implicit bias, it acknowledges the significance of structural and institutional factors, but its primary focus and frame remain the identification, assessment, and redressing of individual psychological states.[126]

Despite Carbado and Roithmayr's thoughtful caveats and the caveats within the article by Kang and his colleagues,[127] the latter article is framed by an assertion that the findings from ISC "are now reshaping the law's fundamental understandings of discrimination and fairness." The article goes on to emphasize "the size and scope of these behavioral effects [of implicit bias] and how to counter them—by altering the implicit biases themselves and by implementing strategies to attenuate their effects," and it later focuses on the initiative from the NCSC to implement three pilot projects in California, Minnesota, and North Dakota to teach judges and court staff about implicit bias.[128]

As laudable as these initiatives are, they are not about addressing structural or institutional racism. They are about developing interventions to alter the individual psychological dispositions of key actors in the criminal justice system. Of course, implicit biases cumulatively have a structural impact, but these articles and the initiatives they hold up as models are grounded in decidedly "thin" conceptions of institutions and structures. They do not view implicit biases in relation to the historical and cultural matrices that have formed and given them meaning over time but instead focus on individuals' cognitive states in the present. As such, they are firmly in the *Davis* tradition of focusing on present intent.

Banaji and Greenwald (Greenwald was also a coauthor of the study just discussed) elevate the significance of individual psychology as the preeminent master explanation for the persistence of racial injustice in America when they assert that "the transforming effect our research has had on our own understanding of discrimination has gradually brought us to the point of believing that . . . *in-group favoritism* . . . may be the largest contributing factor to the relative disadvantages experienced by Black Americans and other already disadvantaged groups"[129]

This statement is, frankly, a stunning dismissal of precisely the sorts of structural and institutional factors that Carbado and Roithmayr so carefully

caution us bout. Yet it is not wholly discontinuous with Carbado and Roithmayr's approach because both they and Greenwald and Banaji (as well as the
article "Implicit Bias in the Courtroom") fail to take into account the historical and cultural situatedness of such "relative disadvantages." This
approach thus reduces the ongoing effects of centuries of racial subordination in the country to a matter of individual cognitive mind bugs.

Moreover, this approach seems wholly oblivious to the work of social scientists from outside the field of psychology, such as Katznelson, Oliver, and
Shapiro, who, as discussed earlier, powerfully demonstrate that what Greenwald and Banaji characterize as "relative disadvantages" have direct and
immediate roots in decades of structural and institutional practices going
back prior to the New Deal that have nothing to do with implicit bias. This
argument brings us full circle back to the issue of time and shows how the
focus on psychology and intent as primary explanatory frames for contemporary racial injustice depends on the erasure of history and the consignment of more explicit and institutional forms of racism to the past.

4

BEHAVIORAL REALISM IN ACTION

Behavioral realists are very emphatic about the immediate, practical legal and policy applications of their work. Their goal is not simply to study a phenomenon or develop a new theory but to intervene actively in specific ways to promote policies they see as advancing a positive agenda of racial progress. In this regard, their work and ambitions are admirable. But their enthusiasm masks the need for a deeper examination of some of the unintended practical consequences of their project.

PRACTICAL LEGAL OUTCOMES

In their article on implicit bias in the courtroom, Jerry Kang and his colleagues offer a thoughtful caveat acknowledging that the Supreme Court decision in "*Wal-Mart Stores, Inc. v. Dukes*, 131 S. Ct. 2541 (2011), made it much more difficult to certify large classes in employment discrimination cases."[1] This case involved an attempt to certify as a class 1.6 million women who were current or former employees of Walmart for the purposes of a gender discrimination lawsuit based on pay and promotion policies and practices in Walmart stores.[2] Under the Federal Rules of Civil Procedure, a group of plaintiffs must show sufficient commonality of questions of law or fact among their claims in order to obtain certification as a class.[3] To establish commonality in this case, the plaintiffs presented precisely the sort of analysis that combined structural factors with ISC research on implicit bias advocated by Kang and his colleagues as well as by Devon Carbado and Daria Roithmayr.[4] The Court noted that the plaintiffs "relied chiefly on three forms of proof: statistical evidence about pay and promotion disparities between men and women at the company, anecdotal reports of discrimination from about 120 of Wal-Mart's female employees, and the testimony of a sociologist, Dr. William Bielby, who conducted a 'social framework analysis' of Wal-Mart's 'culture' and personnel practices, and concluded that the company was 'vulnerable' to gender discrimination."[5] Bielby's "social framework analysis" in particular aimed to connect the theory of implicit bias to larger structural issues at Walmart by proposing that the entire class suffered in common from the consequences of Walmart's strong corporate culture and personnel practices that made it "'vulnerable' to gender discrimination."

Generally speaking, social framework analysis has been used to provide a background for understanding the context within which certain practices may occur.[6] In trying to use such evidence to support the certification of a class, the plaintiffs in *Wal-Mart* needed to move beyond general assertions regarding corporate culture and connect the social framework to specific policies or practices that played a meaningful role in employment decisions affecting all members of the class. In his opinion for the Court, Justice Antonin Scalia emphasized the need to "bridge the gap" between "(a) an individual's claim that he has been denied a promotion [or higher pay] on discriminatory grounds, and his otherwise unsupported allegation that the company has a policy of discrimination, and (b) the existence of a class of persons who have suffered the same injury as that individual, such that the individual's claim and the class claim will share common questions of law or fact and that the individual's claim will be typical of the class claims."[7]

In *Wal-Mart*, the plaintiffs sought to bridge the gap by using Bielby's social framework analysis and other statistical evidence to prove that the employer operated under a "general policy" of discrimination.

Scalia, however, found evidence sufficient to establish "significant proof" that such a policy was "entirely absent here." He noted that although relying on social framework analysis to argue that Walmart has a "'strong corporate culture' that makes it 'vulnerable' to 'gender bias' . . . [Bielby] could not . . .'determine with any specificity how regularly stereotypes play a meaningful role in employment decisions at Wal-Mart.'" Scalia particularly emphasized the fact that "'Dr. Bielby conceded that he could not calculate whether 0.5 percent or 95 percent of the employment decisions at Wal-Mart might be determined by stereotyped thinking.'" If Bielby could not make such a determination, Scalia concluded, "we can safely disregard what he has to say. It is worlds away from 'significant proof' that Wal-Mart 'operated under a general policy of discrimination.'"[8]

Subsequent to *Wal-Mart*, the Iowa Supreme Court dismissed similar evidence in *Pippen v. State* (2014), where plaintiffs offered ISC testimony to support their claims of racial discrimination in employment practices by the State of Iowa. In this case, Anthony Greenwald (one of the originators of the IAT) testified that based on his meta-analysis of IAT results, all persons to some degree had an automatic implicit preference for one race or another. Greenwald claimed that such evidence was strongly presumptive that Iowa managers had made implicitly biased employment decisions. Yet, like Bielby, Greenwald had not reviewed any specific hiring files or any discrete employment decision relating to any of the class members.[9]

The problem of reasoning from the general to the particular as a matter of evidence in these cases is embedded in the nature of the ISC research in general and of the IAT in particular. Ironically, Greenwald's coauthor Mahzarin Banaji has made clear her belief (shared by other prominent ISC researchers) that the IAT is a "research and educational technique" that "should not be used for diagnostic purposes."[10] This qualification mirrors the distinction between using social framework analysis as a tool to provide context for understanding the particular facts of a case and using it to make specific, essentially diagnostic legal claims about particular instances of bias.

I would posit, however, that more basic than the problem of reasoning from general social framework to particular cases is the underlying frame evidenced in Kang's assertion that science—"specifically the remarkable findings of social cognition"—can break through the current "deadlock" of jurisprudence on race and discrimination.[11] This confidence in the power of data-driven metrics to overwhelm resistance to progressive racial programs has facilitated the acceptance of the basic conservative frame of focusing on intent in what could or should be primarily a disparate-impact claim.

Such faith in the power of science to autonomously resolve legal issues is misplaced. As Samuel Bagenstos has observed, "Science does not defeat the implicit bias law-reform program, but science does not establish the case for that program, either. That program depends on a normative judgment that discrimination is not about fault but about a social problem—a normative judgment that is deeply contested among judges and policymakers." Thus, he continues, "science will not save antidiscrimination law. To save antidiscrimination law requires articulating and defending the normative principles that justify and guide the application of that law to newly understood forms of bias, whatever they are, and however they are discovered."[12] Science does not interpret and apply itself. Data may matter, but they do not always matter, and they do not always matter in the same way. In the courtroom, data matter only when and how judges decide they do.

Consider, for example, some cases where the Court has allowed the state to evaluate issues of statistical probability in relation to race-based decision making. In the *Bakke*-era case *United States v. Brignoni-Ponce* (1975), the Supreme Court held that U.S. border-control agents could take race into consideration as a "relevant factor" (much as in *Bakke* [1978] itself[13]) when making decisions about which motorists to stop. In the key language justifying the use of race in the law enforcement context of *Brignoni-Ponce*, Justice Lewis Powell's majority opinion stated, "The likelihood that any given person of Mexican ancestry is an alien is high enough to make Mexican appearance a relevant factor but, standing alone, it does not justify stopping all Mexican-Americans to ask if they are aliens."[14] Likelihood, of course, is a probabilistic concept, but there is no discussion here, as there was later in *Wal-Mart*, of needing to bridge any gap between what we might characterize as the larger "social framework" of immigration and the status of any particular person riding in a car near the Mexican border. Granted, the Court required more than the mere fact of "Mexican appearance" for a stop to be made, but one might well argue that in cases such as *Wal-Mart* the accumulated evidence of gender- or race-based differentials provide precisely the sort of additional evidence particularized to the setting either of employment or of criminal justice that would support seeing implicit bias as tainting the relevant processes at issue.

These cases turn not simply on whether race may be considered a "factor" but also on determining what sort of "factor" race is and how it may be considered. The question is not the existence or absence of specific quantitative data. It is what the Court affirmatively *makes* of such data. For Powell, in *Brignoni-Ponce* general assertions of probability were sufficient to warrant consideration of race as a factor in law enforcement, but in *Bakke* he deemed the reams of accumulated data of past historical injustices visited upon African Americans to be "too amorphous" to be considered in crafting affirmative action remedies.[15] Yet such data are not objectively any more amorphous than the idea of probability relied upon in *Brignoni-Ponce*—or than the millisecond measurements of computer strikes in an IAT.

The limited power of science to resolve the fundamentally ideological issues of racial justice is made strikingly clear in an internal memorandum Justice Scalia wrote in 1987 to support a draft of Justice Powell's majority opinion in *McCleskey v. Kemp*.[16] *McCleskey* predated the advent of social framework analysis or behavioral realism per se, but, like them, it involved a plaintiff who proffered statistical social science evidence of bias to make a claim of racial discrimination. McCleskey, a black man, was convicted of murdering a police officer in Georgia and sentenced to death. McCleskey presented statistical evidence from a social science study (performed by David C. Baldus, Charles Pulaski, and George Woodworth and known as the "Baldus study") showing that in Georgia black defendants who killed white victims were the most likely to receive death sentences. McCleskey's attorneys argued that this evidence demonstrated that McCleskey's sentence violated the Eighth Amendment's prohibition of cruel and unusual punishment and the Equal Protection Clause of the Fourteenth Amendment. Sounding much like Scalia's later opinion in *Wal-Mart*, Justice Powell's majority opinion in *McCleskey* asserted that "to prevail under the Equal Protection Clause, McCleskey must prove that the decisionmakers in *his* case acted with discriminatory purpose. He offers no evidence specific to his own case that would support an inference that racial considerations played a part in his sentence. Instead, he relies solely on the Baldus study." Powell's holding, for a closely divided Court, rejected McCleskey's arguments, finding that the generalized information from the statistical study was "insufficient to support an inference that any of the decisionmakers in his case acted with discriminatory purpose."[17]

In his internal memorandum, Scalia stated,

> I plan to join [Powell's] opinion in this case, with two reservations. I disagree with the argument that the inferences that can be drawn from the Baldus study are weakened by the fact that each jury and each trial is unique, or by the large number of variables at issue. And I do not share the view, implicit in the opinion, that an effect of racial factors upon sentencing, if it could only be shown by sufficiently strong statistical evidence, would require reversal. Since it is my view that unconscious operation of irrational sympathies and antipathies, including racial, upon jury

decisions and (hence) prosecutorial decisions is real, acknowledged in the decisions of this court, and ineradicable, I cannot honestly say that all I need is more proof. I expect to write separately to make these points, but not until I see the dissent.[18]

As Erwin Chemerinsky has noted, "The implications of this memorandum are enormous. . . . Justice Scalia stated that, no matter what the statistical proof, he would not find a denial of equal protection."[19] Or as Ian Haney-López puts it, "For Scalia, racism is simply part of the world in which we live, and the law has no role to play, even when the stakes include state decisions to kill."[20] The broader implications go not to Scalia's personal brand of jurisprudence but to Bagenstos's point about the limited ability of statistics and social science evidence to resolve what are fundamentally normative and often ideological issues. Scalia's memo also provides a clear example of Govind Persad's argument that "even if research on cognitive bias were technically exemplary, it still could not, on its own, justify changes in legal norms. The legal relevance of cognitive bias requires support from an argument that experimental subjects' divergence from certain models of behavior (for instance, rational-choice economic models) constitutes a normative mistake rather than a normatively defensible deviation from an empirical prediction."[21] The mere statistical identification of a bias, as Scalia's memo makes abundantly clear, does not necessitate a conclusion—a *judgment*—that such a bias is illegitimate or constitutionally relevant. The science never speaks for itself. Judges must evaluate its meaning and significance in any given context.

The political analogue of Scalia's stance is perhaps most strikingly manifest in a statement by CNN commentator and Trump campaign surrogate Scottie Nell Hughes, who declared after the presidential election in 2016 that "there's no such thing, unfortunately, anymore as facts." The larger point she was trying to make is that in a politically contested environment everything can be disputed, everything becomes a matter of opinion. Her full statement was: "Well, I think it's also an idea of an opinion. And that's—on one hand, I hear half the media saying that these are lies. But on the other half, there are many people that go, 'No, it's true.' And so one thing that has been interesting this entire campaign season to watch, is that people that say facts are facts—they're not really facts. Everybody has a way—it's kind of like looking at ratings, or looking at a glass of half-full water. Everybody has a way of interpreting them to be the truth, or not truth. There's no such thing, unfortunately, anymore as facts."[22] The significance of this statement is not only that it conflates fact and opinion or reveals the illogic and hypocrisy of a particular Republican campaign operative but also that it shows in high relief the stark Machiavellian reality that "facts" alone rarely resolve contentious political disputes. Facts carry weight only as we weave them into a broader story—whether the story be of a glass half empty versus a glass half full or of the pervasiveness of racial discrimination versus the uniqueness of each distinct jury decision. The battle is not just over evidence; it is over narrative.

Behavioral realists would do well to consider more fully the implications of such sentiments before presenting the science of social cognition as the new magic bullet of equal-protection and antidiscrimination law. Their hope has been that they can use the "hard data" and great authority of science to convince judges to bridge the gap from observed disparate outcome to underlying racial animus. But that gap can never be bridged by data alone. The cost of this misplaced faith in science is realized not simply in its ready dismissal by judges who use different ideological frames to pick and choose which numbers to acknowledge as meaningful and when. It comes also in the form of accepting and legitimating the underlying conservative frame of focusing on intent instead of on impact to evaluate the nature and merits of a claim of discrimination. The search for unconscious bias, however supported, directs attention first and foremost to the mindset, the intent (whether conscious or not), of the accused perpetrator rather than seeking to understand the nature of the harm experienced by the plaintiff.

What if the outcome of *Brown v. Board of Education* (1954) had turned on similar behavioral realist arguments about scientific evidence? Yes, the Court did allude to the famous "doll studies" of psychologist Kenneth Clarke in a footnote,[23] but such evidence was not central by any means to the Court's holding. How might Scalia or Powell have responded to that evidence if they had been on the Court at the time? We can easily imagine them saying, "OK, the studies show that black children in segregated schools generally prefer white dolls to black dolls, but can you connect this to any specific harm suffered by these particular plaintiffs in this case?" The simple fact of the matter is that *Brown*'s finding that separate but equal facilities are inherently unequal did not turn on scientific evidence any more than did *Plessy v.*

Ferguson's finding in 1896 that separate but equal was just fine.[24] Nor did these findings turn on trying to divine the *intent* of the parties involved. These diametrically opposed decisions were not dictated by science or by evidence in itself. They were determined by the justices' exercise of *judgment* in evaluating the context and meaning of the statutes at issue—that is, in reflecting and creating the dominant *common sense* of race and racism at the time. The *Plessy* majority's ideological commitment to white supremacy led it to conclude that any perception or experience of stigma resulting from Jim Crow laws was fundamentally a *private* matter and not the responsibility of the state. The *Brown* Court never spoke of the *intent* behind the segregations laws but found that the stigma these laws imposed on children on account of their race deeply offended the Constitution. Haney-López calls this approach "of measuring alleged discrimination through an examination of the larger context . . . '[c]ontextual intent.'"[25] I think we may simply call it "judgment" because, as Richard Ford has argued, "'discrimination' is not a fact in and of itself; it is a narrative, an interpretation."[26] We need to recognize that contesting equal-protection jurisprudence must be understood as fundamentally an interpretive and normative endeavor. We cannot finesse the necessity of judgment by appealing to some mythical transparent authority of scientific measurement.

PRACTICAL POLICY AND PRACTICE OUTCOMES

Behavioral realism is not simply an abstract theory expounded in law reviews or a subject of academic studies that sometimes play a role in court cases. It has also provided the foundation for several significant initiatives by major institutions to address the problem of implicit bias in the court system, law enforcement, and employment. In response to studies showing that implicit bias colors the actions not only of judges but also of jurors and prosecutors,[27] the NCSC and the American Bar Association have developed resources to promote a variety of diversity-training interventions to help reduce implicit bias in the courtroom.[28] Events since the police shooting of Michael Brown in Ferguson, Missouri, in 2014 have cast a spotlight on implicit bias in law enforcement. Prominent among the numerous police-training programs that suggest particular interventions to address implicit bias is Fair and Impartial Policing (FIP), a project led by University of South Florida professor Lorie Fridell that has developed model curricula for police training with grants from the U.S. Department of Justice and its related Community Oriented Policing Services (COPS) Program.[29] In employment contexts, the field of diversity training has emerged in recent years as a major industry in its own right, devoting much concern to addressing questions of stereotyping and implicit bias in workplace settings.[30] In the context of employment, the U.S. Equal Employment Opportunity Commission has developed the "E-Race" (Eradicating Racism and Colorism from Employment) initiative, a national outreach, education, and enforcement campaign aimed at spreading information and training interventions to address implicit bias in employment contexts nationwide.[31] Each of these initiatives draws heavily on the work of behavioral realists and ISC theorists. Jerry Kang in particular has played a central role in the NCSC project to train judges and jurors to address implicit bias in the courtroom.[32]

In 2006, the NCSC launched the National Campaign to Ensure the Racial and Ethnic Fairness of America's State Courts "to mobilize the significant expertise, experience, and commitment of state court judges and court officers to ensure both the perception and reality of racial and ethnic fairness in the nation's state courts." The campaign developed an extensive database of resources on implicit bias and also oversaw and provided technical support to three substantial state court pilot projects to provide implicit bias training to judges and court staff in California, North Dakota, and Minnesota. The three primary objectives of the training were to enable participants "to demonstrate a basic understanding of implicit bias; identify possible strategies to mitigate the influence of implicit bias on behavior; [and] develop an individualized action plan to address implicit bias."[33]

The California program was offered in video format through the state court system's closed-circuit cable television station. Any member of the judicial branch could participate. It is estimated that between 107 and 350 people viewed the program, including judges, court professionals, attorneys, clerks, and support staff.[34] The Minnesota program was smaller and tailored specifically for Minnesota's Racial Fairness Committee, which consisted of 20 to 25 judges, attorneys, justice system partners, and community representatives.[35] North Dakota targeted attendees of its winter judicial conference. Judges, other judicial officers, court administrators, and a few attorneys were among the 44 participants in the program. Each program offered online IATs to the participants and provided video presentations. Minnesota and North Dakota provided background readings and conducted small-group exercises on implicit bias.[36] Foremost among the reading material provided in North Dakota was the text *Implicit Bias: A Primer for the Courts* by Jerry Kang.[37] The featured video at the training sessions was titled *The Neuroscience and Psychology of Decisionmaking*; it was produced by the Judicial Center of California with a grant from the NCSC and features many leading ISC experts, including Banaji, John Dovidio, and Kang.[38]

The American Bar Association's Litigation Section maintains a website of resources as part of its Implicit Bias Initiative to "to help combat implicit bias in the justice system." The website is meant to "serve as 'one-stop shopping'— the 'go-to' repository for anyone who wants to know more about implicit bias in the justice system or in the ranks of the legal profession." A "centerpiece" of this website is the same video used in the NCSC pilot programs, *The Neuroscience and Psychology of Decisionmaking*. The website also contains a link to take the IAT online and a "toolbox" of resources "for use in exploring implicit bias and approaches to debiasing" that includes a model Power Point presentation and links to readings, including Kang's text *Implicit Bias: A Primer for the Courts*.[39]

The FIP program counts dozens of state and local law enforcement agencies among its clients and since 2009 has been providing services to the U.S. Department of Justice's Office of Community Oriented Policing Services. Echoing some of the core tenets of ISC and behavioral realism, the program emphasizes that "it is based on the science of bias, which tells us that biased policing is not, as some contend, due to widespread racism in policing. In fact, the science tells that even well-intentioned humans (and thus officers) manifest biases that can impact on their perceptions and behavior. These biases can manifest below consciousness."[40] There are five FIP curricula, each customized for distinct audiences, including academy recruits and in-service patrol officers, first-line supervisors, midmanagers, command-level personnel (or command personnel and community leaders), and law enforcement trainers. Each curriculum is "based on the science of bias."[41] Fridell notes that "although still relatively new, the fair and impartial policing perspective is getting a lot of attention and acquiring 'converts' from around the nation. . . . Entire states are adopting the FIP perspective, including Kansas, Rhode Island, Wisconsin and South Carolina."[42]

In January 2010, the U.S. Equal Employment Opportunity Commission established a working group "to identify the obstacles that remain in the federal workplace that hinder equal employment opportunities for African Americans." Foremost among the obstacles identified were "unconscious biases and perceptions about African Americans." The working group report highlighted the IAT as an effective tool to address the problem and recommended "unconscious bias training," much along the same lines as the NCSC and FIP programs for all federal employees, "so they can become aware of their biases."[43]

One notable aspect of all these programs is the similarity of their diagnoses and remedies for the problems of implicit bias. The various interventions proposed across platforms share common roots in the field of "diversity training" that emerged in the 1980s largely as a response to federal policies and court decisions in the field of affirmative action and employment discrimination. Although not originally grounded in ISC theory, the field of diversity training has been heavily informed by the field of psychology and animated by many similar concerns to address subtler forms of bias in the workplace. Moreover, over the past two decades, many diversity-training programs have fully embraced and integrated ISC findings into their programs.[44] We see the full integration of behavioral realism and diversity training in claims such as law professor Justin Levinson's contention that "debiasing techniques, which use interventions such as diversity training to lessen the negative effects of implicit bias, hold promise for at least temporarily reducing the harms of implicit memory bias" in courtroom settings.[45]

What, then, is this thing called "diversity training," and how has it worked? One response for certain is that it is a big business.[46] In 2003, it was estimated to be an $8 billion a year industry.[47] In 2015, Google reported it would be spending $150 million on diversity training and related initiatives.[48] The industry itself emerged out of equal-opportunity programs crafted by personnel experts in the 1960s and 1970s following the passage of the Civil Rights Act of 1964 and related antidiscrimination legislation.[49] Sociologist Frank Dobbin notes that although civil rights activists fought for equal rights and politicians outlawed discrimination, it was largely left to personnel managers to define in practice what job discrimination was and was not. He argues that personnel experts took charge for three reasons: first, the civil rights laws themselves contained only vague standards and did not create an independent regulatory agency comparable to the National Labor Relations Board to set or oversee compliance standards; second, the personnel experts saw this as an opportunity to expand their numbers and influence within the firm; and third, the experts "had something lawyers were not offering, plausible bureaucratic vaccines against litigation" in a legal arena where discrimination came to be defined in terms of the presence or absence of diversity-training programs.[50]

What began as compliance in the 1960s and 1970s moved into diversity training in the 1980s as affirmative action programs came under attack. Significantly, however, Dobbin argues that personnel experts led the courts in this transition rather than vice versa. He notes, for example, that Powell's opinion in Bakke, embracing the concept of diversity, was inspired by a program at Harvard University developed by personnel experts. Tracing the waves of corporate equal-opportunity programs, Dobbin argues that in the 1970s bureaucracy emerged as the "antidote to discrimination." In the 1980s during the Reagan years, "when affirmative action was on the ropes," personnel experts reconfigured "equal-opportunity" programs as "diversity-management" programs and argued that such programs promoted efficiency and gave firms a strategic advantage in the market.[51] It was during this transition that the personnel experts began to embrace findings from the cognitive social sciences. By the 1990s, diversity training was also being touted as a means to boost company morale, enhance productivity, and bring greater access to new segments of the marketplace.[52] By the late 1990s, 70 percent of Fortune 500 companies had diversity initiatives, and 90 percent of large organizations reported having them by 2010.[53]

The story that Dobbin and other scholars tell of the diversity industry provides a significant new perspective on the development of civil rights and racial justice that many analysts from the legal academy have overlooked. For example, in her searing indictment of the criminal justice system, The New Jim Crow, Michelle Alexander attributes much of the faltering of the energy and civil rights advances made through the grassroots activism of the 1950s and 1960s to the fact that "the lawyers took over" after the grand success of cases such as Brown v. Board of Education. "This development," she writes, "enhanced their ability to wage legal battles but impeded their ability to acknowledge or respond to the emergence of a new caste system."[54] Similarly, in *From Jim Crow to Civil Rights*, his magisterial survey of the Supreme Court and civil rights, Michael Klarman argues that "judicial victories may . . . have the more concrete deleterious effect of persuading social protestors to channel energy and resources to the method that has already proven successful: litigation. Yet many objectives of the modern civil rights movement were probably beyond the capacity of the courts to deliver." He notes in particular the importance of follow-up legislation to enforce judicial decrees.[55] In themselves, these observations clearly have much merit, but it was not just the lawyers, the courts, or even the Congress who "took over." As Dobbin's work makes clear, it was also and perhaps predominantly the corporate bureaucrats.

ISC theory and diversity training, then, share much in common. Whereas the courts may have cast a very skeptical eye on such ISC-informed practices as social framework analysis and generalized IAT data, personnel managers embraced them wholeheartedly and incorporated the mantra of identifying and addressing implicit bias as a core tenet of programs affecting millions of workers. Surely this incorporation must count as a major victory for ISC theory and behavioral realism. Perhaps it would if diversity training and its diverse methods of "debiasing" worked. The problem is that for all the behavioral realist talk of counterstereotypical screensavers, IATs, and group exercises to create a "bigger we," the best available evidence shows that diversity training has simply failed to increase workforce diversity.

Dobbin notes that throughout the 1980s diversity consultants built the diversity-training business "not by holding up evidence that [it] worked, but by telling a strong story."[56] In one study done in 2006, Alexandra Kalev, Dobbin, and Erin Kelly found that efforts to "moderate managerial bias" through diversity training were "least effective" in increasing workforce diversity, particularly compared to the impact of federal affirmative action edicts that assigned responsibility for compliance to a specific manager. "At best," they concluded, " 'best practices' are best guesses."[57] A review of 985 studies in 2009 observed that "entire genres of prejudice-reduction interventions, including diversity training, educational programs, and sensitivity training in health and law enforcement professions, have never been evaluated with experimental methods," leading to the conclusion that "the causal effects of many wide-spread prejudice-reduction interventions, such as workplace diversity training and media campaigns, remain unknown."[58] Even proponents of diversity training have acknowledged that "conclusive data on the effectiveness of modern day diversity training is still lacking."[59] Finally, a study by Soohan Kim, Kalev, and Dobbin in 2012 firmly concluded that diversity-training programs "do not lead to improvements in workforce diversity."[60] If these programs do not actually promote diversity, why have they persisted and thrived? One possible answer may come from a study done in 2013, which argues that diversity programs "legitimize existing social arrangements" by providing the "illusion of fairness" through procedural programs that appear fair but do not actually produce substantive results.[61]

Regarding the specific programs discussed earlier, it is worth considering that the NCSC's own evaluation of its three state pilot programs found little or no evidence of efficacy.[62] Ironically, pre- and postprogram assessments filled out by participants in the Minnesota and North Dakota programs actually showed a *decrease* in the percentage of participants responding correctly to two of the six questions asked about their understanding of implicit bias.[63] Although there may be many reasons for counterintuitive results, at a minimum such results call into question the efficacy of these interventions. A recent review of explicitly ISC-formulated interventions to mitigate implicit bias similarly found such measures to be ineffective. This study by Calvin Lai and his colleagues tested nine interventions on 6,321 participants. It found that although all nine interventions immediately reduced implicit bias, none of them was effective after a delay of even several hours or several days.[64]

These programs are the ones we have. Grounded in ISC theory and behavioral realism, they have become the dominant paradigm in addressing issues of race and racism throughout the major institutions in American society. At best, the practical outcomes of behavioral realism, both in law and in society, are in doubt, and the unintended negative consequences of providing an illusion of fairness while draining attention and resources away from other approaches to framing and addressing racism are potentially substantial.

5

DERACINATING THE LEGAL SUBJECT

ehavioral realism not only embraces and reinforces existing aspects of the conservative frame but also *produces* problematic new understandings of race and racism in American society. This chapter addresses behavioral realism's tendency to deracinate the legal subject—that is, to strip the individual of history and identity, much as the color-blind ideal would leave behind society's history of race and racism. In 1984, Michael Sandel published an influential critique of the type of liberal proceduralism exemplified by John Rawls's book *A Theory of Justice*.[1] In "The Procedural Republic and the Unencumbered Self," Sandel characterized the liberal vision's "core thesis": "a just society seeks not to promote any particular ends, but enables its citizens to pursue their own ends, consistent with a similar liberty for all; it therefore must govern by principles that do not presuppose any particular conception of the good. What justifies these regulative principles above all is not that they maximize the general welfare, or cultivate virtue, or otherwise promote the good, but rather that they conform to the concept of right, a moral category given prior to the good, and independent of it."[2]

This characterization is consonant with Rawls's idea of the "original position" from which members of society would be able to construct just principles of governance. In the original position, actors act as if behind a "veil of ignorance" as to their own status and identity in the society for which the principles are being developed. The question being asked, then, is: If no one can know what place he or she will occupy in the society being formed, what arrangement of the society would a rational person choose?[3] Or as Sandel puts it, "The original position works like this: It invites us to imagine the principles we would choose to govern our society if we were to choose them in advance, before we knew the particular persons we would be—whether rich or poor, strong or weak, lucky or unlucky—before we knew even our interests or alms or conceptions of the good." His key point follows upon this clarification, when he argues that these principles "presuppose . . . a certain picture of the person, of the way we must be if we are beings for whom justice is the first virtue. This is the picture of the unencumbered self, a self understood as prior to and independent of purposes and ends."[4]

The unencumbered self is a deracinated self, a self without history or distinct identity—certainly, it is a self without race. As Sandel notes, there is a cost to positing such selves as an ideal, for the unencumbered self is denied "the possibility of membership in any community bound by moral ties antecedent to choice; he cannot belong to any community where the self itself could be at stake."[5] Such moral ties are essential for constructing understandings of ourselves, our place in the world, and the type of world we would like to see. "To imagine a person incapable of constitutive attachments such as these," asserts Sandel, "is not to conceive an ideally free and rational agent, but to imagine a person wholly without character, without moral depth."[6] Yet this is precisely the type of self that behavioral realism posits as the model for its program to address implicit bias. Indeed, in one early article, Mahzarin Banaji, Max Bazerman, and Dolly Chugh explicitly invoked Rawls's "veil of ignorance" as a model of understanding implicit bias and how to address it.[7]

We also see the ideal of the "veil of ignorance" manifesting almost literally in Jerry Kang and Banaji's elevation of the "blind" music audition as a model for addressing implicit bias.[8] As discussed earlier, this practice involves placing a screen between musicians auditioning for places in the orchestra and the judges—literally blinding the judges to the performer's color and gender. Similarly, in discussing the policy implications of ISC, psychologists Brian Nosek and Rachel Riskind adapt this approach to other employment contexts, suggesting that although "the evaluating supervisor cannot easily be blinded to employee identities . . . committees of other supervisors could review performance reports or other performance indicators with identifying information redacted. Comparing identity-conscious and identity-blind evaluations can identify discrepancies and provide fodder for investigating whether social bias could be a contributing factor."[9] Here, blindness to identity is the ideal. Identity is severed from merit and drained of any independent value.

Enacting the ideal of liberal procedural fairness, the veil is meant to ensure that people evaluate only "true merit." But many assumptions and values are packed into that little valise labeled "true merit," for the veil does not simply obscure the identity of the performer; it erases it—rendering it irrelevant and indeed antithetical to constructions and judgments of merit. It also renders merit a sort of universal value, a "thing" that can be objectively verified. Dana-Ain Davis argues that under "neoliberal racism . . . the relevance of the raced subject, racial identity and racism is subsumed under the auspices of meritocracy. For in a neoliberal society, individuals are supposedly freed from identity and operate under the limiting assumptions that hard work will be rewarded if the game is played according to the rules."[10] The neoliberal ideal of merit, evident in Justice Lewis Powell's opinion in *Bakke* and that opinion's subsequent iterations in cases from *Croson* to *Grutter*, depends not only on achieving color blindness, which refers to the viewer or discriminating actor, but also on stripping the subject (or object of discrimination) of his or her identity—of his or her history and place in society, of the constitutive affiliations that Sandel marks as the essential precondition for moral depth. It reduces the subject to nothing more than his or her ability to perform specified tasks, whether playing an instrument or taking a standardized test.

THE VALUE OF SITUATED SELVES

The primary problem with this reduction is that, as legal scholar Martha Minow has noted, there are situations in which identity *should* matter and in which erasing identity does harm to the very subjects it is meant to protect. Minow develops the idea of the "dilemma of difference," which involves "the risk of reiterating the stigma associated with assigned difference either by focusing on it or by ignoring it."[11] The dilemma of difference is relational, not inherent. It arises from two questions: "When does treating people differently emphasize their differences and stigmatize or hinder them on that basis? and when does treating people the same become insensitive to their

difference and likely to stigmatize or hinder them on *that* basis?"[12] At the
level of Supreme Court opinions, we see similar concerns reflected in Justice Harry Blackmun's statement in *Bakke* (1978) that "in order to get beyond
racism, we must first take account of race. There is no other way. And in
order to treat some persons equally, we must treat them differently."[13]

Ralph Richard Banks, Jennifer Eberhardt, and Lee Ross point up this
problem in their article "Discrimination and Implicit Bias in a Racially
Unequal Society," where they write that

> even those who laud the ideal of race blindness would admit, if pressed, that
> in our society one need not, and perhaps cannot, be blind to race. Most of
> us believe that it is proper, desirable even, to pay some attention to race,
> even in ways that burden racial minorities. Indeed, some commentators
> have argued that not noticing race, or acting as though race does not
> matter, is itself a form of racial bias. . . . [I]f the findings of the Race IAT
> constitute evidence of racial bias it cannot be because they confirm that
> people deviate from some ideal of being (nearly) blind to race.[14]

Yet both advocates of "race blindness" (who contend different IAT scores
reflect implicit bias) and critics of IATs (who contend that different scores
may reflect nothing more than awareness of larger social stereotypes) view
such differences—seeing race—as inherently suspect. But seeing black
people (or people of another color, gender, sexual orientation, and so on) as
different is not always a bad thing. Recognition of difference may reflect
prejudice, but it can also involve understanding the significance of race both
in historical and social context and in one's own individual psyche. There
might, for example, be times when it is quite understandable or even appropriate for a white person to react differently to a black person than to another
white person. Even some of the "aversive" behaviors identified by John Dovidio
and Samuel Gaertner,[15] such as averting one's gaze or leaning back or stumbling over words,[16] can be understood not only as aversion (which in many
cases it might be) but also perhaps to some degree in some situations as an
awareness of the awkwardness of living with one's own privilege—an aversion, as it were, not simply to the black person in the room but to the awareness of one's own privileged position in relation to that person. Erasing
aversion thus might also mean erasing awareness of privilege. This is not to

say that aversive racism is not real or that it should not be addressed. It is more to say that aversion itself, unease or dis-ease, might be more complex and contested. One white person might lean away from or smile less at a black person because he is simply unconsciously biased; another may do the same thing because she is uncomfortably aware of her historical privilege; and third may do so from a mix of both and perhaps other reasons. Aversive behaviors, like Clifford Geertz's "wink," can have many and multiple meanings, particularly when situated in context.

Philosopher Anthony Appiah has recognized that racial identity can be a positive source of value and should be acknowledged and engaged as such. He notes that we cannot escape normative stereotypes because "they are central to understanding the place of identity in moral and civic life." The challenge is not to erase or to blind us to such stereotypes but to configure them "in such a way as to serve as potential instruments in the construction of a dignified individuality." Thus, for example, if identifying as an African American "is a source of value in the shaping of the modern identities of at least some Americans of African ancestry, then it seems . . . that we must accept that at least some normative stereotypes—about dress or speech or participation in Kwanza, for example—have value."[17]

In contrast to Appiah, Kang, drawing on ISC theory, refers to stereotypes as "racial schemas" provided to us through "law and culture [that] . . . automatically, efficiently, parse the raw data pushed to our senses. These templates of categorical knowledge are applied to entities, including human targets. Racial schemas, because they are chronically accessible, regularly influence social interactions."[18] Kang's almost mechanistic characterization of the nature and functioning of schemas considers their significance only in terms of how a privileged viewer might construct an image of a racialized "other." Appiah, however, recognizes the potential value of such schemas for the construction of self-identity, not merely as a way to perceive others. In short, we make sense not only of others through stereotypes but also of ourselves.

Kang's focus on cognitive schemas also subtly displaces critiques of structural aspects of racism from social to cognitive structures. Hearkening back to David Wellman as well as to Ralph Richard Banks and Richard Ford, who criticize behavioral realism for diverting attention away from structural racism, we see here how the move to deracinate the human subject, to blind us to stereotypes, is accomplished in part through the simultaneous recognition of structures of "law and culture" and their displacement into the realm of individual cognition. Behavioral realism's focus on individual cognition and the neurological processes underlying perception and categorization also strips racism of its historical identity. This erasure produces an impoverished conception of racism because, as George Frederickson has noted, "racism is always nationally specific."[19] It does not exist in a vacuum, out of place or time. Moreover, with particular reference to the American experience, Michael Omi and Howard Winant have argued that "the state *is* inherently racial. Far from *intervening* in racial conflicts, the state is itself increasingly the preeminent site of racial conflict."[20] Racism cannot be understood and addressed apart from it historical context, nor can policies be developed to address it without understanding the role of the state in defining and constructing racialized practices.

Behavioral realism marginalizes such values and allows racial identity to matter only insofar as it serves the milquetoast goal of diversity. But why *shouldn't* race qua race matter sometimes in making decisions about hiring, admissions, school assignment, and so forth? Why *shouldn't* we sometimes respond differently on an IAT or in an fMRI given the deeply embedded histories of racism in our country? Doesn't erasing race in all such circumstances do violence not only to history but also to the identities of those living among us?

The ideal of color blindness embedded in the use of the IAT (and fMRI measurements of brains on IATs) is predicated on the idea that there is some sort of unencumbered true original cognitive position of pure nonbias from which deviations, designated as implicit biases, can be measured. In practice, the ISC regime governed by the IAT and fMRIs is often predicated on an unstated norm of whiteness. Generally speaking, the measure of racism on an IAT means taking *longer* to make associations between "good" objects and "black" faces than between "good" objects and "white" faces. (The converse is also part of the equation: the quicker speed of association between "bad" words or objects and "black" faces than between "bad" words or objects and "white" faces). The unstated goal of debiasing seems pretty clearly to enable test subjects to associate "good" objects with "black" faces *as quickly or easily* as they do with "white" faces. Certainly in dealing with stereotypes, the ideal is not to have subjects view "white" faces with equal suspicion as "black" faces. The norm, then, is not really neutrality—it is to view all people *as if* they were white. We see a typical statement of this norm in one neurological study finding that "numerous fMRI studies have demonstrated greater amygdala response to African-American faces than [to] Caucasian-American faces."[21] Consider an alternative configuration wherein the racial groups are flipped: "numerous fMRI studies have demonstrated *lesser* amygdala response to *Caucasian-American* faces than African-American faces." This latter frame constructs African American as the norm, but in the actual study the response to Caucasian faces is the baseline from which perception of African American faces deviates.

Martha Minow comments on the power of the unstated norm, whether in terms of race or in terms of gender, noting that "the unstated reference point promotes the interests of some but not others; it can remain unstated because those who do not fit have less power to select the norm than those who fit comfortably within the one that prevails."[22] Perhaps more to the point in the case of the IAT's color-blind ideal, Minow argues that "if to be equal you must be the same, then to be different is to be unequal."[23] The IAT's "equality" is one that not only requires the viewer to respond to black faces as if they were white but also implies (unintentionally, of course) that the embodied sources of those images—black people themselves—should be white. This dynamic implicitly strips people of color of their racial identity while eliding the fact that whiteness is also a racial identity. Under this scheme, nonwhites have their identity devalued. Granted, the ideal is meant to devalue negative stereotypes associated with nonwhite racial identities, but when this devaluation is measured in terms of seeing people as if they were the same, white, the dynamic becomes murkier and more problematic. One might argue that under behavioral realism, the perception of nonwhite race is understood to "taint" the results of these tests—in the case of fMRIs quite literally as manifested by the brain "lighting up" in ways deemed indicative of implicit bias. "Not seeing race" can mean not seeing nonwhite race. In the procedural republic of unencumbered amygdalas, blackness is pollution.

In the case of the music audition, it is clear that orchestras have always done more than simply perform music. They are part of a broader community that they engage on multiple levels. If all orchestras do is perform music, then performances themselves might best be conducted behind screens, but people love music for many reasons. Some of those reasons might include, for example, identifying with virtuoso performers. The virtuoso as a personality has long been part of the lure of Western classical music.[24] A virtuoso, however, is more than just the performance; he or she is a *person*—someone with an identity and a history. The same can be said of conductors, who have long performed multiple roles that take them far beyond the basic act of conducting itself. Given that musical performers are *more* than just the sum of their discrete performances, perhaps considering race or gender or other nonmusical characteristics might on occasion be appropriate and even desirable—not for their ability to "debias" the orchestra but in their own right.

Even calls to explicitly engage race to address implicit bias can, perhaps inadvertently and certainly ironically, reinforce the tendency to deracinate the subject. For example, in a thoughtful article titled "Making Race Salient: Trayvon Martin and Implicit Bias in a Not Yet Post-racial Society," Cynthia Lee draws on ISC research to argue that foregrounding race, making it salient, in the courtroom context can mitigate the effects of implicit bias. The example she works with involves a "run-of-the-mill case" in which a person shoots a young black male, and the jury, judge, and prosecutor have to evaluate his claim that he felt "threatened." Lee suggests making jurors "aware of racial issues that can bias their decision-making, like the operation of racial stereotypes." In many respects, this suggestion is quite reasonable and laudable. Lee goes on, however, to characterize this act as "even[ing] the scales"—that is, "when race is salient, jurors tend to treat similarly situated Black and White defendants the same, as they should when the facts are identical in both cases and the only difference is the race of the defendant. Making race salient does not give the Black defendant an advantage over the similarly situated White defendant. Failing to make race salient, however, seems to lead to unequal treatment of similarly situated defendants, with the Black defendant receiving the short end of the stick."[25]

This characterization begs the question of what it means for a black defendant and a white defendant to be "similarly situated." Given the sort of historically pervasive and structural racism embedded in the criminal justice system cataloged by Michelle Alexander,[26] one might ask whether a black defendant and a white defendant can ever be truly "similarly situated"—at least in the present historical moment. The problem here is not that Lee is arguing for making race salient but that she is limiting her conception of salience to the sort of procedural cognitive "mind bugs" of stereotyping and implicit bias that are so central to the program behavioral realism. Making race salient in this context is simply trying to create an audition screen by other means.

We might also make race salient not only by telling jurors, judges, and prosecutors not only about their own cognitive biases but also about the history and ongoing ubiquity of structurally biased practices and procedures in the criminal justice system. Making race salient might not simply be a matter of getting jurors to treat one individual black person the same as they would treat a white person (effectively erasing the person's racial identity) but of getting jurors (and judges and prosecutors) to understand such things in terms of the fact that due to structurally racist practices a black person is many more times likely to be coming before them for this crime than a white person. Failing to make race salient in *this* way enables the perpetuation of structural racism—a clear example of Minow's concern regarding how ignoring difference can enhance injustice.

A LARGER TOOL KIT THAN INSTRUMENTAL RATIONALITY

I do not mean to say that the IAT is "bad" or useless. It can be a very valuable *part* of a larger tool kit for understanding and addressing racism. The problem comes when it is elevated to a master measurement that somehow transparently reveals the presence and nature of bias. The problem is exacerbated when behavioral realists such as Kang and Banaji propose that the IAT might even be used as a direct guide to terminating the duration of affirmative action programs.[27] Implicit bias exists, and good evidence supports the contention that it affects behavior. Certainly, addressing such bias and behavior is a laudable goal. The question is, *How*? When ISC-informed technical tests such as the IAT and fMRI become the definitive, authoritative markers of such bias, then the implicit assumptions of the white norm and ideal of the unencumbered brain may have a tendency to predominate and undermine this otherwise worthy effort.

Gary Wills notes that "the idea that America has somehow outgrown or transcended racism is an ever renewable delusion."[28] The idea is so appealing precisely because it absolves us of the hard responsibility of *working*

through race, of living with different IATs and fMRIs—with our own ines-
capably complex attitudes toward race—and struggling with them on a daily
basis. The logic of denying the perception of identity again resonates with
Justice Antonin Scalia's declaration that "under our Constitution there can
be no such thing as either a creditor or a debtor race."[29] As Charles Lawrence
III has remarked, "Cognitive research's focus on the process of categorization,
like the [Roberts] Court's focus on the process of classification, skips the
question of our responsibility for what our history has wrought. Both turn
our attention away from the content of the categories and the meaning of
that content. Both take white supremacy (and anti-subordination) off the table
as the central concern of our justice project."[30] One might say that the ideal
of behavioral realism, as refracted through the lens of the IAT and the
fMRI, is to have no debtor or creditor amygdalas—brains that are unencumbered by knowledge or awareness of identity. But this is one sort of transcendence we can do without.

In his critique of the blind music audition model, Robert Post argues that
the abstracted meritocratic ideal of "functional rationality" embedded in the
model rests "on a concept of the person that reduces him or her 'to a bundle
of abilities, an instrument valued according to its capacity for performing
socially valued functions with more or less efficiency.'" The logic of American antidiscrimination law exemplified by the music audition, Post contends, "requires employers to regard their employees as though they did not
display socially powerful and salient attributes, because these attributes may
induce irrational and prejudiced judgments." He goes on to ask the critically
important question: "In what sense does a person without an appearance
remain a person?"[31] The ideal of erasing identity affects not only the perceiver but also the perceived.

Consider one fairly typically ISC-informed admonition that in the
employment context "a decisionmaker's failure to make individual, rather
than stereotyped, assessments of people is the result of a choice, and organizations (employers) can motivate decisionmakers to make accurate, individual assessments. Comments about a person based on his/her membership
in a particular group of people—based on race, sex, age, religion or disability—rather than [on] him/her as an individual are evidence of stereotyping as to a particular group of people. When the comments are
derogatory or negative, they suggest a negative perception of that group."[32]

On its face, this comment is certainly reasonable enough. But what sort of "individual" is here constructed? Race, sex, age, religion, and disability—in short, everything that makes one an individual—are deemed potential sources of stereotyping and so to be avoided. Of course, only "derogatory" or "negative" comments are singled out in the passage, but even identity itself is here made a source of danger, a transgressive boundary that should not be crossed. The category of the "individual" is to be kept pure from all aspects of socially and historically embodied identity. Race and the rest become a sort of pollution, concepts that should not enter into the evaluation of the individual, who, in turn, is reduced to a mere entity of functional rationalism—a job-performing cipher without identity.[33] As Devon Carbado and Mitu Gulati note, in specific employment contexts the need to "fit in" might realistically lead a person to deny core aspects of herself or of her self-conception and identity in a manner that constitutes "a continual harm to that employee's dignity."[34]

The common logic of functional rationalism underlying both conservative jurisprudence and behavioral realism creates individuals unencumbered by identity and reduces them to mere instruments governed under what Banks and Ford have characterized as a trend toward "technocratic authoritarianism" embedded in the discourse of unconscious bias.[35] Rather than try to take antidiscrimination efforts outside the realm of the social by grounding them in some abstract ideal of "science," we would do well to heed Post's admonition that "antidiscrimination law always begins and ends in history, which means that it must participate in the very practices that it seeks to alter and to regulate."[36] To be sure, rational instrumentality and technical authority must necessarily be part of many evaluations in particular contexts, but elevating of them to be the primary concern and fundamental metric of value in decision making and legal judgment is highly problematic. The audition screen might sometimes be appropriate, but not always and forever.

In contrast to the original position, Post suggests an alternative perspective that he characterizes as the "sociological account." Instead of seeking "context-free" transcendence, this account "accepts the inevitability of social practices" and "focuses on how the law reconstructs social practices, even at the sacrifice of instrumental rationality."[37] We cannot escape bias or stereotypes, but we can shape them. As Michael Sandel might say, we cannot shape them constructively without preexisting normative commitments. That is, we cannot shape as disencumbered selves in some Rawlsian original position. To be in the world, Govind Persad points out, is to have "worldview bias."[38]

Ian Haney-López echoes these concerns in his discussion of the "contextual approach" to discrimination cases that "seemed geared toward reaching a conclusion about whether the interests behind the challenged government action were generally legitimate or illegitimate, innocent or tainted by racism—rather than establishing whether prejudice or bias on the part of any individual was directly at work."[39] The focus on articulating normative concerns and explicitly formulating principles for guiding social practice animates both Post's "sociological account" and Haney-López's "contextual approach." Both demand a historical and social situatedness that engages rather than transcends identity. Both, therefore, offer stark contrasts to the procedural, decontextualized approach of behavioral realism.

The audition screen does not simply hide the performer from the judge; it also masks the abstract meritocratic ideal underlying behavioral realism, an ideal that strips the subject of identity and reduces her to an instrument of functional rationality. The remedy is technical, conflict free, and devoid of constitutive affiliations with the underlying nature of the harm being addressed. Such thin, unencumbered proceduralism comports far more with Justice John Roberts's injunction that "the way to stop discrimination on the basis of race is to stop discriminating on the basis of race"[40] than with Justice Sonia Sotomayor's riposte that "the way to stop discrimination on the basis of race is to speak openly and candidly on the subject of race, and to apply the Constitution with eyes open to the unfortunate effects of centuries of racial discrimination."[41]

THE PROBLEM OF INTERSECTIONALITY

Finally, the grounding of behavioral realism in the IAT and related fMRI testing raises a problem of suppressing or eliding intersectional identities while reducing race to a monolithic category. To the extent that the IAT is and can be used in a manner that is not premised on color blindness or an unencumbered amygdala, it nonetheless tends to reduce complex human subjects to one single aspect of their multifarious identities. The IAT and related fMRIs are foundationally constructed around binaries, whether with respect to race, gender, age, sex, or disability: black versus white, male versus female, old versus young, and so on. Insofar as the IAT and behavioral realism operate with reference to an unstated white norm, they also operate within a sort of assimilationist paradigm that obscures the multiplicity of individual identities behind a veil not of ignorance but of an ideal that reconciles the black/white binary into a singular, undifferentiated perception of raceless people (though premised on an implicit white norm).

Legal scholar Kimberlé Crenshaw brought the concept of intersectionality to the fore with a pair of foundational, pathbreaking articles in 1989 and 1991.[42] Intersectionality recognizes the complexity of identity and subordination, arguing that institutions and practices of discrimination can operate along more than the basic binaries white/black, male/female, and so on. Crenshaw provides a concrete example of intersectionality in operation when she suggests that

> Black women can experience discrimination in ways that are both similar to and different from those experienced by white women and Black men. Black women sometimes experience discrimination in ways similar to white women's experiences; sometimes they share very similar experiences with Black men. Yet often they experience double-discrimination—the combined effects of practices which discriminate on the basis of race, and on the basis of sex. And sometimes, they experience discrimination as Black women—not the sum of race and sex discrimination, but as Black women.[43]

For Crenshaw, writing in the late 1980s, legal approaches to sex discrimination, although arrayed on a single axis, male versus female, were actually predicated on an implicit paradigm based on the experiences of white women, just as "the model of race discrimination tend[ed] to be based on the experiences of the most privileged Blacks."[44] The binary approach of discrimination law, in short, failed to account for the multiplicity of lived experiences of subordination. Yet it would be a mistake to see intersectionality as simply understanding individuals as aggregates of distinct, "pure" identities. As Carbado and Gulati note, "Fundamental to intersectionality theory is the notion that race and gender are interconnected; they do not exist as disaggregated identities."[45]

Such interconnections are very difficult (if not impossible) to capture through the methodology of ISC. By its very design, the IAT cannot register or measure intersectionality. The resulting combinatoric nightmare of devising and interpreting an IAT that can measure responses to various combinations of race *and* gender *and* age (e.g., young, black male versus old, white female, and so on) would likely be beyond the ability of any sane person to decipher.[46] Some social psychologists working within the field of ISC have acknowledged this shortcoming. Phillip Atiba Goff and Kimberly Barsamian Kahn in particular have argued that much ISC work on bias "has tended to discount the ways in which race and gender mutually construct each other" and has failed to recognize that "race and gender are interrelated and work together intersectionally." They provide a telling hypothetical in which a researcher "may expose participants to negative stereotypes about Blacks subliminally, and then ask questions about how they feel about Blacks 'in general.' In this case, neither the stereotypes nor 'Blacks in general' specify a gender. However, the stereotypes most often associated with Blacks (e.g. violent, aggressive, uneducated, athletic, and criminal) are more associated with men than women 'in general.' Therefore, even if a researcher is attempting to limit attention to racial stereotypes, people think of non-White stereotypes in gendered terms." Goff and Kahn also recognize that the combinatorics of "fully intersectional approaches to the study of race . . . can be difficult to handle logistically, require complex methodology, and at times be difficult to interpret theoretically."[47]

Beyond the IAT, the foundational theories of cognitive psychology and neuroscience upon which much of behavioral realism is based are similarly dualistic. Recall Daniel Kahneman's two-system model popularized in his highly influential book *Thinking, Fast and Slow*, wherein System 1 thinking operates automatically and quickly, with little or no effort and no sense of voluntary control, and System 2 thinking is more deliberative and reflective.[48] Much of the neuroscience that has explored implicit bias is similarly grounded in the idea of a strict separation between automatically reactive regions of the brain, such as the amygdala, and those regions exercising more deliberative executive functions, such as the DLPFC.[49]

Richard Thaler and Cass Sunstein have built directly on this work in developing their theory of "nudging,"[50] and Mahzarin Banaji and Anthony

Greenwald contrast the "product of our reflective or rational mind, on the one hand, and [the product of] our automatic or intuitive mind on the other."[51] Yet recent work in cognitive neuroscience is emphasizing a more dynamic and interactive model of brain functioning that breaks down the binary of fast/slow thinking and "suggest[s] that human informational processing is better characterized in terms of dynamical systems models rather than dual-process models."[52] Thus, in a recent paper Jay Van Bavel, Jenny Xiao, and Leor Hackel argue that although the dual-system model may be a useful heuristic, it does not accurately depict the actual functioning of the brain. They propose instead that "there is unlikely to be a clear dissociation between explicit and implicit representations in the brain. Rather, we argue that representations are constructed from the dynamic interaction of multiple brain systems, and feature the recursive interaction between bottom-up cues (e.g., skin color or hair length) and top-down cues (e.g., attention or motivations) that interact in cycles until the evaluative system settles on a representation of a target."[53]

Just as individuals should not be reduced to static binaries such as black/white, cognitive function is coming to be understood as more complex, situated, and dynamic than the simple dual-function model.

The problem in this area of investigation in behavioral realism is not, however, simply one of measurement or evaluation of brain function. It is also a question of how we interpret and make meaning of what the IAT and other tools of behavioral realism actually measure—in part by considering what they do *not* measure. In trying to reduce racism to something discrete and measureable in quantitative terms, behavioral realism actually leaves antiracist policies open to new sorts of attacks based on precisely the sorts of concerns for the "individual" articulated by Justice Powell in *Bakke*, by Justice Sandra Day O'Connor in *Grutter*,[54] and by Justice Roberts in *Parents Involved*[55]—that is, the criticism that such measurements do indeed reduce the complexity of individual identity to a single static bounded metric of race. In contrast, Chief Justice Earl Warren's opinion in *Brown* (1954) was not based on discrete measurements; it was based on what Post or Haney-López might characterize as a broad sociological interpretation of the meaning of segregation in context and its impact on the "hearts and minds" of the affected children.[56] Despite many commentators' post hoc references to the importance of Kenneth Clarke's famous doll studies, Warren's conclusion was not, indeed could not be, directly supported by any specific psychological measurements or tests.[57]

Intersectionality is not simply a negative critique of reductive or monolithic constructions of identity; it also affirmatively embraces identity. Like Appiah, for example, Crenshaw sees the potential positive power of foregrounding racial identity. "We can all recognize," she writes,

> the distinction between the claims "I am Black" and the claim "I am a person who happens to be Black." "I am Black" takes the socially imposed identity and empowers it as an anchor of subjectivity. "I am Black" becomes not simply a statement of resistance but also a positive discourse of self-identification, intimately linked to celebratory statements like the Black nationalist "Black is beautiful." "I am a person who happens to be Black," on the other hand, achieves self-identification by straining for a certain universality (in effect, "I am first a person") and for a concomitant dismissal of the imposed category ("Black") as contingent, circumstantial, nondeterminant. There is truth in both characterizations, of course, but they function quite differently depending on the political context. At this point in history, a strong case can be made that the most critical resistance strategy for disempowered groups is to occupy and defend a politics of social location rather than to vacate and destroy it.[58]

Crenshaw casts the entire project of intersectionality as attempting "to unveil the processes of subordination."[59] The trope of unveiling contrasts starkly with the procedural liberalism of behavioral realism, which seeks to place the observer behind a Rawlsian "veil of ignorance." Unveiling opens up not just race but also multiple forms of identity and subordination to explicit scrutiny and engagement. As Crenshaw might observe, there certainly is truth in many of the characterizations of behavioral realism, but I would posit that such characterizations also tend to "vacate and destroy" the politics of social location.

Crenshaw's goal of unveiling subordination also resonates with psychologists Valerie Purdie-Vaughns and Richard Eibach's idea of "intersectional invisibility," by which they mean "the general failure to fully recognize people with intersecting identities as members of their constituent groups."[60] Clearly building on Crenshaw's work, their central argument is that

> androcentrism—the tendency to define the standard person as male—
> ethnocentrism—the tendency to define the standard person as a member of
> the dominant ethnic group (i.e., White Americans in the U.S.)—and het-
> erocentrism—the tendency to define the standard person as heterosexual—
> may cause people who have intersecting identities to be perceived as
> non-prototypical members of their constituent identity groups. Because
> people with multiple subordinate identities (e.g., African-American
> woman) do not usually fit the prototypes of their respective subordinate
> groups (e.g., African-Americans, women), they will experience what we
> have termed "intersectional invisibility."[61]

According to this model, minority women or minority gay men or white lesbian women are examples of people with intersecting subordinate identities as "marginal members within marginal groups," a status that "relegates them to a position of acute social invisibility."[62] Similarly from within the discipline of psychology, Kerry Johnson, Jonathan Freeman, and Kristin Pauker have argued that "race and sex categories are psychologically and phenotypically confounded, affecting social categorizations and their efficiency," and thus have challenged the notion "that social categories are perceived independent of one another," "show[ing], instead, that race is gendered."[63] In many respects, this argument merely echoes or confirms what Crenshaw was saying two decades earlier, but it carries her insights from the law directly into the realm of social psychology—the home turf of the IAT and the science of implicit social cognition.

We can readily see how the binary structure of the IAT and related tools of behavioral realism play into this dynamic and threaten to render invisible those with such intersectional identities or at the very least to reduce them to one single aspect of an otherwise complex identity in a manner that constitutes an ongoing dignitary harm. Furthermore, the predominance of the IAT itself as a mode of constructing and understanding implicit bias reinforces in society at large the tendency to obscure or veil the perception of such intersectional identities both as a matter of understanding one's own implicit biases and of identifying and understanding the nature and dynamics of bias as it operates at broader societal and structural levels.

In contrast, Dorothy Roberts and Sujatha Jesudason argue in discussing "movement intersectionality" that "by acknowledging differences, not transcending them, activists can more effectively grapple with the 'matrix of domination' because an intersectional analysis ultimately reveals how structures of oppression are related and therefore our struggles are linked."[64] Seeing difference, rendering it visible, and embracing its positive value present a very different vision of social progress than, for example, yearning toward a supposedly original position where our biases are transcended and no longer register on an IAT. Once again, however, this is not to say that the IAT-related tools of behavioral realism do not have any place in this struggle but rather to caution against elevating those tools above the many tools in the complex tool kit of racial justice. Thus, for example, Roberts and Jesudason speak of the need for political organizations to "build[] trust by learning about each other's movements and concretely demonstrating solidarity for each other's issues."[65] Trust is not built by taking IATs or undergoing diversity training (though perhaps these practices might have a role to play in the process). It is built by engaging in dialogue and in acts of mutual recognition and support.

6

OBSCURING POWER

mplicit bias is primarily a function of cognition. Racism is a function of power. For historian George Fredrickson, racism "is not merely an attitude or set of beliefs; it also expresses itself in the practices, institutions, and structures that a sense of deep difference justifies or validates." At the heart of racism as a historically situated phenomenon is how it functions to "either directly sustain[] or propose[] to establish a racial order." Fredrickson's theory of racism has two components: difference and power. He argues that racism "originates from a mindset that regards 'them' as different from 'us' in ways that are permanent and unbridgeable. This sense of difference provides a rationale for using our power advantage to treat the ethnoracial Other in ways that we would regard as cruel or unjust if applied to members of our own group."[1] This sense of difference, however, is not automatic or innate. In this understanding of racism, much more than attitude, belief, or cognition, that is at stake. Fredrickson understands racism as an ideological need to rationalize the subjugation of a subordinate caste. In constructing a "them" that is somehow innately and unbridgeably different from "us," racism creates a common sense of difference and power. The common sense of racism in the American context is perpetuated not by ignorance or "mind bugs" but, as sociologist Ruha Benjamin notes, by "a particular way of knowing, however inconsistent and malleable, that makes the existence of racial phenomena real."[2]

To say that racism is about power and difference is, perhaps, to state the obvious. But considerations of power are curiously, one might say, strikingly absent from much of the behavioral realist approach to implicit bias. Behavioral realism constructs perceptions of difference largely as natural, even innate, in a manner that both elides the historical emergence of specific forms of racism and further obscures the power dynamics they construct and perpetuate. The behavioral realist approach thus risks becoming an exercise in what Barbara Fields and Karen Fields have characterized as "race-craft": a social practice that misconstrues racism for race.[3] Insofar as behavioral realism focuses on biological, cognitive processes, it further risks naturalizing the construction and perception of race in a manner that, as Benjamin puts it, "mystif[ies] the underlying power dynamics that produce group differences."[4]

Behavioral realism conflates racism and race first and foremost by reducing racism to a cognitive process of the perception of difference as manifest in differential responses on the IAT or other similar technical measures of implicit bias—particularly when combined with images of brain function produced by fMRI. As behavioral realism reduces racism to perceptions of race, it produces interventions that are geared toward the technical management of such perceptions with little or no attention to underlying questions of the distribution or functioning of power. For example, to address the very real and substantial problem of implicit bias in the court system, the NCSC's project on implicit bias and judicial education proposed the following seven specific interventions:

> *Strategy 1*: Raise awareness of implicit bias.
> *Strategy 2*: Seek to identify and consciously acknowledge real group and individual differences.
> *Strategy 3*: Routinely check thought processes and decisions for possible bias.
> *Strategy 4*: Identify distractions and sources of stress in the decision-making environment and remove or reduce them.
> *Strategy 5*: Identify sources of ambiguity in the decision-making context and establish more concrete standards before engaging in the decision-making process.
> *Strategy 6*: Institute feedback mechanisms.
> *Strategy 7*: Increase exposure to stigmatized group members and counter-stereotypes and reduce exposure to stereotypes.[5]

Thoughtfully sensitive to distinctions among individual versus structural aspects of implicit bias, each strategy suggests particular interventions at both the individual and institutional level. Yet the substance of the interventions remains peculiarly focused on the cognitive processing of perceptions of race with scant consideration given to underlying power dynamics affecting the outcome. For example, one might readily hypothesize that providing adequate funding for well-staffed public-defenders offices or doing away with peremptory challenges in juror selection might do more to affect the racial equity of court outcomes than many of these interventions.[6] Such considerations, however, involve allocations of money and power and so do not enter into the equation. In focusing on cognitive processing, these strategies obscure the deeper power dynamics of the very problem they are laudably trying to address.

More generally, a recent review of a broad range of proposed interventions to address implicit bias highlights the following interventions as being prominent "debiasing" methods:

- Counter-stereotypic training in which efforts focus on training individuals to develop new associations that contrast with the associations they already hold through visual or verbal cues.
- Another way to build new associations is to expose people to counter-stereotypic individuals. Much like debiasing agents, these counterstereotypic exemplars possess traits that contrast with the stereotypes typically associated with particular categories, such as male nurses, elderly athletes, or female scientists.
- Intergroup contact generally reduces intergroup prejudice.
- Education efforts aimed at raising awareness about implicit bias can help debias individuals.
- Having a sense of accountability, that is, "the implicit or explicit expectation that one may be called on to justify one's beliefs, feelings, and actions to others," can decrease the influence of bias.
- Taking the perspective of others has shown promise as a debiasing strategy, because considering contrasting viewpoints and recognizing multiple perspectives can reduce automatic biases.
- Engaging in deliberative processing can help counter implicit biases, particularly during situations in which decision-makers may face time constraints or a weighty cognitive load.[7]

The review later concludes: "Broadly speaking, this research affirms the debiasing effectiveness of exposure to counterstereotypical exemplars, using intentionality to reduce bias, and evaluative conditioning."[8] Much like the interventions in the judicial training program, these approaches to addressing implicit bias focus entirely on the process of cognition and are oriented largely around manipulating the cognitive environment within which a given individual perceives and processes difference. Many of the interventions involve subliminal nudges—manipulating the context within which distinct choices or evaluations are made.

Such behavioral realist approaches pay virtually no attention to the allocation and functioning of power. For example, they give no (or at most minimal) consideration to the underlying conditions that produce situations where particular individuals with specific cognitive biases occupy positions of authority through which the manifestation of those biases may come to have a significant impact on others who have less power. Everybody has biases. Stereotypes and classifications are part of how we make sense of the world. At one point, a child may call any four-legged animal in a field a "cow" but later come to differentiate between cows and horses based on characteristics adults deem typical to each. But racial classifications are not just like any other stereotype. They are freighted with history and the power of turning difference into dominance. Foregrounding the purely cognitive aspects of racial perception threatens to obscure this dynamic of history and power. Behavioral realism's tendency to construct racial classifications as simply one version of more general cognitive processes feeds into what Michael Omi and Howard Winant have characterized as the "false universalism" of neoliberal approaches to racial formations, "which can only serve to mask underlying racial conflicts."[9]

SUBMERGED ANTIRACISM

In her book *The Submerged State: How Invisible Government Policies Undermine American Democracy*, political scientist Suzanne Mettler develops a critique of recent government policies that obscure the workings of state power in a manner that serves conservative antigovernment discourses of privatization and free-market fundamentalism. For Mettler, the "submerged state" includes "a conglomeration of federal policies that function by providing incentives, subsidies, or payments to private organizations or households to encourage or reimburse them for conducting activities deemed to serve a public purpose." These policies operate "through indirect means such as tax breaks to households or payments to private actors who provide services"; they are "submerged" because they "obscure government's role from the view of the general public, including those who number among their beneficiaries."[10]

The policies of the submerged state include social benefits in the form of tax breaks for individuals and families (such as the home-mortgage deduction), the tax-free nature of benefits (such as health-care insurance) provided by employers, and federal subsidies to private enterprises to serve public-policy goals (such as student-loan guarantees).[11] The basic problem with such approaches to implementing major public policies is that they erode civic allegiance and mask the affirmative role the state plays in shaping everyday lives and promoting public goods. As Mettler puts it, "The policies of the submerged state obscure the role of the government and exaggerate that of the market, leaving citizens unaware of how power operates, unable to form meaningful opinions, and incapable, therefore, of voicing their views accordingly."[12]

More-visible government programs, such as those of the New Deal (in which the government directly employed individuals through such programs as the Civilian Conservation Corps and the Public Works Administration), readily attracted group loyalty and fostered a sense that the state had a positive role to play in shaping society. In contrast, government policies of the past several decades, under both Republican and Democratic administrations alike, have masked the workings of the state in providing goods and services in a manner "typically too hidden . . . to generate such affiliations."[13]

More recently, the submerged state has manifested preeminently as one of subliminal "nudges" informed by the work of behavioral economists and championed by, among others, Cass Sunstein, whom President Obama named in 2009 to head the White House Office of Information and Regulatory Affairs. Sunstein defines "nudges" as "interventions that steer people in particular directions but that also allow them to go their own way. A GPS nudges; a default rule nudges. A reminder is a nudge; so is a warning. . . . Some nudges work because they inform people; other nudges work because they make certain choices easier; still other nudges work because of the power of inertia and procrastination."[14]

Sunstein insists that nudges do not undermine human agency or choice. However, in elaborating on the power of developing "choice architectures" that "frame" decision making, he and coauthor Richard Thaler tellingly assert that "framing works because people tend to be somewhat mindless, passive decision makers."[15] Independent of whether this observation is empirically accurate, it reveals a conception of citizens as passive and malleable, in need of having certain choices "made easier" through largely invisible or submerged frameworks developed by experts that "nudge" them toward the decision that the experts deem preferable, although, of course, always leaving them a choice—even if they themselves are largely unaware of the role experts have played in directing them.

Mettler sees a paradigmatic example of such framing in President Obama's Making Work Pay tax cut, a central component of his economic stimulus program passed soon after he entered office. Based on the advice of behavioral economists, advisers in the Obama administration deliberately planned for the tax breaks to be hidden because doing so would nudge recipients toward spending the new infusion of funds. Such arrangements, however, not only affect how individuals spend money but also shape citizens' understandings and views of the political system.[16]

Behavioral economists tend to distrust the citizenry—perhaps because they see citizens as "somewhat mindless." As Mettler observes,

Behavioral economists are generally concerned about whether "choice architecture" prompts desirable social and economic outcomes. . . . While those goals are laudable, pursuing them does not necessarily foster democratic citizenship, for example, by enhancing citizens' ability to be aware of government actions, to form opinions about them, and to be able to take a stand on them. In fact, the pursuit of some policy goals—depending on how it is conducted and the design of the policies created—may inadvertently prove detrimental to citizens' knowledge and agency, as indicated by the example of the stimulus tax breaks.[17]

Submerged policies do not engage the civic imagination or produce civic commitments. Perhaps most perniciously of all, instead of fostering active citizenship, the submerged state "inculcates passivity and resentment." This is so, states Mettler, because "democracy depends, first of all, on citizens having the means and capacity to form meaningful opinions about acts of governance."[18]

The detrimental effect of submerged policies occurs not only with respect to social insurance programs but also with respect to programs to address racial injustice. Just as the submerged state obscures the structures of government policy, so the behavioral realist emphasis on implicit bias tends to obscure the structures of racism—both institutional and personal. By psychologizing racism as implicit bias, this emphasis removes racism from everyday consciousness. This removal obscures relations of power as well because when implicit bias is made everybody's problem, it ceases to be anyone's specific responsibility. Developing "choice architectures" to address implicit bias, whether through counterstereotyping screensavers or color-blind performance evaluations, constitutes a form of "submerged antiracism" that, although perhaps producing some laudable results in the short term, may also "inadvertently prove detrimental to citizens' knowledge and agency." Playing off the idea of aversive racism, one might characterize the submerged approach as "aversive liberalism"—an aversion to making an explicit and forthright case for progressive interventions in society, whether in the form of economic policy or antiracist measures.

Behavioral realism's approach to implicit bias is "submerged" in a dual sense: it submerges both racism and antiracism. First, in marginalizing explicit racism in American society, it directs us to focus on implicit bias, which, by definition, is submerged—it is beyond our conscious ability to recognize or control. Such invisible bias can be brought to light only through expert and technologically mediated interventions such as the IAT or, even more strikingly, fMRIs scans that produce vivid, color-coded depictions purporting to show racism at work in the brain. The IAT and fMRI thus submerge racism within the individual, making it invisible, unaccountable, and palatable.

Second, behavioral realism also submerges antiracist efforts—first, by subordinating citizen action to expert direction; second, by formulating much such direction as subliminal nudges; and third, by denying that these efforts are antiracist at all. We see this submersion in the shift in the rhetoric of affirmative action as it moved from a tool to address racial injustice in the 1960s to a means to enhance corporate bottom lines through "diversity." Thus, for example, Frank Dobbin notes that when "affirmative action came under attack in the early 1980s, human resources experts pointedly argued that diversity training and work-family programs were not affirmative action measures at all, but were there to increase productivity."[19] Mahzarin Banaji and Anthony Greenwald would decades later echo this move to obscure the presence or relevance of racism in their contention that "America is no longer racist,"[20] hence by implication that their interventions are not addressing "racism" per se, but only "implicit bias." As Michelle Alexander has noted, "Affirmative action, particularly when it is justified on grounds of diversity rather than equity (or remedy), masks the severity of racial inequality in America, leading to greatly exaggerated claims of racial progress and overly optimistic assessments of the future for African Americans."[21]

In both senses, behavioral realism creates a danger both of obscuring how dominant power structures perpetuate racial injustice and vitiating citizens' agency and hence power to actively and consciously engage in the hard work of antiracism. In addition, behavioral realism's tendency to marginalize the significance of historical racism (discussed at length in the preceding chapter) can also be understood as an attempt to "submerge" the past—to render it invisible and irrelevant to the present. Behavioral realism obscures the larger structural aspects of racism and similarly obscures the role of the citizenry in constructing policies to address these aspects wholesale rather than on the individual "nudge" level. Nudging individuals away from racism leaves structures intact. Just as the submerged state obscures the good that government does, submerged racism obscures both the harm that racism does and what good government still needs to do.

Eddie Glaude Jr., professor of religion and African American studies at Princeton University, identifies the historical roots of a similar move to obscure a direct engagement with race in the mid-1970s when the Democratic Party adopted a strategy to emphasize "a rising tide lifts all boats" approach to addressing racial inequality that would focus on class over racial issues as a means to deprive the Republican Party of race as a wedge issue. Glaude notes that this strategy assumed that, "inwardly, they [the Democrats] remained committed to racial justice; everyone was just *undercover*."[22] Glaude argues that this flight from explicitly confronting and addressing issues of racial inequality head on has fared poorly, leading to increasing disparities and injustices for blacks. Yet we see this strategy continue today in many of President Obama's class-based framings of issues such as health-care reform and access to college.

Behavioral realism layers this "undercover" approach with a veneer of science and expert authority. Thus, for example, Curtis Hardin and Banaji assert that although "it is nearly impossible" for individuals "to consciously correct for effects of implicit prejudice . . . research shows that changes in social organization predict corresponding changes in implicit prejudice which has promising implications for public policy."[23] Policies that effect "changes in social organization" can be understood largely in terms of Sunstein's nudges and choice architectures: where experts think they cannot expect individuals to address bias, they intervene through policies that change the individual without the individual's awareness.

Hardin and Banaji go on to assert that, "in addition to the real problems that malicious 'bad apples' pose for social policy, research demonstrates that prejudice also lives and thrives in the banal workings of normal, everyday human thought and activity. In fact, an over-emphasis on the bad apples may well be detrimental to considerations of policy because it assumes the problem of prejudice to be that of the few rather than that of the many."[24]

On the one hand, their recognition of continuing malicious prejudices and desire to address the more banal workings of implicit bias in everyday life certainly is important, but their caution to avoid overemphasis on the "bad apples" is highly problematic. Although appearing to broaden the concern to address racism, Hardin and Banaji actually narrow it, first by avoiding the term *racism* in favor of the more decontextualized term *prejudice* and, second, by rendering "malice" anomalous, thereby absolving the mass of citizenry for the continuing existence and effects of racism. Yes, Hardin and Banaji do call upon us all to recognize how we are implicated in continuing implicit prejudice, but if we have no malice and no ability to control our implicit prejudice, do we have any responsibility for our prejudice, and if not, where does the responsibility for the persistence of prejudice lie?

In the behavioral realist view, it lies with the experts. Our duty is to submit unknowingly to submerged nudges devised by experts or to consciously enroll in diversity-training programs or similar interventions devised for our benefit and guidance by these self-same experts or to do both. But the behavioral realists have it backward: an overemphasis on implicit bias may have detrimental implications not only for social policy but also for citizenship to the extent that it obscures the ongoing legacy and practices of explicit racism, in both personal and structural forms, that continue to inform and shape contemporary social, economic, and political relationships of power and meaning.

Behavioral realist debiasing techniques play a significant role in the sorts of diversity training offered to many police departments. Prominent among the numerous police-training programs that suggest particular interventions to address implicit bias is the FIP project led by Lorie Fridell of the University of South Florida, which has developed model curricula for police training with grants from the U.S. Department of Justice and its related COPS Program.[25] Similarly, the Center for Policing Equity at the University of California, Los Angeles, provides expert consultation and training on implicit bias to police departments across the country to help improve racial equity in policing. The center has conducted "hands-on, specialized training sessions for police departments who want evidence-based training" in implicit bias and has performed "climate surveys, focus group interviews, and simulations/experiments with the goal of providing concrete solutions for departmental progress" for police departments across the country.[26] Police departments' interest in such programs has been growing rapidly. As Fridell notes, "The demand for Fair and Impartial Policing started to increase in 2013, really on a geometric trajectory in 2014, and then with Ferguson, absolutely, we're getting a lot more requests."[27] And so in the summer of 2016, we had the U.S. Department of Justice announcing a major new initiative for "department-wide implicit bias training for personnel." The program is intended to build on the work done by the COPS and FIP programs to train some twenty-eight thousand department employees "to recognize and address their own implicit bias, which are the unconscious or subtle associations that individuals make between groups of people and stereotypes about those groups."[28]

The FIP website is rife with articles and references on the psychology of implicit bias. Its six-hour training module for recruits and patrol officers is well representative of the program's general approach. The module works to help them "understand that even well-intentioned people have biases; Understand how implicit biases impact on what we *perceive/see* and can (unless prevented) impact on what we *do*; Understand that fair & impartial policing leads to *effective policing*; and, Use tools that help [them] (1) recognize [their] conscious and implicit biases, and (2) implement "controlled" (unbiased) behavioral responses."[29]

The Center for Police Equity, which characterizes itself as a "research and action think tank," is a bit broader in approach and does more basic research and gathering of data than does FIP. Nonetheless, its work, like FIP's, is grounded in applying insights from the cognitive psychology of implicit bias to policing practices, and it, too, provides training on implicit bias to police personnel.[30] Thus, for example, one of its projects "tested officers for psychological profiles, and then linked those profiles to outcomes in patrol (e.g., efficient stops, commendations, racial bias, complaints, etc.)"[31] The center is also participating (along with experts from John Jay College of Criminal Justice and Yale Law School) in the National Initiative for Building Community Trust and Justice, announced by Attorney General Eric Holder in the aftermath of the shooting of Michael Brown in Ferguson, Missouri, in 2014. This three-year grant of $4.75 million aims to take a "holistic approach . . . [to] simultaneously address[ing] the tenets of procedural justice, reducing implicit bias and facilitating racial reconciliation."[32]

Similarly, in April 2015, California attorney general (now U.S. senator) Kamala D. Harris announced that her office was developing the nation's first certified implicit bias training, with the support of law enforcement officials and Stanford professor of psychology Jennifer Eberhardt. At the heart of the initiative is an eight-hour course that includes taking the IAT and talking about the findings. It also includes scenarios and role playing to help officers build new associations. The training is followed up with measurement tools that gauge whether it has been effective.[33]

Again, this work is laudable on its own terms, but much of the training is not unlike the sort of diversity-management exercises that Frank Dobbin found to be so woefully ineffective at actually promoting diversity in corporate hiring and promotion practices. Moreover, such diversity-training programs also run the serious risk of backlash—that is, resentment that can lead to increased discrimination and confirmation of stereotypes.[34] As one police officer remarked at the prospect of diversity training, "Role-play away, I'll jump through the hoops if that's what you want me to do. But, you know, I would much rather be out there on the street trying to police and trying to protect the community that I work for."[35] We see a troubling, if anecdotal, indication of such limitations in the infamous case from the summer of 2015 in which a video captured Officer Eric Casebolt brutally subduing a black teenage girl at a Texas pool party. News reports of the incident included the information that he had taken eight hours of diversity training at a local community college and had also taken courses on racial profiling and the use of force.[36]

The breadth and depth of *explicitly* biased attitudes among police has been brought into high relief by a series of U.S. Department of Justice investigations of use of force by particular police departments. Most recently, a report of the Justice Department's investigation of the Chicago Police Department (CPD), released on January 12, 2017, found that the CPD "engages in a pattern or practice of force in violation of the Constitution" that is "largely attributable to systemic deficiencies within CPD and the City," including a failure "to hold officers accountable when they use force contrary to CPD policy or otherwise commit misconduct."[37] That is, there was an absence of the firm exercise of *power* to suppress such practices. As for the explicit nature of the bias, consider the following description in the report:

> Our investigation found that this pattern or practice of misconduct and systemic deficiencies has indeed resulted in routinely abusive behavior within CPD, especially toward black and Latino residents of Chicago's most challenged neighborhoods. Black youth told us that they are routinely called "nigger," "animal," or "pieces of shit" by CPD officers. A 19-year-old black male reported that CPD officers called him a "monkey." Such statements were confirmed by CPD officers. One officer we interviewed told us that he personally has heard co-workers and supervisors refer to black individuals as monkeys, animals, savages, and "pieces of shit."[38]

It bears emphasizing that these findings are framed as part of a "pattern or practice." They are not isolated outliers; they are not the abnormal behaviors by the supposedly overt bigots, which hold little interest for some of the IAT researchers. They are the norm. Yet even here the report itself never uses the word *racism*. Rather, it refers only to "bias," and notable among its recommendations is that police board investigators receive "training on implicit bias."[39]

The peculiar lethality of the police force in America, particularly as directed toward racial minorities, is therefore not simply a function of psychological "mind bugs." Such cognitive schemas are presumed to be universal, yet, as Rutgers professor of sociology Paul Hirschfield notes, "fatal police shootings in Europe suggest that American police in 2014 were 18 times more lethal than Danish police and 100 times more lethal than Finnish police, plus they killed significantly more frequently than police in France, Sweden and other European countries."[40] Among the key *structural* differences between European and American policing practices is the fact that in 1989 the U.S. Supreme Court deemed it constitutionally permissible for police to use deadly force when they "reasonably" perceive imminent and grave harm.[41] As Hirschfield observes, "State laws regulating deadly force—in the 38 states where they exist—are almost always as permissive as Supreme Court precedent allows, or more so." Hirschfield contrasts this American standard with the standard in Europe, where most countries "conform to the European Convention on Human Rights, which impels its 47 signatories to permit only deadly force that is 'absolutely necessary' to achieve a lawful purpose."[42]

Killings excused under America's reasonable-belief standards often violate Europe's absolute-necessity standards. Indeed, the concept of "reasonableness" has been at the heart of many of the police killings protested by the Black Lives Matter movement. In the shootings of Michael Brown, Tamir Rice, and others, the key question for investigating authorities was always whether the officers had a "reasonable" fear of imminent bodily harm. The question of whether the use of deadly force was necessary, let alone "absolutely necessary," rarely comes up. The latter standards, however, can be used to hold people accountable, regardless of the individuals' implicit or explicit biases. They are a means to impose and enforce norms of proper conduct— that is, they involve the explicit, open assertion of power.

In contrast to Black Lives Matter, which has manifested as a social movement that openly makes demands on power, behavioral realist approaches to implicit bias do not galvanize; they are not capable of rallying people to support a cause. Rather, experts and technocrats frame and implement what approaches are to be taken in dealing with racism. Moreover, behavioral realist interventions are distinctly calibrated to address individuals *as* individuals—not as citizens or members of a political community. The only civic allegiance or consciousness they demand is that which is sufficient to get someone to sit down in front of a computer to take an IAT or perhaps to enroll in a diversity-training class. Such approaches do not make explicit, overt cases against racism. Rather, they proceed subliminally through submerged nudges and other indirect management techniques that may produce less-biased individual actions yet fail utterly to help people understand and appreciate the historical and political significance of those actions—that is, they fail to enhance people's knowledge and agency as citizens who share a common concern to address racial injustice.

Ironically, tropes of invisibility also play a central role in many critiques of structural racism that might otherwise be seen as taking a very different approach from behavioral realism to construct commonsense understandings of the nature and place of racism in contemporary American society. For example, Eduardo Bonilla-Silva, in his influential book *Racism Without Racists: Color-Blind Racism and the Persistence of Inequality in America*, takes a more structural approach that, instead of looking at attitudes such as "how many hate or love blacks and other minorities," focuses on "examining how many whites subscribe to an ideology that ultimately helps preserve racial inequality."[43] Yet in his analysis he emphasizes that

> the mechanisms to keep blacks in their "place" are rendered invisible in three ways. First, because the enforcement of the racial order from the 1960s onward has been institutionalized, individual whites can express a detachment from the *racialized* way in which social control agencies operate in America. Second, because these agencies are *legally* charged with defending *order* in society, their actions are deemed neutral and necessary. Finally, the white-dominated media depicts incidents that seem to indicate that racial bias is endemic to the criminal justice system as isolated.[44]

This sort of invisibility is not produced through innate cognitive schema beyond conscious control. These mechanisms are artifacts of history and politics, requiring similarly socially situated popular interventions to render them visible and address them. In contrast, implicit bias needs technically constructed IATs and fMRIs administered and interpreted by experts to be made manifest.

In sharing tropes of invisibility, however, both Bonilla-Silva's more structural approach and behavioral realism's cognitive approach perhaps confuse what is invisible with what we as a society (or what dominant members of our society) are willfully or intentionally blind to. In this regard, we might extend to large segments of American society Ian Haney-López's argument that the current Supreme Court "seems intentionally blind to the persistence of racial discrimination against non-Whites. It is this resistance that connects the current assaults on antidiscrimination statutes to the evisceration of affirmative action. It also links both of these to a larger history of reversals in equality law spanning four decades."[45] Such blindness is not a function of the invisibility of racism (whether structural or cognitive) but of the construction of a broader understanding of the common sense of what racism is (or is not) in contemporary America—a common sense that fosters a sort of perceptual inertia that allows those with racial privilege simply to fail to see the racial injustice all around them.

In this regard, we may add a third possibility to interpreting the meaning of the IAT. Advocates of the IAT, such as Greenwald and Banaji, argue that pervasive implicit bias manifests in myriad aversive behaviors. Critics of the IAT, such as Philip Tetlock and Gregory Mitchell, contend that if the IAT results mean anything at all, they may merely reflect awareness of societal stereotypes rather than of actual prejudice. I would suggest the following alternative: the results might also (and not in a mutually exclusive manner) reveal not implicit or unconscious bias but *suppressed* or perhaps *repressed* bias—that is, bias to which we have willfully but perhaps not "consciously" turned a blind eye. We can consider this bias something that we have chosen not to see—much as Haney-López speaks of the intentional blindness of the Supreme Court in areas of equal-protection doctrine. Among society at large, however, the intentional blindness has become a tool or method of plausible deniability that allows those living with race privilege to live normal, everyday lives in the face of ongoing and pervasive racial injustice.

We can see how conservative dog-whistle politics have aided and abetted such repression in a telling anecdote from John Erlichman, who played a prominent role in President Richard Nixon's White House and in the racially coded formulation of the president's war on drugs. As Erlichman acknowledged, Nixon's focus on "law and order" in his campaigns allowed him to make policy statements in such a way that a voter could "avoid admitting to himself that he was attracted by a racist appeal."[46] Again, nobody likes to think of himself or herself as racist, but it is quite possible to act on underlying racist sentiments—so long as the person can fool himself or herself into thinking that the action he or she takes is really about "law and order" or "quality education." As Carol Anderson observes, the effectiveness of Nixon's Southern Strategy and law-and-order campaign was grounded in a maneuver to "redefine racism itself." She notes that, not unlike the social psychologists and neuroscientists who have expressed little interest in studying overt racists, conservative backlash against the 1960s civil rights movement transformed "unflattering portrayals of KKK rallies and jackbooted sheriffs . . . into the sole definition of racism." This focus on extreme manifestations of racism was "first and foremost . . . conscience soothing."[47] It allowed whites to distance themselves from such overt racism even while embracing the coded appeals embedded in policies such as the war on drugs.[48]

The condition of blindness or repression is, perhaps, cognate to that described by Nadine Gordimer in her novel of South African apartheid, *Burger's Daughter*, where the protagonist, discussing the basis of her radical father's difference from those who accepted the regime, observes, "Even animals have the instinct to turn from suffering. The sense to run away. Perhaps it was an illness not to be able to live one's life the way they did . . . with justice defined in terms of respect for property, innocence defended in their children's privileges, love in their procreation, and care only for each other. A sickness not to be able to ignore that condition of a healthy, ordinary life: other people's suffering."[49]

Perhaps this is to say that the intentional blindness of the Roberts Court (its readiness to turn from other people's suffering—from racial injustice) needs to be understood as the norm for sustaining institutions of racial power in America. Moreover, those endowed with the historical privileges of whiteness have a deep incentive not only to turn from other people's suffering but also (and perhaps even more powerfully) to turn from their own implication in that suffering, from the source of their privilege and those aspects of their selves that continue to harbor racist sentiments. This turning is not implicit bias; it is a form of being at war with oneself. In denying one's racism, one turns not only from other people's suffering but from the possibility of having to suffer oneself by confronting such internal tensions.

The sociologist David Wellman has noted, "There is much to suggest that racist beliefs are normal, routine, and acceptable in America, that racist practice is culturally sanctioned, as well as economically and politically profitable."[50] There have been moments of respite, hiatuses from the norm of intentional blindness (as in Reconstruction and the Second Reconstruction), but they seem always to be followed be reversions to the norm. The norm of turning from racial injustice, however, is not static; rather, as Reva Siegel might say, it has adapted through a process of "persistence and transformation."[51] In the late nineteenth century, it involved declaring that we had abolished slavery even while simultaneously embracing Jim Crow. In the mid–twentieth century, it involved declaring we had abolished Jim Crow even while simultaneously embracing such racially conditioned programs as the GI Bill, federal home-mortgage assistance, and, later, the war on drugs. In the late twentieth and early twenty-first century, it has involved celebrating the election of Barack Obama even while simultaneously accepting the demise of affirmative action and the dismantling of the Voting Rights Act of 1965.

None of these stances necessarily involves "unconscious bias"—they simply were how hegemonic discourses of race relations made sense of the world in each era. Each norm had its own peculiar form of blindness that came fully to light only in subsequent generations. But, in any event, behavioral realism tells us we are not responsible for this norm—for our inability to see our own biases or how they affect other people. As behavioral realism obscures relations of power, it erodes any concomitant sense of civic responsibility for addressing them. And so it becomes easy to ignore other people's suffering—because behavioral realism tells each of us to focus on ourselves and our own perceptions above all.

PRIVATIZING ANTIRACISM

Charles Lawrence III expresses a deep concern over a distinct but related type of repression wherein the Supreme Court's "use of legal formalism to repress our consciousness of racism has converged with psychologists' efforts to explain the origins of unconscious bias" as a function primarily of individual cognition. This convergence, he fears, "has served to undermine . . . the chief purpose" of his groundbreaking article "The Ego, the Id, and Equal Protection" (1987)—namely, "to advance the understanding of racism as a societal disease and to argue that the Constitution commands our collective responsibility for its cure."[52] More specifically, Lawrence argues that although behavioral realism's focus on the mechanisms of cognitive categorization has taught us much about how implicit bias works, it may have also undermined my project by turning our attention away from the unique place that the ideology of white supremacy holds in our conscious and unconscious beliefs. I find this outcome unfortunate, if unintended, as the ubiquity and invidiousness of racism was the central lesson of my article. I further express my fear that cognitive psychology's focus on the workings of the individual mind may cause us to think of racism as a private concern, as if our private implicit biases do not implicate collective responsibility for racial subordination and the continued vitality of the ideology and material structures of white supremacy. In its most extreme manifestation, this view of implicit bias, as evidence only of private, individual beliefs, is expressed as a right to be racist.[53]

Behavioral realism's focus on individual cognition not only marginalizes the significance of history and structure in producing racial inequity in American society but also tends to locate responses to racism primarily in the private sphere.

Where collective responsibility is obscured, collective action becomes difficult, even irrelevant. Although a causal relation with the rise of behavioral realism may be difficult to establish, the move toward privatization is reflected in changing public understandings of the nature of racism and appropriate responses to it. The focus on implicit bias as an individual problem also attenuates ties of common experience and feeds a rising sense of alienation and a decline of cross-racial empathy. Thus, for example, a recent analysis of social survey data by Lawrence Bobo and his colleagues found "the sort of socioemotional bond essential to a sense of basic common humanity and worth is lacking for a large number of white Americans regarding their fellow black citizens." They also found that, consonant with this lack of a "socioemotional bond," support among white Americans "for a strong, active government role in ameliorating racial inequality and segregation" has become very limited, in contrast to the support evinced in the 1970s.[54]

We now instead have the rise of a multi-billion-dollar diversity-management and training industry that dissociates diversity from civil rights and casts antiracism as a tool to increase productivity and improve a business's bottom line.[55] One review of diversity-compliance efforts at the Sedexo corporation evaluated their success in terms of "return on investment," which it calculated at a rate of nineteen dollars for every dollar spent.[56] As Banaji, Max Bazerman, and Dolly Chugh put it in an article for the *Harvard Business Review*, implicit bias in a corporation is "likely to be costly" and "erodes the bottom line."[57] In this regard, it is perhaps no coincidence that diversity training came to the fore in the 1980s, soon to be followed by the rise of the IAT and behavioral realism in the 1990s. This was a period of triumphant neoliberalism when privatization reached into many areas of public policy and the market became the measure of all things. During this period, affirmative action, which had once been the province of direct and open government action, was truncated by the courts and largely taken up as a private matter by corporate compliance officers.[58]

In contrast to casting antiracism as a public and political responsibility, behavioral realism, being deeply informed by behavioral economics, can be understood largely as a theory of directing individual behavior in the market, with the market defined largely in terms of the allocation of implicit bias—and in terms of how implicit bias affects economic value. As sociologist Kimberly Krawiec observes concerning the rise of diversity-management initiatives and similar corporate compliance structures, "The interest groups most conspicuously underrepresented during this process are those that may represent the public interest."[59] We see privatization at work in even the court system, where, as Dobbin notes, "human resource experts [have] devised guidelines for corporations, and then the court [has] vetted them. It [is] corporations that guide[] the judiciary, not the other way around."[60] Insofar as behavioral realist interventions are defined, constructed, implemented, and evaluated by experts working for corporate enterprises, we see the business of antiracism in effect being removed from the public sphere and *outsourced* to private technocrats. In this regard, Michelle Alexander's criticism of diversity-driven affirmative action programs as "the epitome of racial justice purchased on the cheap"[61] might be expanded to include the array of behavioral realist interventions that address implicit bias without disrupting any structures of power or imposing any standards of accountability.

The privatization of antiracism also contributes to obscuring power by giving the appearance of serving the ends of racial equity while in fact serving the economic interests of corporate capital. Again, we see this problem in the diversity-management industry, which legal scholar Nancy Leong has characterized as a form of "racial capitalism," or "the process of deriving social and economic value from the racial identity of another person." Leong notes in particular how the concept of "diversity" as propounded by Justice Lewis Powell in the *Bakke* case has been central to the rise of racial capitalism in a diversity-training industry that "degrades nonwhiteness by commodifying it and that relegates nonwhite individuals to the status of 'trophies' or 'passive emblems.'" Leong goes on to argue that "the diversity rationale values nonwhiteness in terms of its worth to white people . . . [and] confers on white people and predominantly white institutions the *power* to determine the value of nonwhiteness. Because nonwhiteness is valued in terms of what it adds to white people's experiences or endeavors, white people determine what nonwhiteness is worth."[62]

Like the neoliberal paradigm of seeing privatization as the key to social and economic advancement, the ideal of privatized antiracism relies largely on an illusion of progress cloaked by a thin proceduralism. As Dobbin notes with respect to the diversity-management industry, "Employers and regulators are still choosing strategies based on spin, rather than evidence."[63] This emphasis on spin has real implications for the legal status of affirmative action programs and related diversity programs. Cheryl Kaiser and her colleagues note, for example, that the mere presence of diversity programs in corporate structures functions as a "signal" to judges and other relevant policy makers "that the organization's treatment of underrepresented groups is *procedurally fair*," but they argue that this image of fairness is largely an illusion when it comes to evaluating substantive outcomes and in fact "causes majority group members to become less sensitive to recognizing discrimination against minorities and leads them to react more negatively toward minority group members who claim discrimination."[64]

Soohan Kim, Alexandra Kalev, and Frank Dobbin further argue that the broad array of standardized procedures elaborated throughout industry to promote diversity has been similarly ineffective at actually increasing diversity and that "the common pattern is that formal bureaucratic procedures may reproduce inequality rather than eradicating it by cloaking unequal treatment of women and minorities in apparently neutral, universal, and rational procedures and practices."[65] Here we see that focusing on procedure over substance can actually make matters worse, yet the thin proceduralism of behavioral realist–informed diversity programs resonates with broader neoliberal rhetoric of guaranteeing equal opportunity—focusing on procedures over outcomes in a manner that obscures power while providing the illusion of progress.

The privatization of antiracism through diversity management and similar behavioral approaches also resonates with an individualistic consumer-based model of the self and citizen. Behavioral realist projects for addressing implicit bias revolve largely around a sort of self-fashioning that calls to mind writings on "biological citizenship" by sociologists Nikolas Rose and Carlos Novas. These researchers focus largely on developments in the field of biotechnology to assert that new solidaristic ties formed through biological commonalities (such as shared genetic conditions) are allowing groups to make certain types of ethical demands—on themselves, on communities, and on the state. They foreground the consumerist attributes of biological citizenship, presenting the human body as an object to be targeted by enhancement technologies in a global market that exists separate from nation-states. As they put it, "This is the citizenship of brand culture, where trust in brands appears capable of supplanting trust in neutral scientific expertise."[66]

Rose and Novas note that biological citizenship also makes demands on a subject "to inform him or herself not only about current illness, but also about susceptibilities and predispositions . . .[and] to take appropriate steps" to minimize the risk of illness and maximize health. As consumers, biological citizens have duties that primarily involve their own self-fashioning rather than their participation in a common enterprise for the greater good.[67] In *Neuro: The New Brain Sciences and the Management of the Mind*, Rose and coauthor Joelle Abi-Rached extend their analysis into the field of neuroscience to argue that given the plasticity of the brain, we now have "an obligation to take care of our brain"—that is, to make choices and take actions with an eye to "nurture and optimize" our brains.[68]

On the one hand, all this sounds reasonable: given scientific advances, the average person is increasingly presented with an array of consumeristic choices in the marketplace that allow her to maximize her cognitive potential. On the other hand, as with Rose's earlier discussion of biological citizenship, this emphasis on the individual and the market locates responsibility for addressing issues such as implicit bias firmly in the private sphere with little or no role for government intervention. Some critics have expressed concerns that Rose's model, with its apparent celebration of citizenship as a function of consumption, is a dangerous departure from more traditional conceptions of social and political citizenship.[69] An overenthusiastic embrace of Foucauldian ideas of "care of the self" here may morph into an abdication of public responsibility for addressing racism.[70]

Like Rose and Novas's "citizenship of brand culture," many behavioral realist interventions adopt an essentially privatized, consumerist model of addressing implicit bias. Consider Linda Krieger, who in her influential article "The Content of Our Categories: A Cognitive Bias Approach to Discrimination and Equal Employment Opportunity" suggests that "the nondiscrimination principle, currently interpreted as a proscriptive duty 'not to discriminate,' must evolve to encompass a prescriptive duty of care to identify and control for category-based judgment errors and other forms of cognitive bias in intergroup settings."[71] Krieger is careful to emphasize that this new duty of care must be grounded in further empirical and theoretical work—largely in the area of cognitive or social psychology.[72] The duty of care she speaks of here is in many respects a legal cognate to the sort of neuronal and genetic care of the self that Rose and Novas advocate, for, after all, what does a duty to "identify and control for . . . cognitive bias" involve but a policing of one's own private cognition?

Victoria Pitts-Taylor situates the idea of brain plasticity, so central to Rose's analysis, "in a context of biomedical neoliberalism, where the engineering and modification of biological life is positioned as essential to selfhood and citizenship." Pitts-Taylor goes on to note that "deployments of plasticity pressure subjects to see themselves not only in biomedical but also in specifically neuronal terms." The neoliberal emphasis on plasticity in turn

> replaces an ethic of state care with an emphasis on individual responsibility and market fundamentalism. In relation to health, neoliberal societies have seen the vast privatization of health care and the escalation of commercial investment in the body and biology. Market-based health care policies construct populations of individuals who are encouraged to ensure their own health and promote their own personal wellness and success in the face of economic insecurity and globalization; they simultaneously render patient populations consumers. Health maintenance becomes a responsibility or a

duty rather than a right, and bodies and selves are targeted for intense personal care and enhancement.[73]

Behavioral realism similarly draws upon findings in cognitive psychology and neuroscience to emphasize the plasticity of cognition and implicit bias as essential preconditions to implementing market-based interventions to nudge individuals toward better care of their neuronal selves.

Just as Pitts-Taylor sees individuals pressured to recognize a duty to respond as consumers to targeted personal care and enhancement programs, behavioral realists see interventions, whether by diversity-management firms, the NCSC, the U.S. Department of Justice, or the American Bar Association, as invoking concepts of duty and responsibility to pressure individuals to consume these particular products and programs. In all of this, then, antiracism is being recast as a largely private, consumer-driven endeavor. In this regard, we may view these various diversity-training initiatives as a form of corporate self-care, not only inoculating businesses against lawsuits or promoting more self-awareness among legal practitioners but also comporting with the new type of duty to address our cognitive mind bugs, as Linda Krieger urged in 1995. Notably, however, this duty is not enforced by legal mandate or direct government policy. Rather, it is crafted as a function of private choice in the marketplace.

7

RECREATIONAL ANTIRACISM AND THE POWER OF POSITIVE NUDGING

The interventions proposed by behavioral realists may also be giving rise to what I characterize as "recreational antiracism." It is a natural extension of the privatization of antiracism. Its preeminent form is perhaps the IAT itself, which millions of people have taken. As one article in the journal *Monitor on Psychology* in 2008 noted, "The Implicit Association Test (IAT) is one of those rare research tools that has transcended the lab to catch the attention of not just the social psychologists, who use it in increasing numbers, but also a large swath of the general public. In fact, the IAT has been written about in newspapers, featured on radio and television and garnered more than 5 million visits to its official Web site (https://implicit .harvard.edu) by people who want to take the test."[1]

Anecdotally, it is clear that many people taking the IAT do so on a whim or perhaps as part of a particular course they are taking (it is very popular on college campuses as well as in diversity-training programs). As the National Alliance for Partnership and Equity puts it, "Many participants find it fun or are curious as to the test results."[2] The test is literally a form of video game that takes the participant about five to ten minutes to complete. Ten minutes in front of a video screen, and you have taken the first step to addressing your own implicit biases—an easy, pain-free, technologically mediated, individualized means to feel connected to the enterprise of addressing racism.

This pain-free approach fits in with the general discomfort expressed by behavioral realists such as Mahzarin Banaji and Anthony Greenwald in calling Americans racist—they don't want to make people feel uncomfortable about their attitudes. They want the process of self-discovery to be nonthreatening, inviting, and relatively painless. We see this approach in the very title of their book *Blind Spot: Hidden Biases of Good People*, which tells readers that they do not need to feel bad about having hidden biases because they are still "good people." The title is also universalizing—we all are "good" people, and we all have these biases. Banaji and Greenwald move further toward make their findings palatable and nonthreatening by emphasizing that they believe that the IAT and related measures of implicit bias "are not the types of negativity or hostility that are generally taken to be characteristic of 'prejudice.' . . . This is why we answer 'no' to the question 'Does automatic White preference mean "prejudice"?'" With the IAT, they were working toward developing a technique that could provide a "kind of aha moment," where there was a "palpable recognition of automatic feelings that go counter to reflective ones."[3] This soft sell allows one to feel comfortable with one's biases. Once readers or test takers experience this "aha" moment, all they have to do is be willing to work on addressing their blind spots.

Moving beyond the IAT, one recent study conducted at Dartmouth used something called "embedded game design" to demonstrate how video games can alter players' implicit biases—literally turning antiracism into a game. The researchers used two party card games meant to challenge gender stereotypes and implicit bias in science, technology, engineering, and math fields. Notably, the study employed a technique researchers called "obfuscating," which involves "using game genres or framing devices that direct players' attention or expectations away from the game's true aims."[4] This approach follows up on an observation made by Nilanjana Dasgupta and Anthony Greenwald in 2001 that "effortful processes may not be the only way to moderate implicit prejudices."[5] The term *effortful* here is indicative of the idea that it might be possible to address bias literally without demanding effort from the subject, as one might, for example, with a game (or with a counterstereotypical image as a screensaver). Although promising when considered in isolation, such games, when viewed in a larger context, not only are a clear example of the problematic idea that racism can be addressed painlessly through recreational pursuits but also further exemplify the submerged approach to antiracism that obscures relations of power and accountability.

Of course, there is nothing inherently wrong with fostering a greater degree of self-knowledge through something that is fun. But the great degree to which this approach provides a template for further types of antibias interventions opens the door to an entire ecosystem of technologically mediated approaches to addressing racism that reduce fighting racism to a recreational pastime. Jerry Kang and Banaji exemplify well this recreational framing in their list of remedies to prevent the influence of implicit bias, where under the heading "Better Debiasing" they suggest, "If images we see and imagine can decrease our implicit bias, an interesting range of possibilities become available for private, individual, voluntary, 'do it yourself' attitude makeovers. How do you decorate your room? What is on your Screensaver? What is the office's decor? We do not yet have definitive evidence that provides an uncontroversial list of best practices. But we do want to highlight the increasing evidence."[6]

This passage reads a bit like a feature in the style section of a newspaper or a Buzzfeed listicle—"DIY Antiracism: 10 Ways You Can Fight Implicit Bias from the Comfort of Your Own Home!" The idea of addressing racism as something akin to getting a personal "makeover" is both facile and insulting. It reduces historical struggles for justice to the equivalent of a fashion choice. But it is also appealing because it is familiar, easy, and nonthreatening. As Kang and Banaji make clear, they are looking for "uncontroversial" best practices.

We see this appeal to easiness also in the NCSC's recommendations for "addressing implicit bias in the courts." The first strategy is "raise awareness of implicit bias," wherein "simply knowing about implicit bias and its potentially harmful effects on judgment and behavior may prompt individuals to pursue corrective action."[7] The phrase "simply knowing" pretty much says it all. The first step toward addressing implicit bias is "simple" and easy to take—all it involves is becoming aware of implicit bias. Subsequent strategies similarly focus on subjects' understandings and attitudes, including such recommendations as "seek to identify and consciously acknowledge real group and individual differences"; "routinely check thought processes and decisions for possible bias"; "identify distractions and sources of stress in the decision-making environment and remove or reduce them"; and "increase exposure to stigmatized group members and counterstereotypes and reduce exposure to stereotypes."[8] Many of these strategies involve trying to manipulate time and space to provide a more conducive "choice architecture" within which court judges may act to improve their attitudes and decision-making processes. Like self-help gurus selling positive psychology, the authors of the NCSC recommendations aim to make the judges the best possible versions of themselves.

The only substantive demands made on the subjects is that they pay attention to what the gurus have to tell them and engage in the self-work the gurus direct. What these strategies very conspicuously do not challenge, manipulate, or even address are the substantive structures and relations of power within which such attitudes are formed and decisions made. Thus, for example, there is no consideration of declining access to adequate legal aid or how the war on drugs has produced the overcrowded dockets that create the sort of time constraints that the recommendations identify as a problem. There is, in short, little or no consideration of the needs or status of the people who are subject to the power exercised over them by the court system. We instead get yet another iteration of "screensaver justice," where judges are encouraged to have their computer screensavers display positive, counterstereotypical images of minorities.

Such strategies give remarkably little consideration to imparting to the subjects a sense of the consequences of their biases—in other words, a sense of the practical effect and historical weight of such stereotypes or "mind bugs" on the lived experience of real human beings. But doing so might make the subjects feel bad, and we are supposed to be positive. We see such concern for the *subjects'* feelings most clearly evidenced in the framing of the evaluation forms handed out to participants in the NCSC pilot programs in California, Minnesota, and North Dakota. The primary outcome measures in these programs were "whether participants were satisfied with the program (e.g., how did they react to a program on this topic) and whether their knowledge of implicit bias increased pre- and postprogram." The focus was on how the participants *felt* about the program—whether they "express[ed] satisfaction with the training." And the responses were indeed positive: 93 percent of the California participants expressed satisfaction with the program, and 81 percent and 84 percent of the Minnesota and North Dakota participants, respectively, were similarly satisfied.[9] Of course, the California program primarily involved having participants simply watch a video on their desk-top computers. But the knowledge outcomes in all three pilot programs were equivocal at best, with questionnaires for North Dakota actually indicating a *decrease* in knowledge in some areas after the program.[10]

But apparently that was OK because all the participants were satisfied with the experience.

Behavioral realism's pronounced optimism and emphasis on self-fashioning calls to mind Barbara Ehrenreich's critique of America's love affair with the "power of positive thinking" in her book *Bright-Sided: How the Relentless Promotion of Positive Thinking Has Undermined America*. Ehrenreich characterizes "positive thinking" as a distinctively American ideology that involves two features: first, a powerful optimism, which she describes as a "cognitive stance, a conscious expectation, which presumably anyone can develop through practice," and second, "the practice, or discipline of trying to think in a positive way." Echoing Nikolas Rose and Carlos Novas on biological citizenship, she notes that the flip side of such positivity is "a harsh insistence on personal responsibility" for cultivating one's own individual practices of positive thinking.[11]

The practice of "bright-siding" also includes online tests like the IAT. Ehrenreich recounts taking the "Authentic Happiness Inventory" developed by psychologist Martin Seligman of the University of Pennsylvania and notes how such approaches "attend[] almost solely to the changes a person can make internally by adjusting his or her own outlook." Ehrenreich sees a close tie between bright-siding and the rise of a brand of American capitalism in which working on the self became an obligation in order to "make that self more acceptable and even likeable to employers, clients, coworkers, and potential customers."[12] Much of the diversity-training industry, with its emphasis on improving workplace morale and productivity, would fit neatly into this model.

Although Ehrenreich does not address behavioral realism per se, we see the logical connection between it and bright-siding in one vignette she gives about someone proposing that positive psychology be renamed "applied behavioral economics." As she focuses on motivational speakers from Norman Vincent Peale to Tony Robbins, she highlights self-monitoring and general work on the self that are cognate to the kind of "attitude make over" proposed by Kang and Banaji.[13] We see these emphases also in a study by leading social psychology researchers on how "lovingkindness mediation training reduces intergroup bias," wherein "growing evidence show[s] implicit bias reduction through unconscious and effortless activation of countergoal . . . stereotypes," and how "lovingkindness meditation" may "improve[]

intergroup orientations without arousing rebound or backlash effects."[14] Here again we find a defensive concern for backlash and the desire to find ways to affect implicit bias without actually requiring effort from subjects. Such attitude makeover and meditation exercises tend to reduce the duties of citizenship to a low-cost exercise in narcissism. As in "bright-siding," the focus is all on "me" and "my progress" toward addressing "my own attitudes." Mirroring the jurisprudence of the conservative Supreme Court, those engaging in attitude makeovers are asked to concentrate on their own *intent* rather than on the *impact* of their biases on other people.

Robin DiAngelo, writing about what she terms "white fragility," observes that "whites often respond defensively when linked to other whites as a group or 'accused' of collectively benefiting from racism." Unlike behavioral realists, however, she characterizes this response as a form of narcissism, which she sees as "a result of the white racial insulation ubiquitous in dominant culture."[15] It is, perhaps, such insulation that undergirds the lack of cross-racial empathy identified by Lawrence Bobo and his colleagues.[16] DiAngelo argues that this insulated environment "builds white expectations for racial comfort while at the same time lowering the ability to tolerate racial stress." White fragility, in short, "is a state in which even a minimum amount of racial stress becomes intolerable, triggering a range of defensive moves . . . [that], in turn, function to reinstate white racial equilibrium."[17]

One difference between bright-siding and behavioral realism is that for the latter much of the work on the self is meant to come about through the power of positive "nudging" rather than the power of positive thinking. Thus, we have Richard Thaler and Cass Sunstein talking about manipulating "choice architectures" to produce better outcomes and Dasgupta and Greenwald developing techniques that focus "on changing the social context that people inhabit rather than [on] directly manipulating their goals or motivations."[18] This indirect approach, however, further reinforces notions of white fragility and fear of backlash. Subliminal nudges, games, meditation, and behavioral realists' general reluctance to invoke the concept of racism do nothing to challenge the cultural insulation DiAngelo identifies. To the contrary, they validate it and may even reinforce it by allowing white subjects to feel good about their position in society and their facile efforts to deal with their biases. In seeking to avoid backlash, such behavioral realist framings may in fact be solidifying the obstacles to real progress by valorizing white fragility.

Behavioral realism, with its defensive concerns not to offend and its effort to make addressing implicit bias palatable to the white majority, accepts and thereby reinforces the frame of acceding to white resentment first articulated by Justice Lewis Powell in *Bakke* and later echoed by Justice Anthony Kennedy in *Schuette*. As Reva Siegel argues, Powell critically reoriented the *Brown* Court's concern for how racially classifications might impose stigma on minorities toward a skeptical view of all uses of race "because of concerns about the 'resentment' and 'outrage' of 'innocent' members of the 'dominant majority.'"[19]

Thirty-six years after *Brown v. Board of Education of Topeka*, Justice Kennedy expressed in *Schuette v. BAMN* (2014) similar concerns that the state's broad use of racial classifications, even if causing no stigma, "might become itself a source of the very resentments and hostilities based on race that this Nation seeks to put behind it."[20] As Siegel notes, in this increasingly dominant account "government classification by race poses risks to social cohesion, threatening balkanization and racial conflict, and so strict judicial oversight is crucial to constrain the practice." The overriding concern of this conservative juridical frame, she argues, is to consider how "majority groups understand and experience state action undertaken for benign, race-conscious reasons."[21]

The upshot is that as behavioral realism reinforces a focus on the majority's feelings, attitudes, and beliefs, it strengthens the conservative solicitude for whites' sensibilities and the concern to avoid any actions that might inflame racial tensions—both Kennedy and the behavioral realists appear to want to avoid conflict at all costs. One can only wonder what Frederick Douglass, who so famously declared that "power concedes nothing without a demand. It never did and it never will,"[22] would make of such sentiments.

Compare the flight from racial discomfort evidenced by Kennedy and the behavioral realists with Justice Sonia Sotomayor's dissent in *Schuette*, where she declared that "race matters."

> Race matters in part because of the long history of racial minorities' being denied access to the political process. . . . Race also matters because of

persistent racial inequality in society—inequality that cannot be ignored and that has produced stark socioeconomic disparities. . . . And race matters for reasons that really are only skin deep, that cannot be discussed any other way, and that cannot be wished away. Race matters to a young man's view of society when he spends his teenage years watching others tense up as he passes, no matter the neighborhood where he grew up. Race matters to a young woman's sense of self when she states her hometown, and then is pressed, "No, where are you *really* from?" regardless of how many generations her family has been in the country. Race matters to a young person addressed by a stranger in a foreign language, which he does not understand because only English was spoken at home. Race matters because of the slights, the snickers, the silent judgments that reinforce that most crippling of thoughts: "I do not belong here."[23]

Sotomayor here is focusing on the *impact* of racism on the history and current lived experience of minorities in America. She sees and engages the tension of race relations. She returns the focus to stigma, directing us away from personal attitudes, and demands that we "confront . . . the racial inequality that exists in our society" directly and explicitly,[24] not through submerged nudges or screensavers.

But, as Siegel notes, Kennedy's view has been ascendant. We see such conservative attitudes reflected in broader surveys of changing public opinion over the past several decades. In their review of results from the General Social Survey since 1972, Bobo and his colleagues find that "despite broad acceptance of principles of equality . . . whites [have been] reluctant to endorse actions challenging the status quo," showing particularly little enthusiasm for endorsing "government action to redress racial inequality." Significantly, they also find that whites have over time become less sympathetic to structural explanations for racial inequality, with two in five whites considering "discrimination" as a cause of inequality in 1997, but only about one in three doing so by 2008.[25] Of course, correlation does not equal causation, but the era of the rise of behavioral realism has coincided with an erosion in a broader commonsense understanding of the significance of racial discrimination as a factor in structuring social relations and equality in America.

It is not that that behavioral realism has necessarily caused or even promoted such changes, but it most certainly resonates with them—particularly with its individualistic framing and care to avoid disturbing the status quo or making whites feel uncomfortable. Moreover, behavioral realism's focus on adjusting individual subjects' attitudes also fits in with the common view among whites, revealed in Bobo and his colleagues' review, that "lack of 'motivation or willpower' is the most commonly endorsed explanation of black disadvantage across the 1977–2008 time span."[26] When fighting racism is made a function of a personal-attitude makeover, then perhaps it becomes easier to see others' failure to overcome inequality as similarly the function of a poor attitude—this, indeed, is the message Ehrenreich identifies as close to the heart of bright-siding.[27] Banaji also invokes the idea that the IAT is an "(un)consciousness-raising device" (a term first coined by John Jost in a paper cowritten with Banaji and Greenwald in 1994).[28]

Of course, this idea harks back to the consciousness-raising movement of second-wave feminism in the late 1960s and early 1970s, but it is different in several key respects—respects that point up the easier, more recreational aspects of many contemporary behavioral realist interventions. One recent article titled "Using the Implicit Association Test as an Unconsciousness Raising Tool in Psychology" picks up on Banaji's characterization to directly argue that the IAT can be useful in "raising students' awareness about their unconscious biases and teaching them about implicit attitudes." This particular experiment involved having students in a classroom take an IAT, answer six essay questions, read two articles on the IAT, and then answer five additional essay questions. After the readings, more students agreed that the IAT measured prejudice than the number who agreed before the readings. The researchers' hope was that "once students have this additional knowledge, they may be more willing to accept that they harbor implicit biases, which is a necessary first step in eradicating prejudice."[29]

On its face, this hope is reasonable enough and generally reflects core behavioral realist beliefs about the value of the IAT. There is a casual elision here, however, between "awareness" and "consciousness." Perhaps because of behavioral realists' primarily psychological focus, consciousness is here in effect reduced to mere awareness—simply knowing about something. Feminist consciousness raising was quite different and, I would argue, much more complex, challenging, and comprehensive. Behavioral realist unconsciousness raising is fundamentally hierarchical and monologic. It involves a subject being guided through a test devised, delivered, and interpreted to them by experts—or, in the case of the classroom IAT experiment, a teacher who ultimately grades them (hence hierarchical). It tends to be apolitical, abstracted from social and political context; atomizing, focusing on the individual subject as he or she takes the test by himself or herself, independently of others; and passive, providing subjects with a test that they take and maybe some additional survey questions to answer but otherwise demanding very little actual work or self-examination from them.[30]

Feminist consciousness raising cannot be reduced to any single formula. Contrast behavioral realist "unconsciousness raising" with feminist consciousness raising as a "radical weapon" that, according to Kathie Sarachild in 1973, involved "studying the whole gamut of women's lives, starting with the full reality of one's own."[31] There is no atomization in the latter, no separation out from politics or history, no removal of the individual from society. Sarachild presented consciousness raising "as a means for the organizers themselves to make an analysis of the situation, and also a means to be used by the people they were organizing and who in turn were organizing more people." It was a self-directed, nonhierarchical enterprise whose purpose "was to get to the most radical truths about the situation of women in order to take radical action." It did not require expert intervention, direction, or interpretation. This brand of consciousness raising was a communal exercise wherein "the importance of listening to a woman's feelings was collectively to analyze the situation, not analyze her."[32] Listening was central here—in contrast to the IAT, feminist consciousness raising was fundamentally and essentially dialogic.

Perhaps the greatest contrast to the psychologized, bright-siding of behavioral realism is to be found in Sarachild's contention that "the idea [of feminist consciousness raising] was not to change women, was not to make 'internal changes' except in the sense of knowing more. It was and is the conditions women face, it's male supremacy, we want to change." Sarachild went on to assert that "the view of consciousness-raising as an end in itself—which happens when consciousness-raising is made into a methodology, a psychology—is as severe and destructive distortion of the original idea and power of the weapon as is seeing consciousness-raising as a stage."[33] Her disdain for psychology is palpable.

Writing in the late 1980s, Catherine MacKinnon explicitly cast consciousness raising as a "form of political practice" that "inquires into an intrinsically social situation, into that mixture of thought and materiality which comprises gender in the broad sense. It approaches its world through a process that shares its determination: women's consciousness, not as individual or subjective ideas, but as collective social being." Above all, perhaps, consciousness raising is hard work. It is "a face-to-face social experience that strikes at the fabric of meaning of social relations between and among women and men by calling their grievances into question and reconstituting their meaning in a transformed and critical way."[34] This type of consciousness raising cannot be reduced to a game or promoted through screensavers. It is not meant to make the subject feel good or to help him or her achieve enlightenment without discomfort. There are no nudges here. Consciousness raising is not about changing individual psychology; it is about community building and empowerment.

We can see, perhaps, a glimpse of the hard work that goes into a white person's real racial consciousness raising in Wendell Berry's reflections on this issue in *The Hidden Wound*: "I am trying to establish the outlines of an understanding of myself in regard to what was fated to be the continuing crisis in my life, the crisis of racial awareness—the sense of being doomed by my history to be, if not always a racist, then a man always limited by the inheritance of racism, condemned to be always conscious of the necessity not to be a racist, to be always dealing deliberately with the reflexes of racism that are embedded in my mind as deeply as the language I speak."[35]

No IATs here, no screensavers, no expert advice. Berry's historically contextualized and deeply personal self-reflection is a work in progress, a ceaseless endeavor that makes demands and requires relentless effort to address. Such critical self-reflection is the antithesis of bright-siding.

By the comparisons discussed here, I do not mean to romanticize feminist consciousness raising as some purer or higher form of engagement. Rather, I mean to contrast the structure and orientation of the original concept of consciousness raising with the idea of unconsciousness raising as invoked by behavioral realists. Where the former was dialogic, engaged, decentralized, collective, contextualized, and political, the latter is monologic, hierarchical, technical, individualistic, passive, and decontextualized. As Nancy

Leong notes, however, improving racial relations "requires hard work."[36] Consciousness raising is hard work—unconsciousness raising, not so much.

PAINLESS JUSTICE

It is also instructive, I think, to contrast the behavioral realist approach to achieving progress toward racial justice with the approaches taken during the civil rights movement of the 1950s and 1960s. Of course, the latter was not a monolith. It contained many different themes and approaches. But indisputably at the heart of most movement actions were confrontation and tension. From A. Phillip Randolph's threat to march on Washington to pressure President Franklin Roosevelt into signing an Executive Order banning employment discrimination in the federal government and defense industries in June 1941 to the Montgomery Bus Boycott in 1956 and the Selma to Montgomery March in 1965, the civil rights movement engaged in actions that provoked, that made people uncomfortable, and that challenged the complacency of the dominant white culture. Did confrontation elicit resentment and backlash? Most certainly, but it also produced progress. In his letter from a Birmingham jail, Martin Luther King Jr. wrote,

> You may well ask: "Why direct action? Why sit-ins, marches and so forth? Isn't negotiation a better path?" You are quite right in calling for negotiation. Indeed, this is the very purpose of direct action. Nonviolent direct action seeks to create such a crisis and foster such a tension that a community which has constantly refused to negotiate is forced to confront the issue. It seeks so to dramatize the issue that it can no longer be ignored. My citing the creation of tension as part of the work of the nonviolent resister may sound rather shocking. But I must confess that I am not afraid of the word "tension." I have earnestly opposed violent tension, but there is a type of constructive, nonviolent tension which is necessary for growth.[37]

Such tension, such confrontation, has no place in the scheme of behavioral realism. Tension does not make people feel good about themselves. It does not allow for "effortless" progress toward greater self-awareness. It does not ask oppressors to examine their attitudes. It demands that they confront issues—issues about the effect those attitudes and attendant privileges have had upon others. Frank Dobbin notes that the rise of diversity-management interventions during the 1990s were made "palatable" by diverting attention away from the concept of prejudice. Even those programs that did address bias were "couched in terms of unwitting stereotypes rather than in terms of knowing prejudice." As a result, he argues, "the programs whitewashed the problem of bias. And so, we no longer hear the word 'prejudice' on the lips of human resource managers."[38] Nor do we hear them, I would submit, on the lips of behavioral realists more generally.

This contrast is not meant to set up an overly stark dichotomy between the civil rights movement and behavioral realism. One need not "choose" between them as to which is better for any given particular purpose. The contrast is meant, rather, to highlight how both are also exercises in meaning making—they are approaches to framing and understanding the nature of a particular problem facing the nation. Many behavioral realists certainly would embrace King's point and are aware of the broader cultural changes that must occur in order to progress toward racial justice.

For example, in discussing the problem of how judges and jurors unknowingly misremember case facts in racially biased ways, Justin Levinson acknowledges the limitations of debiasing techniques and argues that "a permanent elimination of the bias (and implicit biases generally) will best occur through a sustained process of cultural change." Very promisingly, Levinson argues that "dealing with implicit racial biases, then, requires more than a scientific effort at debiasing through cues and primes. It requires a recognition that [the] very existence [of such biases] reflects the state of American culture." And yet when discussing specific strategies to promote such broad cultural change, Levinson falls back on such limited behavioral realist interventions as "informing people about implicit biases, followed by 'efforts to retain and expand policies that serve to override them, including affirmation action'; providing people the opportunity to be more emotionally comfortable with out-group members; and recognizing the cultural influences on the self while striving for a more inclusive society."[39] Apart from the passing reference to affirmative action, none of these interventions actually involves affecting the distribution of goods or power, and they all emphasize once more the importance of making people "comfortable." It seems that even when wanting to address broader structural issues, behavioral realists remain confined by the horizons of their individualistic, psychological frame of reference.

Anthropologist Leith Mullings has noted that new formulations of "color-blind" or "laissez-faire" racism "seek to make the social appear natural and ruthless inequality appear as common sense." She argues that,

> like neoliberalism, these contemporary explanatory frameworks facilitate the denial of racism and conceal the inner workings of the social system by attributing contemporary inequality to individual culture or meritocracy. They simultaneously erase the actual history of racism and the collective histories of struggle against racism by subordinated populations. Perhaps most invidiously—like neoliberalism, which has commandeered the concept of freedom—these doctrines astutely appropriate the language and concepts derived from contemporary oppositional struggles, such as multiculturalism, equal opportunity, and the right to be different. They function not only to rationalize inequality but also to delegitimize antiracist activities.[40]

Mullings is not discussing behavioral realism, but rather the sort of conservative reworkings of racial ideology critiqued by Eduardo Bonilla-Silva and Lawrence Bobo. Nonetheless, the similarities to implicit bias frameworks (with their focus on individual merit, erasure of history, and emphasis on the language of diversity) should give us all pause before too readily embracing behavioral realism as the frame for understanding what ails us. Perhaps of greatest concern is the possibility that behavioral realist approaches to racial inequality, with their emphasis on nonconfrontational, submerged, and expert-directed interventions, may actually be delegitimizing both other antiracist activities such as the Black Lives Matter movement, which surely follow in the tradition of the civil rights movement, and other antiracist legal doctrines such as antisubordination and explicit concerns regarding stigma.

In this regard, another section of King's letter comes to mind—one in which he chastises otherwise well-meaning white moderates for their timidity and complacency:

> I must confess that over the past few years I have been gravely disappointed with the white moderate. I have almost reached the regrettable conclusion

that the Negro's great stumbling block in his stride toward freedom is not
the White Citizen's Counciler or the Ku Klux Klanner, but the white moderate, who is more devoted to "order" than to justice; who prefers a negative
peace which is the absence of tension to a positive peace which is the presence of justice; who constantly says: "I agree with you in the goal you seek,
but I cannot agree with your methods of direct action"; who paternalisti-
cally believes he can set the timetable for another man's freedom; who lives
by a mythical concept of time and who constantly advises the Negro to wait
for a "more convenient season." Shallow understanding from people of
good will is more frustrating than absolute misunderstanding from people
of ill will. Lukewarm acceptance is much more bewildering than outright
rejection.[41]

Behavioral realists agree that the goal is racial equality and certainly would
not place the ideal of "order" over that of "justice"; nonetheless, behavioral
realism's methods evince a similar concern for achieving racial progress
with an "absence of tension" and maintain a somewhat "mythical concept
of time" wherein the past does not matter. Behavioral realists' understanding of contemporary racism may not be "shallow," but it does seem to be
blinkered by an excessive fascination with and faith in the power of technical, scientific interventions administered by experts to bring about the
change we all seek.

Lawyers, of course, litigate. But litigation itself may also often serve as a
means to manage and contain tension. As Michael Klarman observes in his
history of the rise of the Supreme Court and the civil rights movement,
"Judicial victories may also have the more concrete deleterious effect of persuading social protesters to channel energy and resources to the method that
has proven successful: litigation. Yet many objectives of the modern civil
rights movement were probably beyond the capacity of the courts to
deliver."[42] Klarman and Michelle Alexander bemoan the readiness with which
broader social movements for civil rights were over time channeled into the
more contained, controllable, and socially palatable arena of litigation. In the
early days of the civil rights movement, Klarman argues, "direct-action protest more reliably created conflict and incited opponents' violence, which
ultimately proved critical to transforming national opinion on race."[43] But
Alexander notes that with the rise of successful civil rights litigation,

"public attention shifted from the streets to the courtroom[, and] the extraordinary grassroots movement that made civil rights legislation possible faded from public view. The lawyers took over."[44] Samuel Bagenstos suggests that in the end the answer to addressing pervasive racial prejudice "may lie within the broad realm of politics and social change rather than in the narrow confines of legal doctrine."[45]

These critiques have much merit, but they tend to draw an overly stark dichotomy between legal and social change. The two, of course, are not independent of each other. *Brown* could not have happened without the emerging transformation of American society in the aftermath of World War II. But *Brown* in turn played a critical role in reshaping broader social understanding of the common sense of race and racism in America. The critical thing all these scholars identify is that progress in civil rights depends on more than mere technical interventions—whether in the courts or in bureaucracies. They depend on broader engagements to "transform national opinion." Lawsuits and IATs may, in fact, have a constructive role to play in such engagements, but they must do so openly, not through subliminal nudges, and energetically, not by walking on eggshells and seeking to avoid making people feel uncomfortable. Perhaps most of all, they must do so democratically, not by surrendering authority to experts and technocrats to do the work for them.

8

SEEKING A TECHNICAL FIX TO RACISM

iscussing the emergence of modern behavioral psychology, philosopher Tamsin Shaw notes that in 1971 founding father B. F. Skinner "expressed the hope that the vast humanly created problems facing our beautiful planet (famines, war, the threat of nuclear holocaust) could all be solved by new 'technologies of behavior.'"[1] The technical fix to complex social and legal problems holds great appeal. It is neat, clean, seemingly objective, and powerfully authoritative. Behavioral realism's technical fix turns racism into a function of measurement and subordinates legal and political judgment to scientific expertise. To the degree that such subordination comes to dominate strategies of antiracist action, it amounts to outsourcing the hard public and democratic work of addressing injustice to private technocrats.

MEASURING EVERYTHING

Numerous critiques of the neoliberal turn in American politics since the 1980s have decried the "commodification of everything."[2] Similarly, my critique of behavioral realism takes issue with its urge to measure everything. There is, of course, a connection between the two—not only in the impulse toward quantification but also in the fact that diversity management and related applications of behavioral realism have become big business. Behavioral realism is deeply grounded in technologies of measurement. From the millisecond response calculations of the IAT to the glowing images of the fMRI, behavioral realism reduces racism to a metric phenomenon—real or meaningful only to the extent that it can be measured by technological apparatuses devised, implemented, and assessed by experts. Measuring requires the quantification of bias, and as anthropologist Sally Merry notes, "quantification is seductive" because of the ways in which it simplifies knowledge and facilitates decision making. Merry cautions, however, that "counting things requires making them comparable, which means that they are inevitably stripped of their context, history, and meaning."[3]

Social psychologists love to measure prejudice. In a recent article titled "Measures of Stereotyping and Prejudice: Barometers of Bias," Susan Fiske and Michael North note that "social psychologists have measured racial and ethnic bias since the field's origins" and go on to evaluate eleven distinct measures of bias.[4] The methods used vary from survey questionnaires to the IAT's reaction-time measures. Beyond this, a similar review in the *Handbook of Multicultural Measures* evaluated no fewer than *thirty-seven* purported measures of prejudice.[5] Each measure surely has its own particular merits, but together they cumulatively testify to a near fetishization of technologies of measurement as the foundation for social psychological approaches to bias. We see this fascination with measurement foregrounded in the very title of Jerry Kang and Mahzarin Banaji's influential article "Fair Measures: A Behavioral Realist Revision of 'Affirmative Action.'"[6] The contemporary fascination with measuring racism harks back eerily to the nineteenth-century scientific obsession with measuring all aspects of the black body to establish biological racial difference.[7]

Taking up such frameworks, the primary report from the NCSC implicit bias training program summarizes several physiological measures of implicit bias, including "the measurement of sweat production" (alternately referred to as "skin conductance response . . . , galvanic skin response . . . , and electrodermal activity"); "cardiovascular responses," such as heart rate; "facial electromyography," the measurement of electrical activity associated with facial muscle contractions; "startle eyeblink response"; fMRI; and "event-related brain potentials," measurable electrical signals emitted by brain activity.[8]

One recent study went so far as to compare IAT results and fMRIs of subjects acting as jurors in hypothetical employment-discrimination cases and found that with respect to finding correlations with the amount of money awarded to victims of discrimination, fMRI actually "measures racial bias with more practical validity" than the IAT. The authors deem fMRI superior because "implicit behavioral measures like the IAT still require some conscious cognition, but fMRI measures can tap unconscious processes even further along the implicit–explicit spectrum."[9] The more complex the technological intervention, it would seem, the greater the authority of the results. The authors of the study do not suggest that real jurors actually be subject to fMRI screening, not yet at least. But their caveats, as in so much of behavioral realist scholarship, are somewhat half-hearted and technical rather than principled.

For example, the authors first emphasize that given the Sixth Amendment duty to provide a trial by a fair and impartial jury, "courts should strive to select jurors with the least amount of racial prejudice," but then they modestly state, "We are not suggesting that potential jurors be put in an MRI machine during jury selection for cases where race is salient. The cost of doing so would be prohibitive, many people might feel it is overly invasive, and—because of lack of data—courts have been hesitant to allow neuroimaging data to be used in trials, although the acceptance of neuroimaging data by the courts has steadily been increasing."[10]

The authors of this study thus locate the problem with using fMRI to screen jurors not in the technology but in the practical economic and social impediments, such as cost and personal discomfort. They even cast the legal evidentiary requirements as potentially transitory, observing that court acceptance of neuroimaging data is "increasing." The implication here is that all we need is more "data"—that is, more measurement. So, no, they are not suggesting the we use fMRI to screen jurors for bias—not yet, anyway. But certainly the unstated message is that we might able to do so in the future if we can only bring down the cost and overcome people's silly concerns about invasiveness.

Such emphasis on measurement as the appropriate technical fix for bias resonates with current calls for body cameras on police as a remedy to the problems highlighted by the Black Lives Matter movement. On the one hand, such technology obviously has the potential to make a positive contribution to addressing issues of racial profiling and equity in policing. On the other hand, we should keep in mind that the deaths of Eric Garner and Tamir Rice were filmed, but that did not seem to affect the outcome of grand jury proceedings, which failed to return any indictments against the officers involved.[11] The mistaken presumption, again, is that the technology, whether a body camera or an fMRI, renders images that constitute a transparent objective representation of "reality."

Mariame Kaba, a member of the Chicago anti-police-violence organization We Charge Genocide, presented a very different perspective on police body cams, arguing that "this notion that there is a single truth that comes out of a video is interesting to me. People watching the same video can still come to very different conclusions about what happened, just as eyewitnesses see different things in real time. The truth is completely conditioned by your social location and by whether or not you're likely to believe the police. Some people have friendly relations with the police. But others don't. And that affects what they see happening in videos. We've seen this borne out by recent grand jury deliberations."[12] A similar skepticism toward technological fixes is evident in Ta-Nehisi Coates's observation that "talk of diversity training, sensitivity training, and body cameras . . . [is] all fine and applicable, but [it] understate[s] the task and allow[s] the citizens of this country to pretend that there is real distance between their own attitudes and those of the ones appointed to protect them."[13]

The point here is not that Kaba and Coates are necessarily "right" and that advocates of technological interventions are "wrong," but that the issue is legitimately contested, which has significant implications for the relative status of the authority derived from such technologically grounded claims.

We see a similar technophilic impulse in some of the more progressive approaches to law and economics, as in legal scholar Ian Ayers's contention "that objective evidence of race-contingent decisionmaking [sic] is knowable if we as a society have the will to go out and look for it." For Ayers, as for behavioral realists more generally, discrimination is the anomaly, a glitch in the market, a failure to properly measure "true" merit.[14] In all of this, the measurable, particularly as manifested in physiology, is taken as providing a somehow purer, more direct, and unmediated access to some sort of objectively verifiable "reality" of racism. Ayers contends that "race-contingent behavior should not simply be asserted. It needs to be continually reestablished by ongoing testing and ongoing scrutiny of test results."[15] Similarly, Jennifer Eberhardt notes that researchers "consider[] involuntary affective responses (such as [electromyography] measures) to be more valid indicators of affect toward out-group members than self-report measures. Because involuntary affective responses are less controllable, they are thought to be less subject to self-presentational concerns."[16] Behavioral realists see physiology as revealing a deeper, more essential truth of racism, just as nineteenth-century anatomists saw physiological measurements of the body as indicators of the true nature of race.[17]

Finally, behavioral realism privileges technologies of measurement not only as a means to identify racism but also as the basis for assessing when the legal and political system has successfully addressed its causes and effects. As mentioned earlier, Kang and Banaji propose that the IAT (or related measures) might be used as a basis for providing the sort of "ending for affirmative action" called for by Justice Sandra Day O'Connor in *Grutter v. Bollinger* (2003) when she asserted that "race-conscious admissions policies must be limited in time" and suggested that twenty-five more years might be sufficient for affirmative action to play itself out.[18] "In our view," propose Kang and Banaji,

> the lifespan for certain affirmative action programs should be guided by evidence of bias rather than any arbitrary or hopeful deadline. Now that we can measure threats to fair treatment—threats that lie in every mind—such data should be a crucial guide to ending affirmative action. We suggest a terminus when measures of implicit bias for a region or nation are at zero or some rough behavioral equivalent. At this point, implicit bias would align with an explicit creed of equal treatment. It would fulfill collective aspirations to behave in accordance with explicitly held values.[19]

This formulation is not only problematic in how it overlooks structural aspects of racism but also and perhaps even more deeply problematic in its assumptions that the products of such technologies of measurement can be rendered as transparent, unmediated representations of the reality of a complex psychological, social, and historical phenomenon such as racism. It reduces the task of identifying and addressing the legacy and present realities of racism to a function of technocratic management.

The focus on measurement further reinforces the conservative frame of "color-blind merit." Behavioral realism tells us that technologies of measurement make implicit bias real and legally cognizable and asserts that once such bias is identified and addressed, we will then be able to focus on truer, more accurate "fair measures" of merit as the basis for awarding social goods. This brings us back to Ralph Richard Banks and Richard Ford's critique of implicit bias discourse as "further[ing] a trend toward technocratic authoritarianism" by implicitly elevating "a norm of technically rational decision making" that is wholly instrumental in its logic.[20] Such an approach fails to consider or to account for the deeper meaning and significance of racism or, for that matter, for what counts as "merit" in a complex society. In the employment context, it reduces merit purely to how the employer defines the instrumental functions of any given position. In the educational context, it threatens to reduce merit to standardized test scores or grades.

As much as behavioral realists might like to see bias quantifiably manifest in millisecond response times or glowing fMRIs, there is no simple calculus to racial injustice. As Ira Katznelson observes, "In truth, the brutal harms inflicted by slavery and Jim Crow are far too substantial to ever be properly remedied."[21] Here the phrase "too substantial" is not a mere quantitative evaluation; it is a recognition that such harms are ultimately beyond technical measurement. Behavioral realists are much like those racial pragmatists who, Katznelson observes, "fail to argue forthrightly . . . that the purpose of affirmative action is to put a definitive end to the caste status of blacks in American life and thus also to put an end to white privilege." The embrace of conservative frames of "merit" and "diversity" opens up calls for racial justice "to cost–benefit calculations" that abstract such programs from their larger social and historical context, thereby making it impossible to determine or appreciate the depth and significance of the interests at stake.[22] Behavioral realism's definition of measurement as the means to break through the impasse on equal-protection law actually ends up validating and reinforcing the conservative frame Justice Lewis Powell articulated early on in *Bakke* (1978), in which he dismissed the effects of "societal discrimination" as "an amorphous concept of injury."[23] One might just as easily substitute the term *unmeasurable* for the term *amorphous*. For Powell, apparently, if it can't be measured, it doesn't exist.

This is not to say that empirical research into the dynamics of implicit prejudice is unwarranted or will necessarily yield poor data. Rather, it is to point up the tendency in behavioral realism, despite the equivocal caveats that science is not a magic bullet, to claim that such empirical work should have pride of place in establishing the legal baselines for finding discrimination and in crafting legal and policy responses to such findings. Always there is the search for "objective evidence"—something concrete, measureable, quantifiable—the implication being that other more sociologically or historically informed qualitative interpretive methods of understanding and addressing racism should take a back seat to the science.

FOLLOW THE SCIENCE

Behavioral realists embrace scientific authority largely in the name of providing a counterweight to the more conservative quantitative work of law and economics scholars—using the tools of the enemy against him, so to speak. Jerry Kang, for example, sees behavioral realism as so powerful precisely because it is grounded in "those rigorous and quantitative techniques that the Right demanded when dismissing victim accounts about discrimination as mere anecdote."[24] When one thinks about the status of scientific authority in the realm of legal discourse, one usually thinks of the evidentiary issues raised by the Supreme Court case *Daubert v. Merrell Dow Pharmaceuticals* (1993) and its progeny, which set forth the conditions under which a court will admit expert evidence at trial as relevant and reliable.[25] As Sheila Jasanoff notes, "Since the early years of industrialization, belief has grown in legal circles that scientific evidence is one of the most reliable kinds of evidence, and that science can deliver insights into matters otherwise hidden from judicial inquiry."[26]

"The hope," Jasanoff continues, "is that technology, through its mechanical reproducibility, will be impervious to context and will provide unbiased and reliable evidence about the facts of the matter. Human actions, however, can never be entirely ruled out of the picture in the production of evidence."[27] Like Joseph Dumit in his study of PET scans,[28] Jasanoff is keenly aware of the fact that scientifically observed phenomena do not speak for themselves. They are, to the contrary, "for all practical purposes unreadable, unless they are made to speak with the aid of specialized laboratory techniques, scientific instruments, and expert testimony, all of which demand the work of trained professionals."[29] Or, as she states elsewhere, "facts, in other words, are not pure, unmediated renditions of an external reality whose objectivity is secured by a single, transcendent scientific method. In producing scientific facts, especially on previously unstudied problems, scientists must engage in complex debates about the correctness of particular theories, experimental methods, instrumental techniques, validation procedures, statistical analyses, review processes, and the like."[30]

Like science, law and politics have their own institutional constraints and imperatives. Doing justice and promoting public welfare follow different processes and priorities. But the hope and the illusion that science (and scientists) can offer unmediated access to objective truths about social life pervade behavioral realism. Thus, behavioral realism's embrace of measurement, like its acceptance of the conservative framing of affirmative action, provides a foundation for a broader and more problematic elevation of quantitative methods of analysis over qualitative and an attendant subordination of legal to scientific authority.

We can thus return here once again to Banaji and Kang's assertion that

> the methodology of behavioral realism forces the law to confront an increasingly accurate description of human decision making and behavior, as provided by the social, biological, and physical sciences. Behavioral realism identifies naïve theories of human behavior latent in the law and legal institutions. It then juxtaposes these theories against the best scientific knowledge available to expose gaps between assumptions embedded in law and reality described by science. When behavioral realism identifies a substantial gap, *the law should be changed to comport with science.*[31]

This statement is significant not simply because it is uttered by two of the leading proponents of behavioral realism but also because it so clearly sets forth the basic premise common to many behavioral realists: the authority of science should be elevated over that of the law in engaging issues of race and racism in American society. The basic frame here is that the science can fix the law, make it better, bring it more in accord with "reality" if only it is allowed to lead the way. This frame reflects what Sheila Jasanoff has characterized as the "signal disenchantment in contemporary America with the law's capacity to resolve the manifold technical disputes of modernity and a concomitant embrace of the imagined clarity, certainty, and rationality of science."[32] Similarly, it echoes Sally Merry's observation that the move toward empirical, evidence-based governance "moves responsibility from judicial and political decision makers to the experts in quantification who develop and implement measurement systems."[33]

Behavioral realist legal scholars Justin Levinson and Robert Smith posit that the "truth" of implicit bias "is revealed to us through rigorous scientific method used by scores of social scientists to consistently reveal a disquieting but potent truth."[34] Thus, "science" (that is, the science of behavioral realism) and those who wield it gain preeminent authority as purveyors of this seemingly transparent reality. According to behavioral realism, states Ivan Bodensteiner, the experts in possession of this truth "must educate the attorneys, judges and jurors in the psychology of discrimination."[35] The impulse to educate is reasonable, of course, and is at the heart of the programs developed by the NSCS, the U.S. Department of Justice, and other entities to combat implicit bias, but it also replicates Richard Thaler and Cass Sunstein's view of citizens (including attorneys, judges, and jurors) as "somewhat mindless, passive decisions makers" who need to be "nudged" by experts toward better outcomes.[36]

What does it mean as a practical matter to say that law should be made to comport with science? This is a way of saying that science can "see" things about racism that the law cannot, that the "data" of behavioral realism are superior to legal understandings of racism that draw on interpretive understandings of history, culture, and society. Behavioral realism's elevation of scientific authority over legal authority is further premised on a problematically stark separation between the two. This dyadic conceptualization is not unique to behavioral realism. Jasanoff has noted how it also informs the Supreme Court's approach to scientific evidence, arguing that *Daubert* and its progeny "endorsed a separatist model of law and science, presupposing a sharper boundary between the institutions than exists or should exist." She contends that "a better approach is to recognize that law and science are both knowledge generating institutions, but that fact-making serves different functions in these two settings." Such efforts to "make judicial practice more scientific," she comments, "are part of a tectonic shift in US legal and political thought that aims to 'modernize' legal decision-making by making it more efficient, standardized, and predictable."[37]

Such "modernization" is at the heart of behavioral realism. Jasanoff also cautions, however, that "too much concern for the goodness of science runs the risk of tilting the law away from its core concern with doing justice in a modern, high-tech economy."[38] In the realm of something such as affirmative action, the elevation of the "scientific approach" wholly cedes the terrain of redressing discrimination to conservative tropes of "merit" and "objective" measurements of functionalist efficiencies. Behavioral realists do not contest this frame; they do not challenge the assumption underlying the conceptualization of merit as a decontextualized, functionalist, individualized attribute but merely argue for better, more scientific measures of such merit.

Racism, however, needs to be understood as only secondarily an empirical phenomenon measured by IATs or fMRIs. It is first and foremost a function of context, meaning, and power. Measurement necessarily must be secondary because we must employ qualitative knowledge to interpret or argue about what such measurements mean. Technology is never transparent; it never interprets itself or autonomously constructs its own message. This is not to say that technologies or measurements of racial attitudes are not "real" but rather that they are not "pure"—that is, they cannot meaningfully exist outside of value-laden human interpretive enterprises.

Take *Plessy v. Ferguson* (1896) and *Brown v. Board of Education of Topeka* (1954) as paradigmatic examples. The doctrine "separate but equal" may well be understood as a doctrine of measurement—asserting that so long as facilities are measurably equal there can be no offense to the Constitution. The Court used the formal idea of measurable equality to obscure or submerge the deeper *meaning* and *message* of segregation. And so in *Plessy* Justice Henry Billings Brown could write of "the underlying fallacy of the plaintiff's argument" that "the enforced separation of the two races stamps the colored race with a badge of inferiority. If this be so it is not by reason of anything found in the act, but solely because the colored race chooses to put that construction upon it."[39] Justice Brown looked only at the formal text of the act. He accepted the underlying assumption that measurably equal facilities could be provided. He dismissed the significance of interpretation and thereby deemed to be irrelevant the *meaning* of segregation both to those imposing it and to those experiencing it. Justice John Marshall Harlan saw this problem, and so, despite the many flaws of his *Plessy* dissent, he declared that the "true intent and meaning" of the Thirteenth and Fourteenth Amendments to be that "there is no caste here. Our Constitution is color-blind, and neither knows nor tolerates classes among citizens."[40] The reference to being "color-blind," it must be reiterated, has to be understood as being critically modified by the phrase "neither knows nor tolerates classes among citizens." Seeing color offends the Constitution only when it is done to create a subordinate caste. Harlan recognized that the concepts of equal citizenship inscribed in the Reconstruction amendments are not a function of quantifiable equivalence but a function of equal dignity that can be assessed only through an interpretation of "intent and meaning."

Similarly, in *Brown* the Court did not overturn the doctrine of "separate but equal" because of measurable differences between black schools and white schools. The entire logic of the pronouncement that "separate educational facilities are inherently unequal"[41] is premised on the idea that formal measurement alone cannot provide a basis for understanding and assessing the *meaning* of segregation in the context of the specific historical moment that confronted America in 1954. Nor was the somewhat equivocal social science evidence presented by Kenneth Clarke central to the Court's ultimate holding. Rather, it was Justice Earl Warren's interpretative act of asserting the commonsense understanding of how such segregation in context "generates a feeling of inferiority as to [black children's] status in the community that may affect their hearts and minds in a way unlikely ever to be undone."[42]

One might argue that it was precisely the lack of such measureable, quantifiable differences that led Herbert Wechsler in 1959 famously to criticize Earl Warren's opinion for its lack of "neutral principles"—again, the underlying assumption being that quantification is somehow more "neutral" or objective and therefore more authoritative than humanistic legal interpretation. Wechsler noted the thinness of the empirical evidence presented before the Court, asking, "Does the validity of the decision turn then on the sufficiency of evidence or of judicial notice to sustain a finding that the separation harms the Negro children who may be involved?" He concluded, "I find it hard to think the judgment really turned upon the facts. Rather, it seems to me, it must have rested on the view that racial segregation is, in principle, a denial of equality to the minority against whom it is directed; that is, the group that is not dominant politically and, therefore, does not make the choice involved."[43]

Wechsler's conception of "fact" is severely cramped. Good legal scholar that he was, he proposed several hypotheticals to challenge the idea that segregation necessarily, "factually" harmed "the Negro children who may be involved." He asked, for example, whether a particular expert witness was "comparing the position of the Negro child in a segregated school with his position in an integrated school where he was happily accepted and regarded by the whites; or was he comparing his position under separation with that under integration where the whites were hostile to his presence and found ways to make their feelings known? And if the harm that segregation worked was relevant, what of the benefits that it entailed: sense of security, the absence of hostility? Were they irrelevant?"[44] Positing diverse scenarios and evaluating their particular costs and benefits recast equal-protection analysis as a sort of calculus. Warren, however, was engaged in a broad assessment and recognition of the cultural meaning and impact of state-mandated segregation rather than of the particular facts of segregation's distinct manifestations in specific scenarios. Wechsler did not see such engagement as involving "facts" but only "principles"—and nonneutral ones at that because it employed qualitative interpretation, not empirical measurement. But Warren here was applying the underlying constitutional "principle" of equal standing before the law to the commonsense understanding of the "fact" that state-mandated segregation violated that principle by stigmatizing black children.

No more masterful exposition of Wechsler's critique can be found than Charles Black Jr.'s article "The Lawfulness of the Segregation Decisions," published a year after Wechsler wrote his assessment. Black framed his critique with a challenge to abstract principles of neutrality and an appeal to situated common sense:

> Then does segregation offend against equality? Equality, like all general concepts, has marginal areas where philosophic difficulties are encountered. But if a whole race of people finds itself confined within a system which is set up and continued for the very purpose of keeping it in an inferior station, and if the question is then solemnly propounded whether such a race is being treated "equally," I think we ought to exercise one of the sovereign prerogatives of philosophers—that of laughter. The only question remaining (after we get our laughter under control) is whether the segregation system answers to this description.[45]

This challenge, above all, was a call to engage with the social meaning of state-mandated segregation in the social and historical context of twentieth-century

America. Black continued: "it would be the most unneutral of principles, improvised *ad hoc*, to require that a court faced with the present problem refuse to note a plain fact about the society of the United States—the fact that the social meaning of segregation is the putting of the Negro in a position of walled-off inferiority—or the other equally plain fact that such treatment is hurtful to human beings."[46]

Black made it clear that access to such social meaning is not to be had through technical measurements of equality or neutral evaluations of abstract principles. Rather, the answer to the question of what segregation means "can find an answer only on the ground of history and of common knowledge about the facts of life in the times and places aforesaid." Assessing history and common knowledge are interpretative acts, not quantitative evaluations. Black (who participated in the *Brown* litigation) minimized the evidence presented by "scientific" authorities in *Brown* (such as Kenneth Clarke's doll studies), noting that they can be "relegated to a footnote and treated as merely corroboratory of common sense."[47]

As Richard Ford has more recently noted, "'Discrimination' is not a fact in and of itself; it is a narrative, an interpretation."[48] Foreshadowing this observation, Black made it clear that what was really at stake in *Brown* were not neutral principles but the *commonsense story* of race and racism in American society. "The Court that refused to see inequality," he wrote, "would be making the only kind of law that can be unwarranted and outrageous in advance—law based on self-induced blindness, in flagrant contradiction of known fact."[49]

Here we come back to Ian Haney-López's idea of "intentional blindness," this time in the context of arguments over what really are the "known facts" of racism and which of those facts the Court (or society more broadly) is willing to acknowledge. In 1896, Justice Harlan acknowledged in his *Plessy* dissent the "known fact" that the purpose of segregation was to stamp black Americans with a badge of inferiority. "The thin disguise of 'equal' accommodations for passengers in railroad coaches" wrote Harlan, "will not mislead anyone, nor atone for the wrong this day done."[50] Or as Black might have said, the majority opinion was "based on self-induced blindness," whereas by the time Warren wrote the *Brown* opinion, the Court was more willing to see and acknowledge the practical reality of segregation. Haney-López calls the latter approach one of looking for "contextual intent," which he contrasts to the search for "malicious intent." "The former," he asserts, "focuses on motives only in the loosest sense (or sometimes not at all) and emphasizes instead a broadly informed inferential approach to evaluating possible discrimination; the latter declares direct empirical proof of injurious motives a prerequisite and concomitantly declares contextual evidence irrelevant."[51]

Contextual intent relies on broad interpretive approaches to adjudicating claims of racial discrimination. In contrast, behavioral realism, with its focus on measurement, reinforces the preeminence of the malicious-intent approach, which demands direct proof of injurious motive. In eschewing the contextual approach, behavioral realism takes us back to the framework of the majority opinion in *Plessy*, wherein the measureable equality of facilities was assumed and context was deemed legally irrelevant, thus allowing Justice Brown to conclude, "We consider the underlying fallacy of the plaintiff's argument to consist in the assumption that the enforced separation of the two races stamps the colored race with a badge of inferiority. If this be so, it is not by reason of anything found in the act, but solely because the colored race chooses to put that construction upon it." The common sense of black Americans was not Brown's common sense, so he blithely dismissed it.

Wechsler's hypothetical of the black child feeling safer in an all-black school is irrelevant to assessing the commonsense meaning of the legal structure of state-mandated segregation. It might have been possible for some expert to construct a metric of harm or benefit that could find pockets within the Jim Crow system where the chosen items of measurement came out on the plus side for segregation. For example, the shining legacy of many historically black colleges and universities is a testament to the positive possibilities that existed within segregation—but they are examples of triumph *in spite of* the social meaning of segregation, not *because* of it. They do not negate that broader social meaning.

Perhaps nothing in behavioral realism better reflects Wechsler's phantasmagorical quest for the abstract, decontextualized application of neutral principles than Kang and Banaji's contention that "fair measures that target discrimination now can be more objectively designed, implemented, and delimited in scope and duration."[52] We saw in Joseph Dumit's analysis of the actual practices of neuroscience that even when such natural phenomena as those revealed by a PET scan are being studied, the "measures" used by science are never wholly "objectively designed."[53] There are always choices being made about which questions to ask, what parts of the brain to look at, and how to interpret the results. Of course, the scientist aspires toward objectivity, but objectivity is not somehow naturally "there" in scientist's methods if for no other reason that those methods are conceived and implemented *by* the scientist. How much more elusive must we expect the ideal of pure objectivity to be when we are asking the scientist to make choices about how to design and implement methods for measuring racism—a complex social and historical phenomenon that involves the very *subjective* experiences of all people in society, *including the scientist.*

As anthropologist Jonathan Marks observes with respect to scientists studying race, "While the fruitfly biologist has the luxury of studying things that have very limited political meanings, the anthropologist is obliged to study entities that are themselves the products of political history (nation, tribe, state, ethnicity), and produces knowledge that has immediate cultural relevance."[54] An fMRI of a dead salmon may reveal some technical issues with proper calibration of fMRI scans, but it says little about human social relations. An fMRI purporting to show racism at work in the human brain, however, is inherently and unavoidably political for the simple reason that racism is political. The information revealed by such scans might be useful for certain purposes, but the scans themselves should not be granted greater political or legal authority by reason that they are purportedly objectively purer than other methods of legal or political analysis.

Commenting on the "American experiment in desegregation" more than half a century after *Brown*, Curtis Hardin and Mahzarin Banaji assert that "public policies, however noble in intent, may not realize their aspirations if they do not include an understanding of human nature and culture. In other words, they cannot succeed if they are not founded on the relevant science, which reveals the nature of the problem, the likely outcomes, and how social transformation can best be imagined." For them, this science first and foremost is cognitive, involving the psychology of intergroup relations. They go on to lament that, "sadly, this [grounding of public policy in science] has not been the case, both because policy makers are not sufficiently respectful of the importance of science as the guide to social issues, and because academic scientists resist imagining the policy implications of their evidence."[55]

The first thing to note here is how Hardin and Banaji grant pride of place to "science" in the enterprise of understanding human nature and culture. Granted, their extended discussion makes it clear that "science" includes the social as well as cognitive sciences, but they cast it all as science nonetheless, as if science were the only discipline with access to authoritative knowledge about such issues. Second, they presume desegregation to have been a failure that was due in large part to not taking science into account. (This presumption is particularly ironic in light of how so many advocates for empirical sciences in law eagerly claim that social science guided the Court's decision in *Brown*.) This conclusion also implies (incredibly) that massive southern resistance and northern racism—that is, all the political complexities of desegregation—could have been addressed by more scientific research on the subject. Third, they also miss such structural factors as decades of housing, transportation, and employment policies, not to mention the impact of specific Supreme Court decisions, such as *Milliken v. Bradley* (1974) and *Freeman v. Pitts* (1992), that severely constrained the scope and reach of desegregation remedies.[56] Finally, they set up "science" as prior to, independent of, and therefore superior to politics. Policy makers must be "respectful" of science and ground their decisions in it. That is, not only must law be "made to comport with science," but policy must be as well.

Behavioral realism's privileging of science accords with Justice Lewis Powell's reticence in *Bakke* to engage in qualitative interpretations of the meaning and significance of racial classifications in the context of affirmative action. Considering which groups might be deemed appropriately eligible for "preferred status," Powell demurred, asserting that "the kind of variable sociological and political analysis necessary to produce such rankings simply does not lie within the judicial competence—even if they otherwise were politically feasible and socially desirable."[57] The idea of "judicial competence" is central to both behavioral realism and Powell's evisceration of affirmative action in *Bakke*. Both undermine trust in the judgment and discretion of judges when it comes to assessing the nature and dynamics of race relations in American society. By implication, Powell was moving us back toward Wechsler's "neutral principles" ideal. Behavioral realists appear to be fine with this backward move—they simply offer to provide those neutral principles through their scientific findings.

According to Kang's clarification of the behavioral realists' position, they "urge the law to respond to new scientific discoveries about the reality of contemporary discrimination." He argues that "such traditional 'common sense' models [for discrimination] have seriously frayed," while a "burgeoning scientific consensus has triggered calls for the law to become more behaviorally realistic." He denigrates such "intuitive understandings" of human behavior as being based "on models that were not selected through some rigorous scientific competition."[58] As with idea of making the law "comport" with science, Kang here places science first as the leader and driver of legal change. Legal authority, he asserts, does not construct, evaluate, or validate the scientific "discoveries" about bias (at least not beyond the basic evidentiary requirements articulated in *Daubert* and its progeny[59]). This frame also casts science and its practitioners (i.e., behavioral realists) as having privileged access to reality, direct and unmediated by cultural constructions or normative commitments, and not only to reality in general but to such particular manifestations as "bias" and "discrimination," which they purport to define, identify, measure, and evaluate.

This approach is the antithesis of the approach taken by Charles Lawrence III, whose focus on cultural meaning demands a serious engagement with "commonsense" models as a means to understand and address contemporary manifestations of racism. Such culturally engaged understandings derive not from scientific measurements of supposedly "natural" phenomena but from historically informed arguments about the nature and meaning of particular actions, laws, and policies. Behavioral realism may be able to measure different responses to people based on racial perception, but it cannot tell you when such differences become manifestations of racism. Only qualitative interpretation of the historically and culturally situated *meaning* of such responses can do this. The majority opinion in *Plessy* focused on measurements of different treatment and found none. It dismissed black people's commonsense or intuitive understanding of the meaning of segregation as irrelevant. Harlan's dissent in *Plessy*, in contrast, recognized the importance of arguing about the meaning of such segregation, as did Warren's opinion in *Brown*. In short, equal justice is not an equation; it is an argument.

Kang has acknowledged some critiques from the left that question his reliance on science and related concerns that the focus on individual attitudes might be seen as reductionist because it tends to slight larger structural or institutional forces, but he dismisses them as "mostly miss[ing] the mark."[60] He sees behavioral realism as open and pragmatic—a complement to, not a replacement of, structural critiques. He advocates pursuing "multiple methodologies to produce the deepest insight"[61] and asserts that "there is no reason [why,] when terms such as institutional, structural, or societal bias are well-defined and operationalized[,] . . . [they] cannot be integrated with Implicit Social Cognition into the fullest understanding of how multiple causes, at multiple levels, contribute to social inequalities."[62] Certainly, behavioral realism has such potential to be open and pragmatic. But this relatively modest stance is undercut and Kang even approaches a false humility when he precedes such caveats with the following framing statement: "Again, I am merely describing the brute fact that scientific evidence culled through standard hypothesis-testing procedures deploying modern statistics and published in peer-reviewed journals is considered to be the 'gold' standard for policymaking, including legal reform. Accordingly, if the Left wants to be pragmatic about its agenda, it seems sensible to pay attention to what science says. This is not to recommend putting all eggs in the scientific basket, but it is an argument not to abandon it altogether."[63] Kang here presents "science" as some sort of monolithic entity that operates independently of human agency and social or historical context. Moreover, he seems to imply that any critique of science or move to subordinate it to other values or regimes of discursive authority—such as law—is tantamount to "abandon[ing] it altogether." If law is to be made to comport with science, then all those who engage in law-based structural critiques must ultimately subordinate their approaches to Kang's science. This relationship is not one of complementarity; it is the clear privileging of behavioral realism over all other approaches.

In addition, Kang is saying that "science" is on his side. He makes it appear that it is not so much he who is making these points but rather the "brute facts" of science—as if implicit bias is somehow comparable to the second law of thermodynamics. It is one thing for courts or policy makers to take note of such neuroscientific "brute facts" as a lesion to the brain revealed by fMRI as evidence of harm from an accident or a tumor that impairs cognitive function as relevant to assessing the ability to form intent or control actions.[64] It is quite another to rely on fMRIs and IAT results to draw conclusions about the fundamental nature and significance of such overly determined, complex social phenomena as bias, prejudice, and racism. Kang's blurring of this distinction is critical to his construction of an authority for behavioral realist "science" that privileges it over other forms of legal interpretation.

In the case of identifying a brain lesion or tumor (even though fMRI results are not transparent and must be constructed through a variety of human interventions[65]), the observed phenomenon is relatively similar to other sorts of physical "facts" discovered out in the world and assessed by lawyers, judges, and policy makers. Observing and interpreting the significance of a brain lesion may legitimately be within the purview of expert medical and scientific authority from first to last (at least up until the point where lawyers must argue over the implications of such a lesion for assessing culpability or damages). In such an instance, a measure of deference to science is perhaps warranted, provided the evidentiary requirements of *Daubert* are satisfied.

In the case of identifying bias, the observed phenomena providing the basis for guiding law and policy—fMRI and readings of individuals' timed responses in an IAT—are constructed in laboratory settings designed by the scientists themselves. Their meaning and significance for understanding the nature of racism and its implications for law and policy are not directly evident from the science alone. When an fMRI identifies a brain lesion, the significance of that lesion as evidence of injury is relatively self-contained. One need not refer to external social or historical dynamics to understand the nature and significance of the injury. When an fMRI or IAT identifies differential responses to black and white faces, the nature and significance of such scientifically observed differences can be derived *only* through engagement with social and historical formations, values, and practices. This engagement requires *dialogue* between science and the interpretive arts, including law. In such cases, science need not be abandoned, but neither should it simply be followed. It may be used to *inform* legal and policy decisions, but this use is different from having it *direct* such decisions.

Behavioral realists, however, generally want law to emulate science. In many respects, the rise of behavioral realism can be understood as a response from the left to the more conservative tendencies of the law and economics movement that has been gaining ascendance since the 1970s. As Linda Hamilton Krieger and Susan Fiske noted in 2006, "The emergence of law and economics has played a major role in prodding legal scholarship—and, in certain instances, legal reasoning—toward a more scientific method of inquiry." Like Kang, Krieger and Fiske urge that "judges take reasonable steps . . . to make sure they have the science right."[66] Again, this advice presumes that the "science" relevant to legal and policy discussions is prior to and independent of discussion.

Krieger and Fiske also posit a strict dichotomy wherein "law, at root, is normative. Empiricism, at root, is descriptive, and it must remain so to fulfill its proper function."[67] This dichotomy clearly privileges scientific authority as an empirical method for arriving at better, more just decisions. Krieger and Fiske modestly propose, "Behavioral realism does not inject social science theories into legal reasoning. It merely provides a clear and constructive process for recognizing, evaluating, and, where necessary, modifying social science theories that are already there."[68]

But, as in so many behavioral realist caveats, this modesty is false. The search for a value-neutral method, like liberal legal proceduralism, presupposes that there are no issues regarding what is "good" to research but only questions of the "right" method to research them.

Just as in Michael Sandel's critique of John Rawls's "procedural republic," it is almost meaningless to posit an abstract scientific observer in some empirical original position free from normative commitments. Empiricism may be descriptive, but the empiricist must still *choose* what to describe and how to describe it. Sandel speaks of the "unencumbered self";[69] behavioral realism seeks not only a brain unencumbered by racial bias but also a procedural remedy guided by science, which itself is unencumbered by normative commitments—a remedy that is technical, objective, measurable, and ultimately conflict free. But this ideal is a phantom. The questions that scientists pose and the way they frame and pursue them are inevitably affected by prior normative commitments about what matters and what questions are worth asking. This is not to say the "science" and the "scientific method" is somehow corrupt or illusory, merely that they are invariably and inevitably human. "Science" (however construed) may be a valid and important source of authority, but it is not inherently superior to or even entirely distinct from legal authority.

The proceduralism of behavioral realism is evident in Brian Nosek and Rachel Riskind's discussion of the "policy implications of implicit social cognition," where they propose the following "strategies that improve behavioral realism":

First, if particular unwanted biases are identified, then interventions can be designed to change the biases themselves. . . . The main challenges for this strategy are (1) whether the shift will be durable, especially if the social context is temporary, and (2) whether the intervention can change all of the unwanted biases. . . . A second strategy is to teach decision-makers strategies to prevent the unwanted biases from being activated or influence judgment. . . . Finally, a third strategy is to design the behavioral or decision-making context itself so that unwanted biases can be intervened with or prevented from exerting influence in the first place. . . . Together, three approaches—reducing the existence of bias, providing decision-making strategies, and restructuring the decision-making process—provide the means for individuals and organizations to ensure that their judgment or actions reflect their goals and values.[70]

Each stage of this process is dominated by experts: they "identify" biases, "design" interventions, and "teach" decision makers. None of these interventions, however, involves a substantive reallocation of power—they all are procedural, aimed at helping decision makers purify their evaluations of "unwanted biases."

The implications of behavioral realist proceduralism are also evident in corporate diversity-management programs. In their article on the "ironic effects of organizational diversity structures," Cheryl Kaiser and her colleagues argue that judges tend to "defer to the mere presence of diversity programs as an indicator of civil rights compliance without considering whether the program was in fact effective at achieving fair treatment of underrepresented groups" simply because "the presence of diversity structures acts as a *signal* that the organization is committed to treating members of diverse groups with respect and dignity and hence provides an unbiased environment for members of these groups. That is, diversity programs signal to others that the organization's treatment of underrepresented groups is *procedurally fair*." Such diversity programs, often built on behavioral realist foundations, "have the potential to create an illusion of fairness" and thereby to "*legitimize* existing social arrangements within the organization."[71] Such judicial deference is due in no small part to the authority of behavioral science underlying many of these programs. The danger of formalistic procedures legitimizing an illusion of progress starkly illustrates the problematic nature of blanket admonishments that law simply be made to comport with science and of attendant injunctions that legal professionals and policy makers subordinate their authority to scientific experts.

ALGORITHMS AND THE PUBLIC-DEFICIT MODEL OF LEGAL JUDGMENT

We see perhaps the ultimate subordination of legal to scientific authority in Kang's characterization of judicial strict-scrutiny analysis as an "algorithm" to be applied as an "Equal Protection Machine" to "detect concealed intent to harm minorities."[72] Kang's characterization resonates eerily with a neuroscience study that entered "BOLD activation patterns recorded during the presentation of different types of stimuli . . . into a machine-learning algorithm" to predict whether a given subject undergoing fMRI was viewing a black face or a white face[73]—an ultimate algorithmic construction of racial bias in which human judgment need not apply.

Strict scrutiny is typically understood as a method of legal analysis invoked by judges when reviewing a legal classification based on a suspect category, such as race. In these cases, judges require that the racial classification be narrowly tailored to serve a compelling state interest—this is strict scrutiny.[74] An algorithm, of course, is a step-by-step means of solving a problem, but its derivation and prime meaning concern the solving of mathematical problems.[75] Algorithms drive computer programs, not judges. But behavioral realists would have judges act like computers. Like their more conservative counterparts in law and economics, behavioral realists would take the "judgment" out of the act of judging. The idea here is that if you have only the proper metric inputs, then the Equal Protection Machine will provide the true, empirically verifiable answer. But law is not math. Although empirical information may be very important for informing certain legal judgments, it in and of itself cannot make those judgments.

The second Justice Harlan's dissent in *Poe v. Ullman* (1961) speaks in eloquent counterpoint to Kang's idea that strict scrutiny can or should be reduced to an algorithm. "Due process," wrote Harlan,

> has not been reduced to any formula; its content cannot be determined by reference to any code. The best that can be said is that, through the course

of this Court's decisions, it has represented the balance which our Nation, built upon postulates of respect for the liberty of the individual, has struck between that liberty and the demands of organized society. If the supplying of content to this constitutional concept has of necessity been a rational process, it certainly has not been one where judges have felt free to roam where unguided speculation might take them. The balance of which I speak is the balance struck by this country, having regard to what history teaches are the traditions from which it developed as well as the traditions from which it broke. That tradition is a living thing. A decision of this Court which radically departs from it could not long survive, while a decision which builds on what has survived is likely to be sound. No formula could serve as a substitute, in this area, for judgment and restraint.[76]

Yet substituting a formula for judgment is precisely the implication of behavioral realism's fascination with measurement and the application of measurement to law through scientifically guided algorithms. One cannot say that Warren's opinion in *Brown* was empirically correct and Brown's opinion in *Plessy* was empirically incorrect in the same way that one can say Ptolemy was wrong about Earth being at the center of the universe and Copernicus was right about Earth orbiting the sun, for the simple reason that at the core of the difference between Justices Warren and Brown (or, for that matter, between Brown and the first Justice Harlan) was an argument about the *meaning* of legal segregation. Although arguments about the meaning of segregation may be *informed* by empirical data, they cannot be *resolved* by it.

A recent report by investigative journalists at ProPublica casts into high relief some of the pitfalls of ceding too much authority to supposedly objective, metrically based algorithms in the field of criminal justice. Titled "Machine Bias: There's Software Used Across the Country to Predict Future Criminals. And It's Biased Against Blacks," the report examines the practical effects of risk-assessment algorithms that are used "in courtrooms across the nation to inform decisions about who can be set free at every stage of the criminal justice system, from assigning bond amounts to even more fundamental decisions about defendants' freedom."[77] These algorithms, many of them proprietary and beyond public scrutiny, use a variety of factors to predict such things as the risk of recidivism. Race is not explicitly used as a factor, and yet the report shows that the algorithms consistently have disparately harsh impacts on racial minorities. Beyond the criminal justice system, Cathy O'Neil reveals in her recent book *Weapons of Math Destruction* how purportedly objective algorithms similarly produce racially biased results in everything from credit-score reporting to hiring decisions and insurance coverage. This bias is produced for the straightforward reason, O'Neil notes, that "math-powered applications [are] . . . based on choices made by fallible human beings," and so "many of these models encode[] human prejudice, misunderstanding, and bias."[78] Ceding authority to purportedly objective algorithms obscures the fact that algorithms, like fMRI images, are not natural entities but are built upon antecedent human choices and normative commitments about what should be measured and how.

The shortcomings of Kang's algorithmic approach for bias assessment and management can be brought into further relief by science studies scholars' critiques of similar algorithmic approaches to other areas of risk assessment and management.[79] Experts have frequently been baffled by public resistance to accepting their pronouncements regarding a wide range of risks, typically in the fields of health and environmental management (e.g., popular protests over genetically modified foods or nuclear power). This bafflement often takes the form of characterizing the public as suffering from one form of knowledge or understanding deficit or another. That is, popular democratic resistance to unquestioning acceptance of scientific authority is deemed somehow irrational or ignorant on its face. The knowledge-deficit model "is based upon the assumption that expert forms of knowledge . . . provide a sufficient basis for deciding the most important public policy questions. In this view, public perceptions and beliefs that run counter to this expert knowledge provide unacceptable justifications for public policies. Instead, support of expert knowledge needs to be 'built' through education and public relations strategies."[80] This definition nicely describes much of the behavioral realist paradigm.

Sociologist Brian Wynne has observed how this "public-deficit" model has evolved since the 1990s, but all are variations on the theme of the public's lack of understanding of or trust in science and the identification of this failure to acquiesce to experts' recommendations as a function of some defect or lack in the public itself—that is, the model identifies the problem as exterior to the scientific enterprise.[81] For Wynne, however, the misguided premises of an overweening scientism must also be seen as integral to accounting for what scientists cast as a public deficit. "What is typically called 'public rejection of science,'" asserts Wynne,

> is properly described as public rejection of commitments based on value commitments that are misunderstood and misrepresented by scientists and policy experts as if solely scientifically determined. The same entrenched cultural assumption gives rise to the deeply problematic habit of describing public issues involving scientific questions as "scientific issues" (or "risk issues,: and public responses as "perceptions of risk"). This culture of scientism, or institutionalized idolatry of science, is bound to treat public rejection of those things done in the name of science, as rejection of science, because it has already so falsely narrowed its moral imagination to the idea that support for the policy stance is determined by scientific fact, and that no alternative is left. Thus, some kind of public deficit model explanation of public rejection or mistrust "of science" is almost preordained as a function of this scientistic, culturally entrenched premise about the basic meaning of the issue at hand.[82]

The scientism that Wynne describes here resonates with behavioral realism and the idea that the law must be made to comport with science and that challenging science is equivalent to rejecting it. In proposing the "scientific" methods of cognitive psychology and neuroscience as a basis for breaking through the impasse of equal-protection law, behavioral realists imply that *if only conservative jurists and policy makers know the facts*, then they would surely embrace racial amelioration through affirmative action and other related programs. That is, behavioral realists cast the legal community itself as suffering from a knowledge and understanding deficit that can be remedied by embracing the behavior realists' scientific findings.

Not only is this stance empirically questionable, but it also further subordinates legal authority to scientific authority in a manner that blurs the relations both between normative and factual issues as well as between legal and scientific questions. We see this blurring of relations starkly in Jerry Kang and Kristin Lane's declaration that "once upon a time, the central civil rights questions were indisputably normative. What did 'equal justice under law' require? Did it, for example, permit segregation, or was separate never equal? This is no longer the case. Today, the central civil rights questions of our time turn also on the underlying empirics."[83] In the field of equal protection, behavioral realism is trying to make racism into an empirically verifiable "fact" of science in a manner that confuses empirics with meaning and undermines the authority not only of the legal profession but also of the democratic public at large to engage with, assess, and address the nature and significance of racism in contemporary American society.

Just as the risk–benefit analysis of much law and economics research often blurs the distinction between empirical questions of measurement and normative questions of what to measure and how to define its risks or benefits, so too does behavioral realism's focus on gauging millisecond responses to images in an IAT or on reading BOLD patterns in an fMRI image obscure the antecedent normative questions of why we are measuring those outputs and how we define the meaning of the results. Yet Kang characterizes behavioral realism itself as an algorithm that he explicitly contrasts with other more "common sense" forms of judgment based on "naïve psychological theories."[84] As philosopher Conrad Brunk describes the issue here, "Like the proverbial boy with a hammer to whom the whole world looks like a nail, to the expert with an algorithm, the whole world of decision making is reducible to the terms of that algorithm. For this reason, scientists with quantitative algorithms of risk assessment and management will tend to see only harms and probabilities easily reducible to quantitative measures as significant."[85]

Privileging algorithms privileges experts. On this view, experts are accountable primarily to other experts, not to judges and certainly not to "naïve" citizens. Behavioral realism not only elevates scientific authority over legal authority but also elevates unaccountable experts over officers and citizen of a democratic polity. Its valorization of all things metric may thus marginalize interpretive legal authority and the broader democratic impulses upon which it rests.

Such lack of accountability tends to reinforce existing structures of power. As Frank Dobbin and Alexandra Kalev note in their review of diversity-management programs, the programs based on psychological and behavioral interventions to reshape managers' attitudes did not increase workplace diversity but rather applied a mere patina of compliance to ward off lawsuits. Only programs with firm lines of managerial responsibility and accountability showed concrete results.[86] Similarly, many behavioral realist interventions in the legal system are targeted at changing judges' attitudes, not at holding judges or other legal officers *accountable* for racially disparate outcomes. Diversity-training programs, whether those of the NCSC or the U.S. Department of Justice, apply a patina of compliance but ultimately obscure accountability by ceding all authority to identify, measure, interpret, and redress institutional racism to the behavioral realist experts.

To reduce legal and political judgments to an algorithm fed into an Equal Protection Machine is to embrace a false and unobtainable technocratic ideal of conflict-free resolution to contingent and indeterminate social and historical problems. As Theodore Porter argues, the concept or ideal of objectivity "implies nothing about truth or nature. It has more to do with the exclusion of judgment, the struggle against subjectivity."[87] The claim to such objectivity provides the foundation of scientific authority in modern life. But behavioral realists improperly seek to extend the bounds of that sphere of authority to a position of dominance in the realm addressing race and racism in American legal and policy discourse. Behavioral realism's foregrounding of science thus evinces and promotes a deep distrust of the subjective process of judging itself. To exercise authority under this science-based regime, decision makers must subject themselves to the evaluation and direction of technocratic experts in cognitive and social psychology. They must be made to "comport" with science. But I argue here that legal authorities ultimately must strive not toward ending conflict through purportedly objective scientific interventions but toward managing it prudently, humanely, and effectively through, in the second Justice Harlan's words, "reasonable and sensitive judgment."[88] We are not in a conflict-free, postracial era, and we are not likely to enter such a millenarian epoch anytime soon. One thing is for sure, though: no algorithm is going to get us there.

DISTRUSTING JUDGMENT

In his classic book on judicial review, *Democracy and Distrust* (1980), John Hart Ely argued that "unless there is a special reason to distrust the democratic process in a given case, substantive review of its output, no matter how 'weak,' is not justified."[89] Behavioral realism is suffused with such distrust. But where Ely was concerned to address the countermajoritarian difficulty of having judges question laws enacted by democratically elected legislatures,

behavioral realism challenges the foundations of legal and democratic authority. For Ely, distrust involves judges asserting a counterbalance where the democratic process might trend toward majoritarian tyranny. Behavioral realism
distrusts the act of judgment itself—whether by citizens or by judges. It does
not trust citizens to be able to address racism without submerged, subliminal
interventions to nudge them in the right direction, nor does it trust judges to
reach "correct" decisions without the science of implicit bias to direct them.

For behavioral realists, ambiguity, discretion, and judgment are the
enemy because they are the means through which implicit bias enters the
world of behavior and affects people's access to goods and status in society.
They have a very valid point here, but their suggested interventions to
address such challenges tend to devalue, marginalize, and subordinate these
qualitative interpretive enterprises to the discipline of expert authority. Such
interventions are premised on the ideas that ambiguity can be erased
through rigorous measurement, that discretion can be contained through
objective standards, and that judgment can be directed by algorithms. Thus,
for example, beyond basic diversity training, we see among the diverse strategies developed by the NCSC for addressing implicit bias in the courts such
suggestions as "develop guidelines and/or formal protocols for decision
makers to check and correct for implicit bias" and "identify sources of ambiguity in the decision-making context and establish more concrete standards before engaging in the decision-making process."[90]

For the behavioral realist, ambiguity is bad because it creates space for
discretion; discretion is bad because it relies on judgment; and judgment is
bad because it is tainted by implicit biases. Although there is certainly a logic
to this way of thinking and empirical evidence to support the idea that discretion and judgment are often tainted by bias, the logic and evidence do not
necessarily mean that the best or primary way to address such problems is
to eliminate ambiguity, discretion, and judgment. For example, in the messy
reality of real-world interactions, there will always be a measure of ambiguity and uncertainty. The idea that behavioral realist interventions can definitively resolve such ambiguities and somehow purify our judgment carries
with it the danger of providing a false assurance of certainty that can mis-
guide us every bit as much as our implicit biases do. This idea also threatens
to obscure democratic accountability by asserting that expertly defined
metrics can be used to evaluate and address bias definitively, which absolves

political and legal actors of responsibility for the consequences of their actions. Critics of the diversity-management industry make this point when arguing that such programs function primarily to insulate corporations from lawsuits over discriminatory practices.

Perhaps behavioral realists who favor more aggressive responses to persistent racial bias have cause to distrust our current crop of judges and justices. Given the backlash in Supreme Court cases from *Richmond v. Croson* (1989) to *Parents Involved* (2007) and, more recently, *Schuette* (2014),[91] one can see their point. But their answer is to try to use the authority of science to perform a sort of end-run around the consequences of political losses involving both judicial appointments and larger political discourses of race and racism. Yes, if we trust judges, if we acknowledge their interpretive discretion, we risk getting lousy judges who make lousy decisions. But our generation can no more rely on "enlightened" applications of science to automatically guarantee racial progress than earlier generations could rely on "enlightened" applications of legal authority.

Wechsler was right, in a way, when he decried the fact that the Warren Court decisions were not grounded in "neutral principles," if by this phrase we mean the sort of algorithms favored by behavioral realists. How could they be grounded in neutral principles when the law most emphatically is not a science? Always there must be an argument. That is how democracy works, and that is how the interpretive enterprise of jurisprudence works. An uncritical embrace of science may provide the illusion of resolving such arguments, but illusion it is. And to the extent that it diverts us from engaging in the tough, contingent, qualitative work of explicitly contesting commonsense understandings of racism, it is a dangerous illusion.

Powell's opinion in *Bakke* evinces some of the tensions embedded in this distrust of interpretation. One the one hand, he invoked Oliver Wendell Holmes's pragmatism to affirm the imperative of judicial interpretation, declaring, "The concept of 'discrimination,' like the phrase 'equal protection of the laws,' is susceptible of varying interpretations, for as Mr. Justice Holmes declared, '[a] word is not a crystal, transparent and unchanged, it is the skin of a living thought and may vary greatly in color and content according to the circumstances and the time in which it is used.'"[92]

But then as the opinion unfolded, Powell retreated from the challenge of interpretation, seeking refuge in a very Wechslerian search for neutral principles, finding that "there is no principled basis for deciding which groups would merit 'heightened judicial solicitude' and which would not." Without such principles to guide him, he withdrew, modestly finding that "the kind of variable sociological and political analysis necessary to produce such rankings simply does not lie within the judicial competence."[93] But the same criticism could have been mounted (as indeed Wechsler did) against the opinion in *Brown* or against later opinions such as *Loving v. Virginia* (1967), which struck down antimiscegenation laws as unconstitutional despite the fact that they appeared to apply equally to blacks and whites.[94]

Powell feigned a lack of judicial competence, a lack of expertise, to engage in the sort of commonsense interpretive enterprise that led Warren to see segregation as imposing stigma in *Brown* and to see antimiscegenation laws as designed to maintain white supremacy in *Loving*. Here are the seeds of a color-blind constitutionalism that will not trust judges to make commonsense distinctions in the realm of equal protection. The real message here, one that lies at the heart of behavioral realism, is that racial justice is too controversial to be handed over to the vagaries of judicial discretion; rather, it must be contained and controlled by rigid neutral principles and algorithms. As Justice John Roberts emphasized in *Parents Involved*, "'Racial classifications are simply too pernicious to permit any but the most exact connection between justification and classification.'"[95] Exactitude is the operative concept here. Roberts constructed racial classifications as so volatile, so dangerous, so beyond the scope of commonsense judicial knowledge that they may be used only pursuant to findings of exact and, one might readily say, "scientifically verified" connections between justification and classification. Powell's modest demurrer of limited judicial competence is revealed as an abdication of judicial responsibility to engage head on the issues of the relative merits of different forms of racial classification and how they operate in society. Such abdication serves simply to validate and solidify the existing racial status quo.

Contrast Powell's false modesty and Roberts's fetishization of exactitude with Justice Thurgood Marshall's opinion in *Bakke*, where he used history to provide a context for scientific data. In the interpretive tradition of *Brown*, Marshall first stated that Bakke was not "any sense stamped as inferior by the Medical School's rejection of him." Marshall made stigma the gravamen of impermissible racial classifications. He went on to contrast Bakke's situation to "the position of the Negro today in America," which, he asserted, "is the tragic but inevitable consequence of centuries of unequal treatment." Moving on to recite various statistics revealing black disadvantages in income, health, and employment, he concluded that "at every point from birth to death the impact of the past is reflected in the still disfavored position of the Negro."[96]

Marshall did not eschew empirical data provided by experts, but he reserved to himself the right and the power as a *judge* to evaluate and interpret the meaning of such data in light of social and historical experience. Neither he nor Warren was trying to make the law "comport" with the data but rather to use the data to inform his judgment. There is a critical difference between using science to inform one's judgment and "following" the science. The former recognizes a place for scientific *evidence* in the legal system but does not subordinate legal authority to scientific *authority*.

In the *Bakke* decision, Marshall emphasized that Harlan's dissent in *Plessy* was first and foremost about the "real meaning" of the legislation at issue; that is, it demanded that the Court *interpret* the law in context. Harlan's dissent, Marshall noted, "recognized the bankruptcy of the Court's reasoning."[97] Reflexively subordinating legal judgment to expert authority is similarly bankrupt because it erodes the role of judges, undermining their responsibility for articulating principled reasons for their decisions and obscuring accountability behind a facade of "objective" expertise.

Algorithmic approaches to resolving questions of racial justice evince a profound discomfort with the uncertainty inherent in democratic processes and interpretive judgment. They promise risk-free, error-free results that are the antithesis of the messy and necessarily flawed products of all-too-human democratic deliberation. This shift toward making law more predictable and efficient has its roots in the conservative law and economics movement, but, as Jasanoff notes, "efficiency of systems . . . is not necessarily compatible with justice to individuals."[98] Jasanoff is here concerned primarily with addressing questions of expert testimony and the framing of environmental risks under *Daubert*, but her observations illuminate questions of how we deal with risk and uncertainty in spheres of racial justice as well.

Jasanoff's observation of a rising "disenchantment in contemporary America with the law's capacity to resolve the manifold technical disputes of modernity and a concomitant embrace of the imagined clarity, certainty, and rationality of science" resonates powerfully with Kang's declaration that "race talk in legal literature feels like it is at a dead end" and with behavioral realism's consequent ceding of authority to science as a means to further racial progress.[99] But the grand question for law, Jasanoff argues,

> is not how judges can best do justice to science; the more critical concern is how courts can better render justice under conditions of endemic uncertainty and ignorance. Once we focus on the latter question, it becomes clear that the law should not see itself as a simple transcription device for science, automatically writing into legal decisions whatever facts science has—or has not—generated in relation to specific controversies. Rather, the legal process should develop a more searching, self-critical awareness of its own pivotal role in producing new knowledge (and potentially hindering its production). Only by admitting its agency, and its limitations, in this regard will the legal system position itself to use science as it should be used in legal environments: for doing justice.[100]

The imperative is not to flee from uncertainty by asserting the false certitude of science in the social and political realm but rather to embrace uncertainty, to be held accountable for the decisions one makes under conditions of uncertainty, and to develop reasoned arguments to support one's *interpretations* of facts and laws implicating issues of racial justice. This endeavor in itself is risky. It does not guarantee particular results. But the crucial thing to bear in mind is that algorithms do not guarantee results, either—at least not in the realm of law and politics.

We see a well-articulated example of an approach that involves "a more searching, self-critical awareness of its own pivotal role in producing new knowledge" in Charles Lawrence III's discussion of the need to engage with questions of "cultural meaning" in racial law and politics. Lawrence argues that in cases such as *Brown* "the injury of stigmatization consists of forcing the injured individual to wear a badge or symbol that degrades him in the eyes of society. But in most cases the symbol is not inherently pejorative. Rather, the message obtains its shameful meaning from the historical and cultural context in which it is used and, ultimately, from the way it is interpreted by those who witness it." Lawrence consequently emphasizes the distinction between "causal" and "interpretive" analysis. "Causal judgments," he explains, "assert a causal connection between two independently specifiable social phenomena. An interpretive judgment, on the other hand, locates a particular phenomenon within a category of phenomena by specifying its meaning in the society within which it occurs." Behavioral realists are far more concerned with causal analysis, asserting connections between empirically verifiable phenomena such as IAT scores and aversive behavior. Interpretive analysis is, in contrast, grounded far more in disciplines such as history and cultural anthropology that seek to evaluate conduct—say, a law segregating schools—in terms of the "symbolic message to which the culture attaches racial significance."[101]

Lawrence also acknowledges that interpretation is a risky business. It requires us to trust judges and the enterprise of exercising *judgment*. And so he argues that

> it would not be a bad thing for judges to base constitutional decisions on their own sense of what values best reflect our cultural tradition, so long as the conflicting perspectives competing to define those values are made explicit. The search to define those values could then serve a clarifying, rather than a mystifying, role. It should be equally clear that the role of judges as interpreters differs from that of ordinary folks only by virtue of their responsibility to articulate their latest understanding of what we share. Thus, the normative debate would always continue.[102]

Risk here is managed by making judgment explicit—in stark contrast to behavioral realism's more submerged approach, which deals with risk through expert management and algorithms in a realm separate from that of "ordinary folks." The idea of a continuing normative debate is also critical. Racial justice is not something you "achieve" and then are done with. It is a process, a struggle, an argument that must always continue. This understanding of racial justice is antithetical to behavioral realism's use of the IAT to fix an end point for affirmative action remedies and its concomitant acceptance of the conservative frame for dating the exact time when racial justice will simply no longer be an issue.

Ironically, Lawrence makes use of cognitive theory in developing his approach. The very title of his foundational article, "The Id, the Ego, and Equal Protection: Reckoning with Unconscious Racism" (1987), indicates a deep concern for cognition and the psychology of racism. But he does not subordinate interpretative judgment to algorithms or qualitative evaluation to technologically mediated measurements. Kang himself notes this difference, observing that "Lawrence's methodology divines cultural meaning, whereas the 'implicit bias' research measures bias through individuals' reaction-time differentials."[103] The contrast between interpretation and measurement could hardly be clearer. Note Kang's use of the term *divine*, implying that the interpretive enterprise is akin to the oracular readings of sacrificed animals' entrails, whereas behavioral realism is grounded in the hard empirics of "reaction-time differentials."

Revisiting his article twenty years later, Lawrence was careful to distinguish his approach from the work of the implicit bias scholars, expressing concern that the latter may have "undermined" his project "by turning our attention away from the unique place that the ideology of white supremacy holds in our conscious and unconscious beliefs." He further expressed his "fear that cognitive psychology's focus on the workings of the individual mind may cause us to think of racism as a private concern" in a manner that vitiates our appreciation of collective responsibility for racial subordination.[104] Lawrence sees the backlash against affirmative action as indicating a flight from engaging with cultural meaning. We might understand this flight as yet another manifestation of "intentional blindness."[105] It is a refusal, much like the majority's in *Plessy*, to acknowledge or to appreciate the meaning of particular legislative acts as they function in distinct historical and social contexts.

In their study of "race in the American mind," conducted in 2009, sociologists Lawrence Bobo and Camille Charles used social survey data to assess the tenor of racial attitudes in white and black America across the previous four decades. "First and most centrally," they emphasized, "we offer a story of complexity." The study focuses more on explicit than implicit measures of prejudice but notes that "it is in some respects misleading to ask whether people are more or less prejudiced than in the past, since the answer often depends on the domain of life, the specific social context, as well as other individual factors at play, not to mention the exact standard for assessing 'prejudice' one chooses to impose."[106] One of the major premises of implicit bias research is that it purports to reveal prejudices when explicit measures do not. Yet Bobo and Charles's caveats indicate that such divergences are always what they appear to be.

The point here, however, is not to rehash technical issues over the validity of the IAT and related tools of behavioral realism. It is rather to recognize that the terrain upon which such tools work is complex and contested. Such complexity should give us pause before acceding to behavioral realists' calls to subordinate legal to scientific authority in the realm of addressing racial injustice. In the behavioral realists' claims to have mastered the problem of prejudice, their methods resemble what Jasanoff has characterized as "technologies of hubris." Such technologies involve predictive methods (such as risk assessment and cost–benefit analysis) that are designed, says Jasanoff, to "facilitate management and control, even in areas of high uncertainty."[107]

Technologies of hubris derive their authority from claims to objectivity and analytic rigor, but Jasanoff argues that they suffer from three significant limitations. First, "they show a kind of peripheral blindness toward uncertainty and ambiguity . . . producing overconfidence in the accuracy and completeness of the pictures they produce."[108] This might well be said of the sort of blindness to nonquantitative interpretations of cultural meaning that Lawrence identifies in behavioral realism. Second, "the technologies of predictive analysis tend to pre-empt political discussion."[109] This is evident in behavioral realism's demand that law be made to comport with science. Interventions conceived, implemented, and evaluated by experts do not allow for much in the way of democratic deliberation or debate. And third, "predictive technologies are limited in their capacity to internalize challenges that arise outside their framing assumptions." Here Jasanoff provides the example of techniques for assessing chemical toxicity that, although becoming ever more refined, "continue to rest on the demonstrably faulty assumption that people are exposed to one chemical at a time."[110] Similarly, the IAT is limited by its binary framing assumptions of black/white dichotomies that do not allow for considering the impact of intersectional identities on racial perception. Behavioral realism, in short, is overconfident. It makes racism too neat and tidy, too manageable, too convenient, and too governable by experts.

In contrast, Jasanoff argues that there is a growing need for "technologies of humility," which she characterizes as "methods, or better yet institutionalized habits of thought, that try to come to grips with the ragged fringes of human understanding—the unknown, the uncertain, the ambiguous, and the uncontrollable." Such habits of thought do not seek refuge from uncertainty in a false promise of metric exactitude governed by experts. Nor do they eschew expert knowledge and practices. Rather, they "acknowledge the limits of prediction and control" and call for "different forms of engagement between experts, decision-makers, and the public,"[111] where all meet on more or less equal grounds to have their voices heard. Although Jasanoff is speaking more to questions such as citizen participation in addressing the risks of nuclear power or biotechnology, her concern for a more humble approach to acknowledging the limits of expertise bears directly on the validity of the sort of qualitative interpretive enterprise evident in Supreme Court opinions from Harlan's to Warren's and in legal discourse from Black's to Lawrence's. Each opinion or discourse is engaged in constructing and contesting society's commonsense understanding of race and racism.

If we revisit Justice Antonin Scalia's opinion in *Wal-Mart v. Dukes* (2011), we can get a sense of the limits of behavioral realism as a technology of hubris. Recall that *Wal-Mart* involved Justice Scalia's rejection of Dr. William Bielby's expert "social framework analysis" of pervasive implicit bias against women employees at Walmart in order to deny class certification. Jasanoff, though, addresses situations such as citizen participation in notice and comment proceedings before regulatory agencies that develop environmental regulations. At first blush, these situations might seem quite distinct from Bielby's situation. But Jasanoff's concerns revolve around how discourses of expertise can marginalize popular voices and experiences while obscuring the normative implications of the actual limits of expert knowledge and techniques. Scalia's refusal to certify the class of women in *Wal-Mart* effectively amounted to a similar sort of exclusion of nonexpert voices from the table. Having the expert testimony to focus on, Scalia effectively dismissed evidence of individual voices presented by the plaintiffs as merely anecdotal.

In contrast, Justice Ruth Bader Ginsberg, in her dissent in *Wal-Mart*, noted that the "plaintiffs' evidence, including class members' tales of their own experiences, suggests that gender bias suffused Wal-Mart's company culture."[112] Ginsberg was able to meld common voices with statistical evidence, using them to inform each other. She did not elevate one as primarily determinative. Scalia instead adopted a statistical frame for assessing anecdotal evidence from nonexperts and declared that "a few anecdotes selected from literally millions of employment decisions prove nothing at all."[113] Here the technological hubris of behavioral realism's claimed ability to manifest empirical evidence of the objective reality of implicit bias played into Scalia's legal hubris that demanded ever greater assurance of absolute certainty before certifying a class. Ginsburg would have us hear the voices of the people. Scalia silenced and marginalized such voices by demanding statistical proof. He elevated the discourse of expertise to marginalize that discourse of democracy but then rejected the evidence proffered by particular experts as insufficient. Behavioral realism's true hubris, therefore, is its belief that through sheer technological power it can force (or persuade) conservative justices to accept what are ultimately normative claims about bias and discrimination.

Progressive and reactionary understandings of racial justice are always already present in American political and legal life. The challenge of breaking through the current Court's retrograde racial jurisprudence is not simply one of empirical proof; it is one of framing and imagination. This brings us back to Reva Siegel's trenchant critique of the Court's equal-protection jurisprudence. "If our legal culture supplies reasons for adopting the prevailing interpretation of equal protection," argues Siegel,

> it also supplies resources for imagining an alternative interpretation of equal protection. In much the same way, the legal culture of nineteenth-century America supplied reasons for adopting *Plessy's* interpretation of equal protection, as well as the resources for imagining the interpretation of equal protection that Justice Harlan proposed. In matters of constitutional interpretation, no less than in other spheres of life, the nation makes choices for which it can be held morally accountable. We now regularly condemn the interpretive choices the nation made during the Reconstruction era, but how are we to evaluate our own?[114]

By focusing on critical imagination, Siegel understands that engagement with issues of racial justice must ultimately be interpretative and creative acts.

No mere measurements or algorithms can win this argument. Siegel's discussion of the method of interpretive engagement ultimately sounds very much like Jasanoff's call for embracing technologies of humility. "Once we have judged the interpretive choices of our predecessors," urges Siegel, it is just as important to reflect on our *own* acts of interpretive agency: to ask whether we are rationalizing practices that perpetuate historic forms of stratification, as *Plessy* did. If we ask this question with the kind of skeptical or critical detachment that a historical understanding of our position affords, it is clear that having reasons for our interpretive choices is not sufficient; we must also take responsibility for their historical consequences. From this standpoint, it is not enough to condemn *Plessy* a century after the fact. We need also to ask ourselves what opinions like *Davis* and *Feeney* will look like a century hence.[115]

Such qualified, self-aware, and historically informed understandings acknowledge the limits of our ability to resolve questions of racial justice once and for all. There is no "end point" here to be measured by equal IAT scores. What we have instead is an invitation to engage in an ongoing struggle to shape our commonsense understandings of the meanings of race and racism in American society. This is a struggle whose end we can never know if for no other reason than that our knowledge and understanding will always be constrained by our place in history.

9

BIOLOGIZING RACISM

The Ultimate Technical Fix

In the aftermath of World War II and the Holocaust, scientists and social scientists alike worked hard for decades to distance genetic research from its eugenic and racist past. From the Statement on Race by the United Nations Education, Scientific, and Cultural Organization in 1950 to President Bill Clinton's declaration upon the completion of the first draft of the human genome in June 2000 that "in genetic terms, all human beings, regardless of race, are more than 99.8 percent the same,"[1] the primary myth challenged was the idea that human races constituted distinct biological entities.[2] Race reified as a genetic construct has nonetheless proven to be resilient, and like a zombie it seems to keep rising from the dead no matter how many times it has been struck down.[3]

The confluence of cognitive psychology and neuroscience in studies of implicit bias adds a new wrinkle to this dynamic. Where prior battles involved challenging the biologization of *race*, behavioral realism's embrace of neuroscience in exploring the nature of bias threatens to biologize *racism*— that is, to reify it as a material "thing" that can be empirically observed as a biological or physiological phenomenon and quantifiably measured by scientific methods. This tendency is reinforced when such methods as the IAT are paired with fMRI to produce glowing images of racism supposedly at work in the brain. Psychologist Jennifer Eberhardt touts the benefits of neuroimaging and related "psychological measures of racial bias [as] considerable" because "many of these measures are more continuous than traditional behavioral measures, they offer a wealth of information on the time course of responses. Some measures allow researchers to physically locate the phenomena of interest, such that precise predictions can be made regarding when and where race effects will emerge."[4]

Here is where we literally come to find "race on the brain." The idea of "physically locating" manifestations of racism in the brain reduces racism to a decontextualized physiological condition that tends to displace or obscure understandings of it as a socially and historically situated manifestation of power relations.

BIOLOGIZATION AND MEDICALIZATION

This neurophenomenon is related to but distinct from previous debates over whether to characterize racism as some form of mental disease. The medicalization of racism has roots in what John Dovidio characterizes as the "first wave" of psychological research into the nature of prejudice from the 1920s to the 1950s, wherein prejudice was seen as a "psychopathology" that was "simply a disruption in rational processes, [and] a dangerous aberration from normal thinking." It was viewed as a type of "social cancer." Dovidio sees the first wave being followed by a second, in which prejudice was reconceived as rooted in normal rather than abnormal processes, and then a third wave, beginning in the mid-1990s, which "emphasizes the multidimensional aspect of prejudice and takes advantage of new technologies to study processes that were earlier hypothesized but not directly measurable."[5]

These waves were not strictly successive, but rather accretive, with aspects of each wave surviving into the next. For example, the idea of racism as pathological survives not only in the work of specific researchers who continue to characterize it as aberrant and as a disease but also even in the conceptualization of racism in the second and third waves as a problem of cognitive functioning to be explored medically and technologically. The original concept of racism had two components: first, that racism was a problem located in the *body* (the brain) and, second, that it was *abnormal*. The second wave challenged the second component but not the first. The third wave similarly challenged the second component but actually reinforced the first through the introduction of powerful imaging technologies such as fMRI.

The trope of racism as a disease remains powerful and prevalent, as in Jerry Kang's influential behavioral realist article "Trojan Horses of Race," which likens implicit bias to a virus (a computer virus, but a virus nonetheless).[6] Mahzarin Banaji and Anthony Greenwald write of implicit bias as akin to an "infection" that we catch through exposure to negative stereotypes from an early age.[7] Similarly, psychiatrists Carl Bell and Edward Dunbar have an entry in *The Oxford Handbook of Personality Disorders* for 2012 that describes racism as a kind of "public health pathogen."[8] Even Charles Lawrence III, so sensitive to the complex cultural dynamics of racism, refers to it as a "disease" that "infects almost everyone."[9] In contrast to Kang, though, he describes it more as a "societal disorder or sickness" than something manifest primarily in individuals' brains.[10]

Prominent among contemporary proponents of the view of racism as psychopathology is Alvin Poussaint, professor of psychiatry at Harvard Medical School. Poussaint's concern is particularly with extreme forms of racism, which he thinks should be recognized in the *Diagnostic and Statistical Manual of Mental Disorders* as a "delusion" that when extreme may lead to attempts "to harm, and even murder, members of the despised group(s)."[11] As he put it in one interview with the *New York Times*, "If you have a mental process that leads some people to commit genocide, how can you not think that's a mental disorder?"[12] Similarly, James Dobbins and Judith Skillings analogize racism to addiction as a disease and propose "that racism has an etiology and a clinical taxonomy that lends itself to differential diagnosis and treatment of those who manifest symptoms."[13]

There have also been several powerful critiques of such medicalization of racism, however. Sociologist David Wellman argues that the conceptualization of racism as disease is based on four assumptions:

First of all, racism is assumed to be fundamentally a matter of cognition and perception, typically misperception. It is not about practices, hierarchy, domination, or exclusion. . . .

Secondly, since racism is constructed as ideological activity, it is assumed to be a holdover from slavery, a past mistake that has yet to be rectified. . . .

The third assumption is that, since racism in America is an anomaly, it is not normal—that it is, rather, a deviant and abnormal state. . . .

The fourth assumption is that this particular disease takes the form of an addiction, specifically "an addiction to a belief in the American myth that the standard and style of living that is enjoyed by 'successful' Mainstream Americans is due exclusively to their individual efforts."[14]

Recent neuroscience-based approaches to implicit bias share many of these assumptions but differ in one critical respect: they normalize bias as common and pervasive. Thus, for example, the NCSC report on resources for educating courts about implicit bias is premised on an understanding of "social cognitive processes such as implicit bias [as] . . . normal rather than pathological."[15] Similarly, we have Elizabeth Phelps expressing little desire to bring neurotechnologies to bear on the "overtly prejudiced" but rather choosing to concentrate on "'normal' people."[16] Her concern is with society at large rather than with the extreme manifestations identified by Poussaint and his ilk. Nonetheless, they all retain the medicalization frame, characterizing bias as a virus or a public-health problem. Moving from Poussaint's focus on the extreme individual to the typical citizen, behavioral realism actually extends the reach of the medical frame and the authority of the experts overseeing its assessment and redress.

Wellman certainly agrees that "racist beliefs are normal, routine, and acceptable in America."[17] But being pervasive does not mean something must still be understood in medical terms. Drawing on the work of sociologists Peter Conrad and Joseph Schneider, Wellman identifies four central problems with medicalizing racism:

First of all, when a problem is defined as being medical, it is removed from the public realm; it is no longer within the purview or the power of ordinary people. It is put on a plane where only professionals—in this instance, medical or mental health practitioners—can analyze and discuss it. Since the language of expertise is not generally accessible to lay people, the possibility for public debate is diminished.

Secondly, medicalizing racism individualizes troubles shared by all Americans. Causes as well as solutions to a complex problem are located in the individual, seen as problems someone "has," rather than as being rooted in the social system. The goal, then, is to "cure" the affected individual, not the socially constructed hierarchy.

Thirdly, by individualizing racism, the process of medicalization depo-liticizes what is essentially a public issue. Beliefs that exclude certain groups from America's social resources are treated as personal problems rather than political constructions.

Finally, defining racism as illness absolves the citizenry of responsibility for its behavior.[18]

Behavioral realist approaches to implicit bias generally fail to address these problems and may in fact feed into them.

Revealingly, in discussing controversies over the medicalization of racism, psychiatrist Carl Bell first points out that "some psychiatrists have advocated making racism a psychiatric disorder, whereas others have maintained that doing so is inappropriate because it would 'medicalize' a social problem," but then he comments that "it is amazing that neither side is willing to let scientific inquiry answer the question."[19] This sentiment resonates powerfully with behavioral realist contentions that law should follow the science in making claims about discrimination. In both cases, there is an eager desire to subordinate other forms of authority, whether social or legal, to the dictates of scientific experts. Such a move takes racism out of the realm of history and power and instead frames it primarily as a scientific problem, to be identified and addressed through purportedly objective scientific methods. Moreover, a special twist is added when sophisticated technological apparatuses, such as fMRI, are added to the mix. Neuroscience takes medicalized racism out of the sphere of a generalized psychological disorder and biologizes it as a physiologically situated phenomenon that can be observed and measured.

NEURAL NETWORKS OF RACISM

In 2000, Elizabeth Phelps, Mahzarin Banaji, and several other researchers collaborated on one of the first studies combining fMRI with the IAT. In language that would soon become the typical discursive frame for these sorts of studies, they purported to use fMRI "to explore the neural substrates involved in the unconscious evaluation of Black and White social groups." Using the fMRI to focus on the amygdala while subjects were taking an IAT, they first showed "White Americans" pictures of the faces of "unfamiliar Black and White Males" and found that "the strength of amygdala activation to Black-versus-White faces was correlated" with IAT responses. In a second experiment, they did not find similar responses when the stimulus faces "belonged to familiar and positively regarded Black and White individuals."[20] The researchers were concerned primarily to show a correlation between indirect measures of bias, such as the IAT, and fMRI imaging. But the study's underlying frame is what really matters here. Such studies opened the door to the idea that there is something called "neural substrates" to racism. This idea becomes the main theme of follow-up studies that continue to proliferate today. They all assume that there are neural substrates or neural correlates to something we call racism and that by using sophisticated technological interventions, such as fMRI, we can observe "racism" as a physiological phenomenon manifested in distinct regions of the brain.

Thus, twelve years later you have Jennifer Kubota, Banaji, and Phelps writing an article titled "The Neuroscience of Race," in which they discuss the "neural systems of race," by which they mean how "a network of interacting brain regions" light up in an fMRI when an American subject responds to "black and white race categories."[21] Conducting a comprehensive review of "all of the studies using fMRI to examine responses to black and white race categories in American participants," they find race on the brain almost wherever they look. From the amygdala to the DLPFC to the ACC and the FFA, wherever neuroscientists and cognitive psychologists look, they seem to be able to find race—or, rather, evidence of differential responses to perceptions of race made manifest as different BOLD patterns in subjects' brains.[22] That is, they find and, more importantly, construct racial bias as a physiological phenomenon defined in terms of the flow of blood within individual brains.

Behavioral realists have been very excited about applying fMRI to the study of bias because they see it as providing even more direct access to some purported empirical reality of racism than they consider the IAT does already. They are searching, as Jennifer Eberhardt puts it, "to measure pure automatic racial bias." Such technologies, Eberhardt continues, allow "researchers to physically locate the phenomena of interest" in the brain.[23] One recent study using fMRI responses to black and white faces to predict damage awards in hypothetical employment discrimination cases argues that "neuroimaging data can measure a racial bias that is reflected in juror decisions more effectively than a common behavioral measure—the IAT." The basic idea here is that whereas "implicit behavioral measures like the IAT still require some conscious cognition . . . fMRI measures can tap unconscious processes even further along the implicit–explicit spectrum."[24] Such studies are moving beyond simply correlating BOLD patterns observed in the brain with certain IAT-related responses to characterizing such patterns as direct representations of racial prejudice.

The idea of some form of "pure bias" that is accessible only through physiological measurements is particularly striking and revealing here. It implies that technologies such as the fMRI provide direct, unmediated access to some "thing" known as bias in the brain. In addition, the trope of purity casts consciousness as impure, contaminating some distinct, isolated, and somehow more true territory of unconscious bias. In this scheme, technologies such as fMRI have the power to erect and police such boundaries.

Eberhardt is acutely aware of the social dynamics of racism but sees potential in neuroscience to broaden and deepen our understandings of the socially constructed nature of race. Thus, she argues, "in examining changes in blood flow within the brain as people are exposed to race-relevant stimuli under various conditions, researchers can literally see the ways in which social knowledge about race can dictate neurobiological responses. Researchers are tracing the neurobiological effects of people's racial beliefs, attitudes, and knowledge in a manner that appears to highlight (both to scientists and to laypeople) the socially constructed nature of race."[25]

This may be the case, but I believe that Eberhardt and other researchers joining the IAT to fMRI do not sufficiently appreciate the power and unintended consequences of constructing racism as a physiological phenomenon in the brain.

It is striking how readily these researchers characterize racial bias as an empirically observable phenomenon in the brain. Granted, researchers are targeting areas of the brain that they think might be implicated in racial perception, but they seem almost never to have null findings to report. If we look back at some of the technical critiques of this methodology discussed in chapters 1 and 2, we might not be so surprised by their results after all when we consider that the human brain tends to be very good at perceiving *difference* and that society has made stereotypical racial phenotypes a very salient type of difference.[26] But the neuroscience literature generally does not frame the issue this way. Rather, Kubota, Banaji, and Phelps speak of the "neurocircuitry of race" as if it were some sort objectively real thing.[27] Moreover, what they are really talking about here is not the neurocircuitry of race per se but of racial perception and response—that is, racism.

And so you have psychologist David Amodio writing in 2014 of "*a neural network for prejudice*," which he characterizes as "a complex social cognitive process that seems to be supported by a network of neural structures."[28] Ultimately, you have scholars such as Martha Farah, director of the University of Pennsylvania's Center for Neuroscience and Society, declaring in an article on the ethical, legal, and social impact of neuroscience that it "deals with the biological essence of persons, including their minds and behaviors."[29] Similarly, we have Dutch psychologists Daan Scheepers, Naomi Ellemers, and Belle Derks contributing the essay "The 'Nature' of Prejudice" to a recent volume on the "neuroscience of prejudice and intergroup relations," in which they characterize "prejudice as a natural phenomenon."[30] By "prejudice," they mean things such as racism and sexism, and by "natural" they mean biological. This frame moves from observing certain responses to images socially coded as black or white to constructing an understanding of racism as something profoundly and essentially made manifest as a biological phenomenon hard-wired, as it were, into the very synapses of our brain.

Contrast this construction of racism with that provided by anthropologist Leith Mullings in trying to synthesize various approaches to racism grounded in the social sciences and humanities:

> What can we definitively say about racism? Racism is a relational concept. It is a set of practices, structures, beliefs, and representations that transforms certain forms of perceived differences, generally regarded as indelible and unchangeable, into inequality. It works through modes of dispossession, which have included subordination, stigmatization, exploitation, exclusion, various forms of physical violence, and sometimes genocide. Racism is maintained and perpetuated by both coercion and consent and is rationalized through paradigms of both biology and culture. It is, to varying degrees at specific temporal and spatial points, interwoven with other forms of inequality, particularly class, gender, sexuality, and nationality.[31]

Mullings sees racism as grounded in social, cultural, and historical relations. Most neuroscience studies of racism instead reduce the relations of interest to interactions among parts of the brain or, as Kubota, Banaji, and Phelps put it, to "a network of interacting brain regions."[32] These studies examine, for example, how the initial perceptions of racial difference manifest in the FFA activate responses in the amygdala or ACC, reflecting unease or bias, and how these responses then call into play the DFPFC to exercise a command function to suppress the initial bias response.[33] For Mullings, perceived racial differences get translated into inequality through social practices such as stigmatization and subordination; for neuroscience, racism is made manifest through fMRI maps of cognitive function taking place wholly within the individual subject's brain. Of course, neuroscientists and their behavioral realist colleagues are deeply concerned with how these cognitive relations ultimately manifest in individual behavior out in society, but their basic frame for constructing and understanding the nature of racism remains fundamentally oriented toward characterizing it not in terms of social relations but in terms of physiologically manifest phenomena within people's brains.

In the process of being biologized, racism is also naturalized and taken out of history, as if some sort of timeless attribute of the human brain. Like conservative jurisprudence, biologized racism has no need or use for history. It is all about the measurement and representation of racial perceptions in the present. Psychologists and neuroscientists studying prejudice tend to elide the distinctions among perception of difference, fear of outsiders, and racism as we understand it today. This is perhaps most evident in their occasional uses of analytic frames that borrow from evolutionary biology. For example, Damian Stanley, Phelps, and Banaji have asserted that "the linking of race-related implicit attitudes to amygdala function has strengthened claims of those attitudes' unconscious and automatic nature and bolstered arguments that they represent an evolutionarily conserved evaluative process."[34] Similarly, Amodio has argued that "in an era of increasing diversity, international relations, global communication and awareness of civil rights issues, intergroup biases are often deemed to be both personally and socially unacceptable. Preferences based on racial and ethnic categories that may have been adaptive in less complex societies are no longer so."[35]

Researchers using imaging technologies to explore the effects of the hormone oxytocin on racial bias are even more explicit, declaring that observed "racial bias in empathy may reflect an evolutionary strategy to prevent an inappropriate extension of in-group generosity to out-group members in order to benefit the survival of in-group individuals."[36] The concepts "evolutionary conservation" and "adaption" directly draw on the idea that racism is somehow a natural product of human evolution. The problem here is that, evolutionarily speaking, the "strangers" you would likely have been suspicious of were in fact not of different racial or ethnic groups but rather of the group over the next hill, whose members probably looked just like the members of your group. As one science journalist has observed, "Back when the human brain was evolving a few million years ago, our ancestors didn't get around much. They therefore had no chance to encounter people who looked different from themselves."[37] What we today call "racial groups" were historically simply too far removed from each other to provide a basis for evolutionarily adaptive cognitive xenophobic responses.

Mullings points out that "most historians agree that racism (a) is inextricably bound with the historical emergence of nation states, (b) is frequently built on earlier conflicts, and, furthermore, (c) emerges amid contestation."[38] These conclusions are very different from Dutch psychologists' idea of prejudice as a "natural phenomenon." As historian George Fredrickson notes, "To conceive of racism as a natural and virtually inevitable human response to encounters with strangers or aliens is to take the subject outside of history and into the realm of psychology or sociobiology."[39] But this dispute is about more than just disciplinary perspectives. It goes to our core understandings of the nature of the phenomenon being explored and thereby shapes our potential responses to it.

PILLS FOR RACISM

As behavioral realism and neuroscience construct racism as a common biological phenomenon, they render it susceptible to arguments for biological interventions. This step perhaps is where the biologization of racism diverges most significantly from the medicalization of racism. Whereas the latter pathologizes racism as an anomalous and extreme medical condition, the former constructs it as a typical and endemic phenomenon grounded in the cognitive structure of the brain. The concept of "biomedicalization" developed by sociologist Adele Clarke and her colleagues is useful here. In contrast to medicalization, which typically emphasizes "exercising *control over* medical phenomena," biomedicalization practices "emphasize *transformations of* such medical phenomena and of bodies, largely through sooner-rather-than-later technoscientific interventions not only for treatment but also for enhancement."[40]

Once biologized, racism does not need to be "diagnosed" by a medical professional because we all suffer from it due to the structure and functioning of human cognition. That is, cognitive scientists and psychologists have already "diagnosed" the condition as rooted in the very stuff of our gray matter. Racism is thus not some general form of illness but an empirical phenomenon that neuroscientists can localize to specific parts of the brain. The goal here is not to "cure" an anomaly but to modify a "fact of nature." Where medical professionals might come into play is in their role as prescribers of pharmaceutical interventions that might enhance the functioning of the brain, little more.

In biologizing racism, behavioral realism also introduces the possibility of biologizing antiracism. For Kubota, Phelps, and Banaji, "an obvious goal" of this research "is to discover the means by which we can control or eliminate [the] effect [of race attitudes]. Given the overlap in circuitry involved in studies of race and emotion regulation, we can take cues from research on regulation to develop interventions that might alter race attitudes."[41] Similarly, Amodio suggests that "the neuroscientific analysis of prejudice . . . can be used to inform interventions aimed at reducing discrimination."[42] On the one hand, his characterization of neuroscience being used "to inform" policy is far more restrained than Kang's call for law simply to follow the science. On the other hand, his suggested focus on "interventions that enhance the cognitive control of behaviour"[43] firmly situates the responsibility for crafting, implementing, and evaluating such interventions in the hands of psychologists and neuroscientists. Furthermore, it paves the way for interventions based on conceptions of racism as primarily a biological phenomenon to be addressed through biological or, more accurately, biochemical means. Writing in 2008, bioethicist Thomas Douglas suggested that "given this progress in neuroscience, it does not seem unreasonable to suppose that

moral enhancement technologies which operate on relatively simple emotional drives could be developed in the medium term."[44]

Enter Julian Savulescu, professor of practical ethics and director of the
Oxford University Centre for Neuroethics. Together with his former student
Sylvia Terbeck (now a lecturer at Plymouth University) and others at Oxford,
he published a study in 2012 titled "Propranolol Reduces Implicit Negative
Racial Bias." The stated aim of the study was "to examine the role of noradrenergic mechanisms in the generation of implicit racial attitudes."[45] (Noradrenergic mechanisms, generally speaking, involve neurotransmitters such
as norepinephrine, whose release is commonly associated with the fight-or-
flight response in stressful situations.[46]) To do this, the researchers administered a single dose of the beta blocker propranolol to thirty-six volunteers
"of white ethnic origin" in a "randomised, double-blind, parallel group,
placebo-controlled, design." One to two hours after receiving the drug or a
placebo, the participants completed both an explicit measure of prejudice
and took an IAT. The researchers found that, relative to placebo, propranolol "significantly lowered heart rate and abolished implicit racial bias, without affecting the measure of explicit racial prejudice."[47]

Propranolol is a drug commonly prescribed for cardiovascular conditions
such as hypertension. It works by blocking the action of epinephrine and
norepinephrine on both β_1 and β_2 adrenergic receptors so that as a result the
heart beats more slowly and decreases the blood pressure. Notably, propranolol is also used to help with performance anxiety, particularly among
musicians.[48] Basically, beta blockers tend to help people chill out. Therefore,
it might not be too surprising that it affects people's response times on an
IAT, given that such responses appear often to be mediated by feelings akin
to anxiety. As Amanda Pustilnik, senior fellow in law and applied neuroscience at Massachusetts General Hospital's Center for Law, Brain, and Behavior, observed in response to the study, "Because propranolol muffles fear
generally, it reduces automatic negative responses to just about anything."[49]
The real issue, then, is what such findings *mean* in context.

We get the initial indication of how the researchers in the propranolol
study constructed the significance of their findings not in their conclusions
but in their initial framing of the study hypothesis. As noted earlier, they
characterized the aim of the study as looking at the role of noradrenergic
mechanisms in "the *generation* of implicit racial attitudes" (emphasis added

here); that is, they were attempting to locate the generative source of implicit bias at the molecular level in the functioning of the noradrenergic system within individual human bodies. In this biologized framing, racism is not social, it is not historical, nor is it even interpersonal or medical in some general sense; rather, it is constructed mechanistically as being generated by the neurotransmitter norepinephrine.

Beyond this, the researchers asserted that propranolol "abolishes" implicit bias. This claim is critical. They were not simply asserting that propranolol affects response times on an IAT or perhaps masks the effects of implicit bias. No, they were saying that it abolishes implicit bias—the assumption here being that the absence of differential response times on an IAT is equivalent to the absence of implicit bias. By this reckoning, the IAT does not simply measure implicit bias; it is an essential component of the constitution of implicit bias. To deal with IAT response times is thus to deal with implicit bias. In an interview, Savulescu claimed that "such research raises the tantalising possibility that our unconscious racial attitudes could be modulated using drugs, a possibility that requires careful ethical analysis. . . . Biological research aiming to make people morally better has a dark history. And propranolol is not a pill to cure racism. But given that many people are already using drugs like propranolol which have 'moral' side effects, we at least need to better understand what these effects are."[50] On the one hand, Savulescu appears to disavow the notion that he is proposing the idea of a pill to cure racism; on the other, he is clearly stating that that is exactly what he and his colleagues seem to have found with propranolol. Before you know it, you have psychologists Mina Cikara and Jay Van Bavel enthusiastically citing "recent exciting findings . . . [that] may ultimately inform the design of better targeted interventions (including pharmacological interventions) for mitigating prejudice and intergroup conflict."[51]

Thus do we come to pills for racism, the ultimate technical fix. Pills have the initial appeal of being easy. They have the added incentive of being potentially profitable. Somebody has to make and market such pills. Considering that *everybody* has certain implicit biases, the market is potentially boundless. Such pills would be like statins for racism—something you take as a preventative measure every day for the rest of your life. Even if such pills are never fully developed and marketed, the propranolol study and other studies like it nonetheless reinforce a frame that casts racism as a technical problem to be understood and addressed through private means, in particular market interventions. In this regard, this frame is another example of privatizing antiracism and a natural extension of the diversity-training model that has capitalized the business of fighting implicit bias into a multi-billion-dollar industry.

Subsequent to the publication of the propranolol study, we have leading implicit bias researchers Calvin K. Lai, Kelly M. Hoffman, and Brian A. Nosek citing it as possible evidence of interventions that might reduce implicit prejudice.[52] Similarly, bioethicist Thomas Douglas (also at Oxford), referring to the propranolol study, suggested that just as "painkillers can reduce pain without correcting its cause[,] . . . [r]acial aversion, too, might be mitigated by means that leave its putative cognitive causes intact. Likewise, even if racial aversion is *partly constituted* by erroneous beliefs, it might be attenuated without correcting those beliefs. We might instead directly target the noncognitive elements of the aversion; for example, the physiological arousal that occurs when one is confronted with a person of different race."[53]

Just as the diversity rationale in affirmative action law reduces race to merely one of any possible number of individual attributes to be considered by an employer or school admissions committee, Douglas here uses the propranolol study to reduce racism to just another cognitive state—wholly divorced from its social or historical context.

Even more problematic is an article by David DeGrazia, professor of philosophy at George Washington University and senior research fellow in the Department of Bioethics at the National Institutes of Health, that embraces the Savalescu and Terbeck study's findings as demonstrating a form of "moral bioenhancement." DeGrazia includes "moral bioenhancements" among a list of things that "our public policies might support research into and possibly—if and when some forms of [them] are demonstrably safe and effective and the state is prepared to make them universally available—encourage or even require the use of [them] . . . to reduce or eliminate . . . prejudice."[54] Here we enter very treacherous waters.

In writing a letter of critique to the journal that published the Savalescu and Terbeck study, Tabitha Burchett and Lee Glenn argued simply that the IAT has not been sufficiently validated and that "the claim for clinical treatment due to amygdala suppression is unsupported."[55] Chris Chambers from

Cardiff University's School of Psychology cautioned that "we don't know whether the drug influenced racial attitudes only or whether it altered implicit brain systems more generally. And we can't rule out the possibility that the effects were due to the drug incidentally reducing heart rate. So although interesting, in my view these preliminary results are a long way from suggesting that propranolol specifically influences racial attitudes."[56] Similarly, bioethicists Immaculada de Melo-Martin and Arleen Salles noted that "it is implausible that a biomedical intervention would be so finely tuned as to be able to reduce fear to a particular object only."[57] In response to such criticisms, Savalescu, Terbeck, and their colleagues suggested they were referring only to the possibility of clinical treatment "in the abstract" and agreed that, "at this stage, it would indeed be premature for individuals, hospitals and clinicians to modify current practice in response to our study."[58] Of course, "at this stage" is the central modifier to this tepid caveat in which they also call for "further research" into the subject—the implication being that the study was in effect a test of theory paving the way for possible pharmaceutical interventions to treat racism in the future.

"Further research" did not take long to materialize. Taking a cue from work that used fMRI to examine the effects of propranolol on amygdala reactivity,[59] Savalescu, Terbeck, and their colleagues soon took the next logical step and conducted a follow-up study using fMRI to examine the "neural correlates" of the effect they found in their first study of propranolol and implicit bias.[60] In this study, the researchers looked back to Phelps's original study in 2000 using fMRI to examine subjects' brain activity while they were taking an IAT and, in effect, added propranolol to the mix.[61] They had forty subjects (again of "white ethnic origin") view unfamiliar black and white faces while in an fMRI after having taken either propranolol or placebo. They found "significantly reduced activity in the fusiform gyrus and thalamus following propranolol to out-group faces only." And again, as in the first study, they found that "propranolol lowered the implicit attitude score, without affecting explicit prejudice measure." They argue that their findings "support the conjecture that implicit aspects of racial attitudes have an underlying neural component in which face processing in the fusiform gyrus plays an important role" and that future work along these lines "could provide a plausible neurobiological substrate for the ability of propranolol to diminish implicit racial bias."[62]

It is important to emphasize that in their discussion of the findings the authors characterize propranolol as having a mitigating effect on *racism* (or as they put it "modulat[ing] racial bias"[63]), not on patterns of BOLD activation in the brain in response to perceptions of racial difference. This specificity reinforces the idea that racism is primarily a function of phenomena *within* the brain rather than a function of the sort of social and power-based relations discussed by Mullings. As these researchers directly link racism to "neurobiological substrates" that can be modulated through pharmaceutical interventions, they also render the workings of racism in a mechanistic fashion as a series of neurobiological steps (or perhaps, as Kang might have it, algorithms) that can be disrupted by drugs.

Along these same lines, in 2015 a team of Dutch researchers published a study on "reducing prejudice through brain stimulation." Like the propranolol researchers, they built their study around measuring responses to the IAT. Focusing on the role of the medial prefrontal cortex (mPFC) in stereotype activation, they randomly and equally assigned sixty participants to "to receive anodal, cathodal, or sham stimulation over the mPFC while performing an Implicit Association Test (IAT): They were instructed to categorize in-group and out-group names and positive and negative attributes." They found that "anodal excitability-enhancing stimulation decreased implicit biased attitudes toward out-group members compared to excitability-diminishing cathodal and sham stimulation" and concluded that the results "provide evidence for a critical role of the mPFC in counteracting stereotypes activation. Furthermore, our results are consistent with previous findings showing that increasing cognitive control may overcome negative bias toward members of social out-groups."[64] Like the propranolol studies, this work further reinforces the biologized and mechanistic frame within which racism is characterized as a phenomenon physiologically manifest in individual subjects' brains. It also feeds into the idea that similarly mechanistic biomedical interventions can influence or mitigate racism.

Think back to the sorts of implicit bias interventions suggested by the NCSC in its pilot programs for California, Minnesota, and North Dakota. Its focus was on using measures such as counterstereotyping and reducing the frequency of distracted or pressure decision-making circumstances.[65] Now along comes Thomas Douglas, suggesting that the propranolol studies vindicate the "biased judge" scenario he posed in 2008: "James is a district court judge in a multi-ethnic area. He was brought up in a racist environment and is aware that emotional responses introduced during his childhood still have a biasing influence on his moral and legal thinking. For example, they make him more inclined to counsel jurors in a way that suggests a guilty verdict, or to recommend harsher sentencing, when the defendant is African-American. A drug is available that would help to mitigate this bias."[66] For Douglas, taking a pill for racism in such a situation would qualify as a sort of moral bioenhancement that may be "instrumentally good."[67]

At first blush, Douglas's idea of giving pills to judges may seem a far cry from the sort of behavioral realist interventions suggested by the NCSC, but the two are logically connected. As the Dutch brain stimulation researchers noted, "The present results are consistent with previous studies showing that implicit biased attitudes can be controlled in several ways, for example, by emphasizing morality and thus the motivation to suppress them, by interfering with the functioning of cerebral areas devoted to the processing of semantic associations, or by pharmacological interventions."[68] Both the behavioral realist interventions and Douglas aim for a type of "cognitive enhancement" (i.e., reduction of implicit bias) through a sort of "submerged" manipulation of the environment within which judges operate; where one focuses on the external environment of judicial perception (e.g., screensavers), the other focuses on the internal environment of neurochemistry. Each aims to achieve change without requiring judges to discomfit themselves or challenge their understandings of their place in structures of power in the legal justice system, and all interventions are conceived, administered, and evaluated by experts. More to the point, Douglas, the intervention programs, and the Dutch researchers share an embrace of the idea of a technological fix for racism. As one member of the Dutch team put it, "Even if preliminary, these results provide the first evidence that racial biases are not immutable. As such, by means of brain stimulation, the dream of Martin Luther King of a society in which people will not be judged by the color of their skin but by the content of their character, may become a little closer."[69]

Who needs a March on Washington when you have the right pill for the job? Whether by brain stimulation, pills, or screensavers, it seems that the experts will bring about a millennium of racial understanding with little or no effort from the people. All we have to do is follow their directions and buy the products derived from their research.

CONCLUSION

Contesting the Common Sense of Racism

How do we know what we know about racism in contemporary American society? *Implicit* versus *explicit, individual* versus *structural, past* versus *present, law* versus *science*: there are too many binaries here. Each term is useful in its own way, but each directs us toward understandings of racism as a static "thing" that can be cordoned off, defined, and measured. There are no clear dividing lines. Each term constructs and is constructed by the other. Between conscious and unconscious bias there lie myriad way stations of self-delusion, suppression, "intentional blindness," and simple obliviousness. Between individual and structural racism, there is a constant interchange of past individual actions shaping the current structures of individual attitudes. Merely acquiescing to a structure that perpetuates racism might well be understood as a form of racism—but is it individual or structural? Both, of course.

Implicit bias cannot be understood apart from its social and historical context, which has been suffused with explicit bias for generations. Explicit bias is rarely acknowledged by individual subjects and often operates at a tacit, unspoken level of semiconsciousness. It is possible for individuals to benefit from structures that maintain racial privilege without harboring any racial animus. Yet they nonetheless implement and maintain those structures. We may wish to move beyond our troubled racist past, but that past is ever present. Without the past, the present has no meaning; without the present, we have no bearings from which to assess the past. Both law and science produce authoritative discourses of knowledge and power that shape our perceptions and actions in the world. They are distinct, but neither operates in a vacuum, wholly cordoned off from the other. We cannot escape the terms of these binaries, and so we need to set them in dialogue with each other rather than privileging one side over the other. Consider this conclusion a call for a sort of antisubordination theory of constructing and contesting the common sense of racism in American society.

Behavioral realism has much to offer, but we deceive ourselves and risk reinforcing years of racial backlash if we cast the science of implicit social cognition as a magic bullet. Bias may fruitfully be understood as a cognitive process that involves classification and making distinctions; in contrast, racism, although it may at times involve such cognitive processes, involves much more. Raising awareness of implicit bias certainly is a good thing. Using behavioral realist nudges to address "mind bugs" in areas involving discrete consumer-based market choices such as retirement investing and consumer safety might be productive and appropriate in many circumstances. (For example, libertarian paternalist choice architectures may perhaps be productively employed to encourage savings by having contributions to a retirement plan be a default option for employees.[1]) Generally speaking, however, such decisions do not implicate the sorts of complex social and historical meanings and relations of power implicated by choices concerning laws and policies dealing with racial justice. Statistics and measurement also have their place. In the 1990s, the American Civil Liberties Union and other researchers used quantitative analyses to mount effective legal challenges to racial profiling on our nation's highways and brought to light racial bias in pretextual traffic stops.[2] But the totalizing language employed by many behavioral realists raises the specter of mission creep, wherein examples of such productive interventions are extended far beyond their original warrant until we reach a point where we are being told that the "law should be changed to comport with science" and qualitative interpretation and that discretion must yield to algorithmic formulas for justice.

Looking back at Justice Earl Warren's opinion in *Brown*, Bruce Ackerman has recently argued that it was grounded in "two analytically distinct steps: the first, emphasizing the capacity of 'judges, and the rest of us, to make commonsense judgments about the prevailing meaning of social practices'; the second, seeking to determine whether we can 'buttress[] . . . commonsense conclusions with the findings of social science.'"[3] Judges must first of all exercise *judgment*. Science can inform this judgment, not make it. When it comes to racism, judges must interpret the commonsense meaning of a contested law, policy, or practice.

The great danger of uncritically embracing behavioral realism as an answer is that it often asks the wrong question. It presumes to measure racism (or, more tamely, bias) without fully considering the antecedent question of how racism itself is becoming manifest in new and different ways in different times and places. Racism is protean: as you try to grasp it, it changes form. The science of implicit social cognition may have a productive role to play in helping to challenge prevailing commonsense understandings of racism in American society—not by using its technical measurements of reaction times to establish causal connections in order to "prove" specific instances of biased behavior but rather by using such findings to inform broader arguments about the changing nature of racism. Where Anthony Greenwald and Mahzarin Banaji see their findings as supporting the idea that America is not a racist society but rather *only* suffused with implicit bias, I would suggest their findings indicate, to the contrary, that racism merely has taken on new and different forms in our world today.

This is not a simple semantic difference. It goes to the heart of understanding what the findings from the ISC science of *mean* as well as how they should be interpreted and used. First and foremost, this difference goes to make the point that ISC and behavioral realism cannot "solve" the problem of persistent racial injustice through merely technical means. Rather, at most, it can be a useful adjunct to buttress and enhance broader *interpretive* arguments about the ongoing reality of racism in American society today. It can play a role in helping us address the true challenge: gaining the sort of perspective on racism in our own time that Reva Siegel calls for, which is a necessary precondition to addressing it.

For example, we live in a world where juries and prosecutors continue to validate the idea that it is "reasonable" for police officers to be so afraid of young black men that their use of deadly force to subdue them is justified. To challenge this state of affairs, we do not need technical measurements showing that police officers harbor implicit biases. (Indeed, such findings, without more, might be used to validate the idea that their fear is reasonable). But such findings, if used thoughtfully and creatively, can be used to inform and strengthen broader interpretive arguments that such attitudes are *not reasonable*.

Here we might take a lesson from the Supreme Court's opinion in *Palmore v. Sidotti* (1984). This case involved a child-custody dispute in Florida, in which the divorced white father of a three-year-old child sought to have a prior award of custody to the white mother modified because she had moved in with a black man, whom she later married. The Florida trial court awarded custody to the father on the grounds that the best interests of the child would be served by protecting her from the "damaging effects" of being raised in a racially mixed household: "despite the strides that have been made in bettering relations between the races in this country, it is inevitable that Melanie will, if allowed to remain in her present situation and attains school age, and thus more vulnerable to peer pressures, suffer from the social stigmatization that is sure to come."[4]

When the case ultimately wound up at the Supreme Court, the conservative Nixon appointee Chief Justice Warren Burger, writing for a unanimous Court, firmly rejected this reasoning. He readily acknowledged that "it would ignore reality to suggest that racial and ethnic prejudices do not exist, or that all manifestations of those prejudices have been eliminated." But "the question, however, is whether the reality of private biases and the possible injury they might inflict are permissible considerations for removal of an infant child from the custody of its natural mother. We have little difficulty concluding that they are not. The Constitution cannot control such prejudices, but neither can it tolerate them. Private biases may be outside the reach of the law, but the law cannot, directly or indirectly, give them effect."[5]

The same might well be said of the "reasonableness" of perceptions of young black men as dangerous—or, for that matter, of the erasure of police violence against black women.[6] The Supreme Court's unwillingness to give legal effect to societal bias against children in interracial families can and should be extended to resist legally validating the reasonableness of racist stereotypes. Here ISC can help not by providing specific measures of police officers' IAT scores or even by promoting diversity-training programs to mitigate such biases in individual officers' minds, but rather by contributing to a broader discussion of the reality of continuing racism and the need to create standards that reject rather than validate the commonsense racial stereotypes.

Again, consider that in cases such as Michael Brown's, Trayvon Martin's, and Tamir Rice's, findings from ISC *could* have been used to reinforce the idea that the shooter's responses in each case was "reasonable" precisely *because* the shooter harbored implicit biases. Indeed, had evidence of implicit bias been introduced in these cases, the resulting legal exonerations of the shooters might readily be understood as examples of "the law [being made] to comport with [the] science." What is needed in such cases is not to "let the science speak for itself" but to put the science in the service of making a broader point about the pervasive reality of racism and then to take the critical step Burger took in *Palmore* by *refusing* to allow the legal system to become complicit in perpetuating the effects of such racism. Such refusal cannot be arrived at through the application of mechanistic algorithms. It can be made only as an act of judgment.

This is an argument for the long game in fighting for racial justice. Much as Justice Sandra Day O'Connor and others would like to see a temporal terminus for affirmative action, the struggle for racial justice is an ongoing affair. It has been with us for centuries and is not going away anytime soon. Already we see evidence that the current tide of racial backlash may be turning. Black Lives Matter and related movements are challenging decades of dog-whistle politics that have dehumanized African Americans as welfare queens and serial predators.[7] Such movements have created a unique moment to challenge the prevailing common sense of racism that has allowed for the dismantling of affirmative action, voting rights, and antidiscrimination law. But as the recent presidential election has made clear, such progress is not going to proceed unchallenged. ISC findings may yet aid in the process of stripping the veneer off a purportedly postracial, color-blind society—but it cannot do so by leading the way. Rather, its proponents must content themselves with a humbler role for their technology as a helpmeet to the broader, democratically based interpretive enterprise of reshaping the common sense of racism—of making sure that people come to fully understand that indeed black lives do matter.

In the recent case *Obergefell v. Hodges* (2015),[8] Justice Anthony Kennedy grounded his majority opinion declaring that states must allow same-sex marriage in the idea that recognizing basic human dignity is a core constitutional value. State actions that degrade, devalue, or otherwise subordinate individuals based on attributes deemed central to the integrity of their identity as full and equal human beings must be understood as unconstitutional affronts to this basic value.

In writing his opinion, Kennedy traced the history of marriage across millennia as an institution that "always has promised nobility and dignity to all persons, without regard to their station in life." He also characterized the evolution of women's rights as one where "society began to understand that women have their own equal dignity,"[9] thereby leading to the abandonment of understandings of marriage as an institution in which the woman is subordinate to the man.

Kennedy cast his opinion as recognizing the need to similarly move beyond earlier understandings that "did not deem homosexuals to have dignity in their own distinct identity" to the recognition and affirmation that "gays and lesbians [have] a just claim to dignity." Ultimately, Kennedy concluded his opinion by asserting that the petitioners were "ask[ing] for equal dignity in the eyes of the law. The Constitution grants them that right."[10] Kennedy located the constitutional value of dignity in "substantive due process" doctrine. The Fourteenth Amendment guarantees that the state shall not deprive any person of liberty "without due process of law." The basic idea of substantive due process is that the concept of liberty contains certain fundamental values and rights so important that any law affecting them must be subject to a close and searching review by the Court to ensure that they are not being improperly infringed. Kennedy argued in *Obergefell* that just as society's understanding of the nature and value of women's dignity evolved over time, so too has our understanding of the nature and value of the dignity of gay and lesbian people.

Ironically, however, our Supreme Court seems to have forgotten about the constitutional value of the dignity of another marginalized and subordinated group in American society—African Americans. For too long, our legal approach to racial discrimination has focused exclusively on the Fourteenth Amendment's guarantee of "equal protection of the laws." Current equal-protection jurisprudence focuses almost exclusively on whether an actor had the *intent* to discriminate rather than on the *impact* of the law. The Thirteenth, Fourteenth, and Fifteenth Amendments to the Constitution, all passed in the aftermath of the Civil War, should be understood in combination as a formal, constitutional recognition and affirmation of the fundamental value of the dignity of African Americans subject to the jurisdiction of our laws.[11] If we focus on dignity, as Kennedy did in *Obergefell*, the question shifts from one of intent to one of impact.

From *Plessy v. Ferguson* up through *Brown v. Board of Education* and *Loving v. Virginia*, those jurists most concerned for racial justice recognized that the core harm of racial discrimination was *dignitary*. That is, the harm was one that must be understood not only in terms of equal protection but in terms of fundamental rights, which are grounded in the sort of substantive-due-process analysis Kennedy used in *Obergefell*. In 1896, the majority in *Plessy* found no harm in laws that mandated separate but equal public accommodations based on race.[12] By definition, the facilities were equal and so technically did not offend the Fourteenth Amendment's guarantee of equal protection. In his dissent in *Plessy*, Justice John Marshall Harlan asserted that "the arbitrary separation of citizens on the basis of race while they are on a public highway is a badge of servitude wholly inconsistent with the civil freedom and the equality before the law established by the Constitution."[13] His concern was fundamentally *dignitary*—these laws degraded black people. It was grounded in the Thirteenth Amendment's prohibition of slavery and involuntary servitude, which applied not only to states but also to all people. In determining the amendment's meaning as applied to this case, Harlan did not apply technical metrics to gauge formal equality. How, then, did he know these laws were degrading, when the majority of justices seemed so sure they were not? He engaged in an interpretive enterprise to construe the commonsense understanding of the implications of these laws. That is, he engaged in reasoned judgment—in other words, he did what we (should) expect *judges* to do.

In 1954, when the Supreme Court struck down the doctrine of "separate but equal" in *Brown*, Chief Justice Earl Warren focused not on formal equality but on his understanding that "to separate [children] from others of similar age and qualifications solely because of their race generates a feeling of inferiority as to their status in the community that may affect their hearts and minds in a way unlikely ever to be undone." Warren did not declare that separate schools were technically unequal; he declared them to be "*inherently*" unequal.[14] This sort of inequality could not be measured; it had to be interpreted by understanding the commonsense impact that such separation has upon the children. It was the *meaning* of the separation *in context* that created the primary harm here, and that harm was *dignitary*.

A similar dynamic was at work in the case *Loving v. Virginia* in 1967, which struck down antimiscegenation laws. Technically, such laws treated blacks and whites equally—neither could marry a person of the other race—but the Court recognized such laws, when interpreted in context, "as measures designed to maintain White Supremacy."[15] There was no way to technically divine this design as the formal purpose of such laws; rather, the Court did so through an interpretive act that looked at the law in its social and historical context. Although the Court struck down the antimiscegenation laws specifically as a violation of the Fourteenth Amendment's guarantee of equal protection, I think we can also profitably see the Court's identification of the centrality of white supremacy in these laws as the flip side of Harlan's identification of the imposition of a "badge of servitude" as central to the law in *Plessy*—both affront the constitutional value of human dignity central to the Thirteenth Amendment and to all the Civil War amendments when read as a whole.

Trusting judges to judge can be dangerous. We are wary of giving unelected officials with lifetime tenure such power. It feels antidemocratic somehow. Such concerns were at the heart of the various dissents in *Obergefell*, which essentially accused the majority of circumventing the progress of democratic politics and pulling their concerns for the dignity of gay and lesbian people out of thin air. Yet, as Justice Kennedy recognized in this case, "the identification and protection of fundamental rights is an enduring part of the judicial duty to interpret the Constitution." Quoting the second Justice Harlan's dissent in *Poe v. Ullman* (1961), Kennedy recognized that this "responsibility . . . has not been reduced to any formula."[16]

When you have constitutional provisions that are fundamentally grounded in concerns for individual dignity, it is more democratic to trust judges than to rely on wholly unaccountable experts to define equality for us in the technical terms of metrics and algorithms without any concern for their meaning. A judge who merely follows the science is reminiscent of Oscar Wilde's cynic: someone who knows the price of everything and the value of nothing. That way lies the doctrine of separate but equal, with its cold metric logic and blind eye to substantive justice.

Brown and *Loving* were fed by and in turn fed into a growing grassroots civil rights movement in the 1950s and 1960s. One of the iconic images of this movement is a photograph of the Memphis sanitation workers on strike in 1968, wearing placards that declared, "I Am a Man." It was in Memphis that Dr. Martin Luther King Jr. delivered his "mountaintop" speech the day before he was assassinated. "I am a man" (perhaps better rendered today as "I am a human being") has roots in the abolitionist slogan "Am I not a man and a brother?" and in Sojourner Truth's "Ain't I a Woman" speech in 1851. These calls for the recognition of a common, shared humanity are based in the fundamental value of human dignity.

Today, we see this sentiment reflected in the Black Lives Matter movement. The call for racial justice must be understood as one with the calls for women's rights and gay rights. It is not just about equal protection under the law; it is about the substantive constitutional value of not being devalued and humiliated by the state on the basis of the fundamental aspect of one's identity.

The focus of our concerns regarding race needs to be on the harms done to the subjects—not on the perpetrators' intent. The decision in *Brown* did not turn upon the intent of those who passed segregation laws but on the stigma experienced by the children. Justice Kennedy's opinion similarly did not address the intent of marriage laws but the impact those laws had on the dignity of those whom they excluded. The daily indignities visited upon black people in the United States matter most not because of the intent of any given set of racist individuals but because of the impact they have on members of our community who deserve better. Perhaps we may hope that in considering future aspects of racial justice as they come before the Court, Justice Kennedy can expand his conception of the reach of dignity to include this group and these issues and thereby lead us toward a more truly decent society.

Ultimately, this debate is not solely about the law or legal doctrine. It is about how we understand what is at stake in framing and understanding claims for racial justice. The political philosopher Avishai Margalit has characterized a "civilized" society as one whose members do not humiliate one another. In contrast, a "decent" society, he proposes, "is one in which the institutions do not humiliate people."[17] From Ferguson to Charleston, the lives of the individuals killed surely do matter, but they were not just individual lives that were lost—they were black lives. The actions against them constitute dignitary affronts, denials of humanity, attempts to degrade and, in effect, to create or maintain a subordinate caste in society. They are indecent and unworthy of us.

Shared human dignity cannot be measured. Humiliation cannot be quantified. Once we get past all the testing and measurement, the cognitive science, and the social psychology, behavioral realism ultimately is a means to frame and tell a story about the nature of racism and its effects in American society. It is this story, not the technology itself, that needs to be contested. Behavioral realism cloaks its story in appeals to science and objective measurement, but it is a story that dismisses the significance of history and vitiates the significance of distinctive racial identities. When Reva Siegel asks us to "imagine a Court enforcing equal protection by asking whether a law's enforcement 'tells' minorities they are 'unworthy,' or by asking whether a law's enforcement 'demeans' and 'humiliates' them,"[18] she is recognizing that the closely divided Court might actually change in our lifetime. But she is not simply imagining that some future president might get to make some opportune appointments to the Court. She is also calling on all of us to contest the stories that are told about race in racism in our society today. This contestation demands that we situate our understanding of the law in the flow of history and explicitly call out the values upon which the ideals of equal protection of the laws must be based. We must push back against the false ideal of transcending race—we can no more transcend race than we can transcend history. To the contrary, we must double-down on race, as it were. We must recognize and own the continuing reality of racism in American society in all its forms: individual, structural, conscious, unconscious, and everything in between. We must acknowledge racism's past power and continuing salience in our world. And we must engage it forthrightly, without apology, without fear of offending those who would rather not see. Only in this way can we hope to change the story we tell ourselves about race, racism, and justice.

NOTES

PREFACE

1. Sylvia Terbeck, Guy Kahane, Sarah McTavish, Julian Savulescu, Philip J. Cowen, and Miles Hewstone, "Propranolol Reduces Implicit Negative Racial Bias," *Psychopharmacology (Berl)* 222, no. 3 (2012): 419–424.
2. Jonathan Kahn, *Race in a Bottle: The Story of BiDil and Racialized Medicine in a Postgenomic Age* (New York: Columbia University Press, 2013).
3. Michael Omi and Howard Winant, *Racial Formation in the United States: From the 1960s to the 1990s* (New York: Routledge, 1994), 60.

INTRODUCTION: RETHINKING IMPLICIT BIAS—THE LIMITS TO SCIENCE AS A TOOL OF RACIAL JUSTICE

1. *Milliken v. Bradley*, 418 U.S. 717 (1974); *Washington v. Davis*, 426 U.S. 229 (1976); *Regents of the University of California v. Bakke*, 438 U.S. 265 (1978).
2. The literature on the civil rights movement of the so-called Second Reconstruction is vast. A useful review of some key Supreme Court cases of the era can be found in J. Harvey Wilkerson III, *From* Brown *to* Bakke: *The Supreme Court and School Integration: 1954–1978* (New York: Oxford University Press, 1981); see also Michael J. Klarman, Brown v. Board of Education *and the Civil Rights Movement* (New York: Oxford University Press, 2007), which situates the jurisprudence of the era in a broader political context.
3. Ian Haney-López, "Intentional Blindness," *New York University Law Review* 87 (2012): 1779.
4. Owen Fiss, "Groups and the Equal Protection Clause," *Philosophy & Public Affairs* 5 (1976): 107. The literature on antisubordination jurisprudence is vast. A very nice review of some key themes can be found in the symposium volume "The Origins and Fate of Antisubordination Theory," *Issues in Legal Scholarship* 2, no. 1 (2002).

5. On the antisubordination school, see Jack Balkin and Reva B. Siegel, "The American Civil Rights Tradition—Anticlassification or Antisubordination?," *University of Miami Law Review* 58 (2003): 9–33.

6. Fiss, "Groups," 157.

7. *Brown v. Board of Education*, 347 U.S. 483 (1954).

8. *Plessy v. Ferguson*, 163 U.S. 537 (1896), at 559.

9. *City of Richmond v. J. A. Croson Co.*, 488 U.S. 469 (1989), at 494.

10. *Washington v. Davis*, 426 U.S. 229 (1976); *Personnel Administrator of Massachusetts v. Feeney*, 442 U.S. 256 (1979).

11. Haney-López, "Intentional Blindness," 1784–1785.

12. *Shelby County v. Holder*, 133 S. Ct. 2612 (2013).

13. See, for example, Adam Winkler, "The Supreme Court's Ruling and the End of the Civil-Rights Era," *Daily Beast*, June 25, 2013, http://www.thedailybeast.com/articles/2013/06/25/the-supreme-court-s-ruling-and-the-end-of-the-civil-rights-era.html; Scott Lemieux, "The Supreme Court v. Civil Rights," *American Prospect*, October 24, 2013, http://prospect.org/article/supreme-court-v-civil-rights; Patricia Williams, "The Roberts Court's Civil Rights Denialism," *The Nation*, July 2, 2013, http://www.thenation.com/article/175087/roberts-courts-civil-rights-denialism#.

14. Haney-López, "Intentional Blindness," 1783.

15. Ibid., 1783, 1779.

16. Reva Siegel, "Equality Divided," foreword to "The Supreme Court: 2012 Term," special issue of *Harvard Law Review* 127, no. 1 (2013): 4.

17. On the idea that the present conservative majority on the Court is due in part to the fact that liberal justices have been far less attentive to the politics of judicial succession, see David Leonhardt, "The Supreme Court Blunder That Liberals Tend to Make," *New York Times*, June 2, 2014, http://www.nytimes.com/2014/06/03/upshot/the-supreme-court-blunder-that-liberals-tend-to-make.html.

18. Balkin and Siegel, "American Civil Rights Tradition," 10–11.

19. Siegel, "Equality Divided," 94.

20. *Fisher v. University of Texas*, 133 S. Ct. 2411 (2013), aff'd, 136 S. Ct. 2198 (2016).

21. Siegel, "Equality Divided," 94.

22. For the phrase "intentional blindness," see Haney-López, "Intentional Blindness."

23. A foundational ISC article is Anthony G. Greenwald and Mahzarin R. Banaji, "Implicit Social Cognition: Attitudes, Self-Esteem, and Stereotypes," *Psychological Review* 102 (January 1995): 4–27.

24. In 2006, the *California Law Review* published a useful compendium of articles on behavioral realism: see "Symposium on Behavioral Realism," *California Law Review* 94, no. 4 (2006). Particularly useful explications of the idea of behavioral realism in the volume can be found in Linda Hamilton Krieger and Susan T. Fiske, "Behavioral Realism in Employment Discrimination Law: Implicit Bias and Disparate Treatment," 997–1062, and Jerry Kang and Mahzarin R. Banaji, "Fair Measures: A Behavioral Realist Revision of 'Affirmative Action,'" 1063–1118. See also Jerry Kang and Kristin Lane, "Seeing Through

Color Blindness: Implicit Bias and the Law," *UCLA Law Review* 58 (2010): 465–520, and Christine Jolls, Cass R. Sunstein, and Richard Thaler, "A Behavioral Approach to Law and Economics," *Stanford Law Review* 50 (1998): 1471–1550.

25. Jerry Kang, "Trojan Horses of Race," *Harvard Law Review* 118, no. 5 (2005): 1495.

26. Ibid.

27. Kang and Banaji, "Fair Measures," 1064.

28. Linda Hamilton Krieger, "The Content of Our Categories: A Cognitive Bias Approach to Discrimination and Equal Employment Opportunity," *Stanford Law Review* 47 (1995): 1187.

29. Ibid., 1188.

30. Damian Stanley, Elizabeth Phelps, and Mahzarin R. Banaji, "The Neural Basis of Implicit Attitudes," *Current Directions in Psychological Science* 17 (2006): 165.

31. In discussing the concept of "valence," Mahzarin Banaji and Anthony Greenwald note, "When categories can be linked to each other via shared goodness or badness, the shared property is what psychologists call *valence*, or emotional value" (*Blind Spot: Hidden Biases of Good People* [New York: Bantam Books, 2013], 39).

32. One foundational article has exerted a profound influence on the field but appears to be less central to contemporary discussions of implicit bias among psychologists than among behavioral economists. See Amos Tversky and Daniel Kahneman, "Judgment Under Uncertainty: Heuristics and Biases," *Science* 185 (1974): 1124–1131. Contemporary work by psychologists in this area tends to date more from the 1990s. One particularly influential article from this period is Greenwald and Banaji, "Implicit Social Cognition." Banaji and Greenwald recently published the book *Blind Spot* for a popular audience that nicely summarizes much work in this field. A useful overall review of the field can be found in Bertram Gawronski and B. Keith Payne, eds., *Handbook of Implicit Social Cognition* (New York: Guilford, 2010).

33. See, for example, Jennifer T. Kubota, Mahzarin R. Banaji, and Elizabeth A. Phelps, "The Neuroscience of Race," *Nature Neuroscience* 15, no. 7 (2012): 940–948; Stanley, Phelps, and Banaji, "Neural Basis of Implicit Attitudes"; William A. Cunningham, Marcia K. Johnson, Carol L. Raye, J. Chris Gatenby, John C. Gore, and Mahzarin R. Banaji, "Separable Neural Components in the Processing of Black and White Faces," *Psychological Science* 15 (2004): 806–813; and Jennifer L. Eberhardt, "Imaging Race," *American Psychologist* 60 (2005): 181–190.

34. See, for example, Jolls, Sunstein, and Thaler, "A Behavioral Approach to Law and Economics." For a recent review of much of the literature that applies the insights of ISC and behavioral economics to law and policy, see Richard Thaler and Cass Sunstein, *Nudge: Improving Decisions About Health, Wealth, and Happiness* (New Haven: Yale University Press, 2008).

35. Kang, "Trojan Horses," 1494.

36. Krieger, "Content of Our Categories," 1174–1176.

37. Kang, "Trojan Horses," 1499–1500; Kang and Banaji, "Fair Measures," 1068.

38. Greenwald and Banaji, "Implicit Social Cognition," 4–27; Banaji and Greenwald, *Blind Spot*; Project Implicit, "About Us," n.d., https://implicit.harvard.edu/implicit/aboutus.html.

39. Anthony G. Greenwald and Linda Hamilton Krieger, "Implicit Bias: Scientific Foundations," *California Law Review* 94 (2006): 945–968; see also Project Implicit, "Take a Test," n.d., https://implicit.harvard.edu/implicit/iatdetails.html.

40. Krieger, "Content of Our Categories," 1187, 1167.

41. Ibid., 1199, 1201.

42. Kang, "Trojan Horses," 1499–1500, 1508.

43. Ibid., 1499–1500, 1508, 1496 n. 28.

44. Jerry Kang, "The Missing Quadrants of Antidiscrimination: Going Beyond the 'Prejudice Polygraph,'" *Journal of Social Issues* 68, no. 2 (2012): 315.

45. Kang and Banaji, "Fair Measures," 1066.

46. Ibid., 1117.

47. Ibid., 1075–1076.

48. Ibid.; *Grutter v. Bollinger*, 539 U.S. 306 (2003).

49. For this comparison, see, for example, Kang, "Missing Quadrants," 316; Kang and Banaji, "Fair Measures," 1065; Krieger and Fiske, "Behavioral Realism in Employment Discrimination Law," 1001.

50. Krieger and Fiske, "Behavioral Realism in Employment Discrimination Law."

51. Kang and Banaji, "Fair Measures," 1065.

52. Kang, "Trojan Horses," 1496.

53. Quoted in "Clinton on Implicit Bias in Policing," *Washington Post*, September 26, 2016, https://www.washingtonpost.com/video/politics/clinton-on-implicit-bias-in-policing/2016/09/26/46e1e88c-8441-11e6-b57d-dd49277af02f_video.html.

54. National Center for State Courts, "Helping Courts Address Implicit Bias: Resources for Education," n.d., http://www.ncsc.org/ibeducation.

55. American Bar Association, "Implicit Bias Initiative," n.d., http://www.americanbar.org/groups/litigation/initiatives/task-force-implicit-bias.html.

56. U.S. Department of Justice, "COPS: Community Oriented Policing Services," n.d., http://www.cops.usdoj.gov/Default.asp?Item=2618.

57. White House, Office of the Press Secretary, "Presidential Memorandum—Promoting Diversity and Inclusion in the National Security Workforce," October 5, 2016, https://www.whitehouse.gov/the-press-office/2016/10/05/presidential-memorandum-promoting-diversity-and-inclusion-national.

58. Frank Dobbin, *Inventing Equal Opportunity* (Princeton: Princeton University Press, 2009).

59. Michael Omi and Howard Winant, *Racial Formation in the United States: From the 1960s to the 1990s* (New York: Routledge, 1994), 70.

60. Ibid., 55–56, 71, emphasis in original.

61. Thaler and Sunstein, *Nudge*, 4–6.

62. On oxytocin, see, for example, Feng Shenga, Yi Liua, Bin Zhouc, Wen Zhouc, and Shihui Hana, "Oxytocin Modulates the Racial Bias in Neural Responses to Others' Suffering," *Biological Psychology* 92 (2013): 380–386. On propranolol, see, for example, Sylvia Terbeck, Guy Kahane, Sarah McTavish, Julian Savulescu, Philip J. Cowen, and Miles

Hewstone, "Propranolol Reduces Implicit Negative Racial Bias," *Psychopharmacology* 222, no. 3 (2012): 419–424, doi:10.1007/s00213-012-2657-5.

63. Tiffany A. Ito and Bruce D. Bartholow, "The Neural Correlates of Race," *Trends in Cognitive Sciences* 13 (2009): 524–531.

64. Michael J. Sandel, "The Procedural Republic and the Unencumbered Self," *Political Theory* 12, no. 1 (1984): 81–96.

65. Martha Minow, *Making All the Difference: Inclusion, Exclusion, and American Law* (Ithaca: Cornell University Press, 1990), 20.

66. Among the foundational articles on these other categories are two by Kimberlé Williams Crenshaw: "Demarginalizing the Intersection of Race and Sex: A Black Feminist Critique of Antidiscrimination Doctrine, Feminist Theory, and Antiracist Politics," *University of Chicago Legal Forum* 8, no. 1 (1989): 139–167, and "Mapping the Margins: Intersectionality, Identity Politics, and Violence Against Women of Color," *Stanford Law Review* 43, no. 6 (1991): 1241–1299. The journal *Signs* recently dedicated an issue to the discussion of intersectionality: "Intersectionality: Theorizing Power, Empowering Theory," *Signs* 38, no. 4 (2013). It provides a very useful overview of some current scholarship in the area.

67. On the "submerged state," see Suzanne Mettler, "Reconstituting the Submerged State: The Challenges of Social Policy Reform in the Obama Era," *Perspectives on Politics* 8 (2010): 803–824, and *The Submerged State: How Invisible Government Policies Undermine American Democracy* (Chicago: University of Chicago Press, 2011).

68. Barbara Ehrenreich, *Bright-Sided: How Positive Thinking Is Undermining America* (New York: Metropolitan Books, 2010).

69. On "nudging," see Thaler and Sunstein, *Nudge*. On "unconsciousness raising," see Bettina J. Casad, Abdiel J. Flores, and Jessica D. Didway, "Using the Implicit Association Test as an Unconsciousness Raising Tool in Psychology," *Teaching of Psychology* 40, no. 2 (2013): 118–123. On consciousness-raising mobilizations, see, for example, Catherine MacKinnon, *Toward a Feminist Theory of the State* (Cambridge, Mass.: Harvard University Press, 1989), 83–105.

70. See, for example, Sheila Jasanoff, *Science and Public Reason* (New York: Routledge, 2012), and *Science at the Bar: Law, Science, and Technology in America* (Cambridge, Mass.: Harvard University Press, 1995), as well as Brian Wynne, "Public Engagement as a Means of Restoring Public Trust in Science—Hitting the Notes, but Missing the Music?," *Community Genetics* 9 (2006): 211–220.

71. *Schuete v. BAMN*, 134 S. Ct. 1623 (2014), at 1676.

1. DEFINING AND MEASURING IMPLICIT BIAS

1. Jerry Kang and Mahzarin R. Banaji, "Fair Measures: A Behavioral Realist Revision of 'Affirmative Action,'" *California Law Review* 94 (2006): 1064.

2. See Bertram Gawronski and B. Keith Payne, eds., *Handbook of Implicit Social Cognition* (New York: Guilford, 2010).

3. Ralph Adolphs, "Neurobiology of Social Cognition," *Current Opinion in Neurobiology* 23 (2001): 236, 231.

4. John T. Jost, H. Hannah Nam, David M. Amodio, and Jay J. Van Bavel, "Political Neuroscience: The Beginning of a Beautiful Friendship," *Advances in Political Psychology* 35 (February 2014): 4.

5. Curtis D. Hardin and Mahzarin R. Banaji, "The Nature of Implicit Prejudice: Implications for Personal and Public Policy," in *The Behavioral Foundations of Public Policy*, ed. Eldar Shafir (Princeton: Princeton University Press, 2013), 17.

6. Calvin K. Lai, Kelly M. Hoffman, and Brian A. Nosek, "Reducing Implicit Prejudice," *Social and Personality Psychology Compass* 7, no. 5 (2013): 315.

7. John F. Dovidio, "On the Nature of Contemporary Prejudice: The Third Wave," *Journal of Social Issues* 57, no. 4 (2001): 830, 831, 843, 842.

8. Amos Tversky and Daniel Kahneman, "Judgment Under Uncertainty: Heuristics and Biases," *Science* 185 (1974): 1124–1131.

9. Mahzarin R. Banaji and Anthony G. Greenwald, *Blind Spot: Hidden Biases of Good People* (New York: Bantam Books, 2013), 1–20, 4.

10. Richard Thaler and Cass Sunstein, *Nudge: Improving Decisions About Health, Wealth, and Happiness* (New Haven: Yale University Press, 2008), 22–31.

11. Banaji and Greenwald, *Blind Spot*, 16.

12. Thaler and Sunstein, *Nudge*, 23.

13. Banaji and Greenwald, *Blind Spot*, 11.

14. Ibid.

15. Thaler and Sunstein, *Nudge*, 26.

16. Daniel Kahneman, *Thinking, Fast and Slow* (New York: Farrar, Straus and Giroux, 2011), 20–21.

17. Thaler and Sunstein, *Nudge*, 19.

18. David M. Amodio and Saaid A. Mendoza, "Implicit Intergroup Bias: Cognitive, Affective, and Motivational Underpinnings," in *Handbook of Implicit Social Cognition*, ed. Gawronski and Payne, 357.

19. Brian A. Nosek and Rachel G. Riskind, "Policy Implications of Implicit Social Cognition," *Social Issues and Policy Review* 6, no. 1 (2012): 115.

20. Anthony G. Greenwald and Linda Hamilton Krieger, "Implicit Bias: Scientific Foundations," *California Law Review* 94 (2006): 946.

21. Ibid., 949.

22. Ibid., 948. See also Jerry Kang, Judge Mark Bennett, Devon Carbado, Pam Casey, Nilanjana Dasgupta, David Faigman, Rachel Godsil, Anthony G. Greenwald, Justin Levinson, and Jennifer Mnookin, "Implicit Bias in the Courtroom," *UCLA Law Review* 56 (2012): 1124–1186. These authors clarify that "an *attitude* is an association between some concept (in this case a social group) and an evaluative valence, either positive or negative. A *stereotype* is an association between a concept (again, in this case a social group) and a trait" (1128).

23. Greenwald and Krieger, "Implicit Bias," 951.

24. Damian Stanley, Elizabeth Phelps, and Mahzarin R. Banaji, "The Neural Basis of Implicit Attitudes," *Current Directions in Psychological Science* 17 (2006): 164.

25. Greenwald and Krieger, "Implicit Bias," 949.

26. David M. Amodio, "The Social Neuroscience of Intergroup Relations," *European Review of Social Psychology* 19 (2008): 5.

27. See, for example, David Harris, *Driving While Black: Racial Profiling on Our Nation's Highways*, American Civil Liberties Union Special Report (Washington, D.C.: American Civil Liberties Union, June 1999), https://www.aclu.org/racial-justice/driving-while -black-racial-profiling-our-nations-highways; American Civil Liberties Union, "ACLU of NJ Wins $775,000 for Victims of Racial Profiling by State Troopers," press release, January 13, 2001, https://www.aclu.org/racial-justice/aclu-nj-wins-775000-victims-racial -profiling-state-troopers, and "Racial Profiling," n.d., https://www.aclu.org/racial-justice /racial-profiling.

28. John Lamberth, "Driving While Black; a Statistician Proves That Prejudice Still Rules the Road," *Washington Post*, August 16, 1998, http://www.lamberthconsulting.com/uploads /washingtonpost_article.pdf. For a broader discussion of the phenomenon in the 1990s, see U.S. Senate, *Racial Profiling Within Law Enforcement Agencies: Hearing Before the Subcommittee on the Constitution, Federalism, and Property Rights of the Committee on the Judiciary*, 106th Cong., 2nd sess., March 30, 2000, http://www.gpo.gov/fdsys/pkg /CHRG-106shrg72780/pdf/CHRG-106shrg72780.pdf.

29. See, for example, Linda Hamilton Krieger, "The Content of Our Categories: A Cognitive Bias Approach to Discrimination and Equal Employment Opportunity," *Stanford Law Review* 47 (1995): 1161–1248; Christine Jolls, "Antidiscrimination Law's Effects on Implicit Bias," in *NYU Selected Essays on Labor and Employment Law: Behavioral Analyses of Workplace Discrimination*, vol. 3, ed. Mitu Gulati and Michael Yelnosky (Frederick, Md.: Aspen, 2007), 69–102.

30. Banaji and Greenwald, *Blind Spot*, 196.

31. Devah Pager, Bruce Western, and Bart Bonikowski, "Discrimination in a Low-Wage Labor Market: A Field Experiment," *American Sociological Review* 74 (2009): 777–799.

32. On health care, see Michele Goodwin and Naomi Duke, "Health Law: Cognitive Bias in Medical Decision-Making," in *Implicit Racial Bias Across the Law*, ed. Justin D. Levinson and Robert J. Smith (New York: Cambridge University Press, 2012), 95–112. On housing, see Michelle Wilde Anderson and Victoria Plaut, *Property Law: Implicit Bias and the Resilience of Spatial Colorlines* (Berkeley: University of California Press, August 2012), 25–44. On car purchasing, see Banaji and Greenwald, *Blind Spot*, 194–201.

33. Justin D. Levinson, Danielle Young, and Laurie Rudman, "Implicit Racial Bias: A Social Science Overview," in *Implicit Racial Bias Across the Law*, ed. Levinson and Smith, 10.

34. John A. Bargh, Mark Chen, and Lara Burrows, "Automaticity of Social Behavior: Direct Effects of Trait Construct and Stereotype-Activation on Action," *Journal of Personality and Social Psychology* 71 (1996): 230–244.

35. B. Keith Payne, "Prejudice and Perception: The Role of Automatic and Controlled Processes in Misperceiving a Weapon," *Journal of Personality and Social Psychology* 81, no. 2

(2001): 181–192. On the effects of racial priming in criminal justice settings, see also Jennifer L. Eberhardt, Philip Atiba Goff, Valerie J. Purdy, and Paul G. Davies, "Seeing Black: Race, Crime, and Visual Processing," *Journal of Personality & Social Psychology* 87 (2004): 876–893.

36. Banaji and Greenwald, *Blind Spot*, 32, 40.

37. Anthony G. Greenwald, Debbie E. McGhee, and Jordan L. K. Schwartz, "Measuring Individual Differences in Implicit Cognition: The Implicit Association Test," *Journal of Personality and Social Psychology* 74 (1998): 1464–1480.

38. Project Implicit, "About Us," n.d., http://projectimplicit.net/about.html.

39. Project Implicit, "Take a Test," n.d., https://implicit.harvard.edu/implicit/iatdetails.html.

40. Brian A. Nosek and Mahzarin R. Banaji, "The Go/No-Go Association Task," *Social Cognition* 19, no. 6 (2001): 625–664.

41. Banaji and Greenwald, *Blind Spot*, 45–47.

42. See, for example, Kang et al., "Implicit Bias in the Courtroom," 1133–1134. As one sociologist puts it, "This is the central insight of the IAT and implicit cognition research broadly that is most helpful to sociologists: the patterns of cognitive activation that occur without our conscious awareness, and that underlie the way we attach meaning to things, depend on and are organized by our social contexts" (Hana Shepherd, "The Cultural Context of Cognition: What the Implicit Association Test Tells Us About How Culture Works," *Sociological Forum* 26, no. 1 [2011]: 122–123).

43. John T. Jost, Laurie A. Rudman, Irene V. Blair, Dana R. Carney, Nilanjana Dasgupta, Jack Glaser, and Curtis D. Hardin, "The Existence of Implicit Bias Is Beyond Reasonable Doubt: A Refutation of Ideological and Methodological Objections and Executive Summary of Ten Studies That No Manager Should Ignore," *Research in Organizational Behavior* 29 (2009): 60.

44. Quoted in Shankar Vedantam, "See No Bias," *Washington Post*, January 23, 2005, http://www.washingtonpost.com/wp-dyn/articles/A27067-2005Jan21.html.

45. Ed Gordon, "NPR Interview: Are We Hard-Wired to Be Racist?," *News & Notes*, National Public Radio, December 4, 2008, http://www.npr.org/templates/transcript/transcript.php?storyId=97802442.

46. Jennifer T. Kubota, Mahzarin R. Banaji, and Elizabeth A. Phelps, "The Neuroscience of Race," *Nature Neuroscience* 15, no. 7 (2012): 942.

47. As discussed in Shepherd, "Cultural Context of Cognition," 123–126.

48. Banaji and Greenwald, *Blind Spot*, 192–193.

49. Greenwald and Krieger, "Implicit Bias," 954–961.

50. Banaji and Greenwald, *Blind Spot*, 47.

51. Kubota, Banaji, and Phelps, "Neuroscience of Race," 942.

52. Elizabeth A. Phelps and Laura A. Thomas, "Race, Behavior, and the Brain: The Role of Neuroimaging in Understanding Complex Social Behaviors," *Political Psychology* 24, no. 4 (2003): 755.

53. Greenwald and Krieger, "Implicit Bias," 959–960.

54. Anthony G. Greenwald, T. Andrew Poehlman, Eric Luis Uhlmann, and Mahzarin R. Banaji, "Understanding and Using the Implicit Association Test: III. Meta-analysis of Predictive Validity," *Journal of Personality and Social Psychology* 97 (2009): 17, 35, 29. See also Banaji and Greenwald, *Blind Spot*, 49.

55. Nosek and Riskind, "Policy Implications of Implicit Social Cognition," 122.

56. For such criticism of the IAT, see, for example, Philip E. Tetlock and Gregory Mitchell, "Implicit Bias and Accountability Systems: What Must Organizations Do to Prevent Discrimination?," *Research in Organizational Behavior* 29 (2009): 3–38, as well as Hart Blanton, James Jaccard, Erin Strauts, Gregory Mitchell, and Philip E. Tetlock, "Toward a Meaningful Metric of Implicit Prejudice," *Journal of Applied Psychology* 100, no. 5 (2015): 1468–81. Two recent news articles nicely summarize some of the most trenchant current critiques of the IAT's predictive validity: Jesse Singal, "Psychology's Favorite Tool for Measuring Racism Isn't Up to the Job," *New York Magazine*, January 11, 2017, http://nymag.com/scienceofus/2017/01/psychologys-racism-measuring-tool-isnt-up-to-the-job.html, and Tom Bartlett, "Can We Really Measure Implicit Bias? Maybe Not," *Chronicle of Higher Education*, January 5, 2017, http://www.chronicle.com/article/Can-We-Really-Measure-Implicit/238807.

57. Allen R. McConnell and Jill M. Leibold, "Relations Among the Implicit Association Test, Discriminatory Behavior, and Explicit Measures of Racial Attitudes," *Journal of Experimental Social Psychology* 37 (2001): 435.

58. Banaji and Greenwald, *Blind Spot*, 49.

59. Nosek and Riskind, "Policy Implications of Implicit Social Cognition," 123.

60. See, for example, Tori DeAngelis, "Unmasking 'Racial Micro Aggressions,'" *Monitor on Psychology* 40, no. 2 (2009): 42.

61. John F. Dovidio and Samuel L. Gaertner, "Aversive Racism," in *Advances in Experimental Social Psychology*, vol. 36, ed. Mark P. Zanna (San Diego: Academic Press, 2004), 3, 4.

62. Ibid., 4, 18.

63. Banaji and Greenwald, *Blind Spot*, 52, 158–159, 186.

64. Jennifer L. Eberhardt, "Imaging Race," *American Psychologist* 60, no. 2 (2005): 182.

65. Russell H. Fazio and Michael A. Olson, "Implicit Measures in Social Cognition Research: Their Meaning and Use," *Annual Review of Psychology* 54 (2003): 300.

66. Eberhardt, "Imaging Race," 182.

67. American Psychological Association, Science Directorate, "Functional Magnetic Resonance Imaging: A New Research Tool," n.d., http://www.apa.org/research/tools/fmri-adult.pdf; Center for Functional MRI, "What Is Functional Magnetic Resonance Imaging?," n.d., http://fmri.ucsd.edu/Research/whatisfmri.html.

68. Teneille Brown and Emily Murphy, "Through a Scanner Darkly: Functional Neuroimaging as Evidence of a Criminal Defendant's Past Mental States," *Stanford Law Review* 62 (2010): 1119, 1139–1140.

69. Elizabeth A. Phelps, Kevin J. O'Connor, William A. Cunningham, E. Sumie Funayama, J. Christopher Gatenby, John C. Gore, and Mahzarin R. Banaji, "Performance on Indirect

Measures of Race Evaluation Predicts Amygdala Activation," *Journal of Cognitive Neuroscience* 12, no. 5 (2000): 729, 734.

70. For a recent review of such studies, see Kubota, Banaji, and Phelps, "Neuroscience of Race."

71. Stanley, Phelps, and Banaji, "Neural Basis of Implicit Attitudes," 165.

72. Kubota, Banaji, and Phelps, "Neuroscience of Race," 940; Jay J. Van Bavel, Y. Jenny Xiao, and Leor M. Hackel, "Social Identity Shapes Social Perception and Evaluation: Using Neuroimaging to Look Inside the Social Brain," in *Neuroscience of Prejudice and Intergroup Relations*, ed. Belle Derks, Daan Scheepers, and Naomi Ellemers (Hove, U.K.: Psychology Press, 2013), 117–118. Indeed, one study of a white subject with bilateral damage to the amygdala in 2003 found no difference from a control subject's race IAT measures exhibiting an antiblack bias. This result suggested that the amygdala may not be critical to the expression of aversive racist behavior (Phelps and Thomas, "Race, Behavior, and the Brain," 754).

73. See, for example, Darren Schreiber and Marco Iacoboni, "Huxtables on the Brain: An fMRI Study of Race and Norm Violation," *Political Psychology* 33, no. 3 (2012): 313–330.

74. Jay J. Van Bavel, Dominic J. Packer, and William A. Cunningham, "The Neural Substrates of In-Group Bias: A Functional Magnetic Resonance Imaging Investigation," *Psychological Science* 19 (2008): 1135, 1131.

75. Kubota, Banaji, and Phelps, "Neuroscience of Race," 940.

76. Ibid., 940, 942.

77. Kahneman, *Thinking*, 20–21.

78. Kubota, Banaji, and Phelps, "Neuroscience of Race," 942.

79. Ibid., 943.

80. Ibid.

81. Tobias Brosch, Eyal Bar-David, and Elizabeth A. Phelps, "Implicit Race Bias Decreases the Similarity of Neural Representations of Black and White Faces," *Psychological Science* 24 (2013): 160.

82. Amodio, "Social Neuroscience of Intergroup Relations," 4.

83. Jost et al., "Political Neuroscience," 24.

84. Ibid., 29, emphasis in original.

85. See, for example, William A. Cunningham, Marcia K. Johnson, Carol L. Raye, J. Chris Gatenby, John C. Gore, and Mahzarin R. Banaji, "Separable Neural Components in the Processing of Black and White Faces," *Psychological Science* 15 (2004): 806–813 (stating that "these results provide evidence for neural distinctions between automatic and more controlled processing of social groups, and suggest that controlled processes may modulate automatic evaluation" [806]).

86. Van Bavel, Xiao, and Hackel, "Social Identity Shapes Social Perception," 112.

87. William A. Cunningham, Jay J. Van Bavel, Nathan L. Arbuckle, Dominic J. Packer, and Ashley S. Waggoner, "Rapid Social Perception Is Flexible: Approach and Avoidance Motivational States Shape P100 Responses to Other-Race Faces," *Frontiers in Human Neuroscience* 6, no. 140 (2012): 4, doi:10.3389/fnhum.2012.00140.

88. Christian Kaul, Kyle G. Ratner, and Jay J. Van Bavel, "Dynamic Representations of Race: Processing Goals Shape Race Decoding in the Fusiform Gyri," *Social Cognitive & Affective Neuroscience* 9, no. 3 (2013): 5, doi:10.1093/scan/nss138.

89. See, for example, Van Bavel, Xiao, and Hackel, "Social Identity Shapes Social Perception," 110–130. These authors state, "Based on our research on the malleability of automatic evaluations, however, we reasoned that flexibly construing people as in-group members might provide a powerful alternative to the traditional dual process models of control evident in previous research" (116, citation omitted).

90. See, for example, Cunningham et al., "Rapid Social Perception Is Flexible," 1.

91. Amodio, "Social Neuroscience of Intergroup Relations," 39.

92. Mary E. Wheeler and Susan T. Fiske, "Controlling Racial Prejudice: Social-Cognitive Goals Affect Amygdala and Stereotype Activation," *Psychological Science* 16, no. 1 (2005): 56.

93. Amodio and Mendoza, "Implicit Intergroup Bias," 364.

94. Quoted in Sharon Begley, "How Your Brain Looks at Race; Not Even Obama Thinks America Is 'Post Racial.' But Neuroscience, Like the Primary Results, Suggests We Are Not Doomed to See Things in Black and White," *Newsweek*, March 3, 2008. See also Andreas Olsson, Jeffrey P. Ebert, Mahzarin R. Banaji, and Elizabeth A. Phelps, "The Role of Social Groups in the Persistence of Learned Fear," *Science* 309 (2005): 785–787 ("In other words, because of its relatively recent emergence as an important dimension in human social interaction, race inherently cannot be the basis of the outgroup preparedness result" [787]).

95. Eva H. Telzer, Kathryn L. Humphreys, Mor Shapiro, and Nim Tottenham, "Amygdala Sensitivity to Race Is Not Present in Childhood but Emerges over Adolescence," *Journal of Cognitive Neuroscience* 25, no. 2 (2013): 244.

96. Nosek and Riskind, "Policy Implications of Implicit Social Cognition," 122.

97. Quoted in Begley, "How Your Brain Looks at Race."

98. Telzer et al., "Amygdala Sensitivity to Race," 234.

99. Nosek and Riskind, "Policy Implications of Implicit Social Cognition," 114–119, 125, 129–131, 130–131.

100. Adam R. Pearson, John F. Dovidio, and Samuel L. Gaertner, "The Nature of Contemporary Prejudice: Insights from Aversive Racism," *Social and Personality Psychology Compass* 3 (2009): 12.

101. Hardin and Banaji, "Nature of Implicit Prejudice," 22–23.

102. Amodio and Mendoza, "Implicit Intergroup Bias," 364–366. See also Saaid A. Mendoza, Peter M. Gollwitzer, and David M. Amodio, "Reducing the Expression of Implicit Stereotypes: Reflexive Control Through Implementation Intentions," *Personality and Social Psychology Bulletin* 36 (2010): 512–523.

103. Amodio, "Social Neuroscience of Intergroup Relations," 40.

2. THE UPTAKE OF IMPLICIT SOCIAL COGNITION BY THE LEGAL ACADEMY

1. Linda Hamilton Krieger, "The Content of Our Categories: A Cognitive Bias Approach to Discrimination and Equal Employment Opportunity," *Stanford Law Review* 47 (1995): 1164–1167.
2. *Price Waterhouse v. Hopkins*, 490 U.S. 228 (1989).
3. Ibid., at 235–236.
4. Ibid., at 250.
5. Krieger, "Content of Our Categories," 1172, 1183, 1161, 1185, 1201, 1216–1217.
6. Charles Lawrence III, "The Id, the Ego, and Equal Protection: Reckoning with Unconscious Racism," *Stanford Law Review* 39 (1987): 317.
7. Krieger, "Content of Our Categories," 1164 n. 11.
8. Lawrence, "The Id, the Ego, and Equal Protection," 317, 321–322.
9. Ibid., 317, 330.
10. Ibid., 317, 351–359, 324, 317, 358.
11. Charles Lawrence III, "Unconscious Racism Revisited: Reflections on the Impact and Origins of 'The Id, the Ego, and Equal Protection,'" *Connecticut Law Review* 40 (2008): 951.
12. Christine Jolls, "Antidiscrimination Law's Effects on Implicit Bias," in *NYU Selected Essays on Labor and Employment Law: Behavioral Analyses of Workplace Discrimination*, vol. 3, ed. Mitu Gulati and Michael Yelnosky (Frederick, Md.: Aspen, 2007), 75–76, 69.
13. Linda Hamilton Krieger and Susan T. Fiske, "Behavioral Realism in Employment Discrimination Law: Implicit Bias and Disparate Treatment," *California Law Review* 94 (2006): 1013.
14. Jerry Kang, "Trojan Horses of Race," *Harvard Law Review* 118, no. 5 (2005): 1496 n. 28.
15. Krieger and Fiske, "Behavioral Realism in Employment Discrimination Law," 1013.
16. Ibid., 1001, 1002.
17. Jerry Kang and Mahzarin R. Banaji, "Fair Measures: A Behavioral Realist Revision of 'Affirmative Action,'" *California Law Review* 94 (2006): 1065.
18. Jerry Kang, "The Missing Quadrants of Antidiscrimination: Going Beyond the 'Prejudice Polygraph,'" *Journal of Social Issues* 68, no. 2 (2012): 316.
19. Kang and Banaji, "Fair Measures," 1064, 1063, 1064–1065, 1066.
20. Kang, "Missing Quadrants," 324.
21. Kang and Banaji, "Fair Measures," 1067.
22. Jerry Kang and Kristin Lane, "Seeing Through Colorblindness: Implicit Bias and the Law," *UCLA Law Review* 58 (2010): 465.
23. Krieger and Fiske, "Behavioral Realism," 1016.
24. Ibid., 1042.
25. Brief for the American Psychological Association as Amicus Curiae Supporting Respondents, *Grutter v. Bollinger*, 539 U.S. 306 (2003) (Nos. 02-241, 02-516), 2003 LEXIS 179, at 5–6.
26. Brief for the American Psychological Association as Amicus Curiae Supporting Respondents, *Fisher v. University of Texas at Austin*, 133 S.Ct. 2411 (2013) (No. 11-345), LEXIS 3290, at 36–38.

27. Christine Jolls and Cass R. Sunstein, "The Law of Implicit Bias," *California Law Review* 94 (2006): 970.
28. Ibid.
29. See, generally, Nancy Gertner and Melissa Hart, "Employment Law: Implicit Bias in Employment Litigation," in *Implicit Racial Bias Across the Law*, ed. Justin Levinson and Robert Smith (New York: Cambridge University Press, 2012), 80–94.
30. Jolls and Sunstein, "Law of Implicit Bias," 969, 972.
31. Levinson and Smith, *Implicit Racial Bias Across the Law*.
32. Justin Levinson and Robert Smith, "Introduction: Racial Disparities, Social Science, and the Legal System," in *Implicit Racial Bias Across the Law*, ed. Levinson and Smith, 2.
33. Michelle Wilde Anderson and Victoria Plaut, "Property Law: Implicit Bias and the Resilience of Spatial Colorlines," in *Implicit Racial Bias Across the Law*, ed. Levinson and Smith, 35.
34. Charles Ogletree, Robert Smith, and Johanna Wald, "Criminal Law: Coloring Punishment: Implicit Social Cognition and Criminal Justice," in *Implicit Racial Bias Across the Law*, ed. Levinson and Smith, 47–48.
35. Michele Goodwin and Naomi Duke, "Health Law: Cognitive Bias in Medical Decision-Making," in *Implicit Racial Bias Across the Law*, ed. Levinson and Smith, 95–112.
36. Institute of Medicine, *Unequal Treatment: Confronting Racial and Ethnic Disparities in Healthcare* (Washington, D.C.: National Academies Press, 2003), 178. See also Danya Matthew, *Just Medicine: A Cure for Racial Inequality in American Health Care* (New York: New York University Press, 2015).
37. Goodwin and Duke, "Health Law," 111.
38. Jerry Kang, "Communications Law: Bits of Bias," in *Implicit Racial Bias Across the Law*, ed. Levinson and Smith, 132–145.
39. Kang, "Trojan Horses of Race," 1490, 1504.
40. Kang, "Communications Law," 141.
41. Kang and Banaji, "Fair Measures," 1090–1091, 1092.
42. Ibid., 1092. See also Mahzarin R. Banaji and Anthony G. Greenwald, *Blind Spot: Hidden Biases of Good People* (New York: Bantam Books, 2013), 146–147.
43. Kang and Banaji, "Fair Measures," 1093. Kang and Banaji also reasonably note that "our analysis assumes that the social category is in fact irrelevant to merit. If that is not the case for example, gender would be relevant to picking an undercover agent to infiltrate a gang of female bikers—then cloaking social category would be irrational" (1094).
44. Ibid., 1093. A recent edited collection explores the potential of blinding to address bias across a range of domains, from biomedicine to forensics to employment. See Christopher Robertson and Aaron Kesselheim, eds., *Blinding as a Solution to Bias: Strengthening Biomedical Science, Forensic Science, and Law* (Cambridge: Elsevier, 2016).
45. Kang and Banaji, "Fair Measures," 1096; see also "What Is Stereotype Threat?," Reducing StereotypeThreat.org, n.d., http://www.reducingstereotypethreat.org/definition.html.
46. Kang and Banaji, "Fair Measures," 1098–1099.
47. Ibid., 1104–1105.

48. Ibid., citing Nilanjana Dasgupta and Anthony G. Greenwald, "On the Malleability of Automatic Attitudes: Combating Automatic Prejudice with Images of Admired and Disliked Individuals," *Journal of Personality and Social Psychology* 81 (2001): 800, 807.

49. Kang and Banaji, "Fair Measures," 1105–1107, 1108.

50. Kang, "Trojan Horses of Race," 1537.

51. Tabitha C. Peck, Sonia Seinfeld, Salvatore M. Aglioti, and Mel Slater, "Putting Yourself in the Skin of a Black Avatar Reduces Implicit Racial Bias," *Consciousness and Cognition* 22, no. 3 (2013): 779.

52. Kang and Banaji, "Fair Measures," 1109.

53. Ibid., 1109, 1115.

54. On educating personnel in law enforcement and the judiciary, see, for example, Christian M. Halliburton, "Race, Brain Science, and Critical Decision-Making in the Context of Constitutional Criminal Procedure," *Gonzaga Law Review* 47 (2012): 333–334. On educating employers, real estate agents, media executives, and so on, see Levinson and Smith, *Implicit Racial Bias Across the Law,* passim.

55. American Bar Association, "Task Force on Implicit Bias," n.d., http://www.americanbar .org/groups/litigation/initiatives/task-force-implicit-bias.html.

56. Center for Judiciary Education and Research, "The Neuroscience and Psychology of Decisionmaking," n.d., http://www2.courtinfo.ca.gov/cjer/aoctv/dialogue/neuro/index .htm.

57. Center for Judiciary Education and Research, *A New Way of Learning* (video), October 28, 2009, http://www2.courtinfo.ca.gov/cjer/857.htm.

58. Center for Judiciary Education and Research, *The Media, the Brain, and the Courtroom* (video), March 30, 2010, http://www2.courtinfo.ca.gov/cjer/863.htm

59. Center for Judiciary Education and Research, *Dismantling and Overriding Bias* (video), June 29, 2010, http://www2.courtinfo.ca.gov/cjer/864.htm.

60. National Center for State Courts, "Helping Courts Address Implicit Bias: Resources for Education," n.d., http://www.ncsc.org/ibeducation.

61. Pamela M. Casey, Roger K. Warren, Fred L. Cheesman II, and Jennifer K. Elek, *Helping Courts Address Implicit Bias: Resources for Education* (Washington, D.C.: National Center for State Courts, 2012), http://www.ncsc.org/ibreport.

62. Jerry Kang, Judge Mark Bennett, Devon Carbado, Pam Casey, Nilanjana Dasgupta, David Faigman, Rachel Godsil, Anthony G. Greenwald, Justin Levinson, and Jennifer Mnookin, "Implicit Bias in the Courtroom," *UCLA Law Review* 56 (2012): 1174–1176.

63. Ibid., 1176.

64. Justine E. Tinkler, "Controversies in Implicit Race Bias Research," *Sociology Compass* 6, no. 12 (2012): 989.

65. Hal R. Arkes and Philip E. Tetlock, "Attributions of Implicit Prejudice, or 'Would Jesse Jackson Fail the Implicit Association Test?'" *Psychological Inquiry* 15, no. 4 (2004): 257–278.

66. Hart Blanton, James Jaccard, Erin Strauts, Gregory Mitchell, and Philip E. Tetlock, "Toward a Meaningful Metric of Implicit Prejudice," *Journal of Applied Psychology* 100, no. 5 (2015): 1468–1481.

67. See, generally, Gregory Mitchell and Philip E. Tetlock, "Antidiscrimination Law and the Perils of Mindreading," *Ohio State Law Journal* 67 (2006): 1180–1192; Philip E. Tetlock and Gregory Mitchell, "Implicit Bias and Accountability Systems: What Must Organizations Do to Prevent Discrimination?," *Research in Organizational Behavior* 29 (2009): 3–38. See also Phillip Atiba Goff and Kimberly Barsamian Kahn, "How Psychological Science Impedes Intentional Thinking," *Du Bois Review* 10, no. 2 (2013): 365–384 ("There is a disciplinary tendency for social psychological science to value experimental rigor and causality over the ability to generalize beyond the lab" [369]).

68. Tetlock and Mitchell, "Implicit Bias and Accountability Systems," 4.

69. Anthony G. Greenwald, T. Andrew Poehlman, Eric Luis Uhlmann, and Mahzarin R. Banaji, "Understanding and Using the Implicit Association Test: III. Meta-analysis of Predictive Validity," *Journal of Personality and Social Psychology* 97 (2009): 17–41.

70. John T. Jost, Laurie A. Rudman, Irene V. Blair, Dana R. Carney, Nilanjana Dasgupta, Jack Glaser, and Curtis D. Hardin, "The Existence of Implicit Bias Is Beyond Reasonable Doubt: A Refutation of Ideological and Methodological Objections and Executive Summary of Ten Studies That No Manager Should Ignore," *Research in Organizational Behavior* 29 (2009): 39, 60.

71. Kang and Lane, "Seeing Through Colorblindness," 505–508.

72. Daniel Kahneman, "A Proposal to Deal with Questions About Priming Effects," September 26, 2012, quoted in Ed Yong, "Nobel Laureate Challenges Psychologists to Clean Up Their Act," *Nature News*, October 3, 2012, http://www.nature.com/news/nobel-laureate -challenges-psychologists-to-clean-up-their-act-1.11535.

73. Joseph Henrich, Steven J. Heine, and Ara Norenzayan, "The Weirdest People in the World?," *Behavioral and Brain Sciences* 33 (2010): 61.

74. Ibid. See also Robert Burton, *A Skeptics Guide to the Mind* (New York: St. Martin's Press, 2013), 105–107.

75. Katherine S. Button, John P. A. Ioannidis, Claire Mokrysz, Brian A. Nosek, Jonathan Flint, Emma S. J. Robinson, and Marcus R. Munafò, "Power Failure: Why Small Sample Size Undermines the Reliability of Neuroscience," *Nature Reviews Neuroscience* 14 (2013): 1.

76. Daniel Margulies, "The Salmon of Doubt: Six Months of Methodological Controversy Within Social Neuroscience," in *Critical Neuroscience: A Handbook of the Social and Cultural Contexts of Neuroscience*, ed. Suparna Choudhury and Jan Slaby (Hoboken, N.J.: Wiley-Blackwell, 2012), 273–285.

77. Craig M. Bennett, Abigail A. Baird, Michael B. Miller, and George L. Wolford, "Neural Correlates of Interspecies Perspective Taking in the Post-mortem Atlantic Salmon: An Argument for Multiple Comparisons Correction," n.d., http://prefrontal.org/files/post-ers/Bennett-Salmon-2009.pdf.

78. Quoted in Alexis Madrigal, "Scanning Dead Salmon in fMRI Machine Highlights Risk of Red Herrings," *Wired*, September 18, 2009, http://www.wired.com/2009/09/fmrisalmon/.

79. Ibid.

80. Joseph Dumit, "Critically Producing Brain Images of Mind," in *Critical Neuroscience*, ed. Choudhury and Slaby, 198–199.

81. Edward Vul, Christine Harris, Piotr Winkielman, and Harold Pashler, "Puzzlingly High Correlations in fMRI Studies of Emotion, Personality, and Social Cognition," *Perspectives on Psychological Science* 4 (2009): 274–290.

82. Ibid. For a general discussion of the controversy elicited by "Puzzlingly High Correlations in fMRI Studies," see Margulies, "Salmon of Doubt."

83. Lawrence, "Unconscious Racism Revisited," 942, 960, 962–963.

84. Ibid., 964.

85. Eduardo Bonilla-Silva, *Racism Without Racists: Color-Blind Racism and the Persistence of Racial Inequality in America*, 4th ed. (Lanham, Md.: Rowman and Littlefield, 2014).

86. David Wellman, "Unconscious Racism, Social Cognition Theory, and the Legal Intent Doctrine: The Neuron Fires Next Time," in *Handbook of Racial and Ethnic Relations*, ed. Hernán Vera and Joe R. Feagin (New York: Springer Science, 2007), 41, 41–45, 51.

87. Ibid., 48, 51.

88. Ibid., 55–56. See also Lawrence Bobo and Ryan A. Smith, "From Jim Crow Racism to Laissez-Faire Racism: The Transformation of Racial Attitudes," In *Beyond Pluralism: The Conception of Groups and Group Identities in America*, ed. Wendy Katkin, Ned Landsman, and Andrea Tyree (Urbana: University of Illinois Press, 1998), 182–220.

89. Ralph Richard Banks and Richard Thompson Ford, "(How) Does Unconscious Bias Matter? Law, Politics, and Racial Inequality," *Emory Law Journal* 58 (2009): 1058–1065, 1054.

90. Ibid., 1058–1059, 1073, 1074, 1080, 1085.

91. Ibid., 1089–1093. See also *Price Waterhouse v. Hopkins*, 490 U.S. 228 (1989), and *Washington v. Davis*, 426 U.S. 229 (1976).

92. Banks and Ford, "(How) Does Unconscious Bias Matter?," 1113, 1116–1117, 1120–1121.

93. Stephen M. Rich, "Against Prejudice," *George Washington Law Review* 80 (2011): 40, 94, 56.

94. Jerry Kang, "Implicit Bias and the Pushback from the Left," *Saint Louis University Law Journal* 54 (2010): 1142, 1145, 1147, 1148–1149.

3. ACCEPTING CONSERVATIVE FRAMES: TIME, COLOR BLINDNESS, DIVERSITY, AND INTENT

1. Charles Lawrence III, "Education Law: Unconscious Racism and the Conversation About the Racial Achievement Gap," in *Implicit Racial Bias Across the Law*, ed. Justin D. Levinson and Robert J. Smith (New York: Cambridge University Press, 2012), 119.

2. Suzanne Mettler, "20,000 Leagues Under the State," *Washington Monthly*, July–August 2011, http://washingtonmonthly.com/magazine/julyaug-2011/20000-leagues-under-the-state/.

3. Suzanne Mettler, "Reconstituting the Submerged State: The Challenges of Social Policy Reform in the Obama Era," *Perspectives on Politics* 8 (2010): 804.

4. "Cass Sunstein," Harvard Law School Faculty Directory, n.d., http://www.law.harvard.edu/faculty/directory/10871/Sunstein.

5. Jerry Kang and Mahzarin R. Banaji, "Fair Measures: A Behavioral Realist Revision of 'Affirmative Action,'" *California Law Review* 94 (2006): 1065–1066, 1068.

6. Jerry Kang, "The Missing Quadrants of Antidiscrimination: Going Beyond the 'Prejudice Polygraph,'" *Journal of Social Issues* 68, no. 2 (2012): 316.

7. *Regents of University of California v. Bakke*, 438 U.S. 265 (1978), at 308. Justice Clarence Thomas would echo this sentiment decades later, asserting that "general claims that past school segregation affected such varied societal trends are 'too amorphous a basis for imposing a racially classified remedy,' '[i]t is sheer speculation' how decades-past segregation in the school system might have affected these trends" (*Parents Involved in Community Schools v. Seattle School District No. 1*, 551 U.S. 701 [2007], at 760, citations omitted).

8. Jack Balkin and Reva B. Siegel, "The American Civil Rights Tradition—Anticlassification or Antisubordination?," *University of Miami Law Review* 58 (2003): 30.

9. Eduardo Bonilla-Silva, *Racism Without Racists: Color-Blind Racism and the Persistence of Inequality in America*, 4th ed. (Lanham, Md.: Rowman and Littlefield, 2014), 125, 127, 130.

10. So widespread is the concept of a "postracial America" that it has even attained its own *Wikipedia* entry: "Post-Racial America," *Wikipedia*, n.d., http://en.wikipedia.org/wiki/Post-racial_America (accessed July 23, 2014), citing such works as Gregory Parks and Matthew Hughey, eds., *The Obamas and a (Post) Racial America?* Series in Political Psychology (Oxford: Oxford University Press, 2011), and Michael Tesler and David O. Sears, *Obama's Race: The 2008 Election and the Dream of a Post-racial America* (Chicago: University of Chicago Press, 2010).

11. Mahzarin R. Banaji and Anthony G. Greenwald, *Blind Spot: Hidden Biases of Good People* (New York: Bantam Books, 2013), 184.

12. Ibid., 208.

13. Christine Jolls, "Antidiscrimination Law's Effects on Implicit Bias," in *NYU Selected Essays on Labor and Employment Law: Behavioral Analyses of Workplace Discrimination*, vol. 3, ed. Mitu Gulati and Michael Yelnosky (Frederick, Md.: Aspen, 2007), 72.

14. John F. Dovidio, "On the Nature of Contemporary Prejudice: The Third Wave," *Journal of Social Issues* 57, no. 4 (2001): 846.

15. Sophie Trawalter and Jenessa R. Shapiro, "Racial Bias and Stereotyping: Interpersonal Processes," in *Handbook of Implicit Social Cognition*, ed. Bertram Gawronski and B. Keith Payne (New York: Guilford Press, 2010), 378.

16. Mo Costandi, "Interview with Elizabeth Phelps: How the Brain Views Race," *Nature News*, June 26, 2012, http://www.nature.com/news/how-the-brain-views-race-1.10886.

17. Banaji and Greenwald, *Blind Spot*, 184–185.

18. Jennifer T. Kubota, Mahzarin R. Banaji, and Elizabeth A. Phelps, "The Neuroscience of Race," *Nature Neuroscience* 15, no. 7 (2012): 941.

19. Dovidio, "On the Nature of Contemporary Prejudice," 830.

20. Quoted in Adam Nagourney, "A Defiant Rancher Savors the Audience That Rallied to His Side," *New York Times*, April 23, 2014, http://www.nytimes.com/2014/04/24/us/politics/rancher-proudly-breaks-the-law-becoming-a-hero-in-the-west.html?_r=0.

21. Megan Carpentier, "How to Call Cliven Bundy Anything but a Racist: A Lesson in Modern-Day Racism," *Guardian*, April 24, 2014, http://www.theguardian.com/commentisfree/2014/apr/24/cliven-bundy-racist-comments-defenders.

22. Eduardo Bonilla-Silva opens his book *Racism Without Racists* with the following apt epigraph from Albert Memi: "There is a strange kind of enigma associated with the problem of racism. No one, or almost no one, wishes to see themselves as racist; still racism persists, real and tenacious" (1).

23. As another *Guardian* columnist, Gary Younge, noted around the same time in response to a similar furor arising around a Wolfboro, New Hampshire, police commissioner's reference to President Obama as a "fucking nigger," "The magnitude of the response to each incident exemplifies how high the bar is now set for challenging racist behavior and how distorted our understanding has become of what that behavior constitutes" ("Racism Is Far More Than Old White Men Using the N-Word," *Guardian*, May 18, 2014, http://www.theguardian.com/commentisfree/2014/may/18/racism-more-than-old-white-men-using-n-word). Or as Ta-Nehisi Coates has observed, "There are no racists in America, or at least none that the people who need to be white know personally. . . . This is the foundation of the Dream—its adherents must not just believe in it but believe that it is just, believe that their possession of the Dream is the natural result of grit, honor and good works" (*Between the World and Me* [New York: Spiegel and Grau, 2015], 98).

24. John C. Calhoun, "Speech on the Reception of Abolition Petitions, Delivered in the Senate, February 6th, 1837," in *Speeches of John C. Calhoun, Delivered in the House of Representatives and in the Senate of the United States*, ed. Richard R. Cralle (New D. Appleton, 1853), 630.

25. *Plessy v. Ferguson*, 163 U.S. 537 (1896), at 551.

26. Quoted in David Kushner, *Levittown: Two Families, One Tycoon, and the Fight for Civil Rights in America's Legendary Suburb* (New York: Walker, 2009), 112. See also *Brown v. Board of Education of Topeka*, 347 U.S. 483 (1954).

27. John F. Dovidio and Samuel L. Gaertner, "Aversive Racism," in *Advances in Experimental Social Psychology*, vol. 36, ed. Mark P. Zanna (San Diego: Academic Press, 2004), 3.

28. Banaji and Greenwald, *Blind Spot*, 186.

29. Ta-Nehisi Coates, "Cliven Bundy Wants to Tell You All About 'the Negro': This Won't End Well," *Atlantic*, April 24, 2014, http://www.theatlantic.com/politics/archive/2014/04/cliven-bundy-wants-to-tell-you-all-about-the-negro/361152/.

30. Ta-Nehisi Coates, "Bigotry and the English Language," *Atlantic*, December 3, 2013, http://www.theatlantic.com/national/archive/2013/12/bigotryand-the-english-language/281935/.

31. Lawrence D. Bobo and Camille Z. Charles, "Race in the American Mind: From the Moynihan Report to the Obama Candidacy," *ANNALS of the AAPSS* 621 (2009): 244.

32. Ibid., 245–246.

33. Sonya Ross and Jennifer Agiesta, "AP Poll: Majority Harbor Prejudice Against Blacks," Associated Press, October 27, 2012, https://www.yahoo.com/news/ap-poll-majority-harbor-prejudice-against-blacks-073551680--election.html.

34. On these dog-whistle references, see, for example, Heather Digby Parton, "Nothing Left but the Dog Whistle: Trump, 'Real America,' and the Death of the Conservative Movement," *Salon*, September 23, 2016, http://www.salon.com/2016/09/23/nothing-left-but-the -dog-whistle-trump-real-america-and-the-death-of-the-conservative-movement/, and Lucia Graves, "Donald Trump Used to Dog-Whistle Racism. Now He Just Yells It," *Guardian*, July 13, 2016, https://www.theguardian.com/commentisfree/2016/jul/13/don- ald-trump-dog-whistle-racism. For an extensive analysis of the phenomenon of dog-whis- tle politics, see Ian F. Haney-López, *Dog Whistle Politics* (New York: Oxford University Press, 2014).

35. See, for example, Emily Badger, "We're All a Little Biased, Even If We Don't Know It," *New York Times*, October 5, 2016, http://www.nytimes.com/2016/10/07/upshot/were-all-a -little-biased-even-if-we-dont-know-it.html; Jennifer Saul and Michael Brownstein, "Implicit Bias in the Age of Trump," *Oxford University Press Blog*, April 18, 2016, http:// blog.oup.com/2016/04/implicit-bias-racism-trump/; Clarence Page, "My Implicit Bias Against Black People," *Chicago Tribune*, October 7, 2016, http://www.chicagotribune.com /news/opinion/page/ct-implicit-bias-police-kaine-pence-blacks-perspec-1009-jm -20161007-story.html; and Rinku Sen, "Implicit Bias in the Time of Trump," *Colorlines*, March 25, 2016, https://www.colorlines.com/articles/implicit-bias-time-trump.

36. Jennifer Steinhauer, Jonathan Martin, and David M. Herszenhorn, "Paul Ryan Calls Donald Trump's Attack on Judge 'Racist,' but Still Backs Him," *New York Times*, June 7, 2016, http://www.nytimes.com/2016/06/08/us/politics/paul-ryan-donald-trump-gonzalo -curiel.html.

37. Lawrence D. Bobo, Camille Z. Charles, Maria Krysan, and Alicia D. Simmons, "The *Real* Record on Racial Attitudes," in *Social Trends in American Life: Findings from the Gen- eral Social Survey Since 1972*, ed. Peter V. Marsden (Princeton: Princeton University Press, 2012), 62.

38. Michelle Alexander, *The New Jim Crow: Mass Incarceration in the Age of Colorblindness* (New York: Free Press, 2011), 201.

39. Ibid., 21.

40. George Fredrickson, *Racism: A Short History* (Princeton: Princeton University Press, 2002), 93.

41. Reva B. Siegel, "Why Equal Protection No Longer Protects: The Evolving Forms of Status-Enforcing State Action," *Stanford Law Review* 49 (1997): 1113.

42. Ta-Nehisi Coates, "My President Was Black," *Atlantic*, January–February 2017, https:// www.theatlantic.com/magazine/archive/2017/01/my-president-was-black/508793/.

43. Siegel, "Why Equal Protection No Longer Protects," 1113.

44. Ibid., 1111.

45. Rick Perlstein, "Exclusive: Lee Atwater's Infamous 1981 Interview on the Southern Strat- egy," *The Nation*, November 13, 2012, https://www.thenation.com/article/exclusive-lee -atwaters-infamous-1981-interview-southern-strategy/.

46. Leith Mullings, "Interrogating Racism: Toward an Antiracist Anthropology," *Annual Review of Anthropology* 34 (2005): 677, citations omitted.

47. Ian F. Haney-López, "Is the Post in Post-racial the Blind in Colorblind?," *Cardozo Law Review* 32 (2010): 830.

48. *Shelby County v. Holder*, 133 S. Ct. 2612 (2013), at 2625, 2626, 2629, emphasis added ("Regardless of how to look at the record, however, no one can fairly say that it shows anything approaching the 'pervasive,' 'flagrant,' 'widespread,' and 'rampant' discrimination that faced Congress in 1965, and that clearly distinguished the covered jurisdictions from the rest of the Nation at that time" [at 2629]).

49. Reva Siegel, "Equality Divided," foreword to "The Supreme Court: 2012 Term," special issue of *Harvard Law Review* 127, no. 1 (2013): 71.

50. Patricia Williams, "The Roberts Court's Civil Rights Denialism," *The Nation*, July 2, 2013, http://www.thenation.com/article/175087/roberts-courts-civil-rights-denialism#.

51. *Civil Rights Cases*, 109 U.S. 3 (1883), at 25.

52. Coates, *Between the World and Me*, 143.

53. Kang and Banaji, "Fair Measures," 1065–1066.

54. On persisting racial tensions, see Bobo and Charles, "Race in the American Mind," 245–246, and on the Whiggish characterization of racial progress, see, for example, Gary Younge, "The Truth About Race in America: It's Getting Worse, Not Better," *The Nation*, May 21, 2014, http://www.thenation.com/article/179968/truth-about-race-america-its-getting-worse-not-better.

55. Jerome M. Culp Jr., Angela P. Harris, and Francisco Valdes, "Subject Unrest," *Stanford Law Review* 55 (2003): 2445.

56. *Schuette v. BAMN*, 134 S. Ct. 1623 (2014), at 1638.

57. Ibid.

58. Kang and Banaji, "Fair Measures," 1065–1066.

59. *Adarand Constructors, Inc. v. Peña*, 515 U.S. 200 (1995), at 237.

60. *Bakke*, 438 U.S. at 327 (Brennan concurring in the judgment in part and dissenting in part).

61. *Schuette*, 134 S. Ct. at 1676 (Sotomayor, dissenting).

62. David Cole, "The Anti-Court Court," *New York Review of Books*, August 14, 2014, 10, http://www.nybooks.com/articles/archives/2014/aug/14/anti-court-supreme-court/. See also *Bush v. Gore*, 531 U.S. 98 (2000).

63. Ira Katznelson, *When Affirmative Action Was White* (New York: Norton, 2005), 43–48, 112–141.

64. Melvin Oliver and Thomas Shapiro, *Black Wealth/White Wealth: A New Perspective on Racial Inequality* (New York: Routledge, 1997). See also Thomas Shapiro, *The Hidden Cost of Being African American* (Oxford: Oxford University Press, 2005).

65. Ta-Nehisi Coates, "The Case for Reparations," *Atlantic*, May 21, 2014, http://www.theatlantic.com/features/archive/2014/05/the-case-for-reparations/361631/.

66. David R. Williams and Selina A. Mohammed, "Racism and Health I: Pathways and Scientific Evidence," *American Behavioral Scientist* 57, no. 8 (2013): 1152.

67. See, for example, Arline T. Geronimus, Jay A. Pearson, Erin Linnenbringer, Amy J. Schulz, Angela G. Reyes, Elissa S. Epel, Jue Lin, and Elizabeth H. Blackburn, "Race–Ethnicity,

Poverty, Urban Stressors, and Telomere Length in a Detroit Community-Based Sample," *Journal of Health and Social Behavior* 56, no. 2 (2015): 199–224; Virginia Hughes, "Epigenetics: The Sins of the Father," *Nature*, March 2014, http://www.nature.com/news/epigenetics-the-sins-of-the-father-1.14816; Janell Ross, "Epigenetics: The Controversial Science Behind Racial and Ethnic Health Disparities," *National Journal*, March 20, 2014, http://www.nationaljournal.com/next-america/health/epigenetics-the-controversial-science-behind-racial-and-ethnic-health-disparities-20140320.

68. Kang and Banaji, "Fair Measures," 1066–1067, emphasis added.
69. *Grutter v. Bollinger*, 539 U.S. 306 (2003), at 342, 343.
70. *Parents Involved*, 551 U.S. at 731, citations omitted. See also Justice Thomas's concurrence in *Parents Involved*: "Remedial measures geared toward such broad and unrelated societal ills have 'no logical stopping point,' and threaten to become 'ageless in their reach into the past, and timeless in their ability to affect the future'" (at 760, citations omitted).
71. Ibid., at 748.
72. *Shelby v. Holder*, 133 S. Ct. at 2625.
73. Jerry Kang and Kristin Lane, "Seeing Through Colorblindness: Implicit Bias and the Law," *UCLA Law Review* 58 (2010): 465–520.
74. Osagie Obasogie, *Blinded by Sight: Seeing Race Through the Eyes of the Blind* (Stanford, Calif.: Stanford University Press, 2014), 18, 19.
75. *City of Richmond v. J. A. Croson Co.*, 488 U.S. 469 (1989).
76. *Bakke*, 438 U.S. at 291, 312–315 (per Powell, with four justices concurring in the judgment in part and with the chief justice and three justices concurring in the judgment in part).
77. *Croson*, 488 U.S. at 493–496.
78. Ian Haney-López, "Intentional Blindness," *New York University Law Review* 87 (2012): 1825, 1836–1837.
79. See, for example, Balkin and Siegel, "American Civil Rights Tradition."
80. *Croson*, 488 U.S. at 552.
81. Angela Y. Davis, "Recognizing Racism in the Era of Neoliberalism," Vice Chancellor's Oration Presented at Murdoch University, Perth, Western Australia, March 18, 2008, http://www.omi.wa.gov.au/resources/clearinghouse/Recognizing_Racism_in_the_Era_of_Neoliberalism_davis.pdf.
82. See Ralph Richard Banks and Richard Thompson Ford, "(How) Does Unconscious Bias Matter? Law, Politics, and Racial Inequality," *Emory Law Journal* 58 (2009): 1053–1122.
83. Kang and Banaji, "Fair Measures," 1066, emphasis in original.
84. Ibid., 1067.
85. Banaji and Greenwald, *Blind Spot*, 147. See also Kang and Lane, "Seeing Through Colorblindness," 511, and Jerry Kang, *Implicit Bias: A Primer for the Courts*, prepared for the National Campaign to Ensure the Racial and Ethnic Fairness of America's State Courts, August 2009, 7, http://www.americanbar.org/content/dam/aba/migrated/sections/criminaljustice/PublicDocuments/unit_3_kang.authcheckdam.pdf.
86. Brian A. Nosek and Rachel G. Riskind, "Policy Implications of Implicit Social Cognition," *Social Issues and Policy Review* 6, no. 1 (2012): 130.

87. *Croson*, 488 U.S. at 552; *Parents Involved*, 551 U.S. at 748.
88. Theodor Geisel, *The Sneetches and Other Stories* (New York: Random House, 1961), quoted in Banaji and Greenwald, *Blind Spot*, 124.
89. Banaji and Greenwald, *Blind Spot*, 124.
90. Kubota, Banaji, and Phelps, "Neuroscience of Race," 945.
91. Neuroskeptic, "The Racist Brain?," *Discover* magazine, blog, July 5, 2012, http://blogs .discovermagazine.com/neuroskeptic/2012/07/05/the-racist-brain/#.UmrgD1NrTbw.
92. Ralph Richard Banks, Jennifer L. Eberhardt, and Lee Ross, "Discrimination and Implicit Bias in a Racially Unequal Society," *California Law Review* 94 (2006): 1185.
93. David M. Amodio, "The Social Neuroscience of Intergroup Relations," *European Review of Social Psychology* 19 (2008): 4; Kubota, Banaji, and Phelps, "Neuroscience of Race," 940; Eva H. Telzer, Kathryn L. Humphreys, Mor Shapiro, and Nim Tottenham, "Amygdala Sensitivity to Race Is Not Present in Childhood but Emerges Over Adolescence," *Journal of Cognitive Neuroscience* 25, no. 2 (2013): 234; Jay J. Van Bavel, Dominic J. Packer, and William A. Cunningham, "The Neural Substrates of In-Group Bias: A Functional Magnetic Resonance Imaging Investigation," *Psychological Science* 19 (2008): 1131–1136.
94. Elizabeth A. Phelps and Laura A. Thomas, "Race, Behavior, and the Brain: The Role of Neuroimaging in Understanding Complex Social Behaviors," *Political Psychology* 24, no. 4 (2003): 755.
95. Clifford Geertz, *The Interpretations of Cultures* (New York: Basic Books, 1973), 6.
96. Ibid., 7.
97. Banks, Eberhardt, and Ross, "Discrimination and Implicit Bias," 1171.
98. Joseph Dumit, "Critically Producing Brain Images of Mind," in *Critical Neuroscience: A Handbook of the Social and Cultural Contexts of Neuroscience*, ed. Suparna Choudhury and Jan Slaby (Hoboken, N.J.: Wiley-Blackwell, 2012), 198–199.
99. Gregory Mitchell and Philip E. Tetlock, "Antidiscrimination Law and the Perils of Mindreading," *Ohio State Law Journal* 67 (2006): 1180–1192; Philip E. Tetlock and Gregory Mitchell, "Implicit Bias and Accountability Systems: What Must Organizations Do to Prevent Discrimination?," *Research in Organizational Behavior* 29 (2009): 3–38.
100. Anthony G. Greenwald, T. Andrew Poehlman, Eric Luis Uhlmann, and Mahzarin R. Banaji, "Understanding and Using the Implicit Association Test: III. Meta-analysis of Predictive Validity," *Journal of Personality and Social Psychology* 97 (2009): 17–41.
101. Kang and Lane, "Seeing Through Colorblindness," 468.
102. Kang and Banaji, "Fair Measures," 1117.
103. Kang and Lane, "Seeing Through Colorblindness," 519.
104. American Bar Association, "Task Force on Implicit Bias," n.d., http://www.americanbar .org/groups/litigation/initiatives/task-force-implicit-bias.html. For another program, see National Center for State Courts, "Helping Courts Address Implicit Bias: Resources for Education," n.d., http://www.ncsc.org/ibeducation.
105. Kang and Lane, "Seeing Through Colorblindness," 465, 519.
106. On the importance of contextual analysis in antisubordination jurisprudence, see Haney-López, "Intentional Blindness," 1784–1798.

107. Balkin and Siegel, "American Civil Rights Tradition," 15.
108. *Bakke*, 438 U.S. at 315, emphasis added (Powell concurring).
109. Ibid., at 317, 314.
110. *Grutter*, 539 U.S. at 325.
111. Justices John Paul Stevens, Byron White, Brennan, and Marshall wrote separate opinions, some concurring in part and dissenting in part (*Bakke*, 438 U.S.).
112. *Grutter*, 539 U.S. at 338.
113. Banaji and Greenwald, *Blind Spot*, 158–159.
114. *Parents Involved*, 551 U.S. at 720.
115. Ibid., at 723.
116. Charles Lawrence III, "Unconscious Racism Revisited: Reflections on the Impact and Origins of 'The Id, the Ego, and Equal Protection,'" *Connecticut Law Review* 40 (2008): 940–941.
117. Christine Jolls and Cass R. Sunstein, "Debiasing Through Law," *Journal of Legal Studies* 35 (January 2006): 199.
118. Kang and Banaji, "Fair Measures," 1102–1109.
119. Kang and Lane, "Seeing Through Colorblindness," 502.
120. Banaji and Greenwald, *Blind Spot*, 159.
121. Haney-López, "Intentional Blindness," 1783, emphasis in original.
122. Ibid., 1784.
123. Lawrence, "Racism Revisited," 964.
124. *Washington v. Davis*, 426 U.S. 229 (1976).
125. Devon W. Carbado and Daria Roithmayr, "Critical Race Theory Meets Social Science," *Annual Review of Law and Social Science* 10 (2014): 149, 159–160, 149.
126. Jerry Kang, Judge Mark Bennett, Devon Carbado, Pam Casey, Nilanjana Dasgupta, David Faigman, Rachel Godsil, Anthony G. Greenwald, Justin Levinson, and Jennifer Mnookin, "Implicit Bias in the Courtroom," *UCLA Law Review* 56 (2012): 1132–1133.
127. See, for example, ibid., 1152 n. 111.
128. Ibid., 1126, 1130–1131, 1175.
129. Banaji and Greenwald, *Blind Spot*, 162.

4. BEHAVIORAL REALISM IN ACTION

1. Jerry Kang, Judge Mark Bennett, Devon Carbado, Pam Casey, Nilanjana Dasgupta, David Faigman, Rachel Godsil, Anthony G. Greenwald, Justin Levinson, and Jennifer Mnookin, "Implicit Bias in the Courtroom," *UCLA Law Review* 56 (2012): 1152 n. 111.
2. *Wal-Mart Stores, Inc. v. Dukes*, 131 S. Ct. 2541 (2011).
3. FED. R. CIV. P. 23(b).
4. Devon W. Carbado and Daria Roithmayr, "Critical Race Theory Meets Social Science," *Annual Review of Law and Social Science* 10 (2014): 149–167; Kang et al., "Implicit Bias in the Courtroom," 1132–1133.

5. *Wal-Mart*, 131 S. Ct. at 2549.

6. John Monahan, Laurens Walker, and Gregory Mitchell, "Contextual Evidence of Gender Discrimination: The Ascendance of 'Social Frameworks,'" *Virginia Law Review* 94 (2008): 1716–1720.

7. *Wal-Mart*, 131 S. Ct. at 2553–2554, quoting *General Telephone Co. of Southwest v. Falcon*, 457 U.S. 147 (1982), at 157–158.

8. *Wal-Mart*, 131 S. Ct. at 2553–2554, citing 222 F.R.D. 189, 192 (N.D. Cal. 2004). Scalia noted that "Bielby's conclusions in this case have elicited criticism from the very scholars on whose conclusions he relies for his social-framework analysis. See Monahan, Walker, & Mitchell, Contextual Evidence of Gender Discrimination: The Ascendance of 'Social Frameworks,' 94 Va. L. Rev. 1715, 1747 (2008) ('[Bielby's] research into conditions and behavior at Wal-Mart did not meet the standards expected of social scientific research into stereotyping and discrimination'); *id.*, at 1745, 1747 ('[A] social framework necessarily contains only general statements about reliable patterns of relations among variables . . . and goes no further. . . . Dr. Bielby claimed to present a social framework, but he testified about social facts specific to Wal-Mart'); *id.*, at 1747–1748 ('Dr. Bielby's report provides no verifiable method for measuring and testing any of the variables that were crucial to his conclusions and reflects nothing more than Dr. Bielby's "expert judgment" about how general stereotyping research applied to all managers across all of Wal-Mart's stores nationwide for the multi-year class period')" (*Wal-Mart*, 131 S. Ct. at 2554 n. 8).

9. *Pippen v. State*, 854 N.W.2d 1 (2014), at 6. See also Christine A. Amalfe, "The Limitations on Implicit Bias Testimony Post-*Dukes*," March 2013, 6, http://www.americanbar.org /content/dam/aba/events/labor_law/2013/03/employment_rightsresponsibilitiescommitteemidwintermeeting/1_amalfe.authcheckdam.pdf.

10. Damien A. Stanley, Peter Sokol-Hessner, Mahzarin R. Banaji, and Elizabeth A. Phelps, "Reply to Krueger: Good Point, Wrong Paper," *Proceedings of the National Academy of Sciences* 108 (2011): E411, doi:10.1073/pnas.1107937108.

11. Jerry Kang, "Trojan Horses of Race," *Harvard Law Review* 118, no. 5 (2005): 1495.

12. Samuel Bagenstos, "Implicit Bias, 'Science,' and Antidiscrimination Law," *Harvard Law and Policy Review* 1 (2007): 491, 493.

13. *Regents of University of California v. Bakke*, 438 U.S. 265 (1978).

14. *United States v. Brignoni-Ponce*, 422 U.S. 873 (1975), at 876–877.

15. *Bakke*, 438 U.S. at 308. Justice Clarence Thomas would echo this sentiment decades later, asserting that "general claims that past school segregation affected such varied societal trends are 'too amorphous a basis for imposing a racially classified remedy,' '[i]t is sheer speculation' how decades-past segregation in the school system might have affected these trends" (*Parents Involved in Community Schools v. Seattle School District No. 1*, 551 U.S. 701 [2007], at 760, citations omitted).

16. Justice Scalia to the Conference, memorandum, Re: No. 84-6811, *McCleskey v. Kemp* (Jan. 6, 1987), reprinted in Erwin Chemerinsky, "Eliminating Discrimination in Administering the Death Penalty: The Need for the Racial Justice Act," *Santa Clara Law Review* 35 (1995): 519, 528; *McCleskey v. Kemp*, 481 U.S. 279 (1987), at 279.

17. *McCleskey v. Kemp*, 481 U.S. at 292–293, 279.

18. Justice Scalia to the Conference, in Chemerinsky, "Eliminating Discrimination in Administering the Death Penalty," 528.

19. Chemerinsky, "Eliminating Discrimination in Administering the Death Penalty," 528.

20. Ian Haney-López, "Intentional Blindness," *New York University Law Review* 87 (2012): 1860.

21. Govind Persad, "When, and How, Should Cognitive Bias Matter to Law?," *Minnesota Journal of Law and Inequality* 32 (2014): 103.

22. Quoted in Aimée Lutkin, "Trump Surrogate: 'There's No Such Thing' as Facts," *Jezebel*, December 2, 2016, http://jezebel.com/trump-surrogate-theres-no-such-thing-as-facts -1789600509.

23. *Brown v. Board of Education of Topeka*, 347 U.S. 483 (1954), at 495 n. 11.

24. *Plessy v. Ferguson*, 163 U.S. 537 (1896).

25. Haney-López, "Intentional Blindness," 1796.

26. Richard Thompson Ford, "Bias in the Air: Rethinking Employment Discrimination Law," *Stanford Law Review* 66 (2014): 1396.

27. See, for example, Charles Ogletree, Robert Smith, and Johanna Wald, "Criminal Law: Coloring Punishment: Implicit Social Cognition and Criminal Justice," in *Implicit Racial Bias Across the Law*, ed. Justin D. Levinson and Robert J. Smith (New York: Cambridge University Press, 2012), 45–60.

28. Pamela M. Casey, Roger K. Warren, Fred L. Cheesman II, and Jennifer K. Elek, *Helping Courts Address Implicit Bias: Resources for Education* (Washington, D.C.: National Center for State Courts, 2012), http://www.ncsc.org/ibreport; Pamela M. Casey, Roger K. Warren, Fred L. Cheesman II, and Jennifer K. Elek, "Addressing Implicit Bias in the Courts," *Court Review* 49 (2013): 64–70; American Bar Association, "Implicit Bias Initiative," n.d., http://www.americanbar.org/groups/litigation/initiatives/task-force-implicit -bias.html.

29. For these programs, see the Fair and Impartial Policing website at http://fairandimpar-tialpolicing.com/; Lorie Fridell, "This is Not Your Grandparents' Prejudice: The Implications of Modern Science of Bias for Police Training," *Translational Criminology*, Fall 2013, 10–11; and U.S. Department of Justice, "COPS: Community Oriented Policing Services," n.d., http://www.cops.usdoj.gov/Default.asp?Item=2618.

30. Frank Dobbin, *Inventing Equal Opportunity* (Princeton: Princeton University Press, 2009).

31. U.S. Equal Employment Opportunity Commission, "E-RACE Goals and Objectives," n.d., http://www.eeoc.gov/eeoc/initiatives/e-race/goals.cfm.

32. Casey et al., *Helping Courts Address Implicit Bias*, i, acknowledging Kang as an expert adviser for the project.

33. Ibid., i, 6, 7.

34. Ibid., 9.

35. Ibid., 13–14.

36. Ibid., 7–20.

37. Jerry Kang, *Implicit Bias: A Primer for the Courts*, prepared for the National Campaign to Ensure the Racial and Ethnic Fairness of America's State Courts, August 2009, http://www.americanbar.org/content/dam/aba/migrated/sections/criminaljustice/PublicDocuments/unit_3_kang.authcheckdam.pdf.

38. Judicial Council of California, *The Neuroscience and Psychology of Decisionmaking: A New Way of Learning* (video), n.d., http://www2.courtinfo.ca.gov/cjer/857.htm.

39. American Bar Association, "Implicit Bias Initiative."

40. Fair and Impartial Policing, home page, n.d., http://fairandimpartialpolicing.com/.

41. Lorie Fridell, "Overview to Fair and Impartial Policing," n.d., 3, https://static1.square space.com/static/54722818e4b0b3ef26cdc085/t/5623ec8ce4b0099ac9caaada/1445194 892676/Extended_About+FIP_2015.pdf.

42. Ibid., 7.

43. U.S. Equal Employment Opportunity Commission, "African American Workgroup Report 2012," executive summary, n.d., http://www.eeoc.gov/federal/reports/aawg.cfm (see also the press release announcing the publication of the report, March 14, 2013, https://www.eeoc.gov/eeoc/newsroom/release/3-14-13.cfm).

44. See, in general, Dobbin, *Inventing Equal Opportunity*.

45. Justin D. Levinson, "Forgotten Racial Equality: Implicit Bias, Decisionmaking, and Mis-remembering," *Duke Law Journal* 57 (2007): 345–346.

46. Cheryl R. Kaiser, Brenda Major, Ines Jurcevic, Tessa L. Dover, Laura M. Brady, and Jenessa R. Shapiro, "Presumed Fair: Ironic Effects of Organizational Diversity Structures," *Journal of Personality and Social Psychology* 104, no. 3 (2013): 504–519.

47. Rohini Anand and Mary-Frances Winters, "A Retrospective View of Corporate Diversity Training from 1964 to the Present," *Academy of Management Learning and Education* 7, no. 3 (2008): 356.

48. Jessica Guynn, "Exclusive: Google Raising Stakes on Diversity," *USA Today*, May 6, 2015, http://www.usatoday.com/story/tech/2015/05/05/google-raises-stakes-diversity -spending/26868359/.

49. Dobbin, *Inventing Equal Opportunity*, 1, 71.

50. Ibid., 220, 4–6.

51. Ibid., 4, 12–13, 15, 17, 133.

52. Erin L. Kelly and Frank Dobbin, "How Affirmative Action Became Diversity Management: Employer Response to Antidiscrimination Law, 1961–1996," *American Behavioral Scientist* 41 (1998): 973.

53. Victoria C. Plaut, Sapna Cheryan, and Flannery G. Stevens, "New Frontiers in Diversity Research: Conceptions of Diversity and Their Theoretical and Practical Implications," in *APA Handbook of Personality and Social Psychology*, vol. 1: *Attitudes and Social Cognition*, ed. Mario Mikulincer, Phillip R. Shaver, Eugene Borgida, and John A. Bargh (Washington, D.C.: American Psychological Association, 2015), 595.

54. Michelle Alexander, *The New Jim Crow: Mass Incarceration in the Age of Colorblindness* (New York: Free Press, 2011), 225, 226.

55. Michael J. Klarman, *From Jim Crow to Civil Rights: The Supreme Court and the Struggle for Racial Equality* (New York: Oxford University Press, 2004), 95.

56. Dobbin, *Inventing Equal Opportunity*, 96.

57. Alexandra Kalev, Frank Dobbin, and Eric Kelly, "Best Practices or Best Guesses? Assessing the Efficacy of Corporate Affirmative Action and Diversity Policies," *American Sociological Review* 71 (2006): 589. See also Susan Bisom-Rapp, "Fixing Watches with Sledgehammers: The Questionable Embrace of Employee Sexual Harassment Training by the Legal Profession," *University of Arkansas Little Rock Law Review* 24 (2001): 147–168, which finds anti–sexual harassment training programs to be ineffective.

58. Elizabeth Levy Paluck and Donald P. Green, "Prejudice Reduction: What Works? A Review and Assessment of Research and Practice," *Annual Review of Psychology* 60 (2009): 360, 339.

59. Anand and Winters, "A Retrospective View of Corporate Diversity Training," 371.

60. Soohan Kim, Alexandra Kalev, and Frank Dobbin, "Progressive Corporations at Work: The Case of Diversity Programs," *N.Y.U. Review of Law and Social Change* 36 (2012): 197.

61. Kaiser et al., "Presumed Fair," 506.

62. Casey et al., *Helping Courts Address Implicit Bias*, app. H, p. 7 (discussing the need for further studies to find any measurable impact from the training).

63. Ibid., 11, 19.

64. Calvin K. Lai, Allison L. Skinner, Erin Cooley, Sohad Murrar, Markus Brauer, Thierry Devos, Jimmy Calanchini, et al., "Reducing Implicit Racial Preferences: II. Intervention Effectiveness Across Time," *Journal of Experimental Psychology: General* 145 (2016): 1011–1016.

5. DERACINATING THE LEGAL SUBJECT

1. John Rawls, *A Theory of Justice* (Cambridge, Mass.: Harvard University Press, 2009).

2. Michael J. Sandel, "The Procedural Republic and the Unencumbered Self," *Political Theory* 12, no. 1 (1984): 82.

3. Rawls, *Justice*, 116.

4. Sandel, "Procedural Republic," 86.

5. Ibid.

6. Ibid., 90–91.

7. Mahzarin R. Banaji, Max H. Bazerman, and Dolly Chugh, "How (Un)Ethical are You?," *Harvard Business Review* 81, no. 12 (2003): 63–64.

8. Jerry Kang and Mahzarin R. Banaji, "Fair Measures: A Behavioral Realist Revision of 'Affirmative Action,'" *California Law Review* 94 (2006): 1092. See also Mahzarin R. Banaji and Anthony G. Greenwald, *Blind Spot: Hidden Biases of Good People* (New York: Bantam Books, 2013), 146–147, and Jerry Kang and Kristin Lane, "Seeing Through Colorblindness: Implicit Bias and the Law," *UCLA Law Review* 58 (2010): 511.

9. Brian A. Nosek and Rachel G. Riskind, "Policy Implications of Implicit Social Cognition," *Social Issues and Policy Review* 6, no. 1 (2012): 131.

10. Dana-Ain Davis, "Narrating the Mute: Racializing and Racism in a Neoliberal Moment," *Souls* 9, no. 4 (2007): 350.

11. Martha Minow, "Learning to Live with the Dilemma of Difference: Bilingual and Special Education," *Law and Contemporary Problems* 48 (1985): 202.

12. Martha Minow, *Making All the Difference: Inclusion, Exclusion, and American Law* (Ithaca: Cornell University Press, 1990), 51.

13. *Regents of University of California v. Bakke*, 438 U.S. 265 (1978), at 407 (Blackmun concurring in part, dissenting in part).

14. Ralph Richard Banks, Jennifer L. Eberhardt, and Lee Ross, "Discrimination and Implicit Bias in a Racially Unequal Society," *California Law Review* 94 (2006): 1185.

15. John F. Dovidio and Samuel L. Gaertner, "Aversive Racism," in *Advances in Experimental Social Psychology*, vol. 36, ed. Mark P. Zanna (San Diego: Academic Press), 1–51.

16. See, for example, Allen R. McConnell and Jill M. Leibold, "Relations Among the Implicit Association Test, Discriminatory Behavior, and Explicit Measures of Racial Attitudes," *Journal of Experimental Social Psychology* 37 (2001): 435–442.

17. K. Anthony Appiah, "Stereotypes and the Shaping of Identity," in Robert Post, with K. Anthony Appiah, Judith Butler, Thomas Grey, and Reva Siegel, *Prejudicial Appearances: The Logic of American Antidiscrimination Law* (Durham, N.C.: Duke University Press, 2001), 68, 69.

18. Jerry Kang, "Trojan Horses of Race," *Harvard Law Review* 118, no. 5 (2005): 1502.

19. George Fredrickson, *Racism: A Short History* (Princeton: Princeton University Press, 2002), 75.

20. Michael Omi and Howard Winant, *Racial Formation in the United States: From the 1960s to the 1990s* (New York: Routledge, 1994), 82, emphasis in original.

21. Jaclyn Ronquillo, Thomas F. Denson, Brian Lickel, Zhong-Lin Lu, Anirvan Nandy, and Keith B. Maddox, "The Effects of Skin Tone on Race-Related Amygdala Activity: An fMRI Investigation," *SCAN* 2, no. 1 (2007): 39.

22. Minow, *Making All the Difference*, 51.

23. Martha Minow, "Learning to Live with the Dilemma of Difference: Bilingual and Special Education," *Law and Contemporary Problems* 48 (1985): 203.

24. Sudip Bose, "On Virtuosity," *American Scholar*, Summer 2005, http://theamericanscholar.org/on-virtuosity/.

25. Cynthia Lee, "Making Race Salient: Trayvon Martin and Implicit Bias in a Not Yet Postracial Society," *North Carolina Law Review* 91 (2013): 1563, 1586.

26. Michelle Alexander, *The New Jim Crow: Mass Incarceration in the Age of Colorblindness* (New York: Free Press, 2011).

27. Kang and Banaji, "Fair Measures," 1067.

28. Gary Wills, "The Triumph of the Hard Right," *New York Review of Books*, February 11, 2016, 6.

29. *Adarand Constructors, Inc. v. Peña*, 515 U.S. 200 (1995), at 237.

30. Charles Lawrence III, "Unconscious Racism Revisited: Reflections on the Impact and Origins of 'The Id, the Ego, and Equal Protection,'" *Connecticut Law Review* 40 (2008): 962–963.

31. Robert Post, "Prejudicial Appearances: The Logic of American Antidiscrimination Law," in Post, *Prejudicial Appearances*, 18, 15, quoting John Schaar, *Legitimacy in the Modern State* (New Brunswick, N.J.: Transaction, 1981), 203.

32. Ivan E. Bodensteiner, "The Implications of Psychological Research Related to Unconscious Discrimination and Implicit Bias in Proving Intentional Discrimination," *Missouri Law Review* 73 (2008): 106.

33. On "pollution," see, generally, Mary Douglas, *Purity and Danger: An Analysis of Concepts of Pollution and Taboo* (New York: Routledge, 2003).

34. Devon W. Carbado and Mitu Gulati, "The Fifth Black Woman," *Journal of Contemporary Legal Issues* 11 (2001): 720.

35. Ralph Richard Banks and Richard Thompson Ford, "(How) Does Unconscious Bias Matter? Law, Politics, and Racial Inequality," *Emory Law Journal* 58 (2009): 1089. On the reduction to "instruments," see Post, "Prejudicial Appearances," 18.

36. Post, "Prejudicial Appearances," 22.

37. Ibid., 40.

38. Govind Persad, "When, and How, Should Cognitive Bias Matter to Law?," *Minnesota Journal of Law and Inequality* 32 (2014): 122.

39. Ian Haney-López, "Intentional Blindness," *New York University Law Review* 87 (2012): 1797.

40. *Parents Involved in Community Schools v. Seattle School District No. 1*, 551 U.S. 701 (2007), at 748.

41. *Schuette v. BAMN*, 134 S. Ct. 1623 (2014), at 1676.

42. Kimberlé Williams Crenshaw, "Demarginalizing the Intersection of Race and Sex: A Black Feminist Critique of Antidiscrimination Doctrine, Feminist Theory, and Antiracist Politics," *University of Chicago Legal Forum* 8, no. 1 (1989): 139–167, and "Mapping the Margins: Intersectionality, Identity Politics, and Violence Against Women of Color," *Stanford Law Review* 43, no. 6 (1991): 1241–1299.

43. Crenshaw, "Demarginalizing the Intersection of Race and Sex," 149.

44. Ibid., 151.

45. Carbado and Gulati, "Fifth Black Woman," 706.

46. See, for example, Ian Ayers, "Is Discrimination Elusive?," *Stanford Law Review* 55, (2003): 2423–2424.

47. Phillip Atiba Goff and Kimberly Barsamian Kahn, "How Psychological Science Impedes Intersectional Thinking," *Du Bois Review* 10, no. 2 (2013): 365, 372, 369, citations omitted.

48. Daniel Kahneman, *Thinking, Fast and Slow* (New York: Farrar, Straus, and Giroux, 2011), 20–21.

49. See, for example, William A. Cunningham, Marcia K. Johnson, Carol L. Raye, J. Chris Gatenby, John C. Gore, and Mahzarin R. Banaji, "Separable Neural Components in the Processing of Black and White Faces," *Psychological Science* 15 (2004): 806–813 ("These results provide evidence for neural distinctions between automatic and more controlled

processing of social groups, and suggest that controlled processes may modulate automatic evaluation" [806]).

50. Richard Thaler and Cass Sunstein, *Nudge: Improving Decisions About Health, Wealth, and Happiness* (New York: Penguin, 2008).

51. Banaji and Greenwald, *Blind Spot*, 58.

52. William A. Cunningham, Jay J. Van Bavel, Nathan L. Arbuckle, Dominic J. Packer, and Ashley S. Waggoner, "Rapid Social Perception Is Flexible: Approach and Avoidance Motivational States Shape P100 Responses to Other-Race Faces," *Frontiers in Human Neuroscience* 6, no. 140 (2012): 4, doi:10.3389/fnhum.2012.00140.

53. Jay J. Van Bavel, Y. Jenny Xiao, and Leor M. Hackel, "Social Identity Shapes Social Perception and Evaluation: Using Neuroimaging to Look Inside the Social Brain," in *Neuroscience of Prejudice and Intergroup Relations*, ed. Belle Derks, Daan Scheepers, and Naomi Ellemers (New York: Psychology Press, 2013), 112.

54. *Grutter v. Bollinger*, 539 U.S. 306 (2003).

55. In *Parents Involved*, consider also Justice Anthony Kennedy's concurrence, where he criticized the school district's use of "the crude racial categories of 'white' and 'non-white' as the basis for assignment decisions" (551 U.S. at 786).

56. *Brown v. Board of Education*, 347 U.S. 483 (1954), at 494.

57. James T. Patterson and William W. Freehling, Brown v. Board of Education: *A Civil Rights Milestone and Its Troubled Legacy* (Oxford: Oxford University Press, 2001), 45; Charles L. Black, "The Lawfulness of the Segregation Decisions," *Yale Law Journal* 69, no. 3 (1960): 430n25.

58. Crenshaw, "Mapping the Margins," 1297.

59. Ibid., 1296.

60. Valerie Purdie-Vaughns and Richard P. Eibach, "Intersectional Invisibility: The Distinctive Advantages and Disadvantages of Multiple Subordinate-Group Identities," *Sex Roles* 57 (2008): 382.

61. Ibid., 378.

62. Ibid., 382.

63. Kerri L. Johnson, Jonathan B. Freeman, and Kristin Pauker, "Race Is Gendered: How Covarying Phenotypes and Stereotypes Bias Sex Categorization," *Journal of Personality and Social Psychology* 102, no. 1 (2012): 116.

64. Dorothy Roberts and Sujatha Jesudason, "Movement Intersectionaltiy: The Case of Race, Gender, Disability, and Genetic Technologies," *Du Bois Review* 10, no. 2 (2013): 319.

65. Ibid.

6. OBSCURING POWER

1. George Fredrickson, *Racism: A Short History* (Princeton: Princeton University Press, 2002), 7, 9.

2. Ruha Benjamin, "Conjuring Difference, Concealing Inequality: A Brief Tour of Racecraft," *Theory and Society* 43, no. 6 (2014): 685.

3. Barbara J. Fields and Karen Fields, *Racecraft: The Soul of Inequality in American Life* (New York: Verso, 2012).

4. Benjamin, "Conjuring Difference," 683.

5. National Center for State Courts, *Strategies to Reduce the Influence of Implicit Bias* (Washington, D.C.: National Center for State Courts, 2012), 6–17, http://www.ncsc.org/IBstrategies, with the strategies combined into a list here.

6. On adequate funding and peremptory challenges, see, for example, Michelle Alexander, *The New Jim Crow* (New York: Free Press, 2011), 120–123.

7. Cheryl Staats, *State of the Science: Implicit Bias Review 2014* (Columbus, Ohio: Kirwan Institute, 2014), 20–21, http://kirwaninstitute.osu.edu/implicit-bias-review/.

8. Ibid., 32.

9. Michael Omi and Howard Winant, *Racial Formation in the United States: From the 1960s to the 1990s* (New York: Routledge, 1994), 152.

10. Suzanne Mettler, *The Submerged State: How Invisible Government Policies Undermine American Democracy* (Chicago: University of Chicago Press, 2011), 4–5.

11. Suzanne Mettler, "Reconstituting the Submerged State: The Challenges of Social Policy Reform in the Obama Era," *Perspectives on Politics* 8 (2010): 804.

12. Mettler, *Submerged State*, 6.

13. Mettler, "Reconstituting the Submerged State," 809.

14. Cass R. Sunstein, "Nudges Do Not Undermine Human Agency: A Note," *Journal of Consumer Policy* 38, no. 3 (2015): 207.

15. Richard Thaler and Cass Sunstein, *Nudge: Improving Decisions About Health, Wealth, and Happiness* (New York: Penguin, 2008), 37.

16. Mettler, *Submerged State*, 48–49.

17. Ibid., 52.

18. Ibid., 26.

19. Frank Dobbin, *Inventing Equal Opportunity* (Princeton: Princeton University Press, 2009), 2.

20. Mahzarin R. Banaji and Anthony G. Greenwald, *Blind Spot: Hidden Biases of Good People* (New York: Bantam Books, 2013), 184.

21. Alexander, *New Jim Crow*, 265.

22. Eddie Glaude Jr., *Democracy in Black: How Race Still Enslaves the American Soul* (New York: Crown, 2016), 165, emphasis added.

23. Curtis D. Hardin and Mahzarin R. Banaji, "The Nature of Implicit Prejudice: Implications for Personal and Public Policy," in *The Behavioral Foundations of Public Policy*, ed. Eldar Shafir (Princeton: Princeton University Press, 2013), 17, 22.

24. Ibid., 15.

25. Fair and Impartial Policing, home page, n.d., http://fairandimpartialpolicing.com/; U.S. Department of Justice, "COPS: Community Oriented Policing Services," n.d., http://www.cops.usdoj.gov/Default.asp?Item=2618.

26. Center for Policing Equity, "Center for Policing Equity," n.d., http://cpe.psych.ucla.edu/.

27. "Police Officers Debate Effectiveness of Anti-bias Training," National Public Radio, April 9, 2015, http://www.npr.org/2015/04/06/397891177/police-officers-debate-effectiveness-of-anti-bias-training.

28. U.S. Department of Justice, "Department of Justice Announces New Department-Wide Implicit Bias Training for Personnel," press release, June 27, 2016, https://www.justice.gov /opa/pr/department-justice-announces-new-department-wide-implicit-bias-training -personnel.
29. Fair and Impartial Policing, "Recruit and Patrol officer Training," n.d., http://www .fairimpartialpolicing.com/training-programs/.
30. Center for Policing Equity, "Center for Policing Equity."
31. Center for Policing Equity, "What We've Done," n.d., http://cpe.psych.ucla.edu/what -weve-done.
32. U.S. Department of Justice, "Justice Department Announces National Effort to Build Trust Between Law Enforcement and the Communities They Serve," press release, September 18, 2014, http://www.justice.gov/opa/pr/justice-department-announces-national -effort-build-trust-between-law-enforcement-and.
33. California Department of Justice, "Attorney General Kamala D. Harris Releases Results of 90-Day Review of Special Agent Training on Implicit Bias and Use of Force," press release, April 17, 2015, https://oag.ca.gov/news/press-releases/attorney-general-kamala-d -harris-releases-results-90-day-review-special-agent. See also California Department of Justice, "Attorney General Kamala D. Harris Kicks Off First-of-Its-Kind Law Enforcement Training on Implicit Bias & Procedural Justice," press release, November 17, 2015, https://oag.ca.gov/news/press-releases/attorney-general-kamala-d-harris-kicks-first-its -kind-law-enforcement-training.
34. On diversity-training programs and the backlash they can produce, see, for example, Laura S. Abrams and Jené A. Moio, "Critical Race Theory and the Cultural Competence Dilemma in Social Work Education," *Journal of Social Work Education* 45, no. 2 (2009): 248; Kristen P. Jones, Eden B. King, Johnathan Nelson, David S. Geller, and Lynn Bowes-Sperry, "Beyond the Business Case: An Ethical Perspective of Diversity Training," *Human Resource Management* 52, no. 1 (2013): 55–74; Kecia M. Thomas, ed., *Diversity Resistance in Organizations* (New York: Lawrence Erlbaum, 2012); Michael Rowe and Jon Garland, "Police Diversity Training: A Silver-Bullet Tarnished?," in *Policing Beyond Macpherson: Issues in Policing, Race, and Society*, ed. Michael Rowe (New York: Routledge, 2013), 43.
35. Interviewed in "Police Officers Debate Effectiveness of Anti-bias Training."
36. "Texas Pool Party Incident Sparks Protests—and Police Support," *CBS News*, June 9, 2015, http://www.cbsnews.com/news/texas-officer-drawing-gun-on-black-teens-at-pool -party-sparks-protests-and-police-support/.
37. U.S. Department of Justice, Civil Rights Division, and U.S. Attorney's Office, Northern District of Illinois, *Investigation of the Chicago Police Department* (Washington, D.C.: U.S. Department of Justice, January 13, 2017), 5, https://www.justice.gov/opa/file/925846 /download.
38. Ibid., 146.
39. Ibid., 155.
40. Paul Hirschfield, "Why American Cops Kill so Many Compared to European Cops," *The Conversation*, November 25, 2015, http://theconversation.com/why-do-american-cops -kill-so-many-compared-to-european-cops-49696.

41. *Graham v. Connor*, 490 U.S. 386 (1989).

42. Hirschfield, "Why American Cops Kill."

43. Eduardo Bonilla-Silva, *Racism Without Racists: Color-Blind Racism and the Persistence of Inequality in America*, 4th ed. (Lanham, Maryland : Rowman and Littlefield, 2014), 15.

44. Ibid., 53, emphasis in original.

45. Ian Haney-López, "Intentional Blindness," *New York University Law Review* 87 (2012): 1779.

46. Quoted in Carol Anderson, *White Rage: The Unspoken Truth of Our Racial Divide* (New York: Bloomsbury, 2016), 105.

47. Ibid., 100.

48. Consider, in addition, the following quote from John Erlichman about the war on drugs: "The Nixon campaign in 1968, and the Nixon White House after that, had two enemies: the antiwar left and black people. You understand what I'm saying? We knew we couldn't make it illegal to be either against the war or blacks, but by getting the public to associate the hippies with marijuana and blacks with heroin, and then criminalizing both heavily, we could disrupt those communities. We could arrest their leaders, raid their homes, break up their meetings, and vilify them night after night on the evening news. Did we know we were lying about the drugs? Of course we did" (quoted in Dan Baum, "Legalize It All: How to Win the War on Drugs," *Harper's Magazine Online*, April 2016, http://harpers.org/archive/2016/04/legalize-it-all/).

49. Nadine Gordimer, *Burger's Daughter* (New York: Penguin, 1979), 72.

50. David Wellman, "From Evil to Illness: Medicalizing Racism," *American Journal of Orthopsychiatry* 70 (2000): 30.

51. Reva B. Siegel, "Why Equal Protection No Longer Protects: The Evolving Forms of Status-Enforcing State Action," *Stanford Law Review* 49 (1997): 1113.

52. Charles Lawrence III, "Unconscious Racism Revisited: Reflections on the Impact and Origins of 'The Id, the Ego, and Equal Protection,'" *Connecticut Law Review* 40 (2008): 942.

53. Ibid.

54. Lawrence D. Bobo, Camille Z. Charles, Maria Krysan, and Alicia D. Simmons, "The Real Record on Racial Attitudes," in *Social Trends in American Life: Findings from the General Social Survey Since 1972*, ed. Peter V. Marsden (Princeton: Princeton University Press, 2012), 65, 74.

55. Victoria C. Plaut, Sapna Cheryan, and Flannery G. Stevens, "New Frontiers in Diversity Research: Conceptions of Diversity and Their Theoretical and Practical Implications," in *APA Handbook of Personality and Social Psychology*, vol. 1: *Attitudes and Social Cognition*, ed. Mario Mikulincer, Phillip R. Shaver, Eugene Borgida, and John A. Bargh (Washington, D.C.: American Psychological Association, 2015), 596.

56. Rohini Anand and Mary-Frances Winters, "A Retrospective View of Corporate Diversity Training from 1964 to the Present," *Academy of Management Learning and Education* 7, no. 3 (2008): 365.

57. Mahzarin R. Banaji, Max H. Bazerman, and Dolly Chugh, "How (Un)Ethical Are You?," *Harvard Business Review* 81, no. 12 (2003): 58, 60.

58. Dobbin, *Inventing Equal Opportunity*, 12. See also Soohan Kim, Alexandra Kalev, and Frank Dobbin, "Progressive Corporations at Work: The Case of Diversity Programs," *N.Y.U. Review of Law and Social Change* 36 (2012): 171.

59. Kimberly D. Krawiec, "Cosmetic Compliance and the Failure of Negotiated Governance," *Washington University Law Quarterly* 81 (2003): 543.

60. Dobbin, *Inventing Equal Opportunity*, 12.

61. Alexander, *New Jim Crow*, 249.

62. Nancy Leong, "Racial Capitalism," *Harvard Law Review* 126 (2013): 2152, 2171, emphasis in original.

63. Dobbin, *Inventing Equal Opportunity*, 21.

64. Cheryl R. Kaiser, Brenda Major, Ines Jurcevic, Tessa L. Dover, Laura M. Brady, and Jenessa R. Shapiro, "Presumed Fair: Ironic Effects of Organizational Diversity Structures," *Journal of Personality and Social Psychology* 104, no. 3 (2013): 505, 516. See also Kim, Kalev, and Dobbin, "Progressive Corporations at Work": "We also find that some of the most popular equal opportunity programs are not actually the most effective. Formalized hiring and promotion procedures, diversity training, and grievance procedures do not lead to improvements in workforce diversity" (171).

65. Kim, Kalev, and Dobbin, "Progressive Corporations at Work," 196.

66. Nikolas Rose and Carlos Novas, "Biological Citizenship," in *Global Assemblages: Technology, Politics, and Ethics as Anthropological Problems*, 2nd ed., ed. Aihwa Ong and Stephen J. Collier (Malden, Mass.: Blackwell, 2008), 439, 448.

67. Ibid., 451.

68. Nikolas Rose and Joelle Abi-Rached, *Neuro: The New Brain Sciences and the Management of the Mind* (Princeton: Princeton University Press, 2013), 223.

69. Roger Cooter, "Biocitizenship," *Lancet* 372 (2008): 1725, http://www.thelancet.com/journals/lancet/article/PIIS0140-6736(08)61719-5/fulltext.

70. See Michel Foucault, *The History of Sexuality*, vol. 3: *The Care of the Self* (New York: Vintage, 1988).

71. Linda Hamilton Krieger, "The Content of Our Categories: A Cognitive Bias Approach to Discrimination and Equal Employment Opportunity," *Stanford Law Review* 47 (1995): 1166.

72. Ibid.

73. Victoria Pitts-Taylor, "The Plastic Brain: Neoliberalism and the Neuronal Self," *Health* 14, no. 6 (2010): 635, 639.

7. RECREATIONAL ANTIRACISM AND THE POWER OF POSITIVE NUDGING

1. Beth Azar, "IAT: Fad or Fabulous?," *Psychology Monitor* 39 (2008): 44.

2. National Alliance for Partnership in Equity, "Discover Your Biases: The Implicit Association Test," n.d., http://www.careertechpa.org/Portals/0/Nontraditional/Discover%20Your%20Biases.pdf.

3. Mahzarin R. Banaji and Anthony G. Greenwald, *Blind Spot: Hidden Biases of Good People* (New York: Bantam Books, 2013), 52, 66.

4. Geoff Kaufman and Mary Flanagan, "A Psychologically 'Embedded' Approach to Designing Games for Prosocial Causes," *Cyberpsychology: Journal of Psychosocial Research on Cyberspace* 9, no. 3 (2015): article 1, doi: 10.5817/CP2015-3-5.

5. Nilanjana Dasgupta and Anthony G. Greenwald, "On the Malleability of Automatic Attitudes: Combating Automatic Prejudice with Images of Admired and Disliked Individuals," *Journal of Personality and Social Psychology* 81, no. 5 (2001): 800.

6. Jerry Kang and Mahzarin R. Banaji, "Fair Measures: A Behavioral Realist Revision of 'Affirmative Action,'" *California Law Review* 94 (2006): 1108.

7. Pamela M. Casey, Roger K. Warren, Fred L. Cheesman, and Jennifer K. Elek, "Addressing Implicit Bias in the Courts," *Court Review* 49 (2013): 66, http://aja.ncsc.dni.us/publications/courtrv/cr49-1/CR49-1Casey.pdf.

8. Ibid., 65–68.

9. Pamela M. Casey, Roger K. Warren, Fred L. Cheesman II, and Jennifer K. Elek, *Helping Courts Address Implicit Bias: Resources for Education* (Washington, D.C.: National Center for State Courts, 2012), 8, 22, http://www.ncsc.org/ibreport.

10. Ibid., 19.

11. Barbara Ehrenreich, *Bright-Sided: How the Relentless Promotion of Positive Thinking Has Undermined America* (New York: Macmillan, 2009), 4, 8.

12. Ibid., 155, 171, 96.

13. Ibid., 176, 94.

14. Kang Yoona, Jeremy R. Gray, and John F. Dovidio, "The Nondiscriminating Heart: Lovingkindness Meditation Training Decreases Implicit Intergroup Bias," *Journal of Experimental Psychology: General* 143, no. 3 (2014): 1311.

15. Robin DiAngelo, "White Fragility," *International Journal of Critical Pedagogy* 3, no. 3 (2011): 60.

16. Lawrence D. Bobo, Camille Z. Charles, Maria Krysan, and Alicia D. Simmons, "The Real Record on Racial Attitudes," in *Social Trends in American Life: Findings from the General Social Survey Since 1972*, ed. Peter V. Marsden (Princeton: Princeton University Press, 2012), 74.

17. DiAngelo, "White Fragility," 54 .

18. Richard Thaler and Cass Sunstein, *Nudge: Improving Decisions About Health, Wealth, and Happiness* (New York: Penguin, 2008), 4–6, 13; Dasgupta and Greenwald, "On the Malleability of Automatic Attitudes," 801.

19. Reva Siegel, "Equality Divided," foreword to "The Supreme Court: 2012 Term," special issue of *Harvard Law Review* 127, no. 1 (2013): 35.

20. *Schuette v. BAMN*, 134 S. Ct. 1623 (2014), at 1638.

21. Siegel, "Equality Divided," 42, 61.

22. Frederick Douglass, "West India Emancipation Speech, Delivered at Canandaigua, New York (Aug. 4, 1857)," in *The Life and Writings of Frederick Douglass*, 5 vols., ed. Philip S. Foner (Washington, D.C.: Association for the Study of African American Life and History, 1950), 2:437.

23. *Schuette v. BAMN*, 134 S. Ct. at 1638, 1675–1676.

24. Ibid., at 1638, 1676.

25. Bobo et al., "The *Real* Record," 46, 62.

26. Ibid., 61–62.

27. Ehrenreich, *Bright-Sided*, 8, 43, 96.

28. Mahzarin R. Banaji, "Implicit Attitudes Can Be Measured," in *The Nature of Remembering: Essays in Honor of Robert G. Crowder*, ed. Henry L. Roediqer, James S. Nairne, Ian Neath, and Aimée M. Suprenant (Washington, D.C.: American Psychological Association, 2001), 136, citing John T. Jost, Mahzarin R. Banaji, and Anthony G. Greenwald, "Experiments on (Un)Consciousness Raising: Exploiting the Fake Fame Bias in Feminist Samples," paper presented at the annual meeting of the American Psychological Society, Washington, D.C., June 1994.

29. Bettina J. Casad, Abdiel J. Flores, and Jessica D. Didway, "Using the Implicit Association Test as an Unconsciousness Raising Tool in Psychology," *Teaching of Psychology* 40, no. 2 (2013): 118.

30. Behavioral realists are part of a century-old tradition of elite progressive reformers who have thought that the various ills of American democracy can be cured through providing the unenlightened masses with information identified, selected, organized, and disseminated by experts in a similarly monologic manner. See, for example, Jonathan Kahn, *Budgeting Democracy* (Ithaca: Cornell University Press, 1997).

31. Kathie Sarachild, "Consciousness-Raising: A Radical Weapon," in *Feminist Revolution*, ed. Redstockings (New York: Random House, 1978), 145.

32. Ibid., 148.

33. Ibid.

34. Catherine MacKinnon, *Toward a Feminist Theory of the State* (Cambridge, Mass.: Harvard University Press, 1989), 84, 95.

35. Wendell Berry, *The Hidden Wound* (New York: Counterpoint, 2010), 49, quoted in Eddie Glaude Jr., *Democracy in Black: How Race Still Enslaves the American Soul* (New York: Crown, 2016), 64.

36. Nancy Leong, "Reflections on Racial Capitalism," *Harvard Law Review Forum* 127, (2013): 37.

37. Martin Luther King Jr., "Letter from a Birmingham Jail, April 16, 1963," facsimile, Martin Luther King Jr. Research and Education Institute, Stanford University, http://okra.stanford.edu/transcription/document_images/undecided/630416-019.pdf.

38. Frank Dobbin, *Inventing Equal Opportunity* (Princeton: Princeton University Press, 2009), 232.

39. Justin D. Levinson, "Forgotten Racial Equality: Implicit Bias, Decisionmaking, and Misremembering," *Duke Law Journal* 57 (2007): 417, 420, 418–419.

40. Leith Mullings, "Interrogating Racism: Toward an Antiracist Anthropology," *Annual Review of Anthropology* 34 (2005): 679.

41. King, "Letter from a Birmingham Jail."

42. Michael Klarman, *From Jim Crow to Civil Rights: The Supreme Court and the Struggle for Racial Equality* (New York: Oxford University Press, 2004), 95.
43. Ibid., 467.
44. Michelle Alexander, *The New Jim Crow: Mass Incarceration in the Age of Colorblindness* (New York: Free Press, 2011), 225.
45. Samuel R. Bagenstos, "The Structural Turn and the Limits of Antidiscrimination Law," *California Law Review* 94 (2006): 45.

8. SEEKING A TECHNICAL FIX TO RACISM

1. Tamsin Shaw, "The Psychologists Take Power," *New York Review of Books*, February 25, 2016, 38.
2. See, for example, Robert Kuttner, *Everything for Sale: The Virtues and Limits of Markets* (Chicago: University Of Chicago Press, 1999), and Michael Sandel, *What Money Can't Buy: The Moral Limits of Markets* (New York: Farrar, Straus and Giroux, 2013).
3. Sally Merry, *The Seductions of Quantification* (Chicago: University of Chicago Press, 2016), 1.
4. Susan T. Fiske and Michael S. North, "Measures of Stereotyping and Prejudice: Barometers of Bias," in *Measures of Personality and Social Psychological Constructs*, ed. Gregory Boyle, Donald H. Saklofske, and Gerald Matthews Pages (London: Academic Press, 2014), 684.
5. Glenn C. Gamst, Christopher T. H. Liang, and Aghop Der-Karabetian, *Handbook of Multicultural Measures* (Thousand Oaks, Calif.: Sage, 2011), 251–255.
6. Jerry Kang and Mahzarin R. Banaji, "Fair Measures: A Behavioral Realist Revision of 'Affirmative Action,'" *California Law Review* 94 (2006): 1063–1118.
7. See, for example, Evelynn Hammonds and Rebecca Herzig, eds., *The Nature of Difference: Sciences of Race in the United States from Jefferson to Genomics* (Cambridge, Mass.: MIT Press, 2008).
8. Pamela M. Casey, Roger K. Warren, Fred L. Cheesman II, and Jennifer K. Elek, *Helping Courts Address Implicit Bias: Resources for Education* (Washington, D.C.: National Center for State Courts, 2012), app. B, pp. 5–6.
9. Harrison A. Korn, Micah A. Johnson, and Marvin M. Chun, "Neurolaw: Differential Brain Activity for Black and White Faces Predicts Damage Awards in Hypothetical Employment Discrimination Cases," *Social Neuroscience* 7, no. 4 (2011): 398, 399.
10. Ibid., 407.
11. J. David Goodman and Al Baker, "Wave of Protests After Grand Jury Doesn't Indict Officer in Eric Garner Chokehold Case," *New York Times*, December 12, 2014, http://www.nytimes.com/2014/12/04/nyregion/grand-jury-said-to-bring-no-charges-in-staten-island-chokehold-death-of-eric-garner.html?_r=0.
12. Quoted in Osita Nwanevu, "Police Body Cams: Solution or Scam? Debating the Technophiles' Favorite Fix for Police Violence," *In These Times*, January 20, 2015, http://inthesetimes.com/article/17546/police_body_cams_solution_or_scam.

13. Ta-Nehisi Coates, *Between the World and Me* (New York: Spiegel and Grau, 2015), 78.

14. Ian Ayers, "Is Discrimination Elusive?," *Stanford Law Review* 55 (2003): 2420. For a critique of Ayers's approach from the perspective of antisubordination theory, see Jerome M. Culp Jr., Angela P. Harris, and Francisco Valdes, "Subject Unrest," *Stanford Law Review* 55 (2003): 2435–2452.

15. Ayers, "Is Discrimination Elusive?," 2420.

16. Jennifer L. Eberhardt, "Imaging Race," *American Psychologist* 60 (2005): 182.

17. See, for example, Hammonds and Herzig, *The Nature of Difference*.

18. *Grutter v. Bollinger*, 539 U.S. 306 (2003), at 342.

19. Kang and Banaji, "Fair Measures," 1067.

20. Ralph Richard Banks and Richard Thompson Ford, "(How) Does Unconscious Bias Matter? Law, Politics, and Racial Inequality," *Emory Law Journal* 58 (2009): 1116–1117.

21. Ira Katznelson, *When Affirmative Action Was White* (New York: Norton, 2005), 157.

22. Ibid., 158.

23. *Regents of University of California v. Bakke*, 438 U.S. 265 (1978), at 308.

24. Jerry Kang, "Implicit Bias and the Pushback from the Left," *Saint Louis University Law Journal* 54 (2010): 1141.

25. *Daubert v. Merrell Dow Pharmaceuticals*, 509 U.S. 579 (1993). On *Daubert* and its progeny in general, see, for example, Margaret Berger, "The Supreme Court's Trilogy on the Admissibility of Expert Testimony," in *Reference Manual on Scientific Evidence*, ed. Federal Judicial Center (Washington, D.C.: Federal Judicial Center, 2002), 9–38.

26. Sheila Jasanoff, "Just Evidence: The Limits of Science in the Legal Process," *Journal of Law, Medicine, and Ethics* 34 (2006): 330.

27. Ibid.

28. Joseph Dumit, "Critically Producing Brain Images of Mind," in *Critical Neuroscience: A Handbook of the Social and Cultural Contexts of Neuroscience*, ed. Suparna Choudhury and Jan Slaby (Hoboken, N.J.: Wiley-Blackwell, 2012), 195–225.

29. Jasanoff, "Just Evidence," 330.

30. Sheila Jasanoff, "Law's Knowledge: Science for Justice in Legal Settings," *American Journal of Public Health* 95 (2005): S54.

31. Kang and Banaji, "Fair Measures," 1065, emphasis added.

32. Jasanoff, "Law's Knowledge," S50.

33. Merry, *Seductions of Quantification*, 12.

34. Justin D. Levinson and Robert J. Smith, "Introduction: Racial Disparities, Social Science, and the Legal System," in *Implicit Racial Bias Across the Law*, ed. Justin D. Levinson and Robert J. Smith (New York: Cambridge University Press, 2012), 2.

35. Ivan E. Bodensteiner, "The Implications of Psychological Research Related to Unconscious Discrimination and Implicit Bias in Proving Intentional Discrimination," *Missouri Law Review* 73 (2008): 108.

36. Richard Thaler and Cass Sunstein, *Nudge: Improving Decisions About Health, Wealth, and Happiness* (New York: Bantam Books, 2008), 38.

37. Jasanoff, "Law's Knowledge," S49.
38. Ibid., S50.
39. *Plessy v. Ferguson*, 163 U.S. 537 (1896), at 551.
40. Ibid., at 559.
41. *Brown v. Board of Education of Topeka*, 347 U.S. 483 (1954), at 494.
42. Ibid.
43. Herbert Wechsler, "Toward Neutral Principles of Constitutional Law," *Harvard Law Review* 73, no. 1 (1959): 32, 33.
44. Ibid., 33.
45. Charles L. Black Jr., "The Lawfulness of the Segregation Decisions," *Yale Law Journal* 69 (1960): 424.
46. Ibid., 427.
47. Ibid., 427, 430 n. 25.
48. Richard Thompson Ford, "Bias in the Air: Rethinking Employment Discrimination Law," *Stanford Law Review* 66 (2014): 1396.
49. Black, "Lawfulness of the Segregation Decisions," 426.
50. *Plessy*, 163 U.S. at 562.
51. Ian Haney-López, "Intentional Blindness," *New York University Law Review* 87 (2012): 1795–1796.
52. Kang and Banaji, "Fair Measures," 1075.
53. Dumit, "Critically Producing Brain Images of Mind."
54. Jonathan Marks, "The Biological Myth of Human Evolution," in *Biologising the Social Sciences: Challenging Darwinian and Neuroscience Explanations*, ed. David Canter and David Turner (New York: Routledge, 2015), 49.
55. Curtis D. Hardin and Mahzarin R. Banaji, "The Nature of Implicit Prejudice: Implications for Personal and Public Policy," in *The Behavioral Foundations of Public Policy*, ed. Eldar Shafir (Princeton: Princeton University Press, 2013), 18, 19.
56. *Milliken v. Bradley*, 418 U.S. 717 (1974); *Freeman v. Pitts*, 498 U.S. 1081 (1992).
57. *Bakke*, 438 U.S. at 297.
58. Jerry Kang, "The Missing Quadrants of Antidiscrimination: Going Beyond the 'Prejudice Polygraph,'" *Journal of Social Issues* 68, no. 2 (2012): 314–315.
59. *Daubert*, 509 U.S. at 579.
60. Kang, "Implicit Bias," 1142.
61. Jerry Kang, "Trojan Horses of Race," *Harvard Law Review* 118, no. 5 (2005): 1496.
62. Kang, "Implicit Bias,"1147.
63. Ibid., 1145.
64. See, for example, Owen Jones and Christopher Sundby, "Neuroscience in the Law," *SciTech Lawyer* 11 (2015): 4, 6; Amanda Pustilnik, "Pain as Fact and Heuristic: How Pain Neuroimaging Illuminates Moral Dimensions of Law," *Cornell Law Review* 97 (2012): 801; and Sara Reardon, "Neuroscience in Court: The Painful Truth," *Nature* 518 (2015): 474.
65. Dumit, "Critically Producing Brain Images of Mind," 198–199.

66. Linda Hamilton Krieger and Susan T. Fiske, "Behavioral Realism in Employment Discrimination Law: Implicit Bias and Disparate Treatment," *California Law Review* 94 (2006): 1007, 1002.
67. Ibid., 1002.
68. Ibid., 1007–1008.
69. Michael J. Sandel, "The Procedural Republic and the Unencumbered Self," *Political Theory* 12, no. 1 (1984): 81–96.
70. Brian A. Nosek and Rachel G. Riskind, "Policy Implications of Implicit Social Cognition," *Social Issues and Policy Review* 6, no. 1 (2012): 129–131.
71. Cheryl R. Kaiser, Brenda Major, Ines Jurcevic, Tessa L. Dover, Laura M. Brady, and Jenessa R. Shapiro, "Presumed Fair: Ironic Effects of Organizational Diversity Structures," *Journal of Personality and Social Psychology* 104, no. 3 (2013): 505, emphasis in original.
72. Jerry Kang, "Rethinking Intent and Impact: Some Behavioral Realism About Equal Protection," *Alabama Law Review* 66 (2014): 639–640.
73. Tobias Brosch, Eyal Bar-David, and Elizabeth A. Phelps, "Implicit Race Bias Decreases the Similarity of Neural Representations of Black and White Faces," *Psychological Science* 24 (2013): 161.
74. See, for example, Laurence Tribe, *American Constitutional Law* (New York: Foundation Press, 1988), 1452–1454.
75. "Algorithm," *Merriam Webster's Dictionary* (2017), http://www.merriam-webster.com/dictionary/algorithm.
76. *Poe v. Ullman*, 367 U.S. 497 (1961), at 542.
77. Julia Angwin, Jeff Larson, Surya Mattu, and Lauren Kirchner, "Machine Bias: There's Software Used Across the Country to Predict Future Criminals. And It's Biased Against Blacks," ProPublica, May 23, 2016, https://www.propublica.org/article/machine-bias-risk-assessments-in-criminal-sentencing. See also Cathy O'Neil, *Weapons of Math Destruction: How Big Data Increases Inequality and Threatens Democracy* (New York: Crown, 2016).
78. O'Neil, *Weapons of Math Destruction*, 112–117, 149, 161–162, 3.
79. See, for example, Ulrich Beck, *Risk Society: Towards a New Modernity* (Thousand Oaks, Calif.: Sage, 1992), 19; Claus Møldrup and Janine Marie Morgall, "Risk Society—Reconsidered in a Drug Context," *Health, Risk, and Society* 3, no. 1 (2001): 59, 72; and Bryan S. Turner, "Risks, Rights, and Regulation: An Overview," *Health, Risk, and Society* 3, no. 1 (2001): 9.
80. Conrad G. Brunk, "Public Knowledge, Public Trust: Understanding the 'Knowledge Deficit,'" *Community Genetics* 9, no. 3 (2006): 178.
81. Brian Wynne, "Public Engagement as a Means of Restoring Public Trust in Science—Hitting the Notes, but Missing the Music?," *Community Genetics* 9 (2006): 211–220.
82. Ibid., 214.
83. Jerry Kang and Kristin Lane, "Seeing Through Colorblindness: Implicit Bias and the Law," *UCLA Law Review* 58 (2010): 519.

84. Kang, "Missing Quadrants of Antidiscrimination," 316.

85. Brunk, "Public Knowledge, Public Trust," 179. Brunk provides the telling example of Mexican farmers' resistance to genetically modified crops: "They did not believe that the experts understood the nature of the risks the way they understood them. For the campesinos, the risks posed by transgenes in their native maize were defined in terms of a cultural framework that was neither shared nor respected, even if vaguely understood, by the experts examining the issue. For the campesinos, the values put 'at risk' by transgenes in their maize were deeply embedded in the profound cultural and religious significance of maize as an ancestral heritage. . . . Viewed from this deeper, almost metaphysical perspective, what was placed 'at risk' by the Bt transgenes invading their native maize varieties was not only the health of their population and the natural environment, as these are defined in the quantitative algorithms invoked in the scientific background papers and the risk assessments, but also, and more importantly, the *integrity* of this cultural and ancestral heritage" (182).

86. Frank Dobbin and Alexandra Kalev, "The Origins and Effects of Corporate Diversity Programs," in *The Oxford Handbook of Diversity and Work*, ed. Quinetta M. Roberson (Oxford: Oxford University Press, 2013), 274.

87. Theodore Porter, *Trust in Numbers: The Pursuit of Objectivity in Science and Public Life* (Princeton: Princeton University Press, 1995), ix.

88. *Poe v. Ullman*, 367 U.S. at 543.

89. John Hart Ely, *Democracy and Distrust: A Theory of Judicial Review* (Cambridge, Mass.: Harvard University Press, 1980), 251 n. 69.

90. Pamela M. Casey, Roger K. Warren, Fred L. Cheesman, and Jennifer K. Elek, "Addressing Implicit Bias in the Courts," *Court Review* 49 (2013): 66, 68.

91. *City of Richmond v. J. A. Croson Co.*, 488 U.S. 469 (1989); *Parents Involved in Community Schools v. Seattle School District. No. 1*, 551 U.S. 701 (2007); *Schuette v. BAMN*, 134 S. Ct. 1623 (2014).

92. *Bakke*, 438 U.S. at 284.

93. Ibid., at 296, 297.

94. *Loving v. Virginia*, 388 U.S. 1 (1967).

95. *Parents Involved*, 551 U.S. at 720, quoting *Grutter v. Bollinger*, 539 U.S. at 270.

96. *Bakke*, 438 U.S. at 375, 295, 396.

97. Ibid., at 292.

98. Jasanoff, "Law's Knowledge," S57.

99. Ibid.; Kang, "Trojan Horses of Race," 1495.

100. Jasanoff, "Law's Knowledge," S50.

101. Charles R. Lawrence III, "The Id, the Ego, and Equal Protection: Reckoning with Unconscious Racism," *Stanford Law Review* 39, no. 2 (1987): 352, 361, 356.

102. Ibid., 386.

103. Kang, "Trojan Horses of Race," 1496 n. 28. Linda Hamilton Krieger draws a similar contrast, noting that "it is here that my perspective differs from that so compellingly offered by Professor Charles R. Lawrence III in 'The Id, the Ego, and Equal Protection: Reckoning

with Unconscious Racism,' 39 Stan. L. Rev. 317 (1987). Drawing on psychoanalytic theory, Professor Lawrence argues that much of what is classified as disparate treatment discrimination results from subconscious instincts and motivations. While Professor Lawrence does mention cognitive bias as a potential source of discriminatory decision-making, he focuses primarily on discussing motivational rather than cognitive anteced-ents" ("The Content of Our Categories: A Cognitive Bias Approach to Discrimination and Equal Employment Opportunity," *Stanford Law Review* 47 [1995]: 1164 n. 11). The focus on cognition reflects the interest in the causal mechanisms of bias in contrast to Lawrence's interest in the interpretive approach.

104. Charles Lawrence III, "Unconscious Racism Revisited: Reflections on the Impact and Origins of 'The Id, the Ego, and Equal Protection,'" *Connecticut Law Review* 40 (2008): 942.

105. Haney-López, "Intentional Blindness," 1783.

106. Lawrence D. Bobo and Camille Z. Charles, "Race in the American Mind: From the Moynihan Report to the Obama Candidacy," *ANNALS of the AAPSS* 621 (2009): 244.

107. Sheila Jasanoff, *Science and Public Reason* (New York: Routledge, 2012), 178.

108. Ibid.

109. Ibid., 179.

110. Ibid.

111. Ibid., 169.

112. *Wal-Mart Stores, Inc. v. Dukes*, 131 S. Ct. 2541 (2011), at 2563.

113. Ibid.

114. Reva B. Siegel, "Why Equal Protection No Longer Protects: The Evolving Forms of Status-Enforcing State Action," *Stanford Law Review* 49 (1997): 1145.

115. Ibid., 1147. See also *Washington v. Davis*, 426 U.S. 229 (1976), and *Personnel Administrator of Massachusetts v. Feeney*, 442 U.S. 256 (1979).

9. BIOLOGIZING RACISM: THE ULTIMATE TECHNICAL FIX

1. White House, Office of the Press Secretary, "Remarks by the President, Prime Minister Tony Blair of England (via satellite), Dr. Francis Collins, Director of the National Human Genome Research Institute, and Dr. Craig Venter, President and Chief Scientific Officer, Celera Genomics Corporation, on the Completion of the First Survey of the Entire Human Genome Project," June 26, 2000, http://clinton5.nara.gov/WH/New/html/genome-20000626.html.

2. See, generally, Ashley Montagu, *Man's Most Dangerous Myth: The Fallacy of Race* (1942; reprint, Walnut Creek, Calif.: Altamira Press, 2001); Jenny Reardon, *Race to the Finish: Identity and Governance in an Age of Genomics* (Princeton: Princeton University Press, 2009); and Catherine Bliss, *Race Decoded: The Genomic Fight for Social Justice* (Stanford, Calif.: Stanford University Press, 2012).

3. A recent example of the continued existence of this myth is the book *A Troublesome Inheritance: Genes, Race, and Human History* (New York: Penguin, 2014) by longtime

New York Times science writer Nicholas Wade. The book, purporting to show the genetic reality of race, was met with widespread contempt by social scientists and outright scorn by molecular biologists and other natural scientists, more than 140 of whom signed an open letter to the *New York Times* decrying the inaccuracies and misrepresentations in the book. See Graham Coop et al., "Letter: 'A Troublesome Inheritance,'" *New York Times*, August 10, 2014, http://www.nytimes.com/2014/08/10/books/review/letters-a -troublesome-inheritance.html?_r=1.

4. Jennifer L. Eberhardt, "Imaging Race," *American Psychologist* 60 (2005): 182.

5. John F. Dovidio, "On the Nature of Contemporary Prejudice: The Third Wave," *Journal of Social Issues* 57, no. 4 (2001): 830, 831, 842.

6. Jerry Kang, "Trojan Horses of Race," *Harvard Law Review* 118, no. 5 (2005): 1489–1593.

7. Mahzarin R. Banaji and Anthony G. Greenwald, *Blind Spot: Hidden Biases of Good People* (New York: Bantam Books, 2013), 105.

8. Carl C. Bell and Edward Dunbar, "Racism and Pathological Bias as a Co-occurring Problem in Diagnosis and Assessment," in *The Oxford Handbook of Personality Disorders*, ed. Thomas A. Widiger (Oxford: Oxford University Press, 2012), 694.

9. Charles R. Lawrence III, "The Id, the Ego, and Equal Protection: Reckoning with Unconscious Racism," *Stanford Law Review* 39, no. 2 (1987): 321.

10. Charles Lawrence III, "Unconscious Racism Revisited: Reflections on the Impact and Origins of 'The Id, the Ego, and Equal Protection,'" *Connecticut Law Review* 40 (2008): 960.

11. Alvin F. Poussaint, "Is Extreme Racism a Mental Illness? Yes: It Can Be a Delusional Symptom of Psychotic Disorders," *Western Journal of Medicine* 176 (2002): 4.

12. Quoted in Emily Eakin, "Bigotry as Mental Illness or Just Another Norm," *New York Times*, January 15, 2000, http://www.nytimes.com/2000/01/15/arts/bigotry-as-mental -illness-or-just-another-norm.html?pagewanted=all&src=pm.

13. James E. Dobbins and Judith H. Skillings, "Racism as a Clinical Syndrome," *American Journal of Orthopsychiatry* 70 (2000): 14.

14. David Wellman, "From Evil to Illness: Medicalizing Racism," *American Journal of Orthopsychiatry* 70, no. 1 (2000): 29, quoting Judith H. Skillings and James E. Dobbins, "Racism as a Disease: Etiology and Treatment Implications," *Journal of Counseling and Development* 70, no. 1 (1991): 210.

15. Pamela M. Casey, Roger K. Warren, Fred L. Cheesman II, and Jennifer K. Elek, *Helping Courts Address Implicit Bias: Resources for Education* (Washington, D.C.: National Center for State Courts, 2012), 4, http://www.ncsc.org/ibreport.

16. Mo Costandi, "Interview with Elizabeth Phelps: How the Brain Views Race," *Nature News*, June 26, 2012, http://www.nature.com/news/how-the-brain-views-race-1.10886.

17. Wellman, "From Evil to Illness," 30.

18. Ibid.

19. Carl Bell, "Racism: A Mental Illness?," *Psychiatric Services* 55, no. 12 (2004): 1343, http:// ps.psychiatryonline.org.

20. Elizabeth A. Phelps, Kevin J. O'Connor, William A. Cunningham, E. Sumie Funayama, J. Christopher Gatenby, John C. Gore, and Mahzarin R. Banaji, "Performance on Indirect Measures of Race Evaluation Predicts Amygdala Activation," *Journal of Cognitive Neuroscience* 12, no. 5 (2000): 729.
21. Jennifer T. Kubota, Mahzarin R. Banaji, and Elizabeth A. Phelps, "The Neuroscience of Race," *Nature Neuroscience* 15, no. 7 (2012): 940.
22. Ibid., passim.
23. Eberhardt, "Imaging Race," 182.
24. Harrison A. Korn, Micah A. Johnson, and Marvin M. Chun, "Neurolaw: Differential Brain Activity for Black and White Faces Predicts Damage Awards in Hypothetical Employment Discrimination Cases," *Social Neuroscience* (2011): 399.
25. Eberhardt, "Imaging Race," 189.
26. For one such critique, see Neuroskeptic, "The Racist Brain?," *Discover* magazine, blog, July 5, 2012, http://blogs.discovermagazine.com/neuroskeptic/2012/07/05/the-racist-brain/.
27. Kubota, Banaji, and Phelps, "Neuroscience of Race," 945.
28. David M. Amodio, "The Neuroscience of Prejudice and Stereotyping," *Nature Reviews Neuroscience* 15 (2014): 675, emphasis in original.
29. Martha J. Farah, "Neuroethics: The Ethical, Legal, and Societal Impact of Neuroscience," *Annual Review of Psychology* 63 (2012): 572–573.
30. Daan Scheepers, Naomi Ellemers, and Belle Derks, "The 'Nature' of Prejudice: What Neuroscience Has to Offer to the Study of Intergroup Relations," in *Neuroscience of Prejudice and Intergroup Relations*, ed. Belle Derks, Daan Scheepers, and Naomi Ellemers (New York: Psychology Press, 2013), 2.
31. Leith Mullings, "Interrogating Racism: Toward an Antiracist Anthropology," *Annual Review of Anthropology* 34 (2005): 684.
32. Kubota, Banaji, and Phelps, "Neuroscience of Race," 940.
33. For descriptions of this process, see, for example, ibid., passim; Jennifer A. Richeson, Abigail A. Baird, Heather L. Gordon, Todd F. Heatherton, Carrie L. Wyland, Sophie Trawalter, and J. Nicole Shelton, "An fMRI Investigation of the Impact of Interracial Contact on Executive Function," *Nature Neuroscience* 6, no. 12 (2003): 1323–1328; and Chad E. Forbes, Joshua C. Poore, Aron K. Barbey, Frank Krueger, Jeffrey Solomon, Robert H. Lipsky, Colin A. Hodgkinson, David Goldman, and Jordan Grafman, "BDNF Polymorphism—Dependent OFC and DLPFC Plasticity Differentially Moderates Implicit and Explicit Bias," *Cerebral Cortex* 22 (2012): 2602–2609.
34. Damian Stanley, Elizabeth Phelps, and Mahzarin R. Banaji, "The Neural Basis of Implicit Attitudes," *Current Directions in Psychological Science* 17 (2006): 168.
35. Amodio, "Neuroscience of Prejudice and Stereotyping," 667.
36. Feng Shenga, Yi Liua, Bin Zhouc, Wen Zhouc, and Shihui Hana, "Oxytocin Modulates the Racial Bias in Neural Responses to Others' Suffering," *Biological Psychology* 92 (2013): 385.
37. Sharon Begley, "How Your Brain Looks at Race; Not Even Obama Thinks America Is 'Post Racial.' But Neuroscience, Like the Primary Results, Suggests We Are Not Doomed to See Things in Black and White," *Newsweek*, March 3, 2008.

38. Mullings, "Interrogating Racism," 684.
39. George Fredrickson, *Racism: A Short History* (Princeton: Princeton University Press, 2002), 99.
40. Adele E. Clarke, Laura Mamo, Jennifer Fosket, Jennifer Fishman, and Janet Shim, *Biomedicalization: Technoscience, Health, and Illness in the US* (Durham, N.C.: Duke University Press, 2010), 2, emphasis in original.
41. Kubota, Banaji, and Phelps, "Neuroscience of Race," 945.
42. Amodio, "Neuroscience of Prejudice and Stereotyping," 679.
43. Ibid.
44. Thomas Douglas, "Moral Enhancement," *Journal of Applied Philosophy* 25, no. 3 (2008): 233. See also Edward Dunbar, "Reconsidering the Clinical Utility of Bias as a Mental Health Problem: Intervention Strategies for Psychotherapy Practice," *Psychotherapy: Theory, Research, Practice* 41 (2004): 97–111. Dunbar argues, "Given that pathological forms of bias include a variety of cognitions, behaviors, and affects, with multiple etiologies and varying levels of severity, it follows that differing pharmacological strategies may need to be followed. Pharmacological treatments that target identified symptoms of clinical bias may well provide a reduction in ideation and behavioral disturbance" (104).
45. Sylvia Terbeck, Guy Kahane, Sarah McTavish, Julian Savulescu, Philip J. Cowen, and Miles Hewstone, "Propranolol Reduces Implicit Negative Racial Bias," *Psychopharmacology* 222, no. 3 (2012): 419, doi:10.1007/s00213-012-2657-5.
46. "Noradrenergic System," *Access Science*, 2014, http://www.accessscience.com/content/Noradrenergic-system/456150.
47. Terbeck et al., "Propranolol," 419.
48. "Propranolol," *MedlinePlus*, n.d., https://www.nlm.nih.gov/medlineplus/druginfo/meds/a682607.html.
49. Amanda Pustilnik, "Racey, Racey Neuro-hype! Can a Pill Make You Less Racist?," *Concurring Opinions*, March 2012, http://www.concurringopinions.com/archives/2012/03/racey-racey-neuro-hype-can-a-pillmake-you-less-racist.html.
50. Quoted in Stephen Adams, "Blood Pressure Drug 'Reduces In-Built Racism,'" *Telegraph*, March 7, 2012, http://www.telegraph.co.uk/health/healthnews/9129029/Bloodpressure-drug-reduces-in-built-racism.html.
51. Mina Cikara and Jay J. Van Bavel, "The Neuroscience of Intergroup Relations: An Integrative Review," *Perspectives on Psychological Science* 9 (2014): 246, 256.
52. Calvin K. Lai, Kelly M. Hoffman, and Brian A. Nosek, "Reducing Implicit Prejudice," *Social and Personality Psychology Compass*, July 5, 2013, 318.
53. Thomas Douglas, "Moral Enhancement Via Direct Emotion Modulation: A Reply to John Harris," *Bioethics* 27, no. 3 (2013): 164.
54. David DeGrazia, "Moral Enhancement, Freedom, and What We (Should) Value in Moral Behavior," *Journal of Medical Ethics* 40, no. 6 (2013): 364.
55. Tabitha S. Burchett and L. Lee Glenn, "Letter to the Editor: Measurement Validity of Tests for Implicit Negative Bias," *Psychopharmacology* 222, no. 4 (2012): 721–722.
56. Quoted in Adams, "Blood Pressure Drug 'Reduces In-Built Racism.'"

57. Inmaculada de Melo-Martin and Arleen Salles, "Moral Bioenhancement: Much Ado About Nothing?," *Bioethics* 29, no. 4 (2015): 230.

58. Sylvia Terbeck, Guy Kahane, Sarah McTavish, Julian Savulescu, Phil Cowen, and Miles Hewstone, "Reply to T. S. Burchett and L. L. Glenn, 'Measurement Validity of Tests for Implicit Negative Bias,'" *Psychopharmacology* 222, no. 4 (2012): 724.

59. René Hurlemann, Henrik Walter, Anne K. Rehme, Juraj Kukolja, S. C. Santoro, C. Schmidt, Knut Schnell, Frank Musshoff, Christian Keysers, W. Maier, Keith M. Kendrick and Oezguer A. Onur, "Human Amygdala Reactivity Is Diminished by the β-Noradrenergic Antagonist Propranolol," *Psychological Medicine* 40 (2010): 1839–1848.

60. Sylvia Terbeck, Guy Kahane, Sarah McTavish, Robert McCutcheon, Miles Hewstone, Julian Savulescu, L. P. Chesterman, Philip J. Cowen, and R. Norbury, "β-Adrenoceptor Blockade Modulates Fusiform Gyrus Activity to Black Versus White Faces," *Psychopharmacology* 232, no. 16 (2015): 2951, http://link.springer.com/article/10.1007/s00213-015-3929-7/fulltext.html.

61. Ibid., 2952, citing Phelps et al., "Performance on Indirect Measures of Race Evaluation."

62. Terbeck et al., "β-Adrenoceptor Blockade Modulates Fusiform Gyrus Activity," 2951, 2957.

63. Ibid., 2951.

64. Roberta Sellaro, Belle Derks, Michael A. Nitsche, Bernhard Hommel, Wery P. M. van den Wildenberg, Kristina van Dam, and Lorenza S. Colzato, "Reducing Prejudice Through Brain Stimulation," *Brain Stimulation* 8 (2015): 891.

65. Casey et al., *Helping Courts Address Implicit Bias.*

66. Douglas, "Moral Enhancement Via Direct Emotion Modulation," 161.

67. Ibid.

68. Roberta Sellaro, Belle Derks, Michael A. Nitsche, Bernhard Hommel, Wery P. M. van den Wildenberg, Kristina van Dam, and Lorenza S. Colzato, "Reducing Prejudice Through Brain Stimulation," *Brain Stimulation* 8, no. 5 (2015): 891.

69. "Press Release: Nederlandse Vereniging voor Psychonomie (NVP), 'Reducing Prejudice Through Brain Stimulation,'" *ScienceDaily*, May 4, 2015, http://www.sciencedaily.com/releases/2015/05/150504082600.htm.

CONCLUSION: CONTESTING THE COMMON SENSE OF RACISM

1. Richard H. Thaler and Cass R. Sunstein, *Nudge: Improving Decisions About Health, Wealth, and Happiness* (New York: Bantam Books, 2008), 105–119.

2. See, for example, David A. Harris, *Driving While Black: Racial Profiling on Our Nation's Highways*, American Civil Liberties Union Special Report (Washington, D.C.: American Civil Liberties Union, June 1999), https://www.aclu.org/report/driving-while-black-racial-profiling-our-nations-highways.

3. Bruce Ackerman, "De-schooling Constitutional Law," *Yale Law Journal* 123 (2014): 3133, quoting Bruce Ackerman, *We the People: The Civil Rights Revolution* (Cambridge, Mass.: Harvard University Press, 2014), 131.

4. *Palmore v. Sidoti*, 466 U.S. 429 (1984), at 431, quoting App. to Pet. for Cert., 26–27.

5. Ibid., at 433.

6. See, for example, Kimberlé Williams Crenshaw, Andrea J. Ritchie, Rachel Anspach, Rachel Gilmer, and Luke Harris, *Say Her Name: Resisting Police Brutality Against Black Women* (New York: African American Policy Forum, 2015), http://static1.squarespace .com/static/53f20d90e4b0b80451158d8c/t/55a810d7e4b058f342f55873/1437077719984/ AAPF_SMN_Brief_full_singles.compressed.pdf.

7. See Ian Haney-López, *Dog Whistle Politics: How Coded Racial Appeals Have Reinvented Racism and Wrecked the Middle Class* (Oxford: Oxford University Press, 2013).

8. *Obergefell v. Hodges*, 135 S. Ct. 2584 (2015).

9. Ibid., at 2594, 2595.

10. Ibid., at 2596, 2608.

11. See Charles Black, *A New Birth of Freedom* (New Haven: Yale University Press, 1997).

12. *Plessy v. Ferguson*, 163 U.S. 537 (1896).

13. Ibid., at 555.

14. *Brown v. Board of Education*, 347 U.S. 483 (1954), at 494, emphasis added.

15. *Loving v. Virginia*, 388 U.S. 1 (1967), at 11.

16. *Obergefell*, 135 S. Ct. at 2598.

17. Avishai Margalit, *The Decent Society* (Cambridge, Mass.: Harvard University Press, 1996), 1.

18. Reva Siegel, "Equality Divided," foreword to "The Supreme Court: 2012 Term," special issue of *Harvard Law Review* 127, no. 1 (2013): 94.

INDEX

CPSIA information can be obtained
at www.ICGtesting.com
Printed in the USA
LVOW11*0833060318
568830LV00001B/2/P